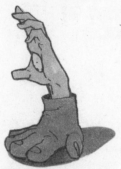

Thanks for buying volume 18!!
My schedule's gotten insanely full!
Plus Ultra!

KOHEI HORIKOSHI

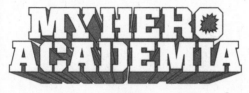

SHONEN JUMP Manga Edition

STORY & ART KOHEI HORIKOSHI

TRANSLATION & ENGLISH ADAPTATION **Caleb Cook**
TOUCH-UP ART & LETTERING **John Hunt**
DESIGNER **Julian [JR] Robinson**
SHONEN JUMP SERIES EDITOR **John Bae**
GRAPHIC NOVEL EDITOR **Mike Montesa**

BOKU NO HERO ACADEMIA © 2014 by Kohei Horikoshi
All rights reserved.
First published in Japan in 2014 by SHUEISHA Inc., Tokyo.
English translation rights arranged by SHUEISHA Inc.

The stories, characters and incidents mentioned in this publication are entirely fictional.

No portion of this book may be reproduced or transmitted in any form
or by any means without written permission from the copyright holders.

Printed in the U.S.A.

Published by VIZ Media, LLC
P.O. Box 77010
San Francisco, CA 94107

10 9 8 7 6
First printing, April 2019
Sixth printing, September 2022

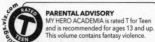

PARENTAL ADVISORY
MY HERO ACADEMIA is rated T for Teen
and is recommended for ages 13 and up.
This volume contains fantasy violence.

My Hero Academia

vol. 18

Bright Future

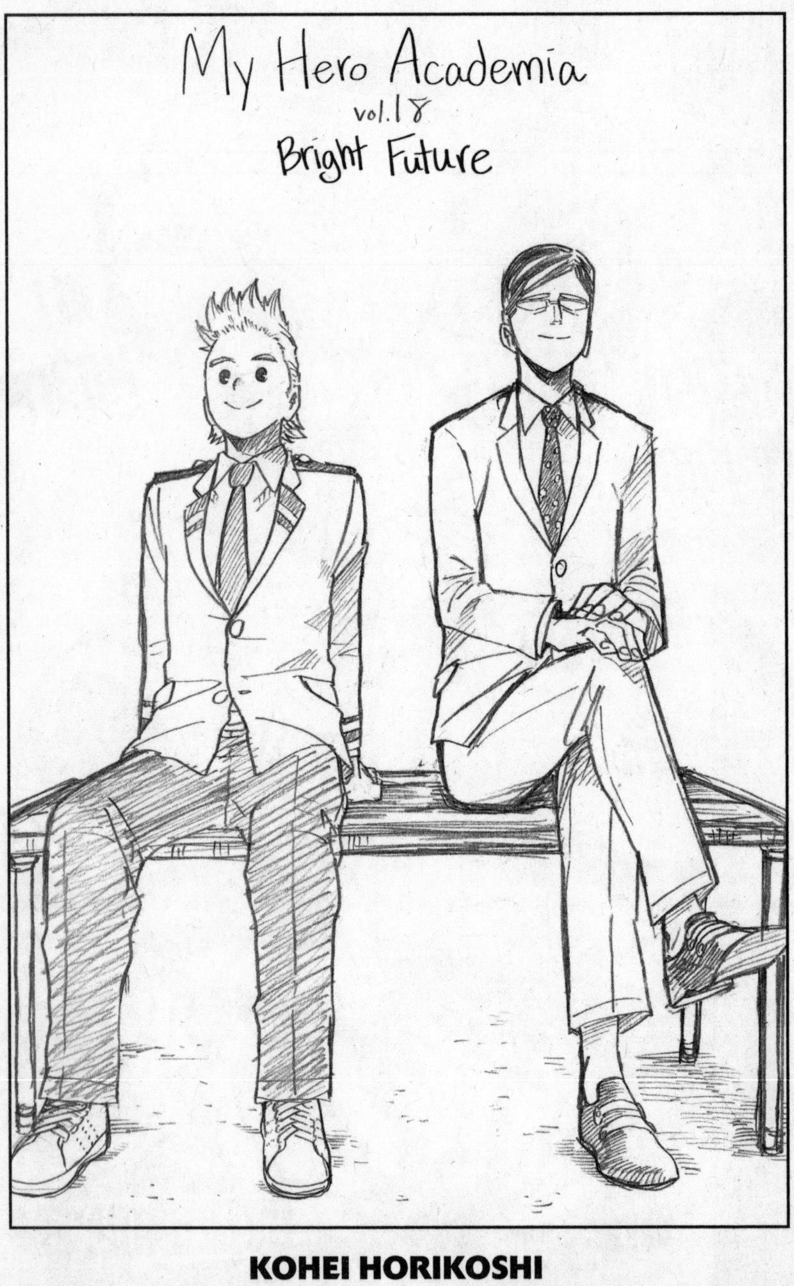

KOHEI HORIKOSHI

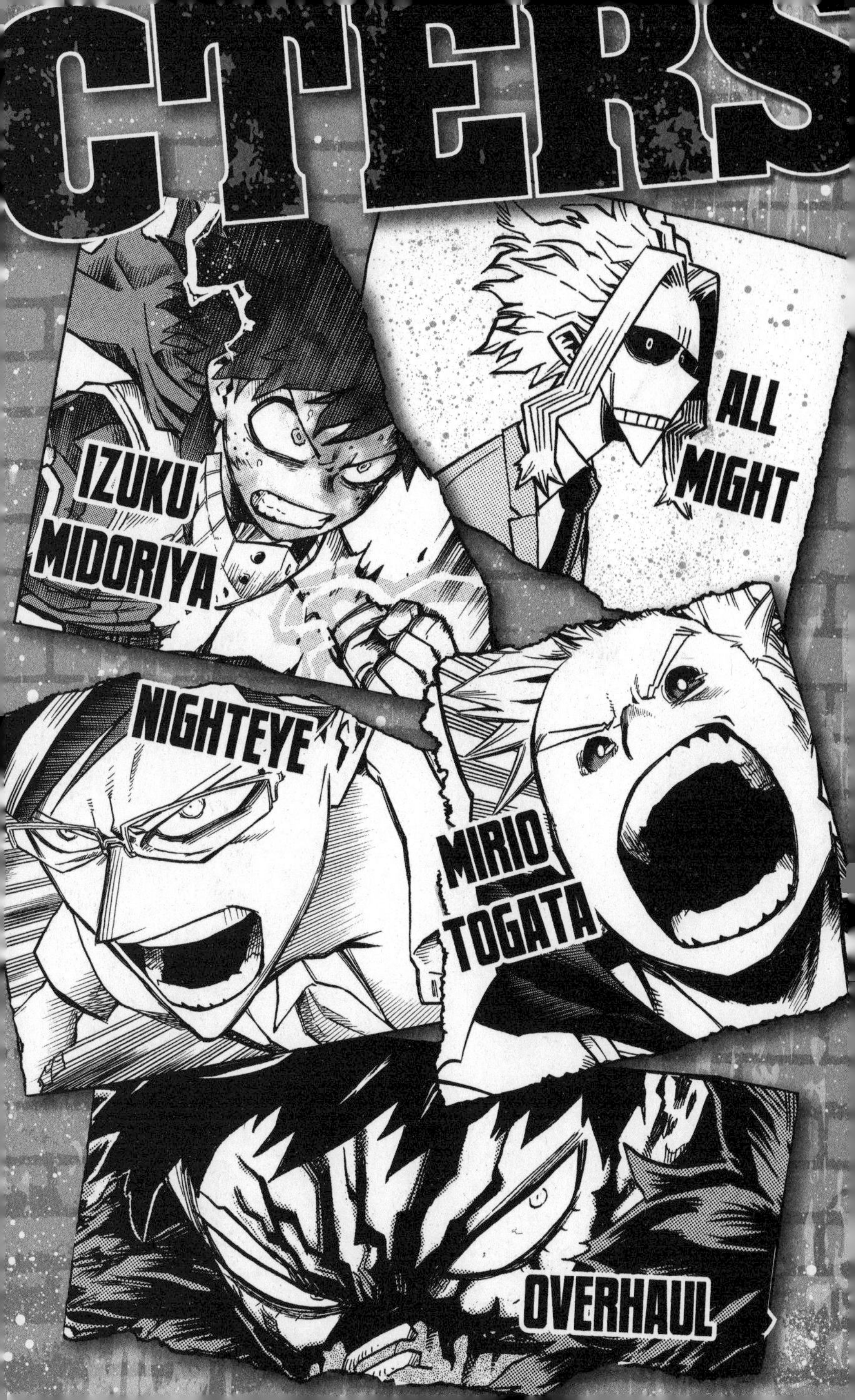
CTERS
ALL MIGHT
IZUKU MIDORIYA
MIRIO TOGATA
NIGHTEYE
OVERHAUL

CHARA

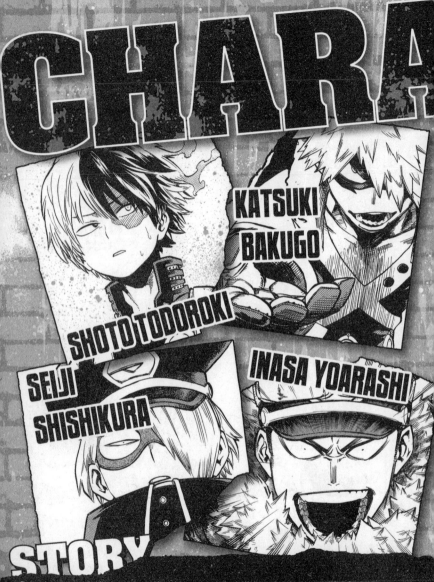

KATSUKI BAKUGO
SHOTO TODOROKI
INASA YOARASHI
SEIJI SHISHIKURA

STORY

One day, people began manifesting special abilities that came to be known as "Quirks," and before long, the world was full of superpowered humans. But with the advent of these exceptional individuals came an increase in crime, and governments alone were unable to deal with the situation. At the same time, others emerged to oppose the spread of evil! As if straight from the comic books, these heroes keep the peace and are even officially authorized to fight crime. Our story begins when a certain Quirkless boy and lifelong hero fan meets the world's number one hero, starting him on his path to becoming the greatest hero ever!

Vol. 18

MY HERO ACADEMIA

CONTENTS

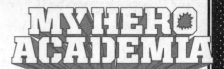

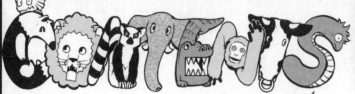

Bright Future

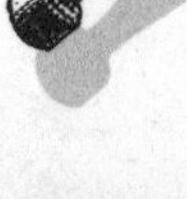

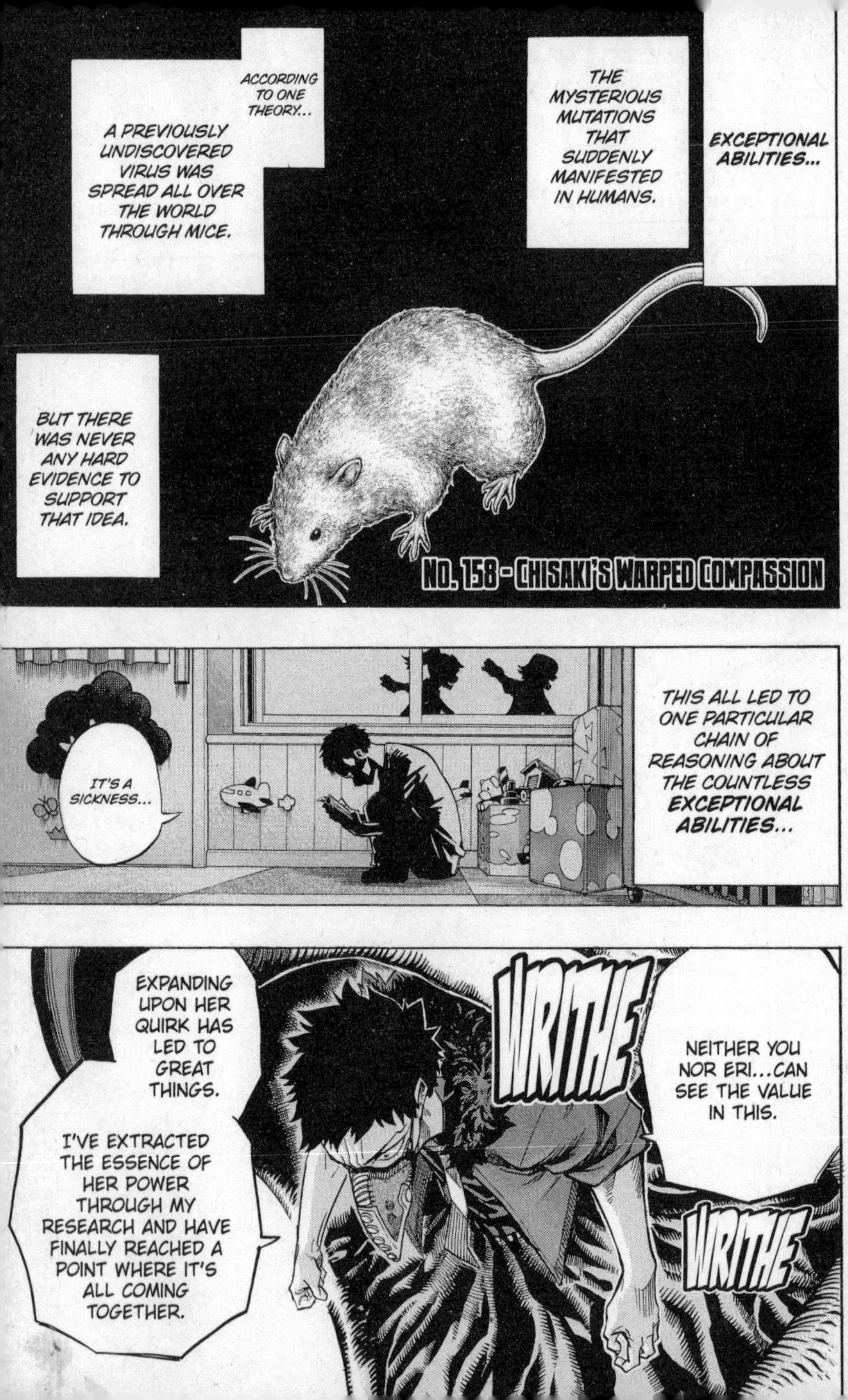
EXCEPTIONAL ABILITIES...
THE MYSTERIOUS MUTATIONS THAT SUDDENLY MANIFESTED IN HUMANS.
ACCORDING TO ONE THEORY...
A PREVIOUSLY UNDISCOVERED VIRUS WAS SPREAD ALL OVER THE WORLD THROUGH MICE.
BUT THERE WAS NEVER ANY HARD EVIDENCE TO SUPPORT THAT IDEA.
NO. 158 - CHISAKI'S WARPED COMPASSION
THIS ALL LED TO ONE PARTICULAR CHAIN OF REASONING ABOUT THE COUNTLESS EXCEPTIONAL ABILITIES...
IT'S A SICKNESS...
NEITHER YOU NOR ERI...CAN SEE THE VALUE IN THIS.
WRITHE
EXPANDING UPON HER QUIRK HAS LED TO GREAT THINGS.
WRITHE
I'VE EXTRACTED THE ESSENCE OF HER POWER THROUGH MY RESEARCH AND HAVE FINALLY REACHED A POINT WHERE IT'S ALL COMING TOGETHER.

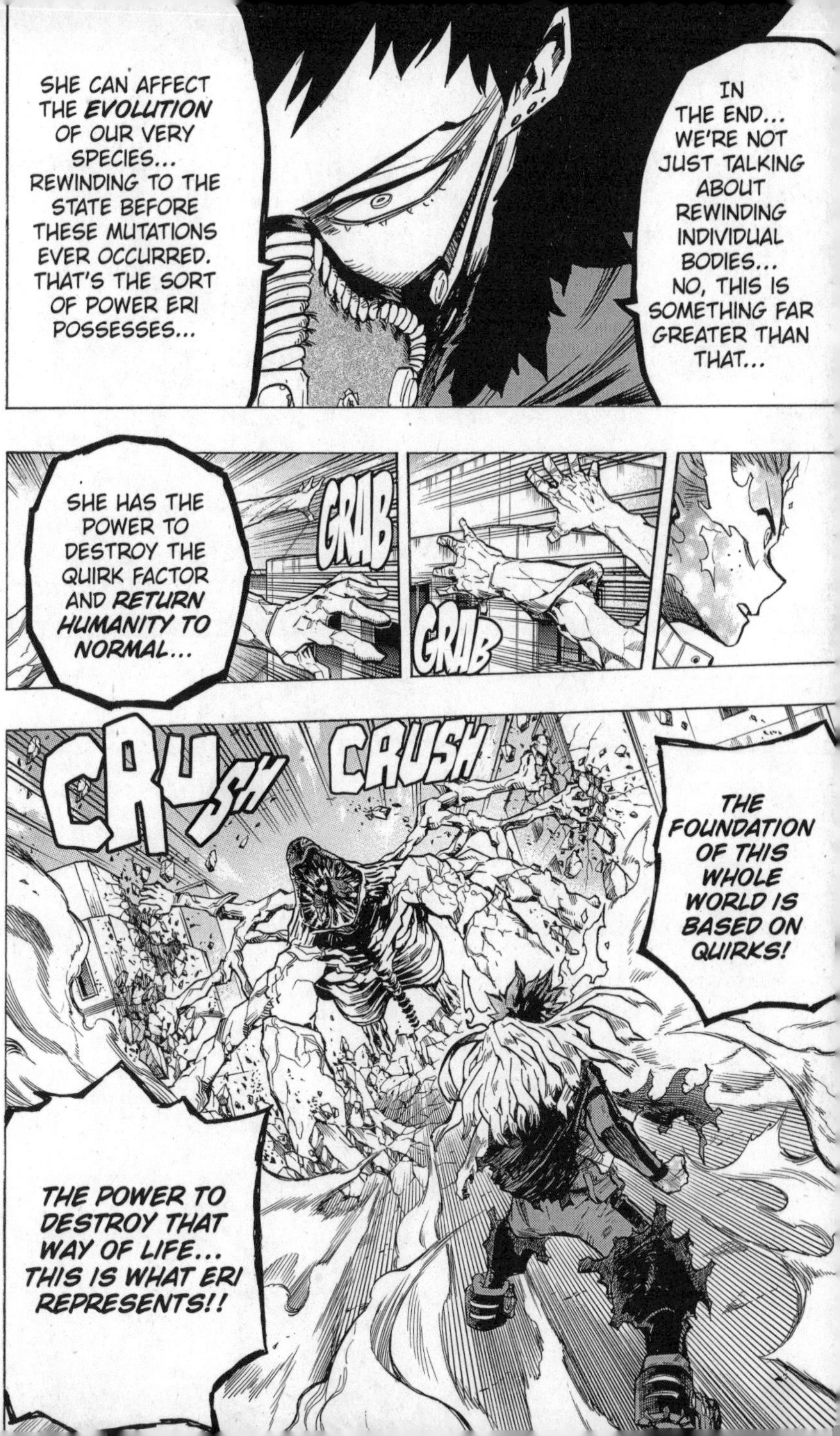
IN THE END... WE'RE NOT JUST TALKING ABOUT REWINDING INDIVIDUAL BODIES... NO, THIS IS SOMETHING FAR GREATER THAN THAT...
SHE CAN AFFECT THE *EVOLUTION* OF OUR VERY SPECIES... REWINDING TO THE STATE BEFORE THESE MUTATIONS EVER OCCURRED. THAT'S THE SORT OF POWER ERI POSSESSES...
GRAB
GRAB
SHE HAS THE POWER TO DESTROY THE QUIRK FACTOR AND *RETURN HUMANITY TO NORMAL...*
THE FOUNDATION OF THIS WHOLE WORLD IS BASED ON QUIRKS!
CRUSH
CRUSH
THE POWER TO DESTROY THAT WAY OF LIFE... THIS IS WHAT ERI REPRESENTS!!

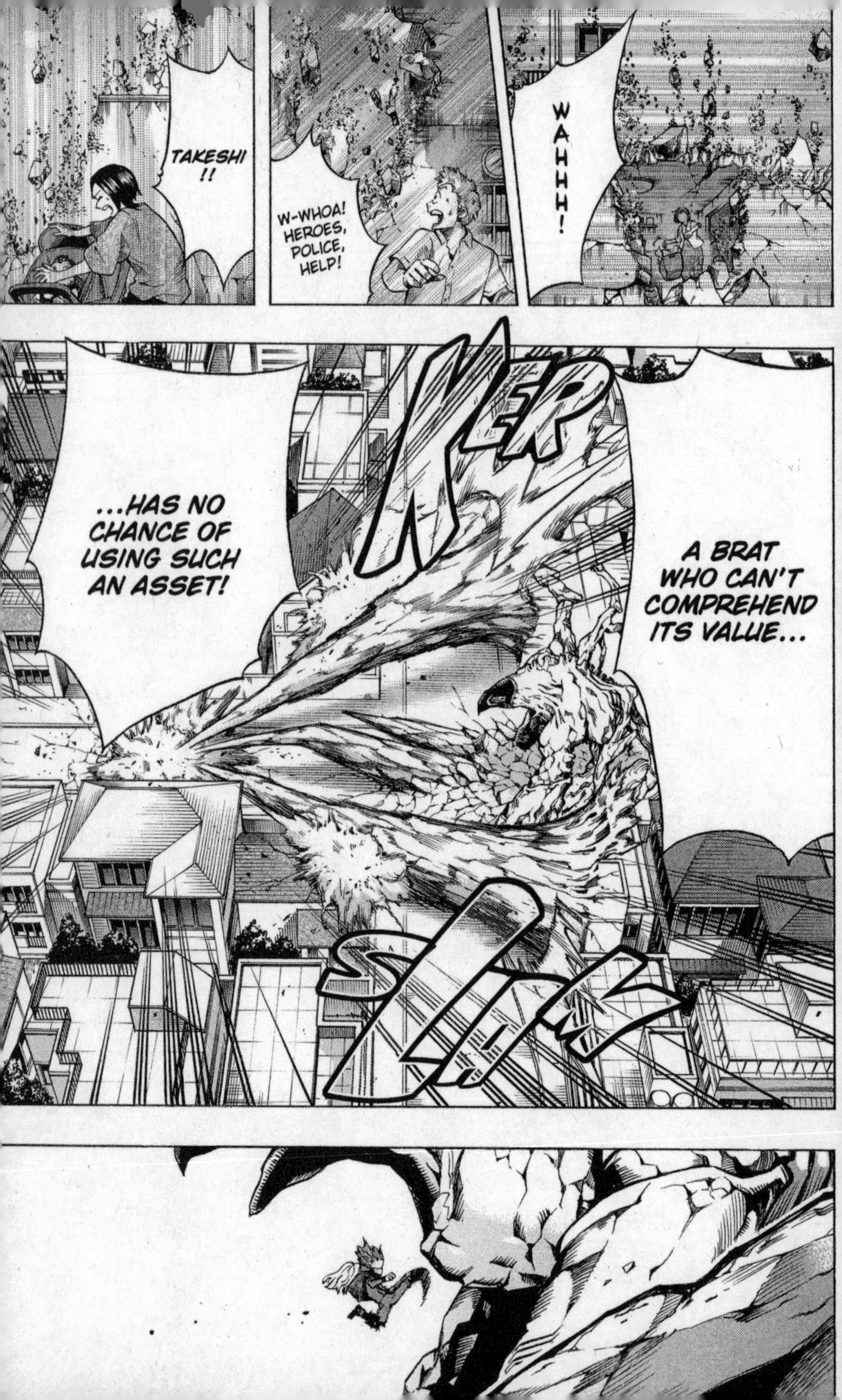
WAHHHH!
W-WHOA! HEROES, POLICE, HELP!
TAKESHI !!
A BRAT WHO CAN'T COMPREHEND ITS VALUE...
...HAS NO CHANCE OF USING SUCH AN ASSET!

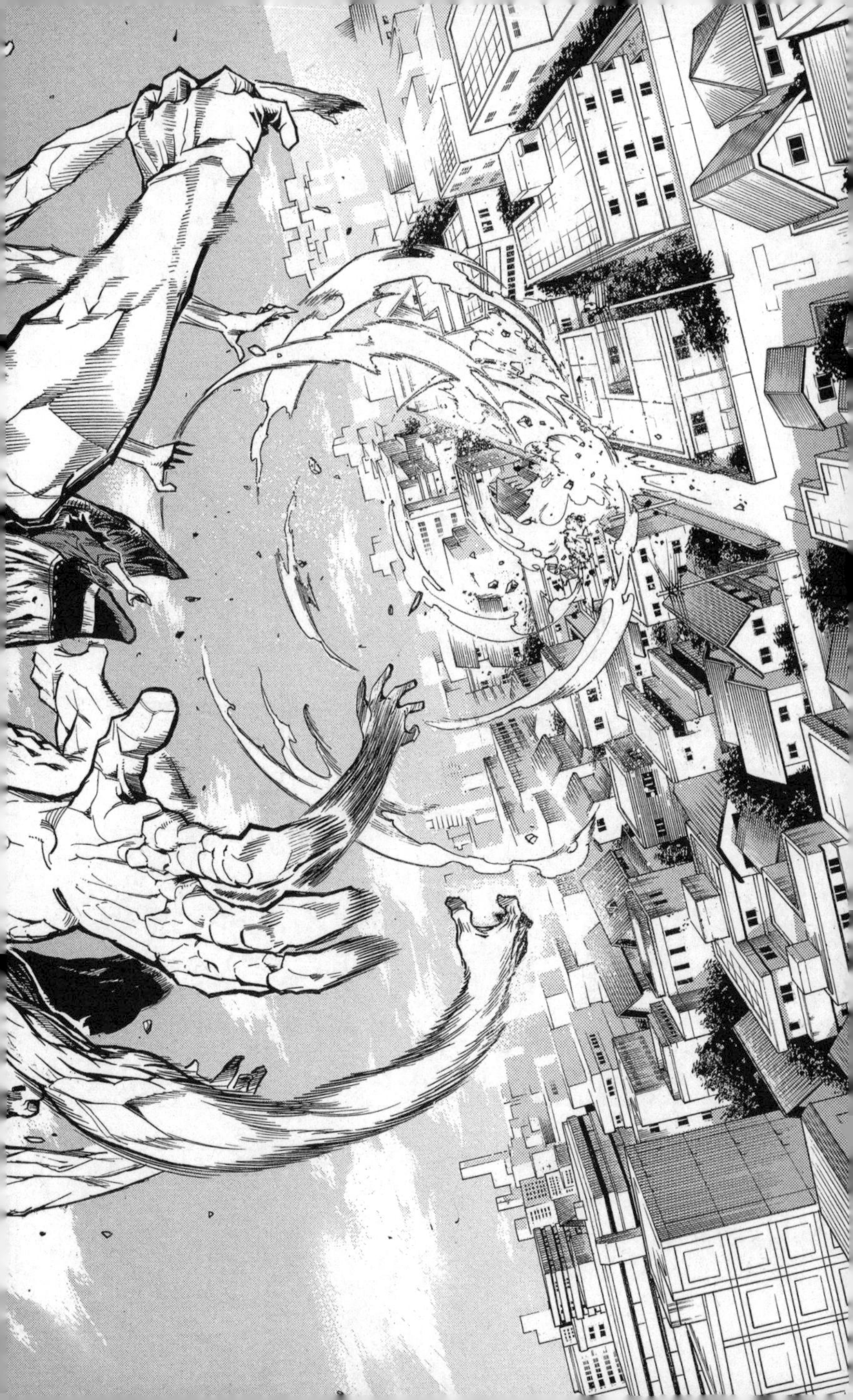

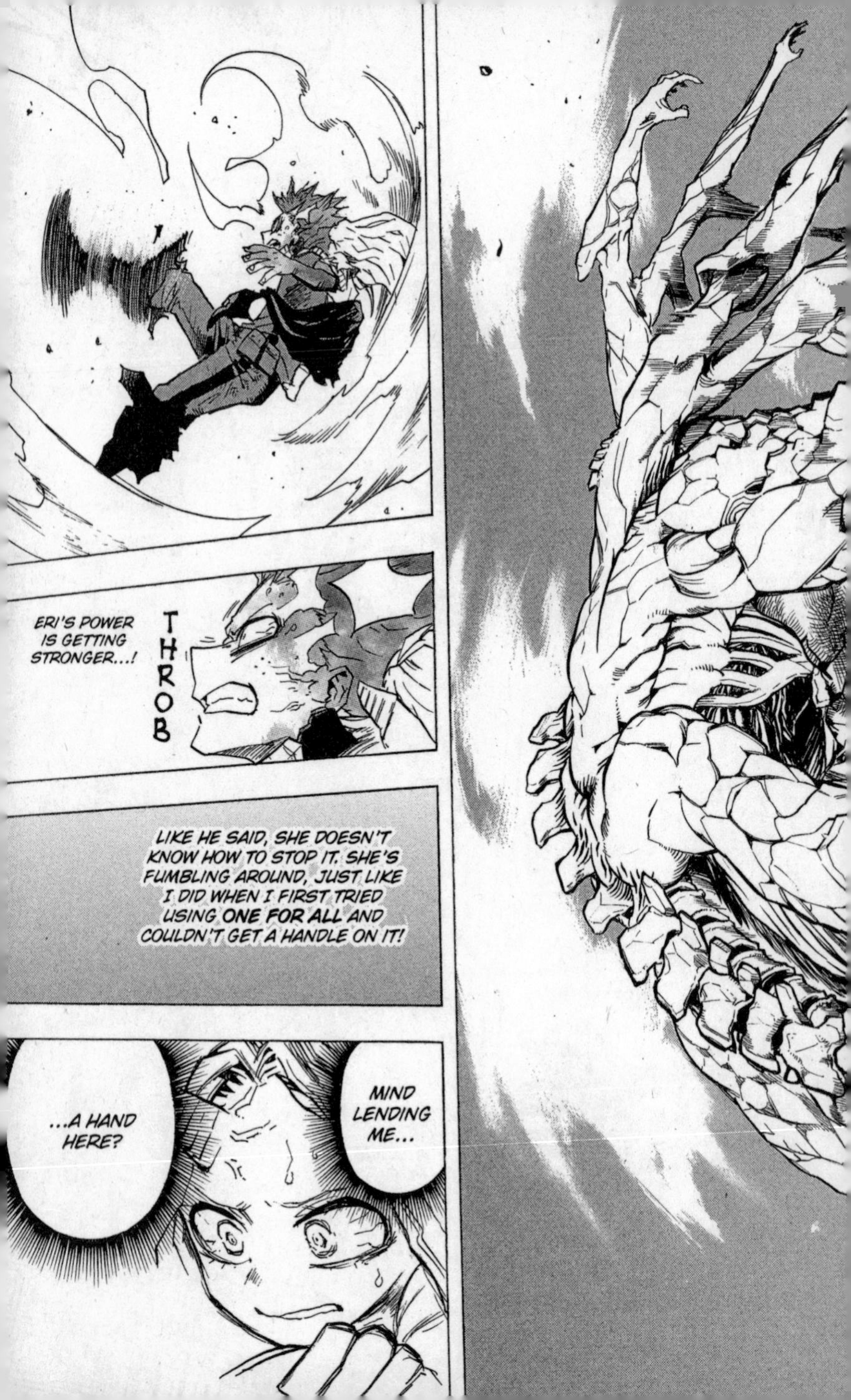
THROB
ERI'S POWER IS GETTING STRONGER...!
LIKE HE SAID, SHE DOESN'T KNOW HOW TO STOP IT. SHE'S FUMBLING AROUND, JUST LIKE I DID WHEN I FIRST TRIED USING ONE FOR ALL AND COULDN'T GET A HANDLE ON IT!
MIND LENDING ME...
...A HAND HERE?

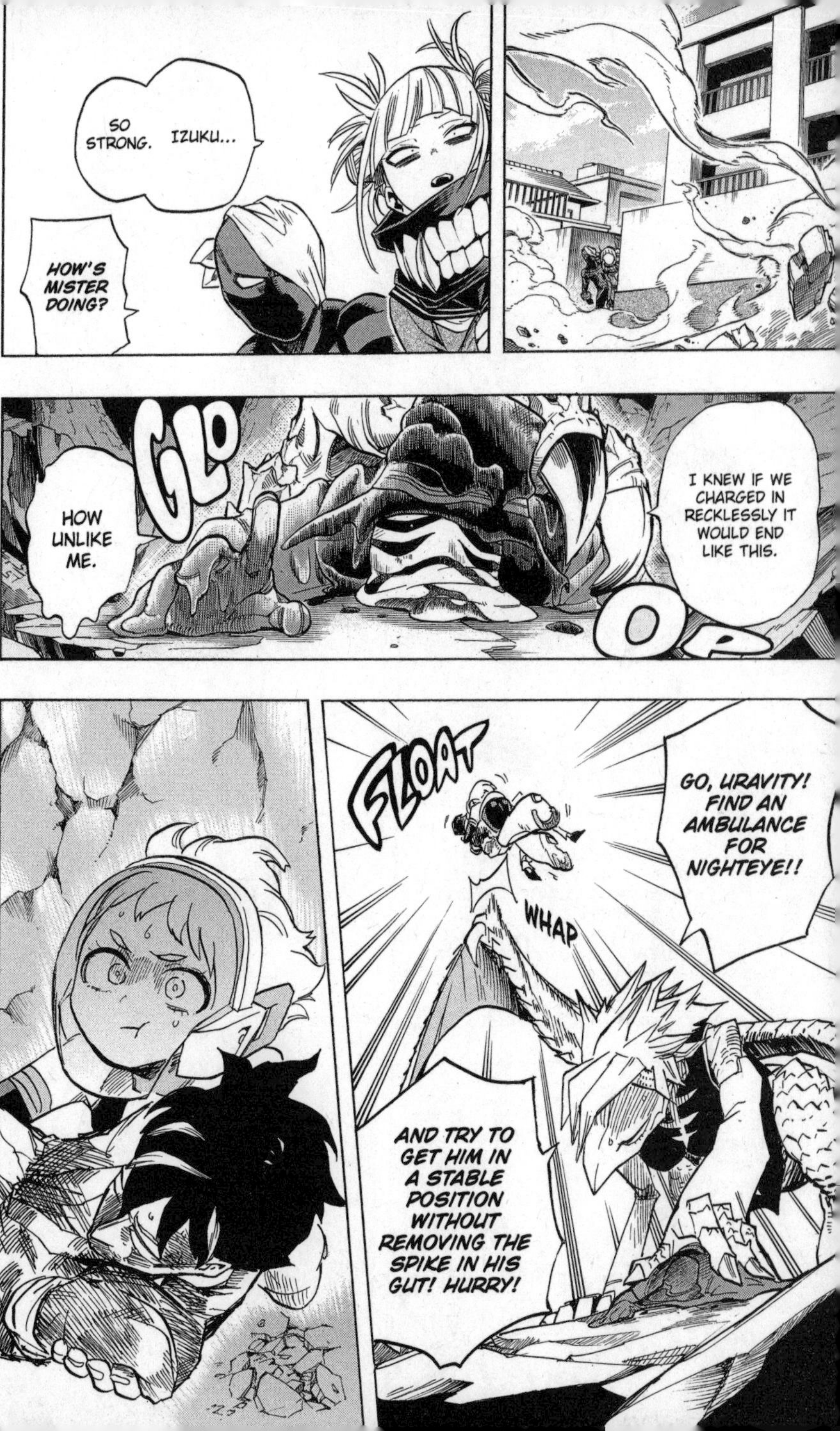
SO STRONG. IZUKU...
HOW'S MISTER DOING?
I KNEW IF WE CHARGED IN RECKLESSLY IT WOULD END LIKE THIS.
OP
GLO
HOW UNLIKE ME.
GO, URAVITY! FIND AN AMBULANCE FOR NIGHTEYE!!
FLOAT
WHAP
AND TRY TO GET HIM IN A STABLE POSITION WITHOUT REMOVING THE SPIKE IN HIS GUT! HURRY!

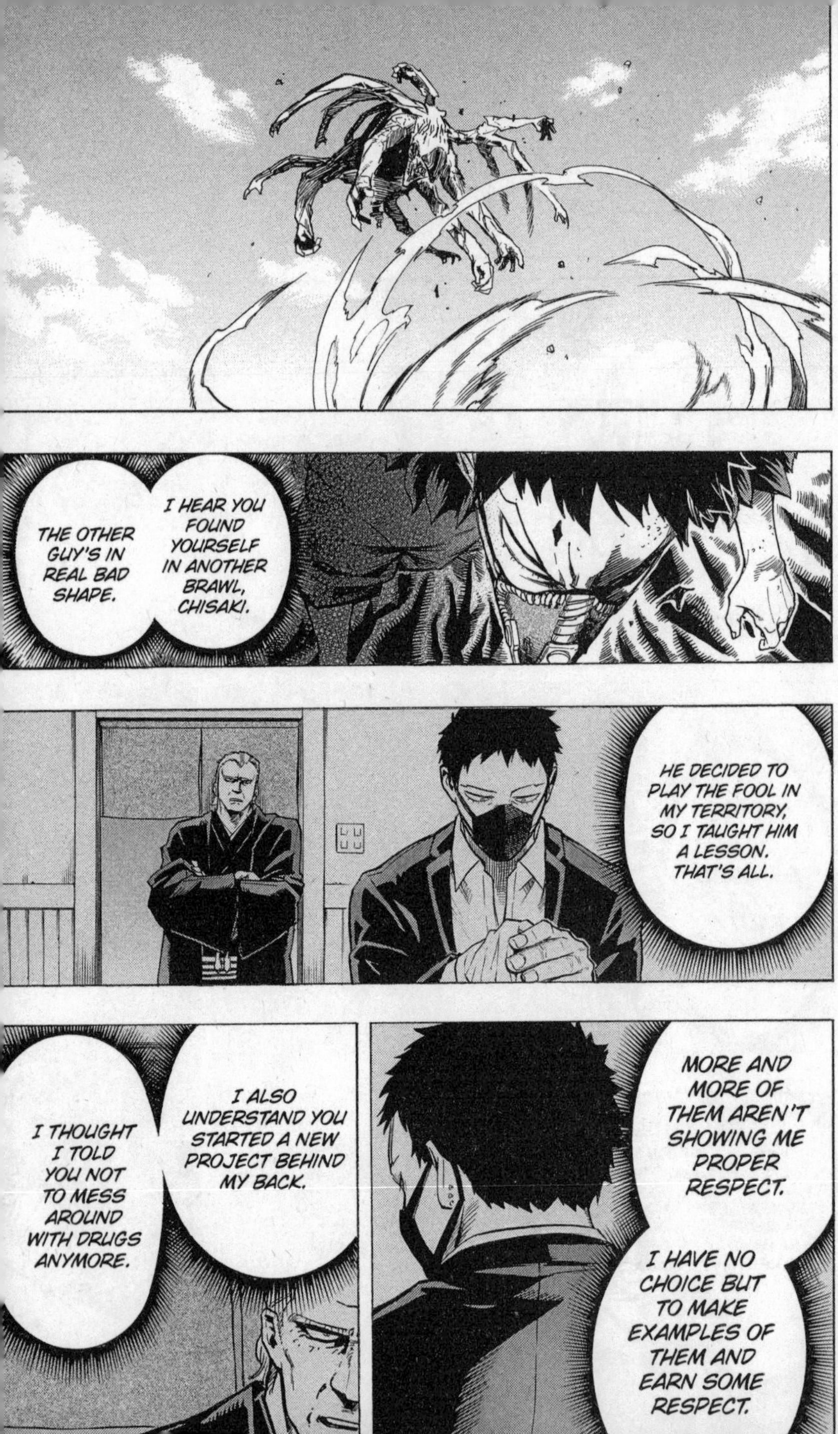
I HEAR YOU FOUND YOURSELF IN ANOTHER BRAWL, CHISAKI.
THE OTHER GUY'S IN REAL BAD SHAPE.
HE DECIDED TO PLAY THE FOOL IN MY TERRITORY, SO I TAUGHT HIM A LESSON. THAT'S ALL.
MORE AND MORE OF THEM AREN'T SHOWING ME PROPER RESPECT.
I HAVE NO CHOICE BUT TO MAKE EXAMPLES OF THEM AND EARN SOME RESPECT.
I ALSO UNDERSTAND YOU STARTED A NEW PROJECT BEHIND MY BACK.
I THOUGHT I TOLD YOU NOT TO MESS AROUND WITH DRUGS ANYMORE.

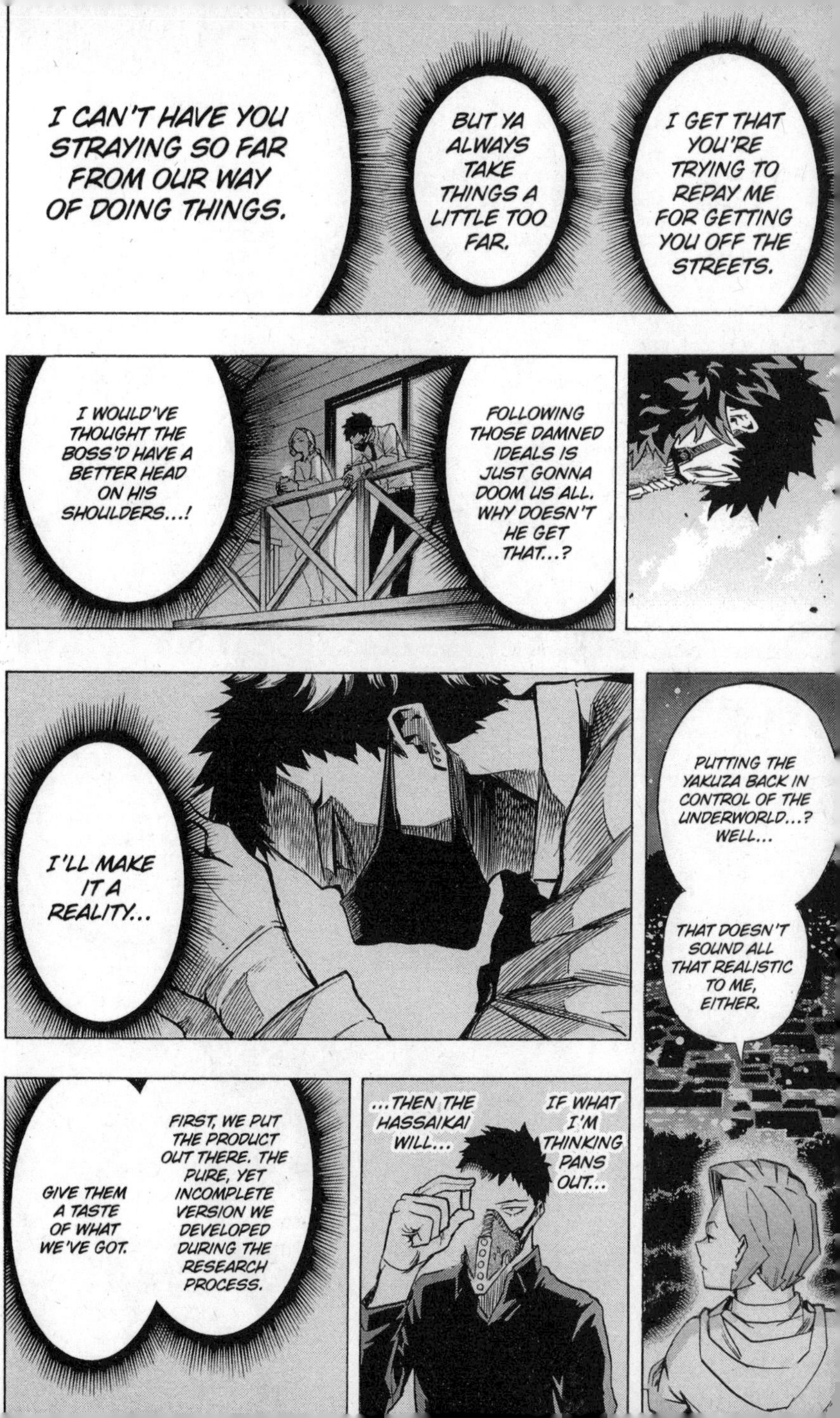
I GET THAT YOU'RE TRYING TO REPAY ME FOR GETTING YOU OFF THE STREETS.
BUT YA ALWAYS TAKE THINGS A LITTLE TOO FAR.
I CAN'T HAVE YOU STRAYING SO FAR FROM OUR WAY OF DOING THINGS.
FOLLOWING THOSE DAMNED IDEALS IS JUST GONNA DOOM US ALL. WHY DOESN'T HE GET THAT...?
I WOULD'VE THOUGHT THE BOSS'D HAVE A BETTER HEAD ON HIS SHOULDERS...!
PUTTING THE YAKUZA BACK IN CONTROL OF THE UNDERWORLD...? WELL...
THAT DOESN'T SOUND ALL THAT REALISTIC TO ME, EITHER.
I'LL MAKE IT A REALITY...
IF WHAT I'M THINKING PANS OUT...
...THEN THE HASSAIKAI WILL...
FIRST, WE PUT THE PRODUCT OUT THERE. THE PURE, YET INCOMPLETE VERSION WE DEVELOPED DURING THE RESEARCH PROCESS.
GIVE THEM A TASTE OF WHAT WE'VE GOT.

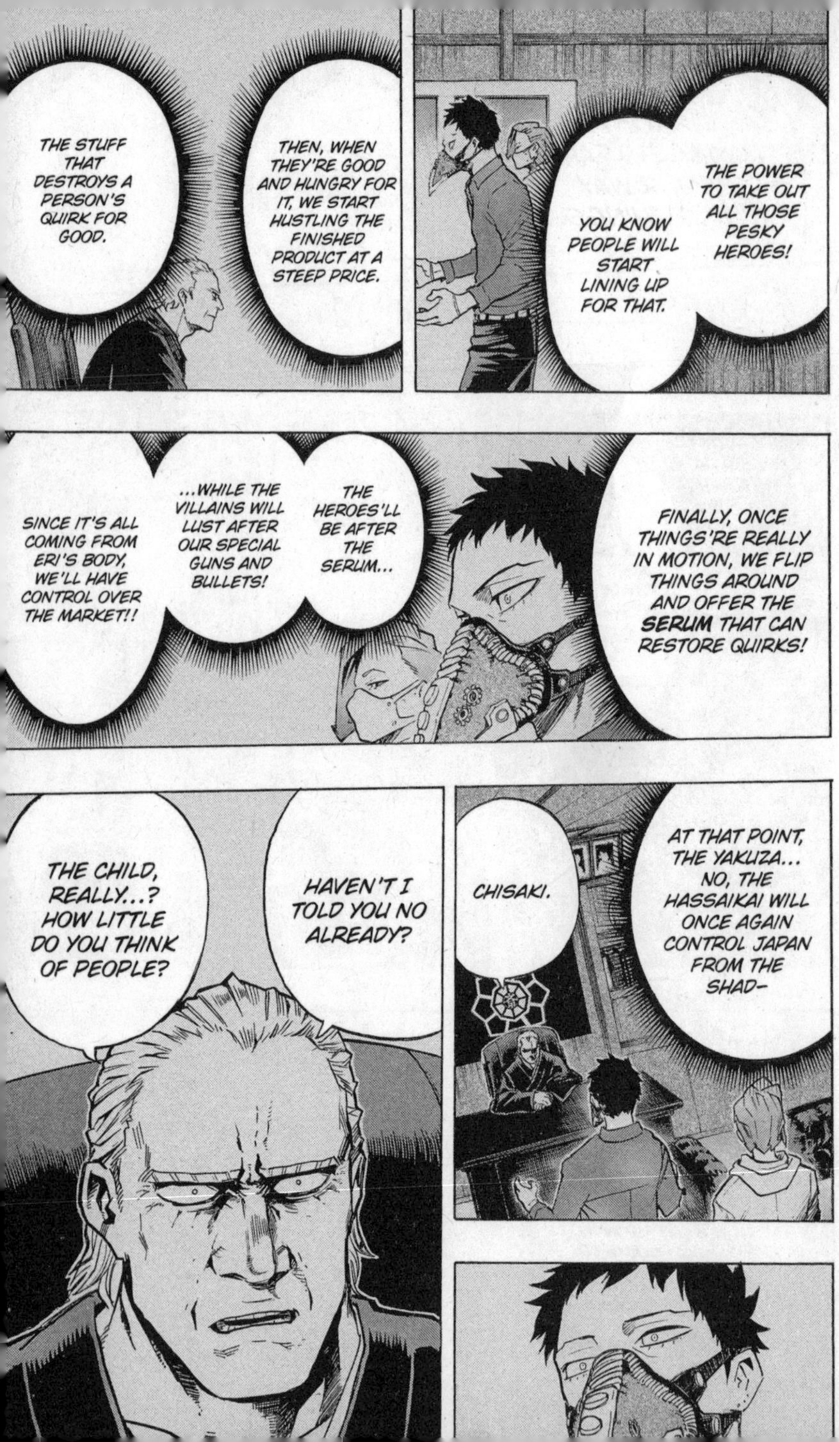
THE POWER TO TAKE OUT ALL THOSE PESKY HEROES!
YOU KNOW PEOPLE WILL START LINING UP FOR THAT.
THEN, WHEN THEY'RE GOOD AND HUNGRY FOR IT, WE START HUSTLING THE FINISHED PRODUCT AT A STEEP PRICE.
THE STUFF THAT DESTROYS A PERSON'S QUIRK FOR GOOD.
FINALLY, ONCE THINGS'RE REALLY IN MOTION, WE FLIP THINGS AROUND AND OFFER THE **SERUM** THAT CAN RESTORE QUIRKS!
THE HEROES'LL BE AFTER THE SERUM...
...WHILE THE VILLAINS WILL LUST AFTER OUR SPECIAL GUNS AND BULLETS!
SINCE IT'S ALL COMING FROM ERI'S BODY, WE'LL HAVE CONTROL OVER THE MARKET!!
AT THAT POINT, THE YAKUZA... NO, THE HASSAIKAI WILL ONCE AGAIN CONTROL JAPAN FROM THE SHAD-
CHISAKI.
HAVEN'T I TOLD YOU NO ALREADY?
THE CHILD, REALLY...? HOW LITTLE DO YOU THINK OF PEOPLE?

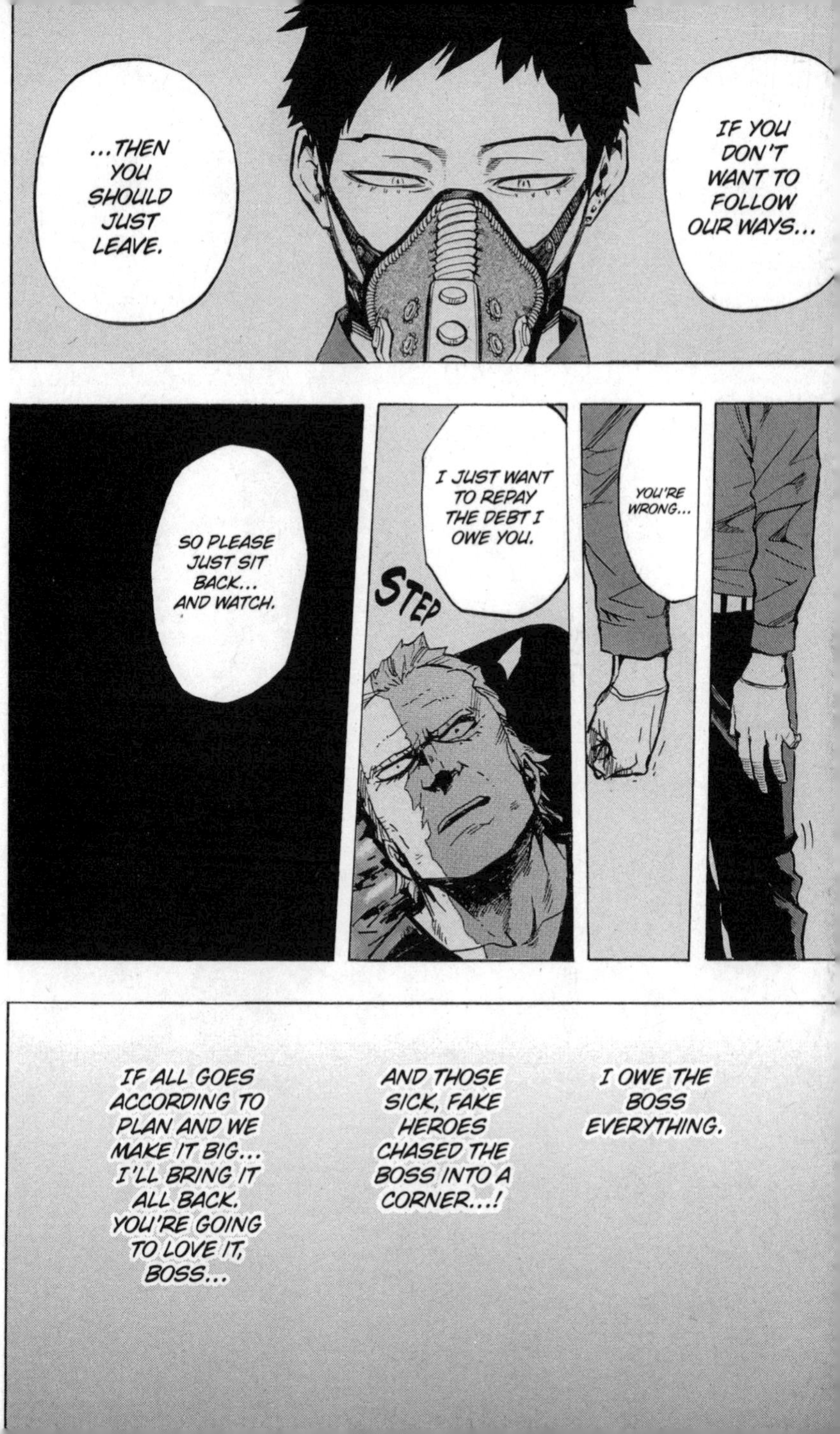
IF YOU DON'T WANT TO FOLLOW OUR WAYS...
...THEN YOU SHOULD JUST LEAVE.
YOU'RE WRONG...
I JUST WANT TO REPAY THE DEBT I OWE YOU.
STEP
SO PLEASE JUST SIT BACK... AND WATCH.
I OWE THE BOSS EVERYTHING.
AND THOSE SICK, FAKE HEROES CHASED THE BOSS INTO A CORNER...!
IF ALL GOES ACCORDING TO PLAN AND WE MAKE IT BIG... I'LL BRING IT ALL BACK. YOU'RE GOING TO LOVE IT, BOSS...

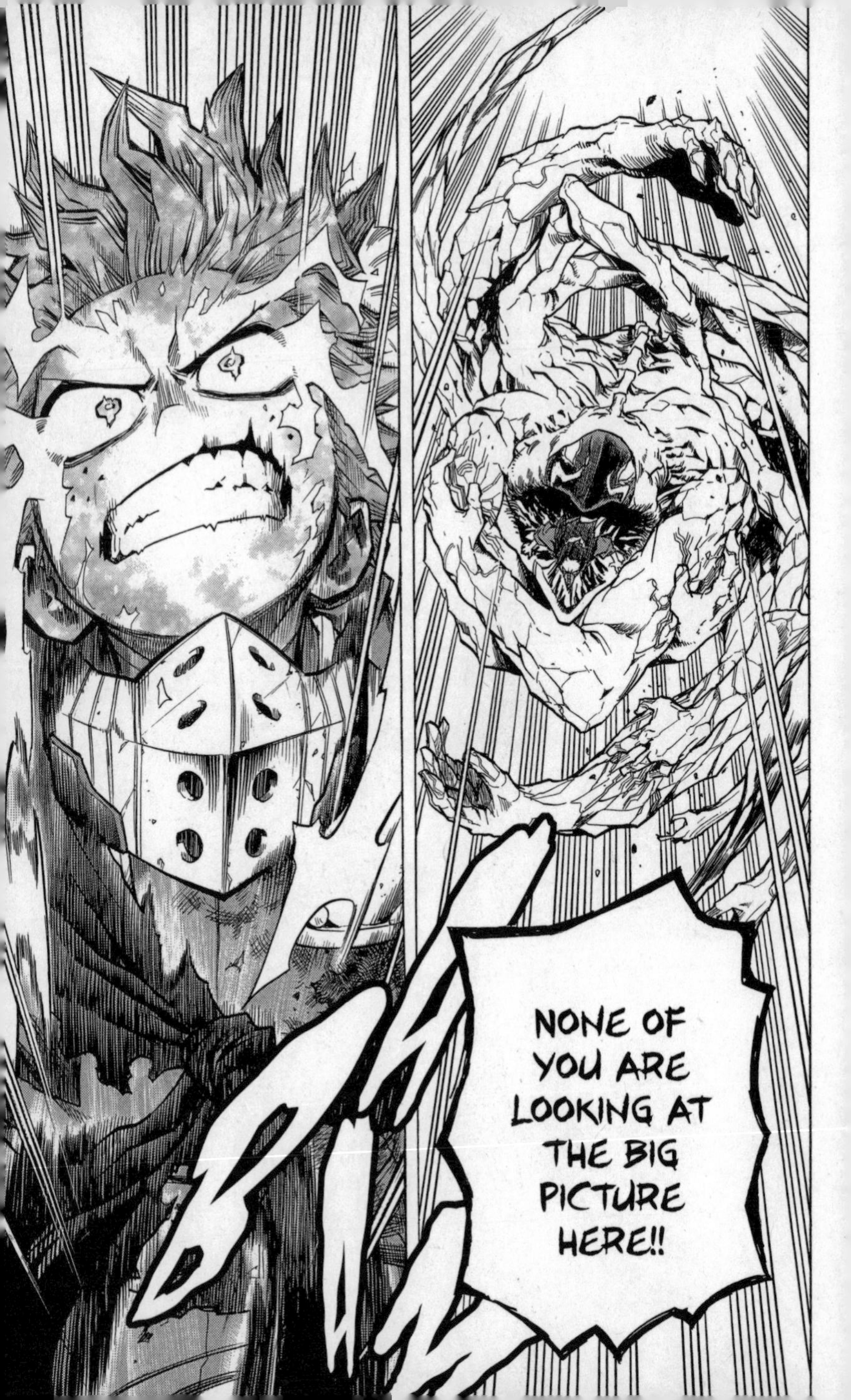
NONE OF YOU ARE LOOKING AT THE BIG PICTURE HERE!!

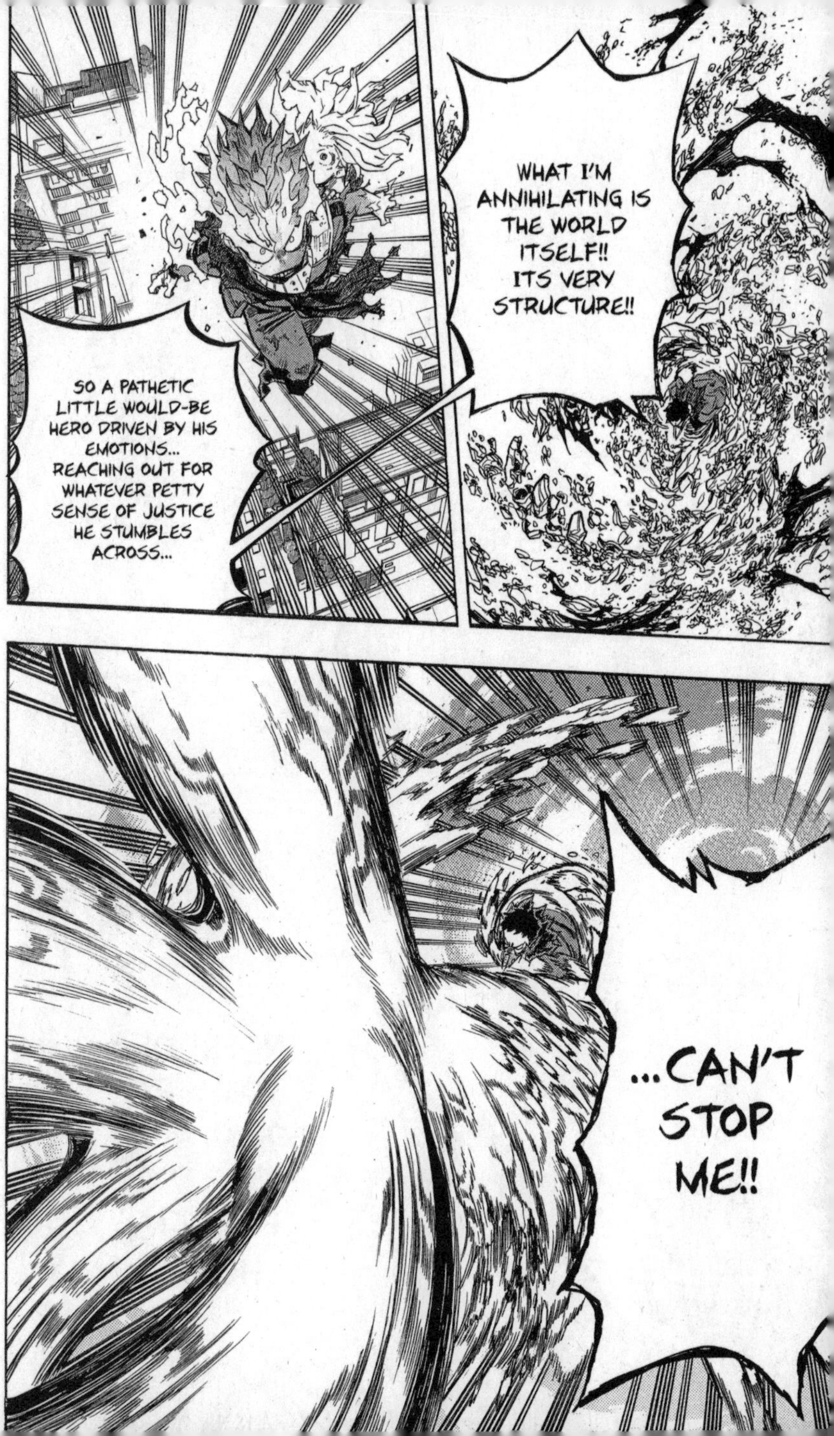
WHAT I'M ANNIHILATING IS THE WORLD ITSELF!! ITS VERY STRUCTURE!!
SO A PATHETIC LITTLE WOULD-BE HERO DRIVEN BY HIS EMOTIONS... REACHING OUT FOR WHATEVER PETTY SENSE OF JUSTICE HE STUMBLES ACROSS...
...CAN'T STOP ME!!

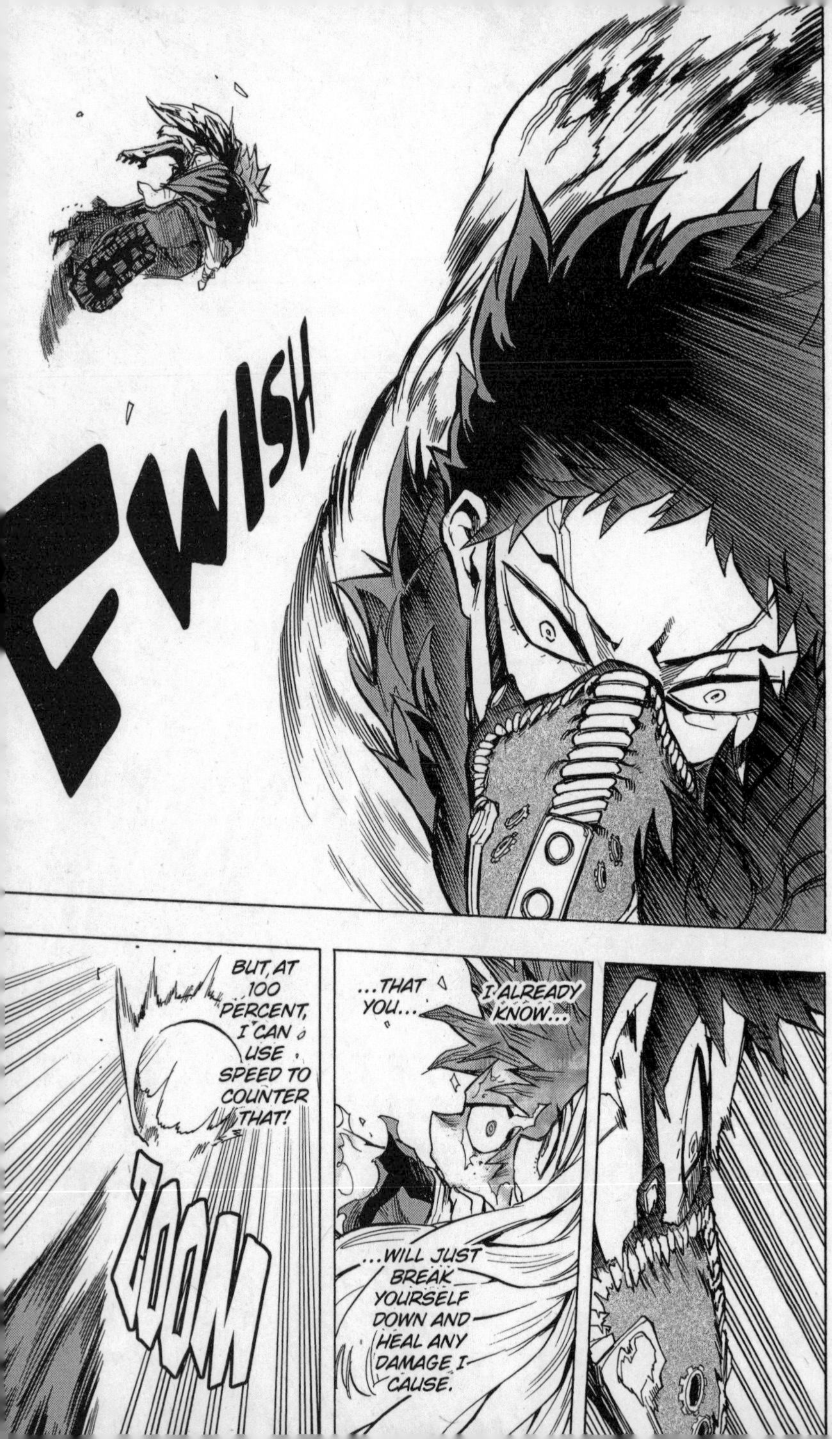
FWISH
I ALREADY KNOW...
...THAT YOU...
...WILL JUST BREAK YOURSELF DOWN AND HEAL ANY DAMAGE I CAUSE.
BUT, AT 100 PERCENT, I CAN USE SPEED TO COUNTER THAT!
ZOOM

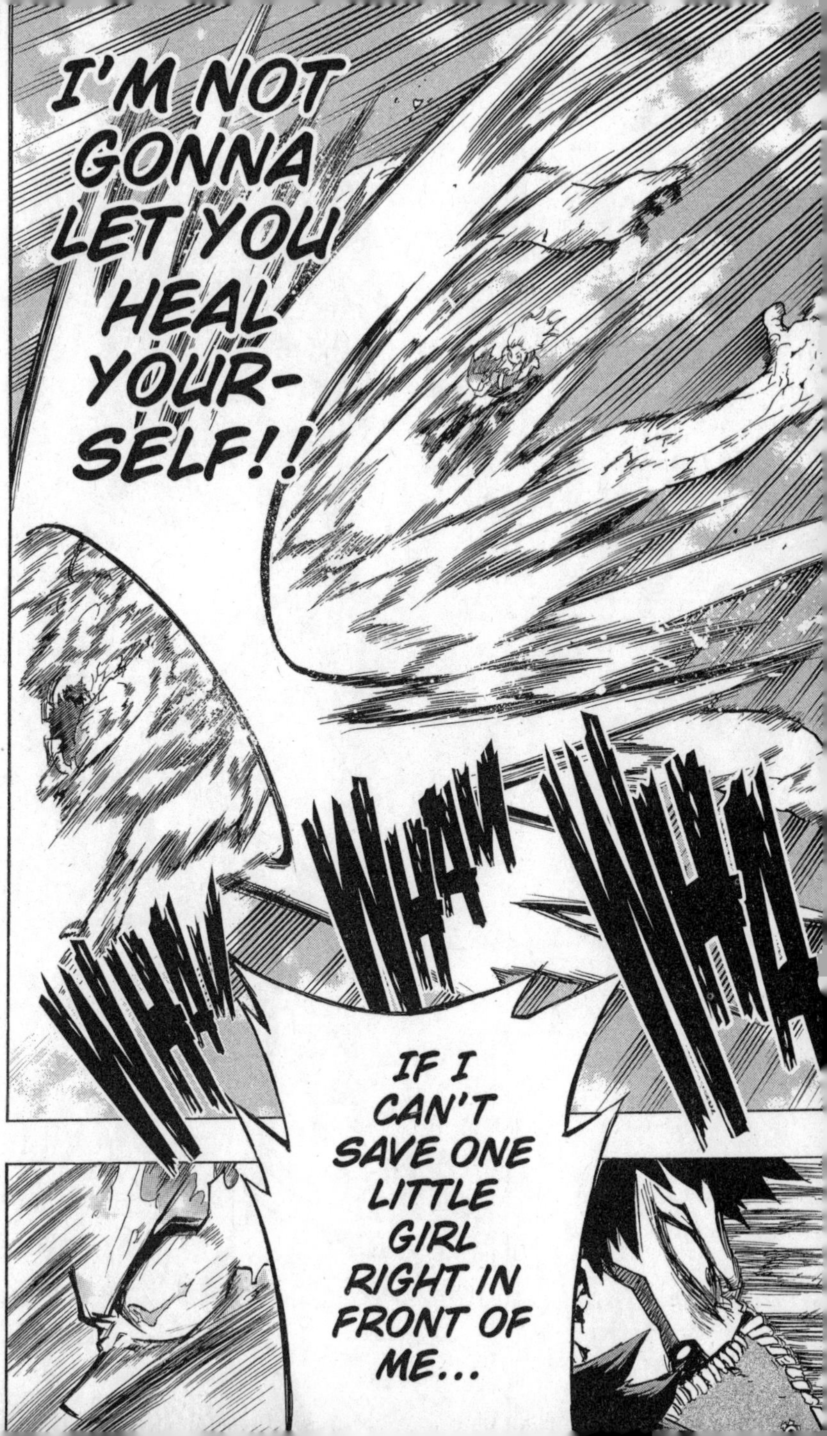
I'M NOT GONNA LET YOU HEAL YOURSELF!!
WHAM
WHAM
WHAM
IF I CAN'T SAVE ONE LITTLE GIRL RIGHT IN FRONT OF ME...

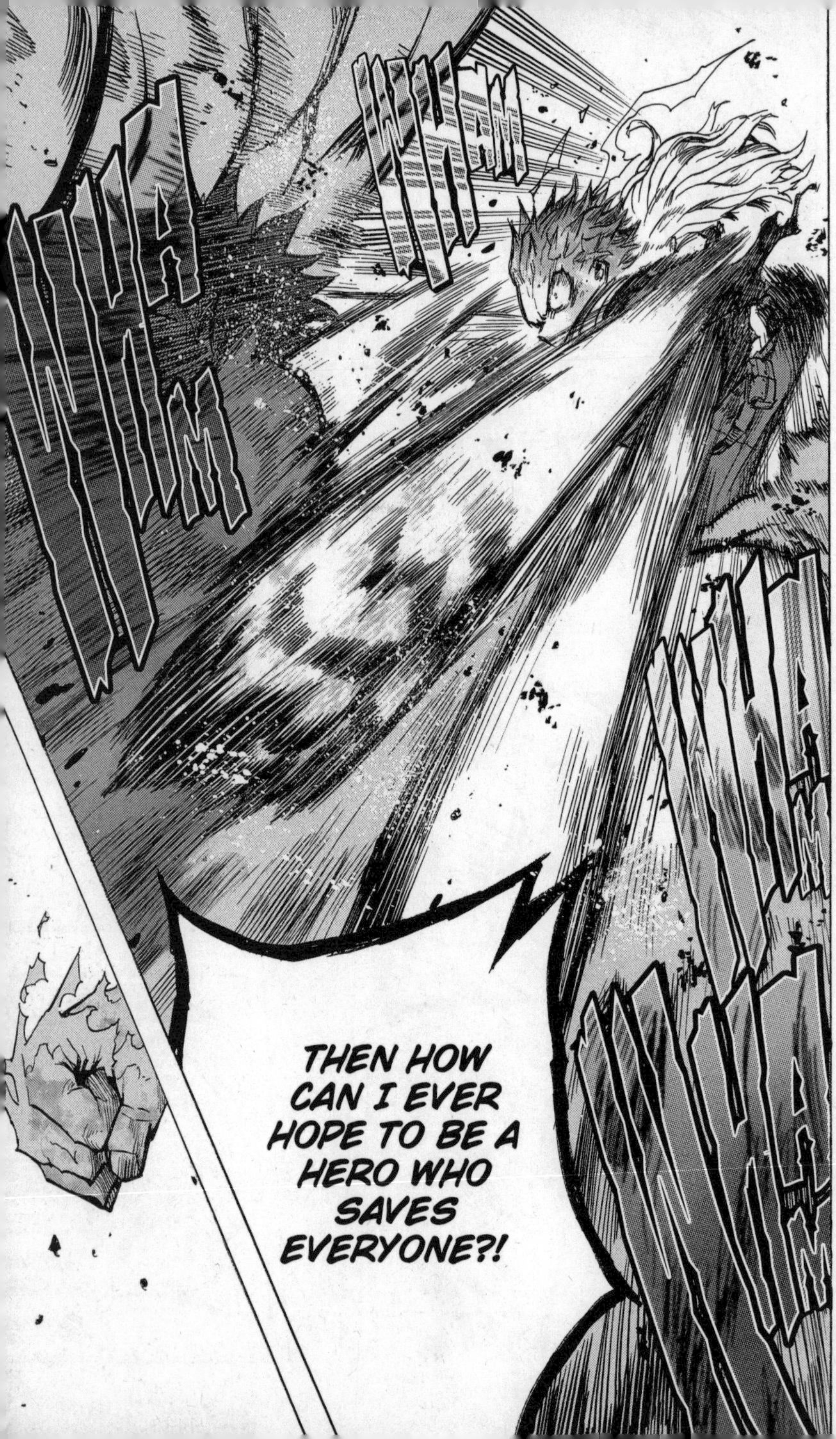
THEN HOW CAN I EVER HOPE TO BE A HERO WHO SAVES EVERYONE?!

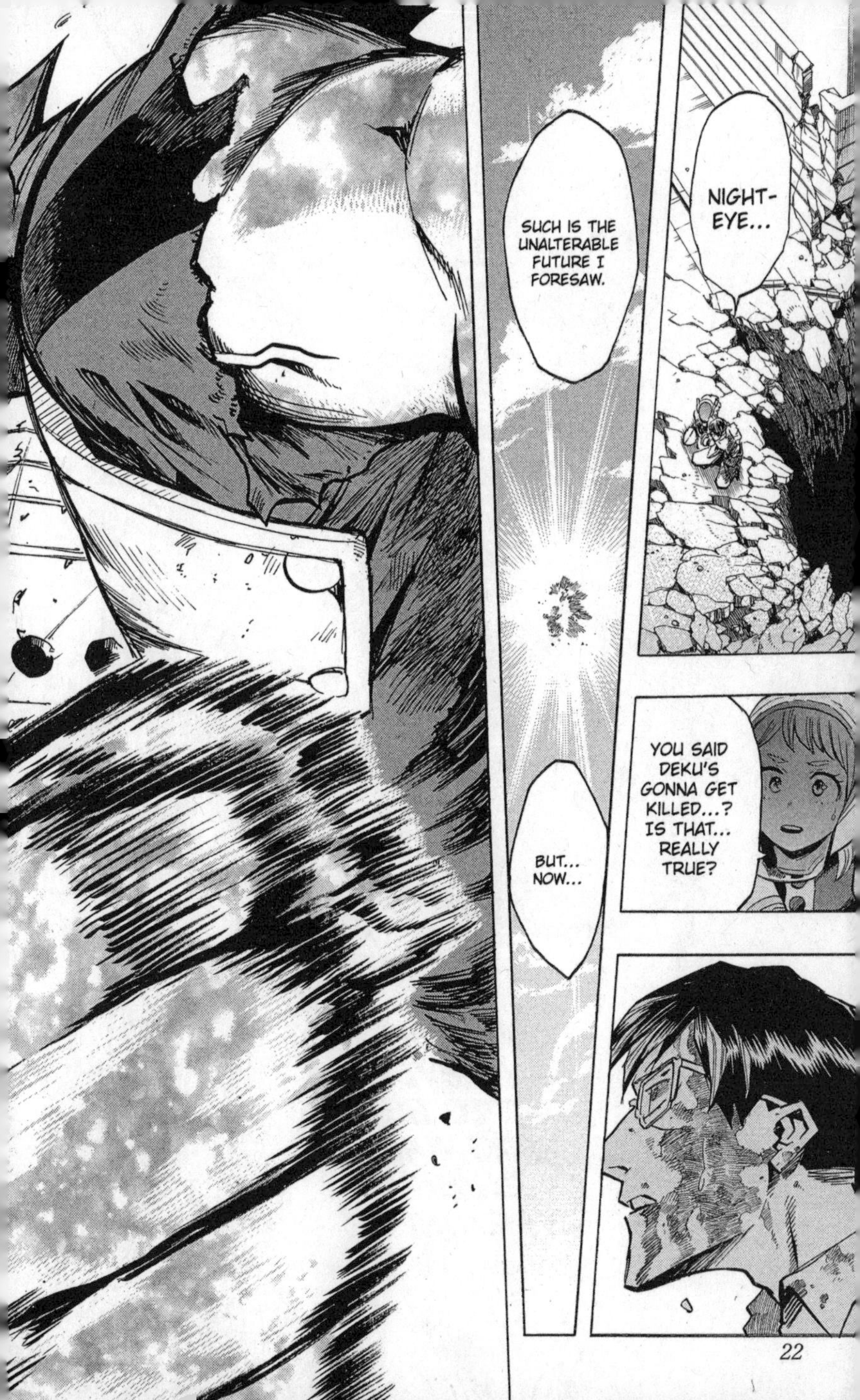
NIGHT-EYE...
YOU SAID DEKU'S GONNA GET KILLED...? IS THAT... REALLY TRUE?
SUCH IS THE UNALTERABLE FUTURE I FORESAW.
BUT... NOW...

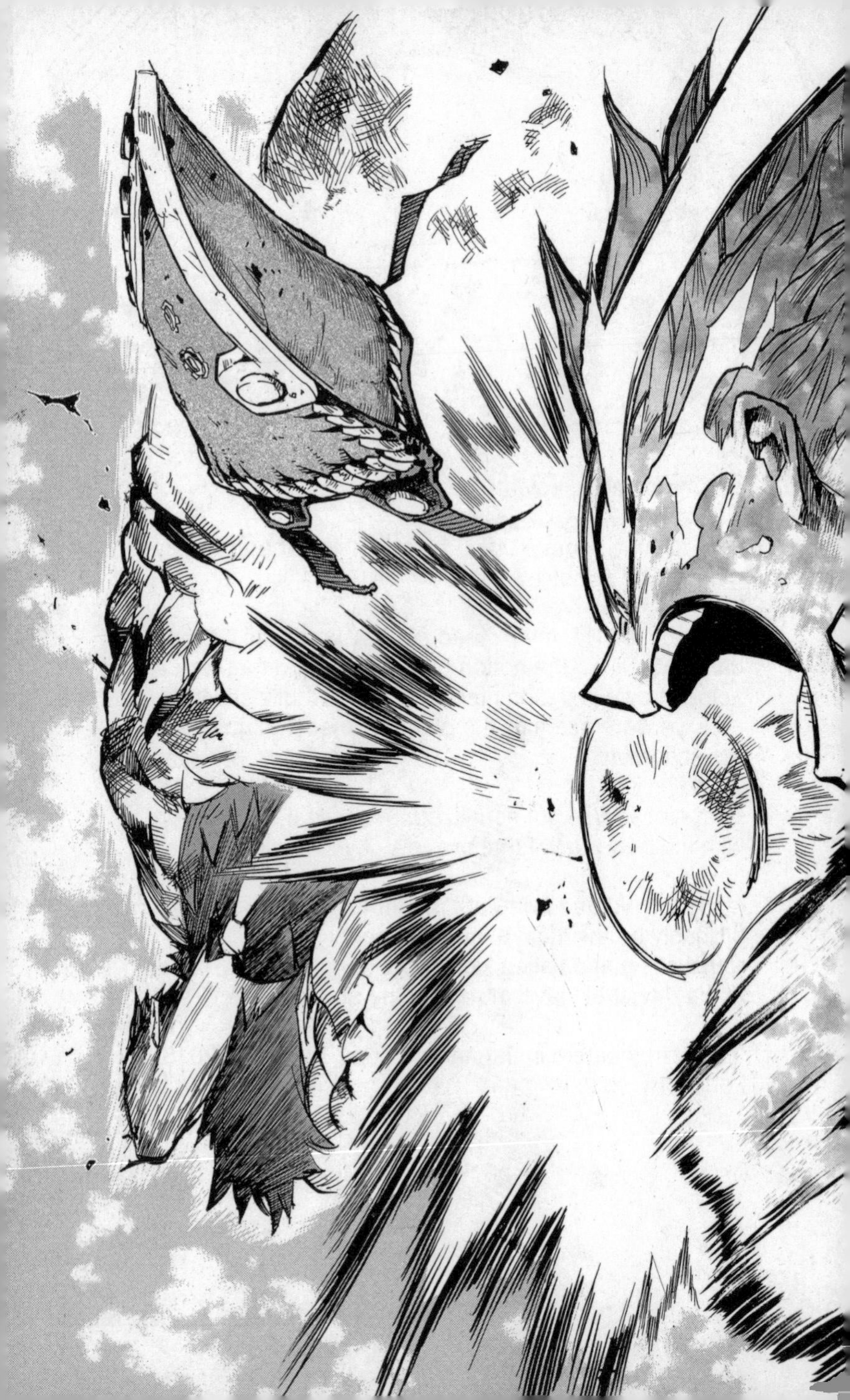

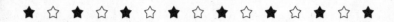

THE·MOVIE

We're getting a movie!!

This all may seem a bit sudden, but yes–there's really going to be a movie.

I already felt like my life had peaked when the anime came about, so the notion of going beyond that with an actual movie just didn't feel real. I didn't fully accept it until we were actually in a planning meeting, going over the script, etc.

Ever since *MHA* got serialized, every year has brought with it a new peak, I guess.

Once I'm old and living out my remaining years, I'll probably be the local pseudo celebrity, known for reminiscing and telling kids in the neighborhood, "Back in the day, they gave me an anime and a movie to boot."

It's out in theaters in Japan on Friday, August 3, 2018. Look forward to it!!

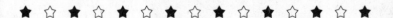

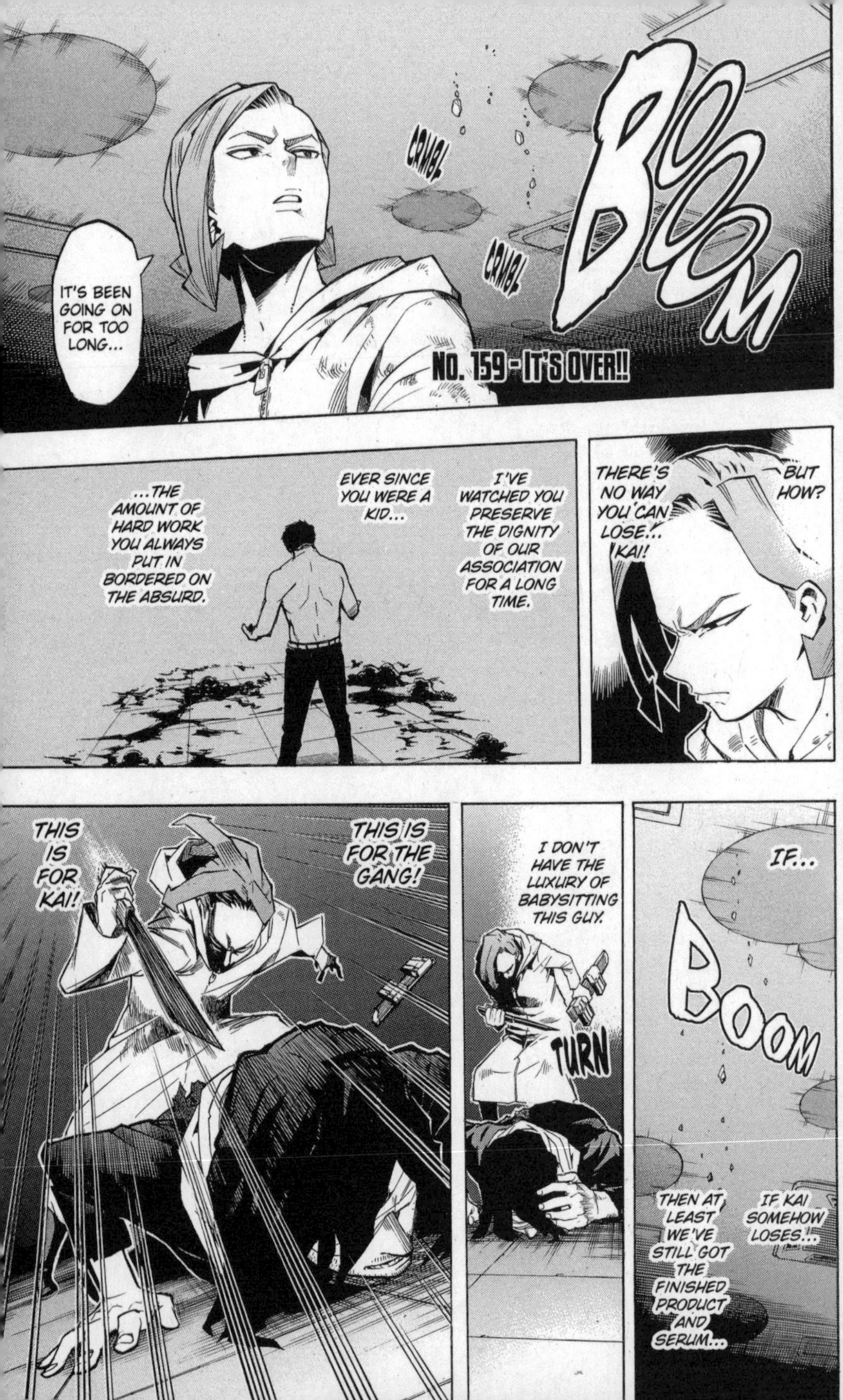
BOOM
CRMBL
CRMBL
NO. 159 - IT'S OVER!!
IT'S BEEN GOING ON FOR TOO LONG...
BUT HOW?
THERE'S NO WAY YOU CAN LOSE... KAI!
I'VE WATCHED YOU PRESERVE THE DIGNITY OF OUR ASSOCIATION FOR A LONG TIME.
EVER SINCE YOU WERE A KID...
...THE AMOUNT OF HARD WORK YOU ALWAYS PUT IN BORDERED ON THE ABSURD.
IF...
BOOM
IF KAI SOMEHOW LOSES...
THEN AT LEAST WE'VE STILL GOT THE FINISHED PRODUCT AND SERUM...
I DON'T HAVE THE LUXURY OF BABYSITTING THIS GUY.
TURN
THIS IS FOR THE GANG!
THIS IS FOR KAI!

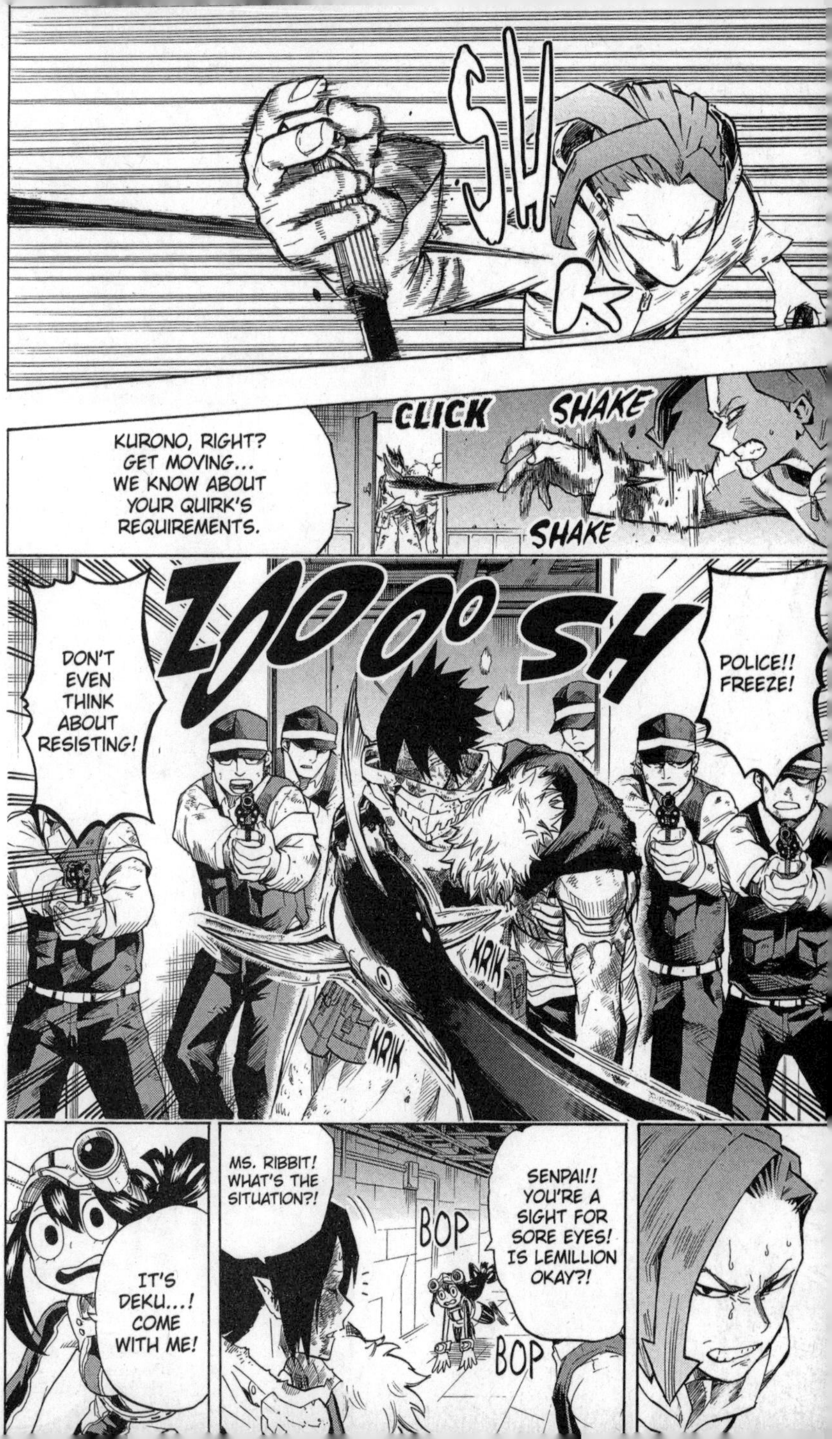
SHK
SHAKE
CLICK
KURONO, RIGHT? GET MOVING... WE KNOW ABOUT YOUR QUIRK'S REQUIREMENTS.
SHAKE
ZOOOOSH
POLICE!! FREEZE!
DON'T EVEN THINK ABOUT RESISTING!
KRIK
KRIK
SENPAI!! YOU'RE A SIGHT FOR SORE EYES! IS LEMILLION OKAY?!
MS. RIBBIT! WHAT'S THE SITUATION?!
BOP
BOP
IT'S DEKU...! COME WITH ME!

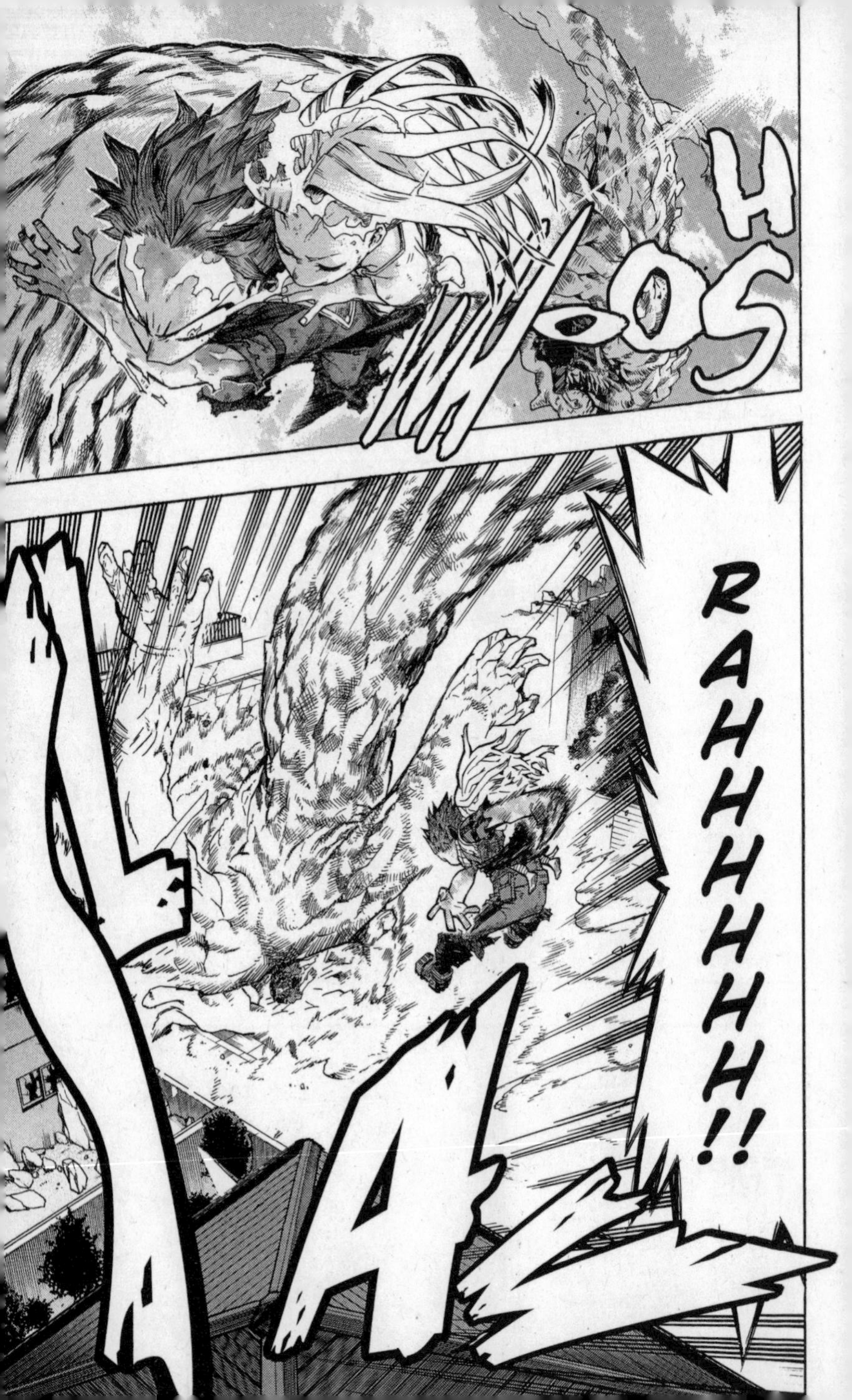
WOOSH
RAHHHHHH!!

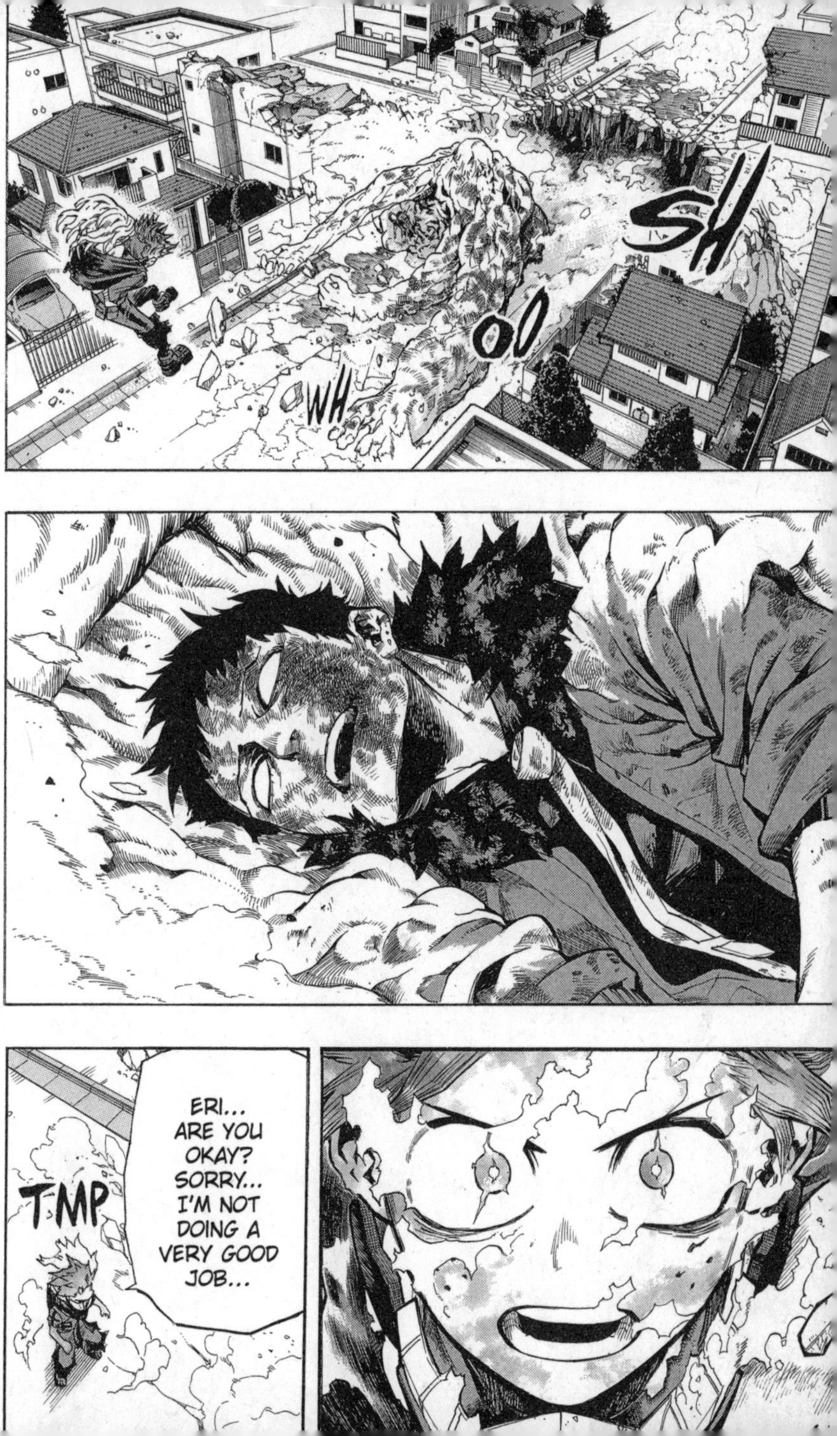
WHOOSH
ERI... ARE YOU OKAY? SORRY... I'M NOT DOING A VERY GOOD JOB...
TMP

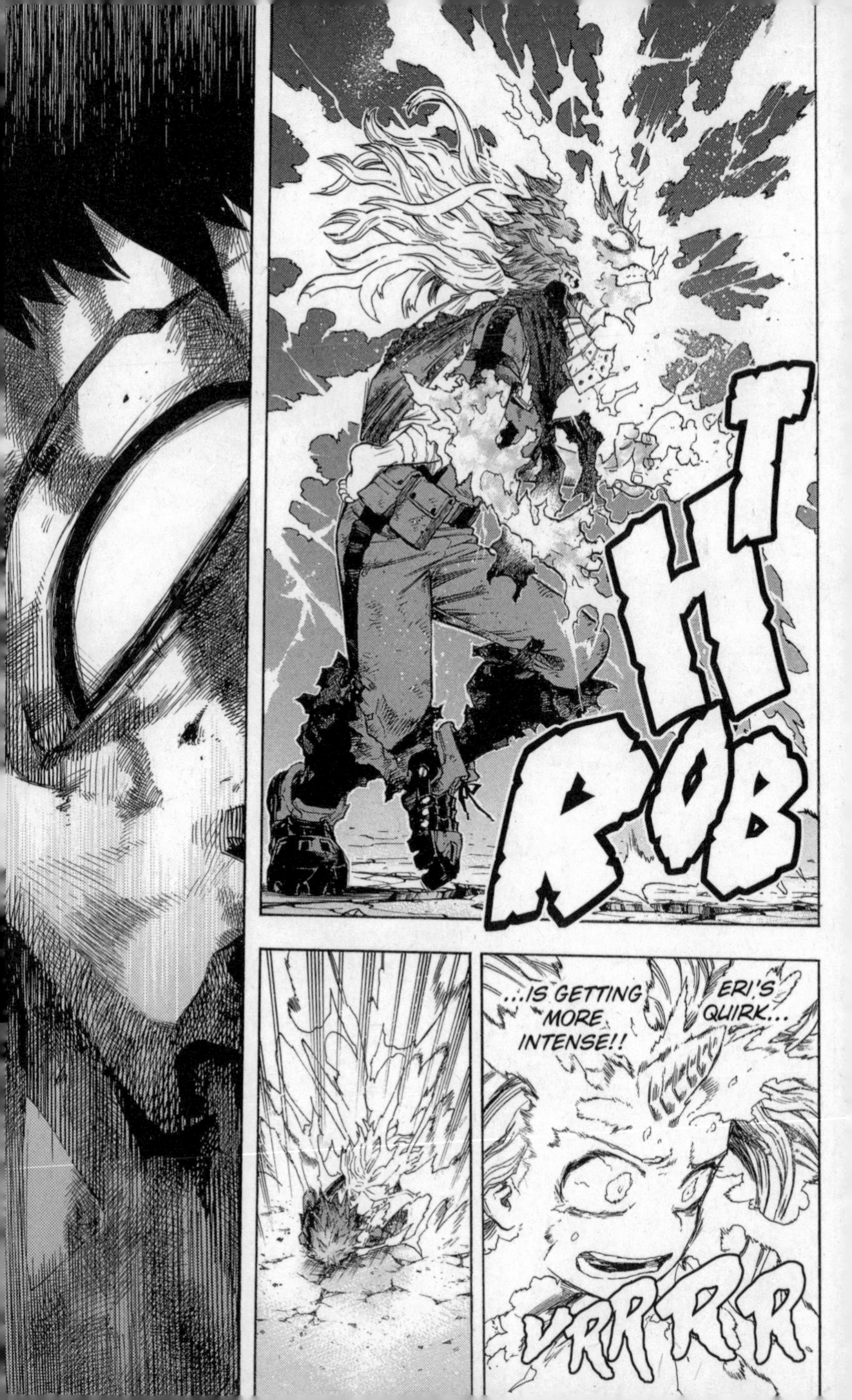
THROB
ERI'S QUIRK...
...IS GETTING MORE INTENSE!!
VRRRRR

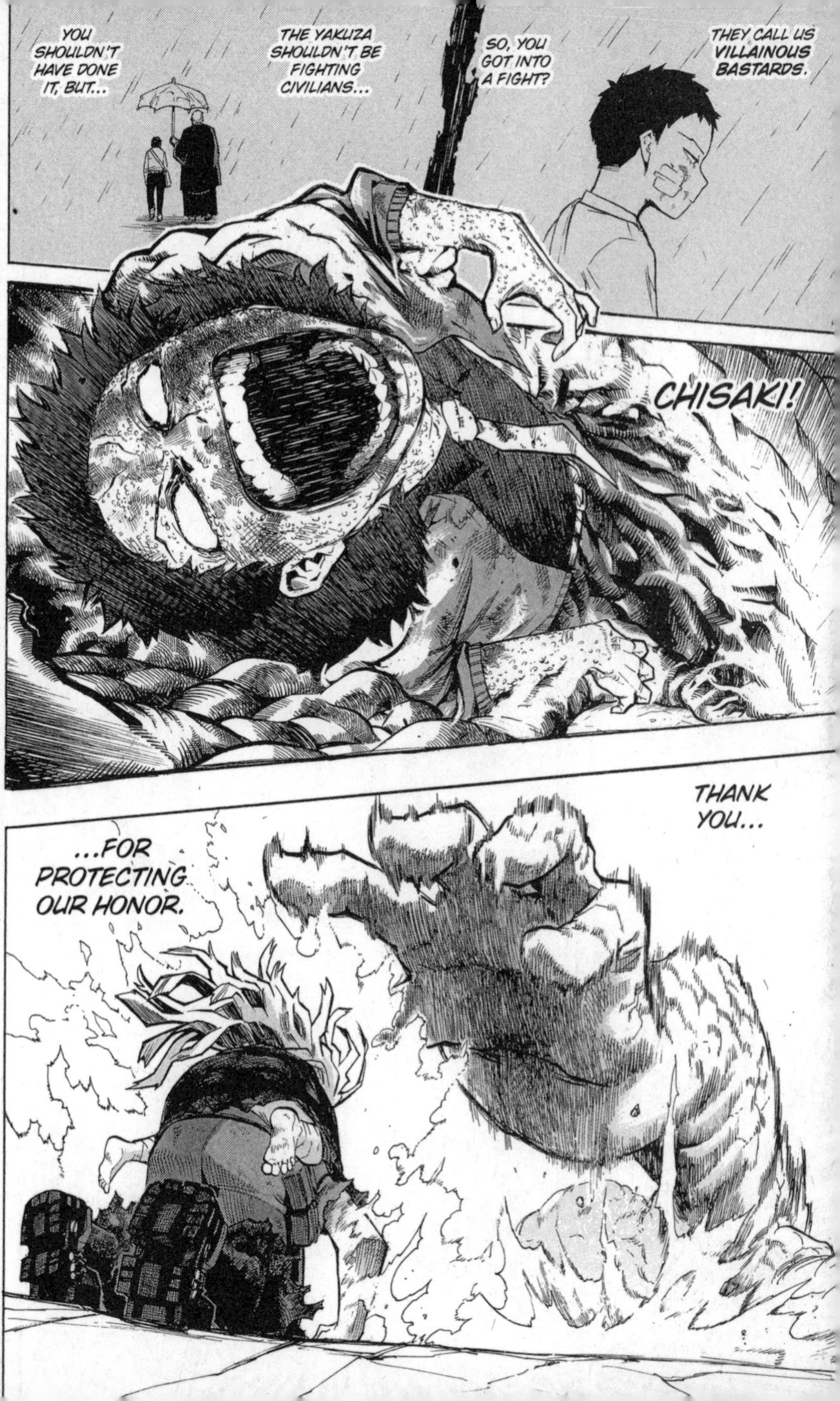
THEY CALL US VILLAINOUS BASTARDS.
SO, YOU GOT INTO A FIGHT?
THE YAKUZA SHOULDN'T BE FIGHTING CIVILIANS...
YOU SHOULDN'T HAVE DONE IT, BUT...
CHISAKI!
THANK YOU...
...FOR PROTECTING OUR HONOR.

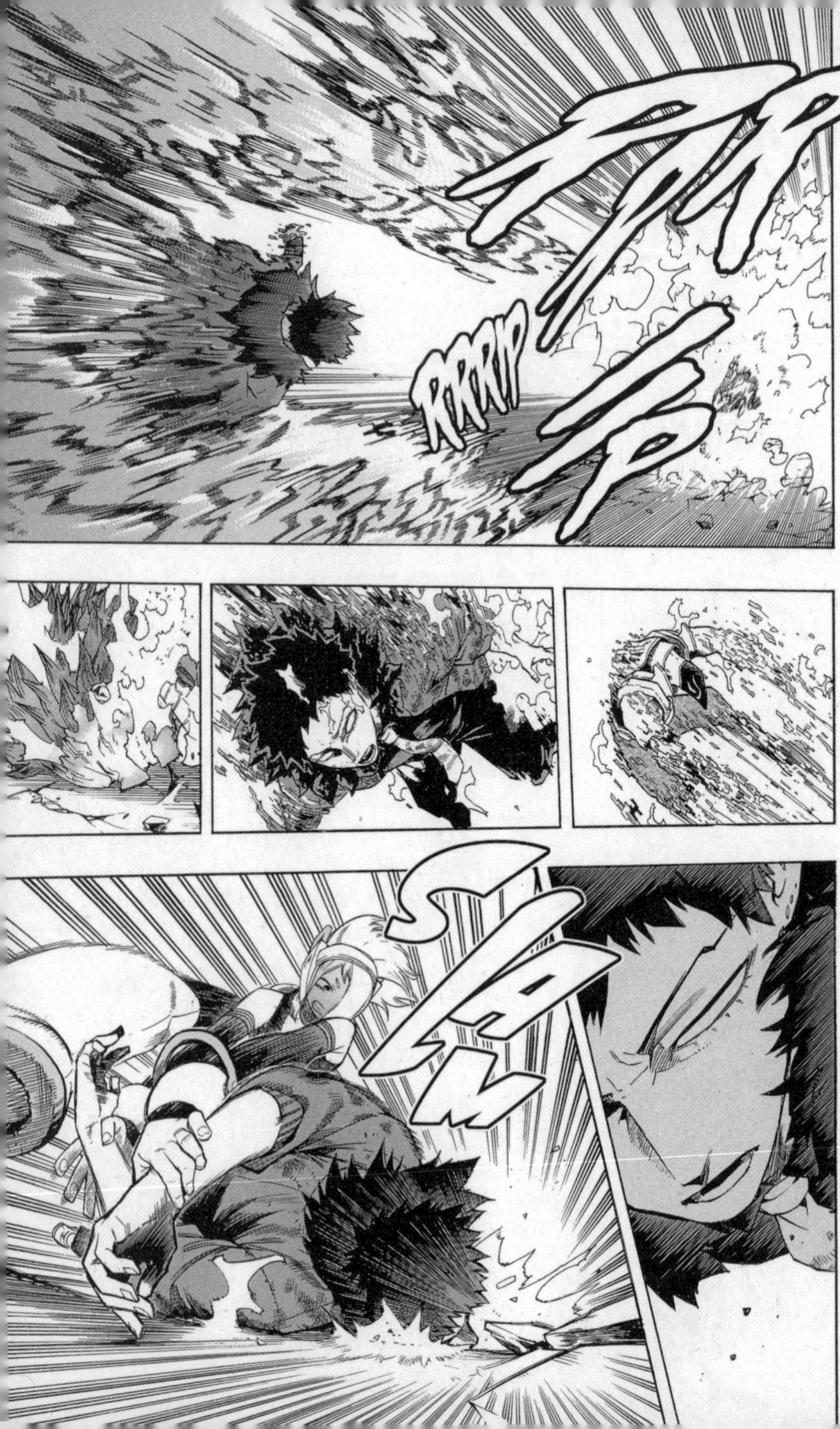
RRIP
RRRRIP
SLAM

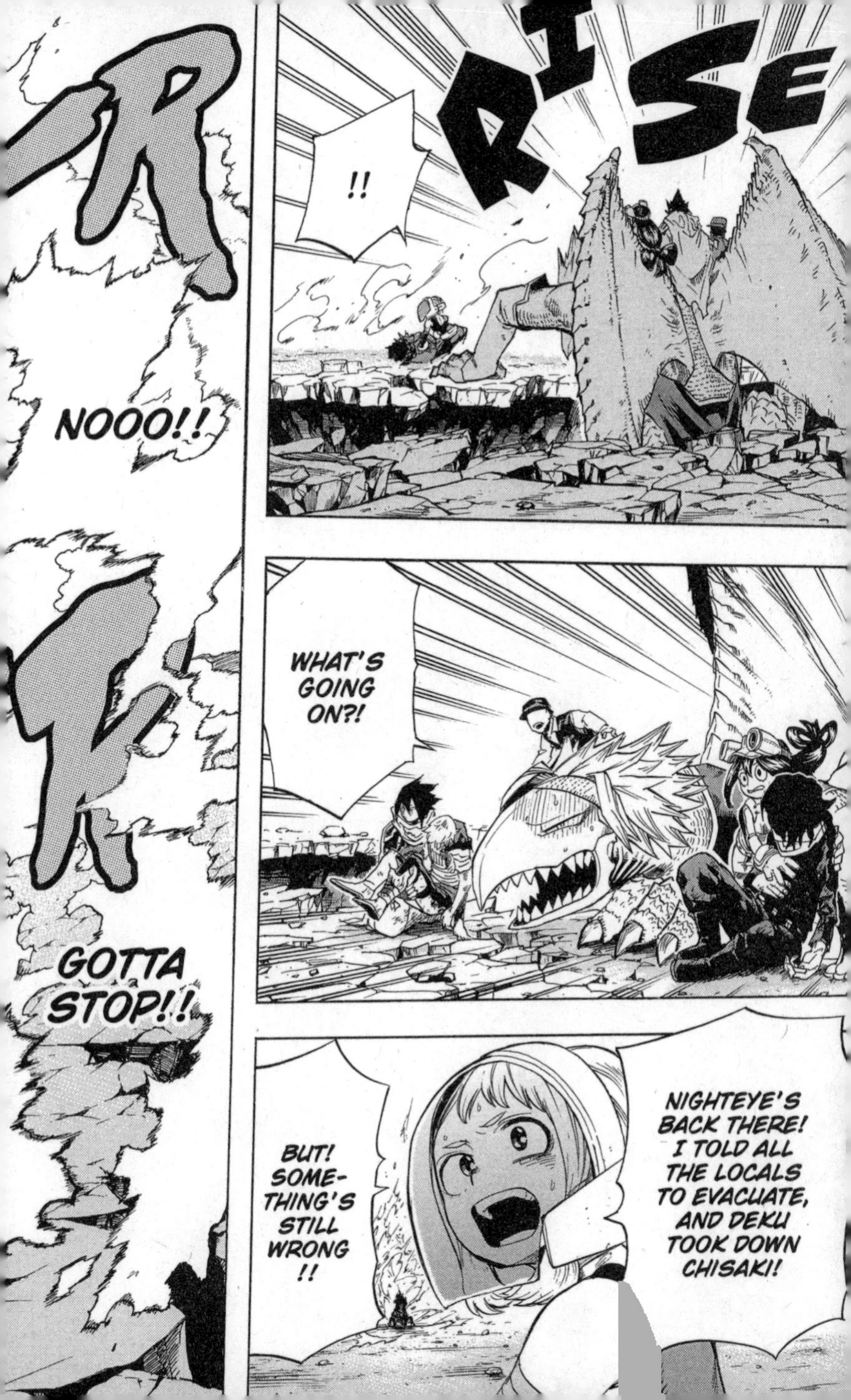
RISE
!!
WHAT'S GOING ON?!
NIGHTEYE'S BACK THERE! I TOLD ALL THE LOCALS TO EVACUATE, AND DEKU TOOK DOWN CHISAKI!
BUT! SOME-THING'S STILL WRONG!!
NOOO!!
GOTTA STOP!!

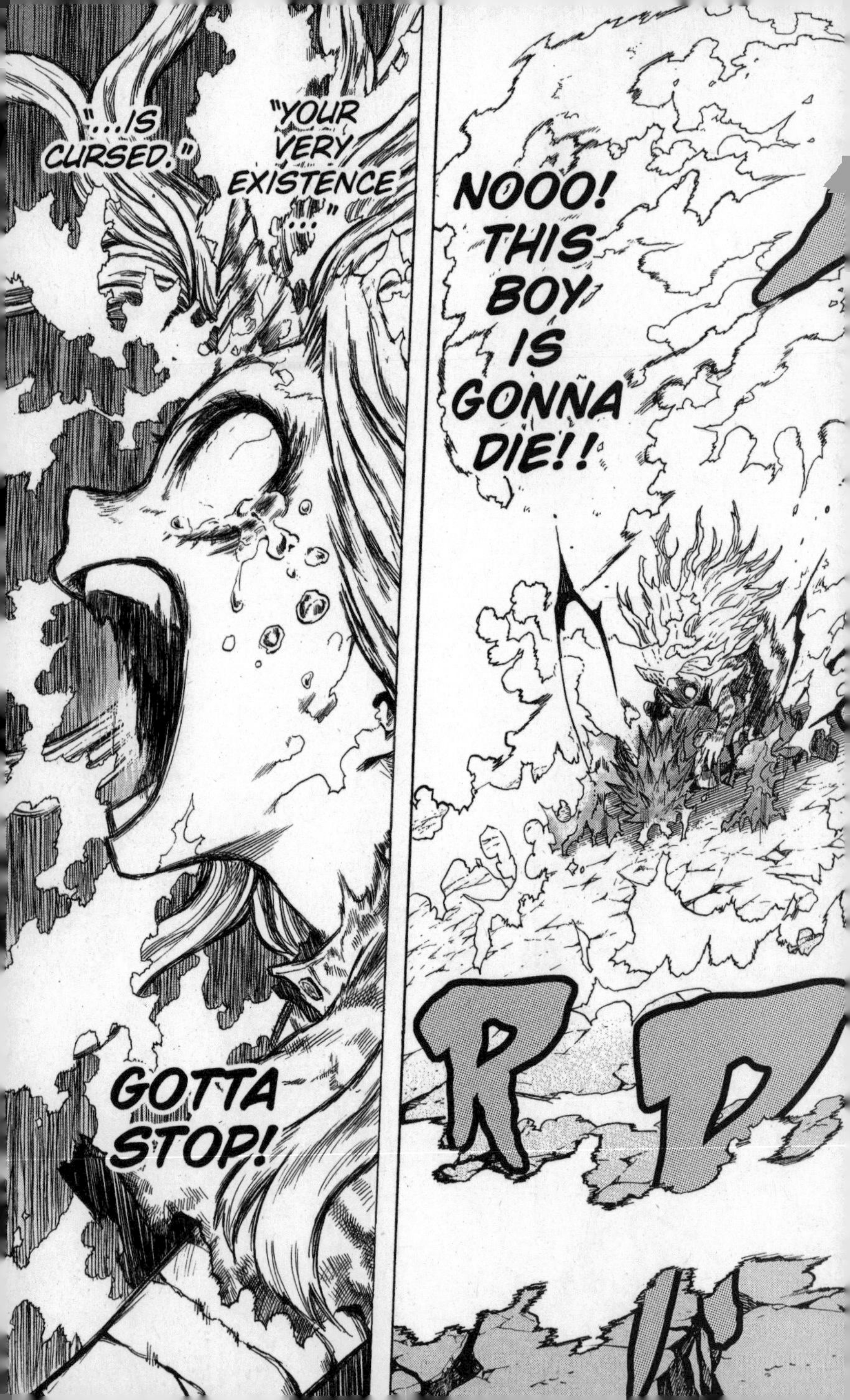
NOOO! THIS BOY IS GONNA DIE!!
"YOUR VERY EXISTENCE..."
"...IS CURSED."
GOTTA STOP!

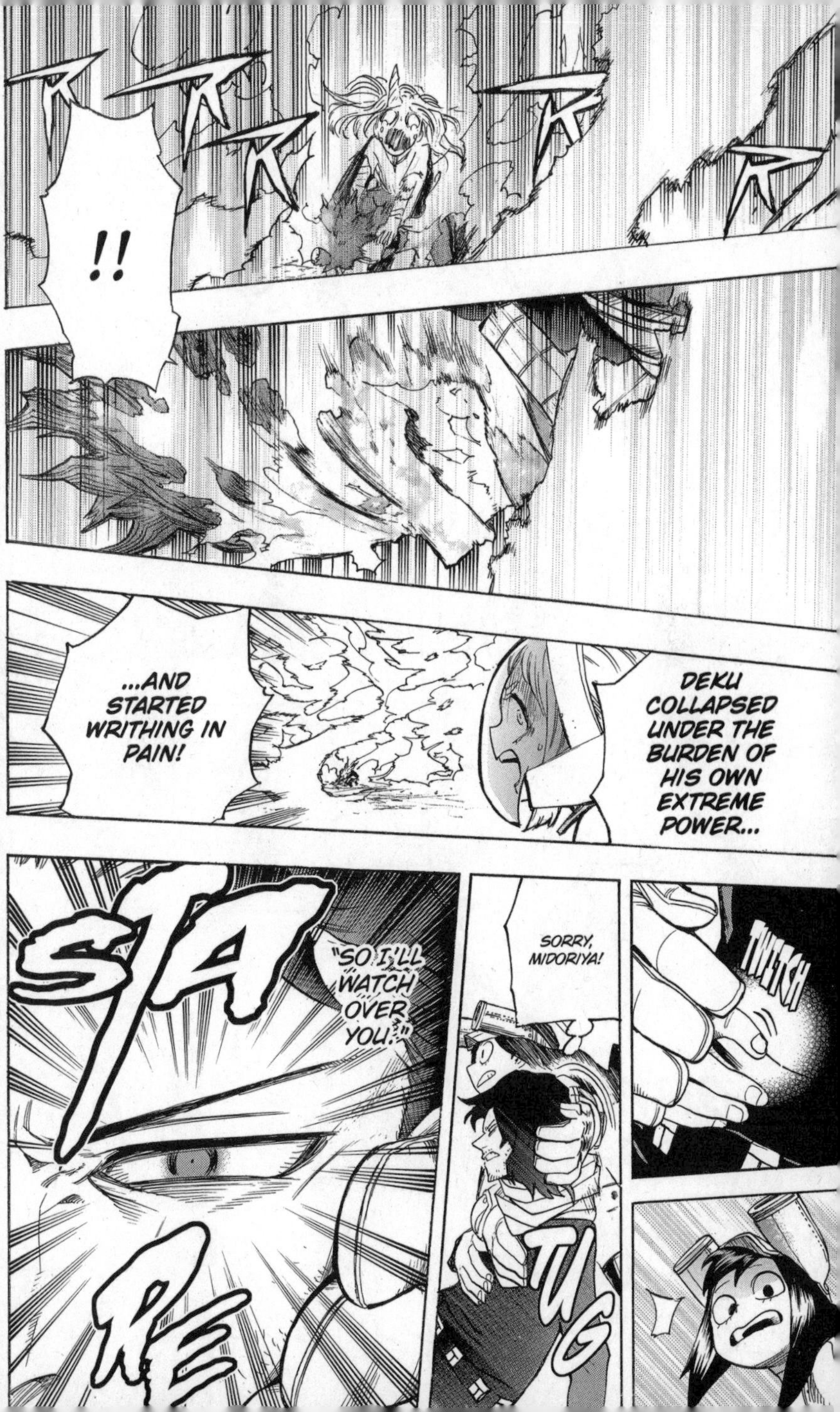

R R R
R R R
!!
DEKU COLLAPSED UNDER THE BURDEN OF HIS OWN EXTREME POWER...
...AND STARTED WRITHING IN PAIN!
TWITCH
SORRY, MIDORIYA!
TUG
"SO I'LL WATCH OVER YOU."
STARE

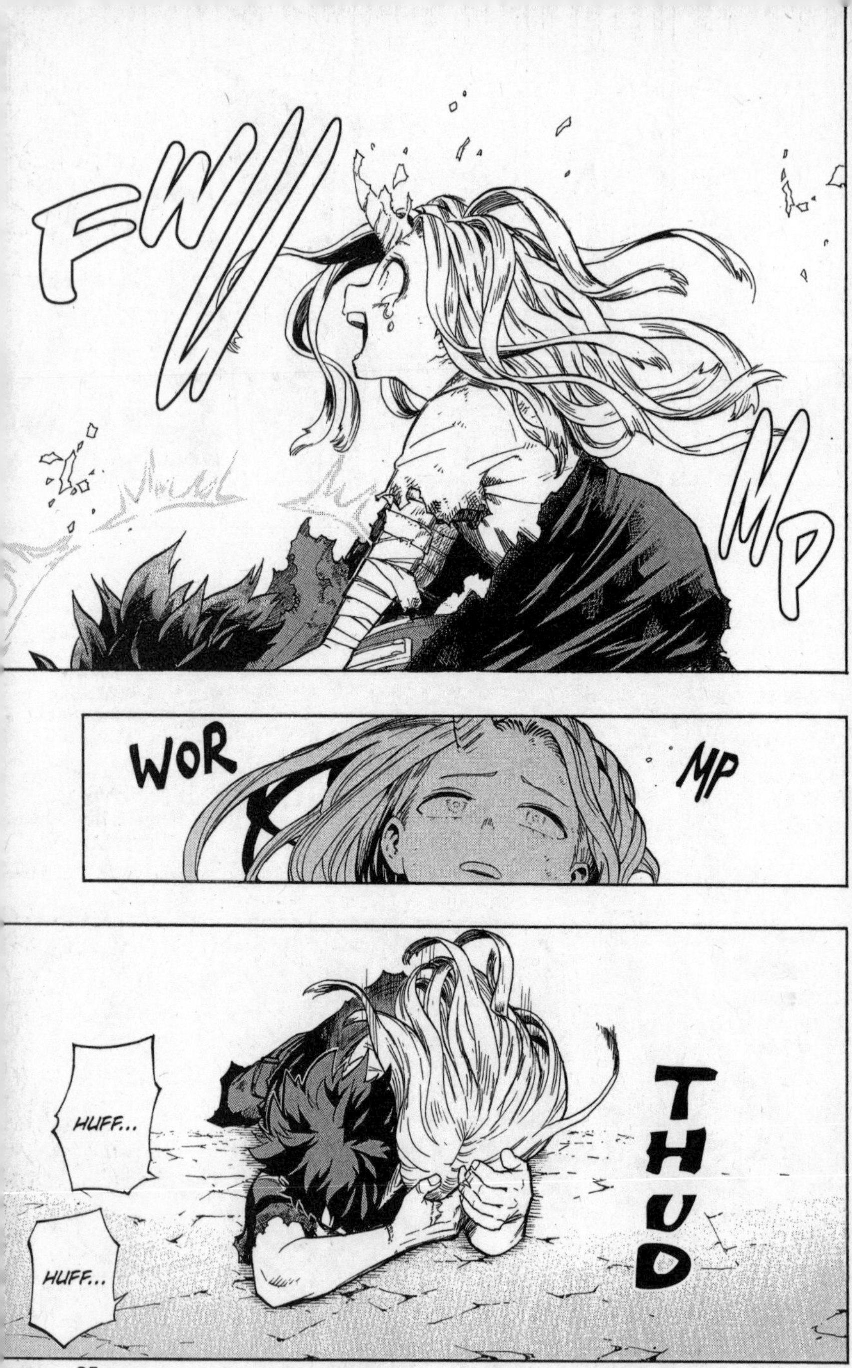
FW
MP
WOR
MP
THUD
HUFF...
HUFF...

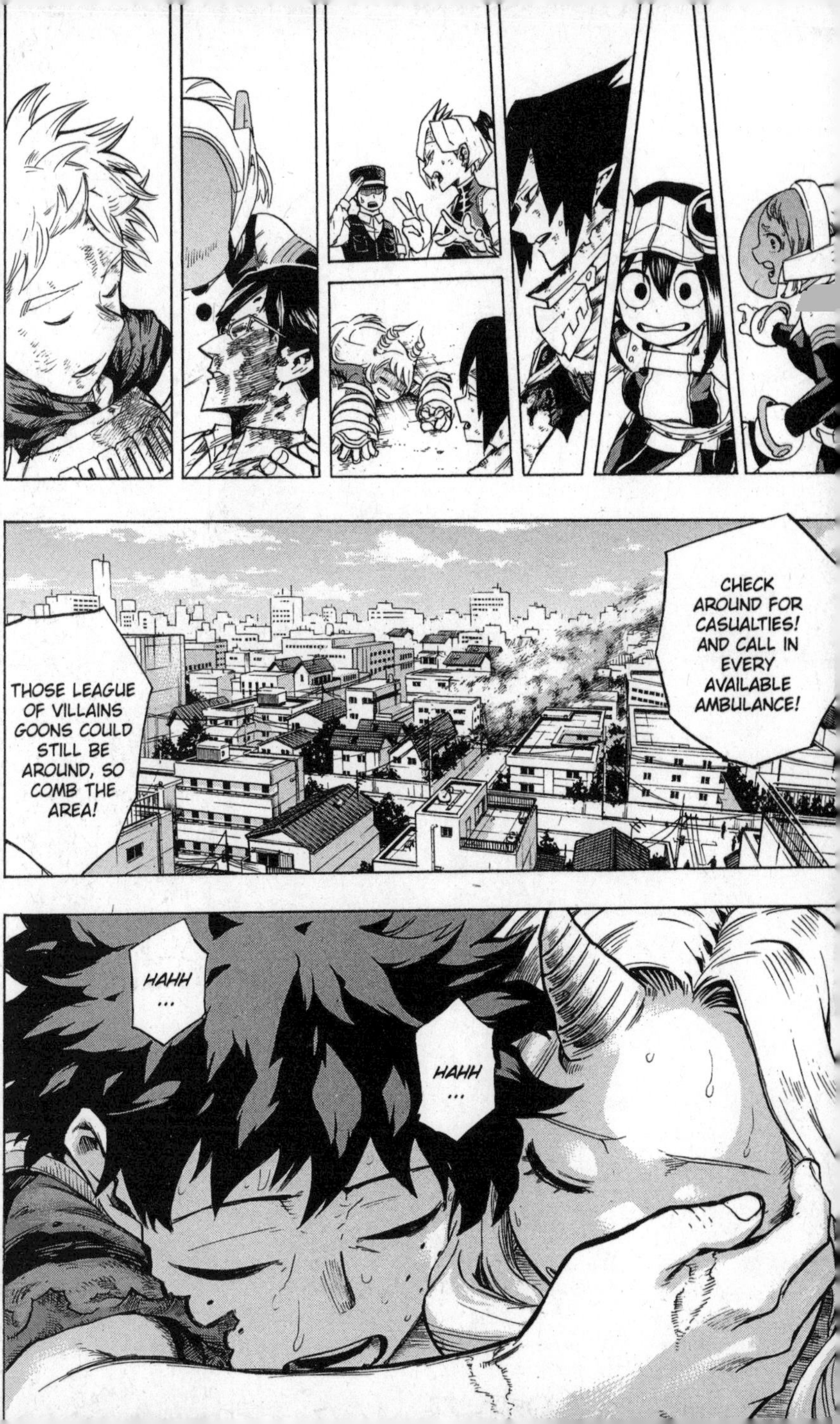
CHECK AROUND FOR CASUALTIES! AND CALL IN EVERY AVAILABLE AMBULANCE!
THOSE LEAGUE OF VILLAINS GOONS COULD STILL BE AROUND, SO COMB THE AREA!
HAHH ...
HAHH ...

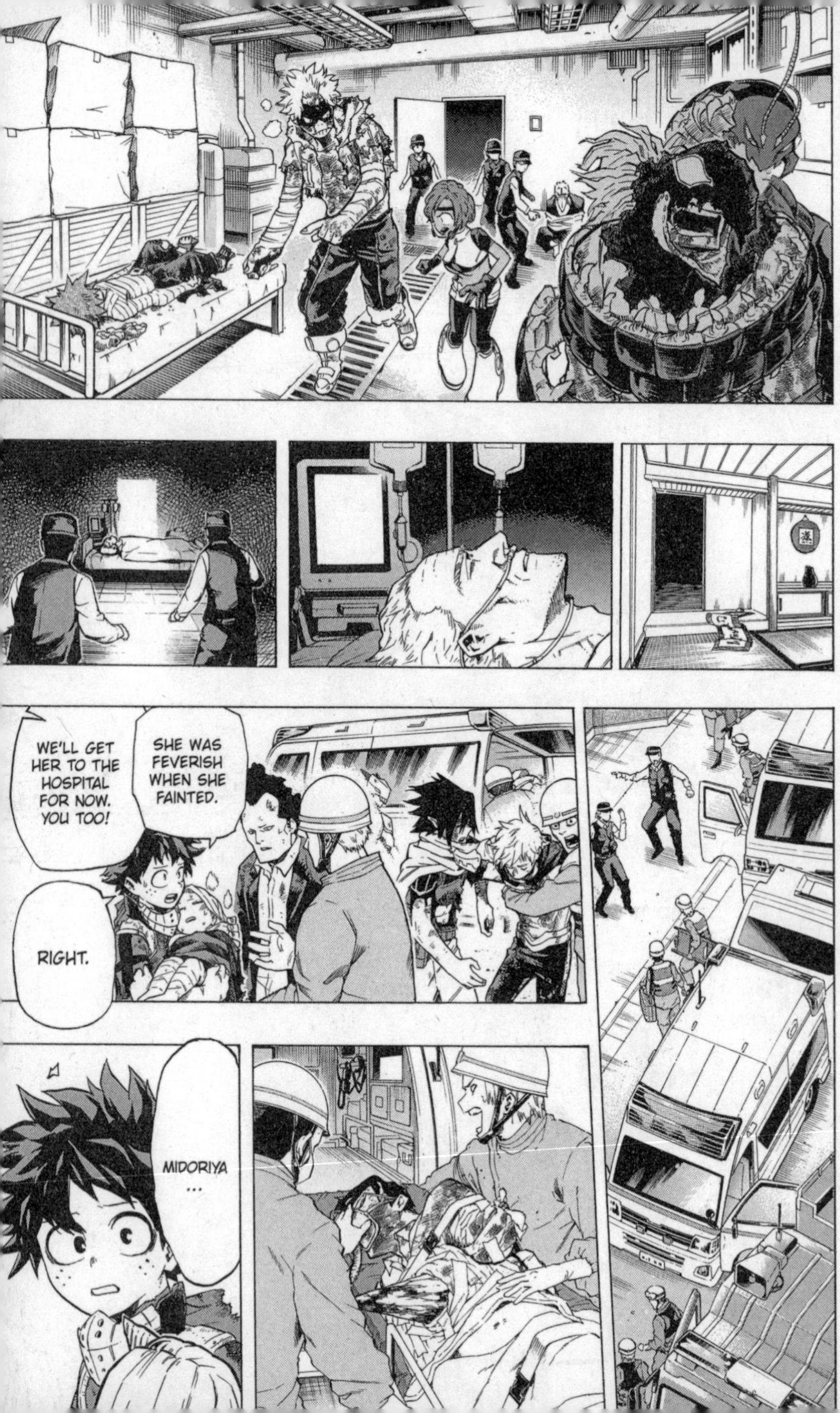
SHE WAS FEVERISH WHEN SHE FAINTED.
WE'LL GET HER TO THE HOSPITAL FOR NOW. YOU TOO!
RIGHT.
MIDORIYA ...

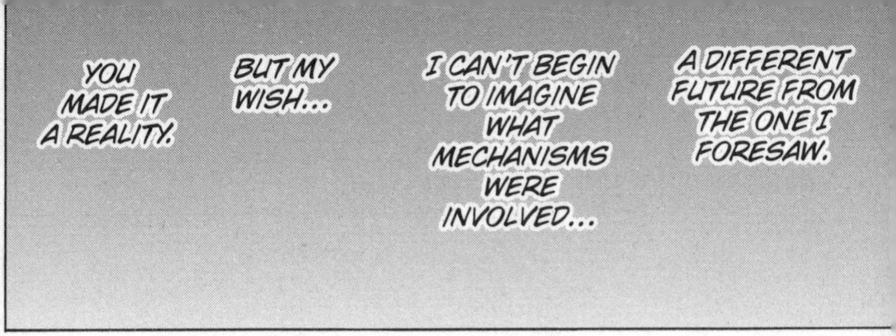
A DIFFERENT FUTURE FROM THE ONE I FORESAW.
I CAN'T BEGIN TO IMAGINE WHAT MECHANISMS WERE INVOLVED...
BUT MY WISH...
YOU MADE IT A REALITY.

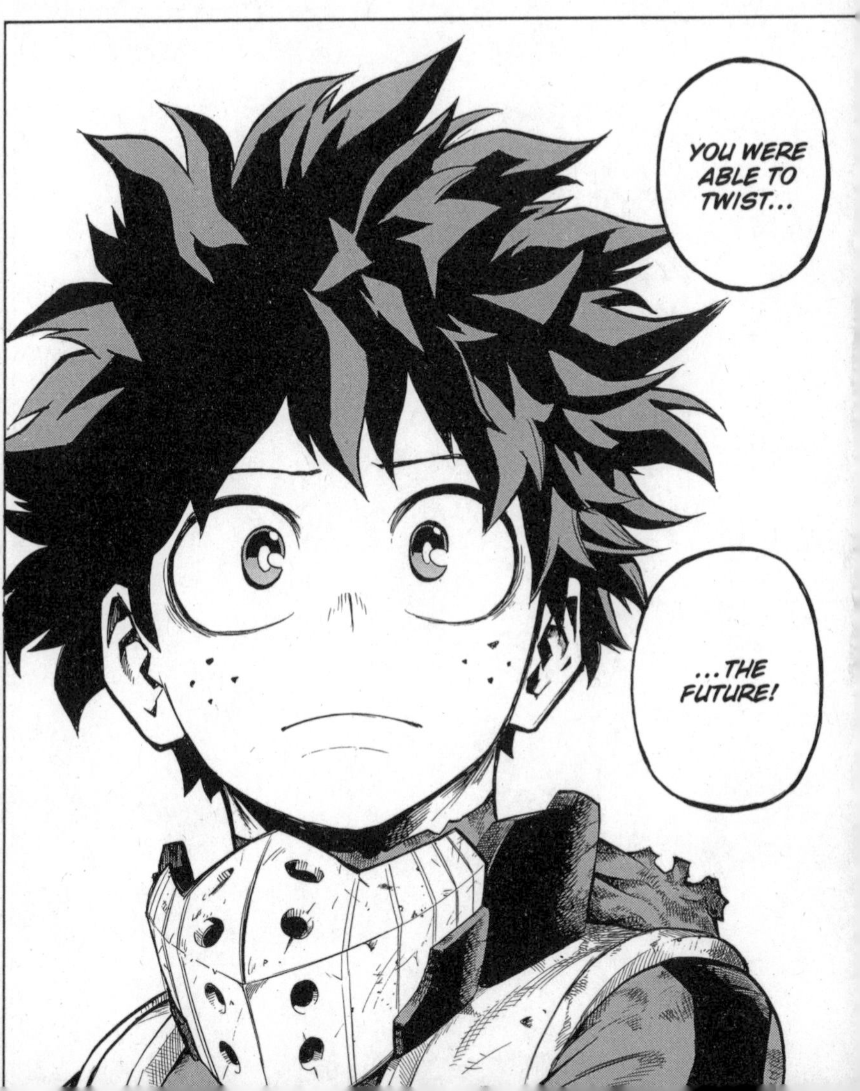
YOU WERE ABLE TO TWIST...
...THE FUTURE!

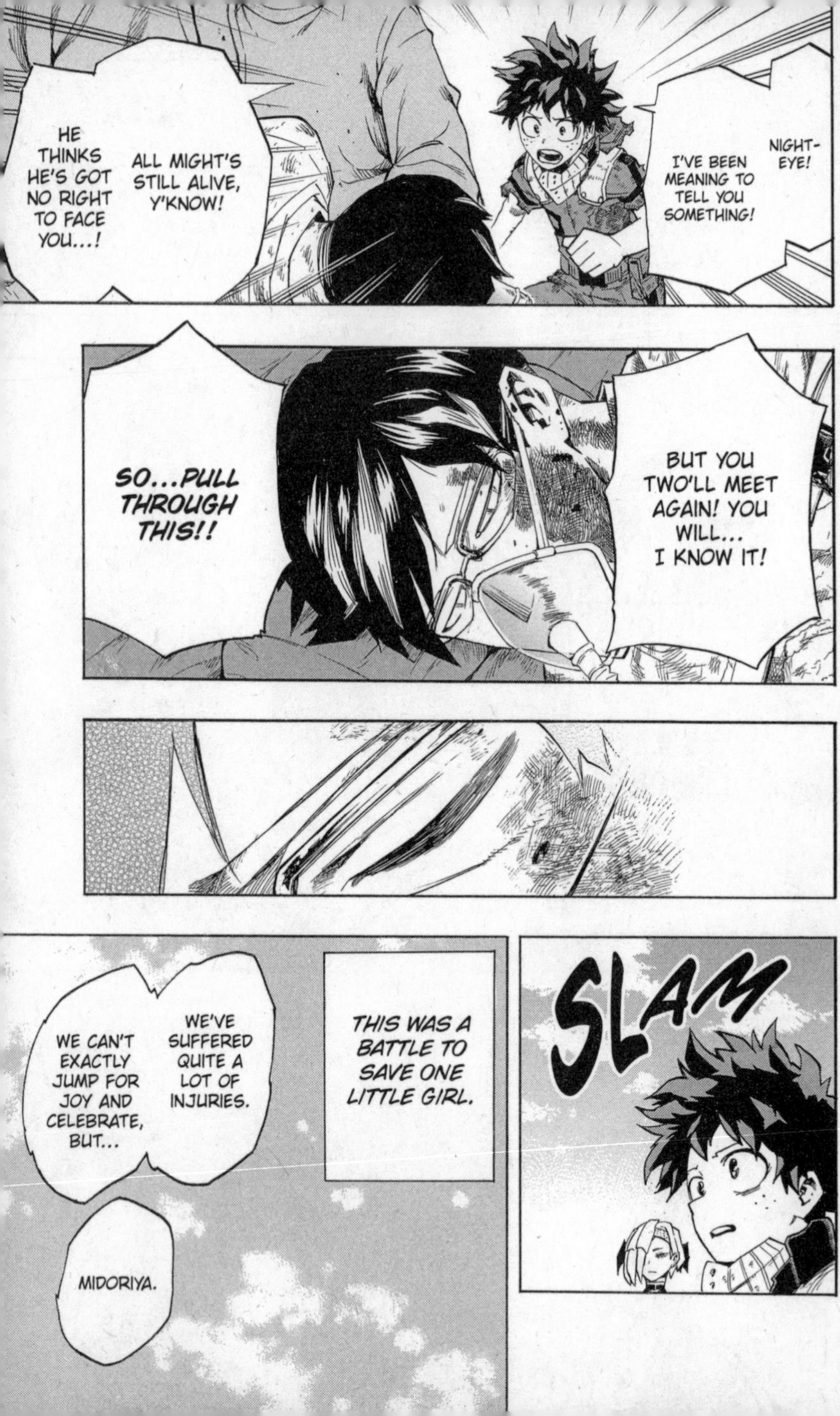
NIGHT-EYE!
I'VE BEEN MEANING TO TELL YOU SOMETHING!
ALL MIGHT'S STILL ALIVE, Y'KNOW!
HE THINKS HE'S GOT NO RIGHT TO FACE YOU...!
BUT YOU TWO'LL MEET AGAIN! YOU WILL... I KNOW IT!
SO...PULL THROUGH THIS!!
SLAM
THIS WAS A BATTLE TO SAVE ONE LITTLE GIRL.
WE'VE SUFFERED QUITE A LOT OF INJURIES.
WE CAN'T EXACTLY JUMP FOR JOY AND CELEBRATE, BUT...
MIDORIYA.

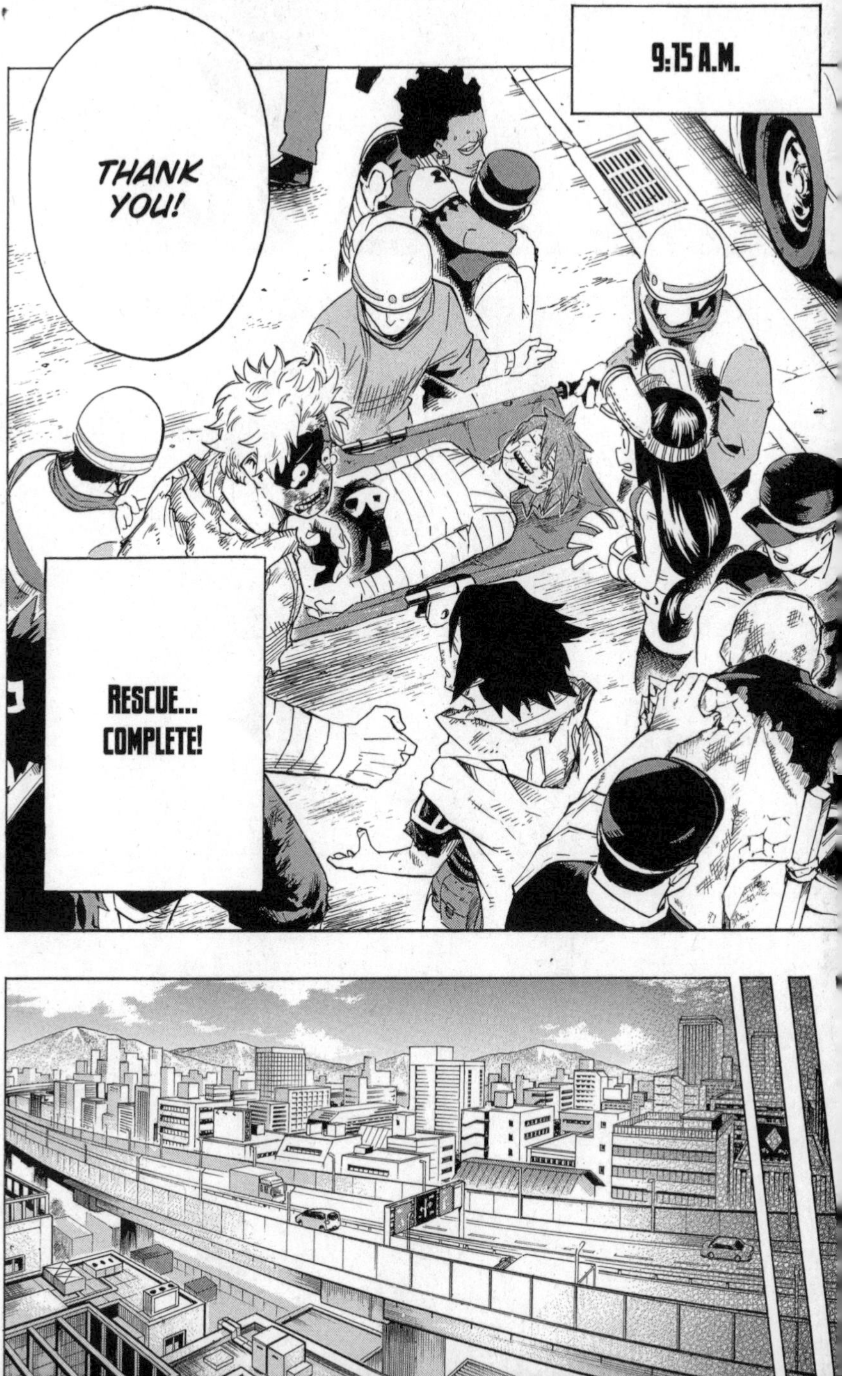
9:15 A.M.
THANK YOU!
RESCUE... COMPLETE!

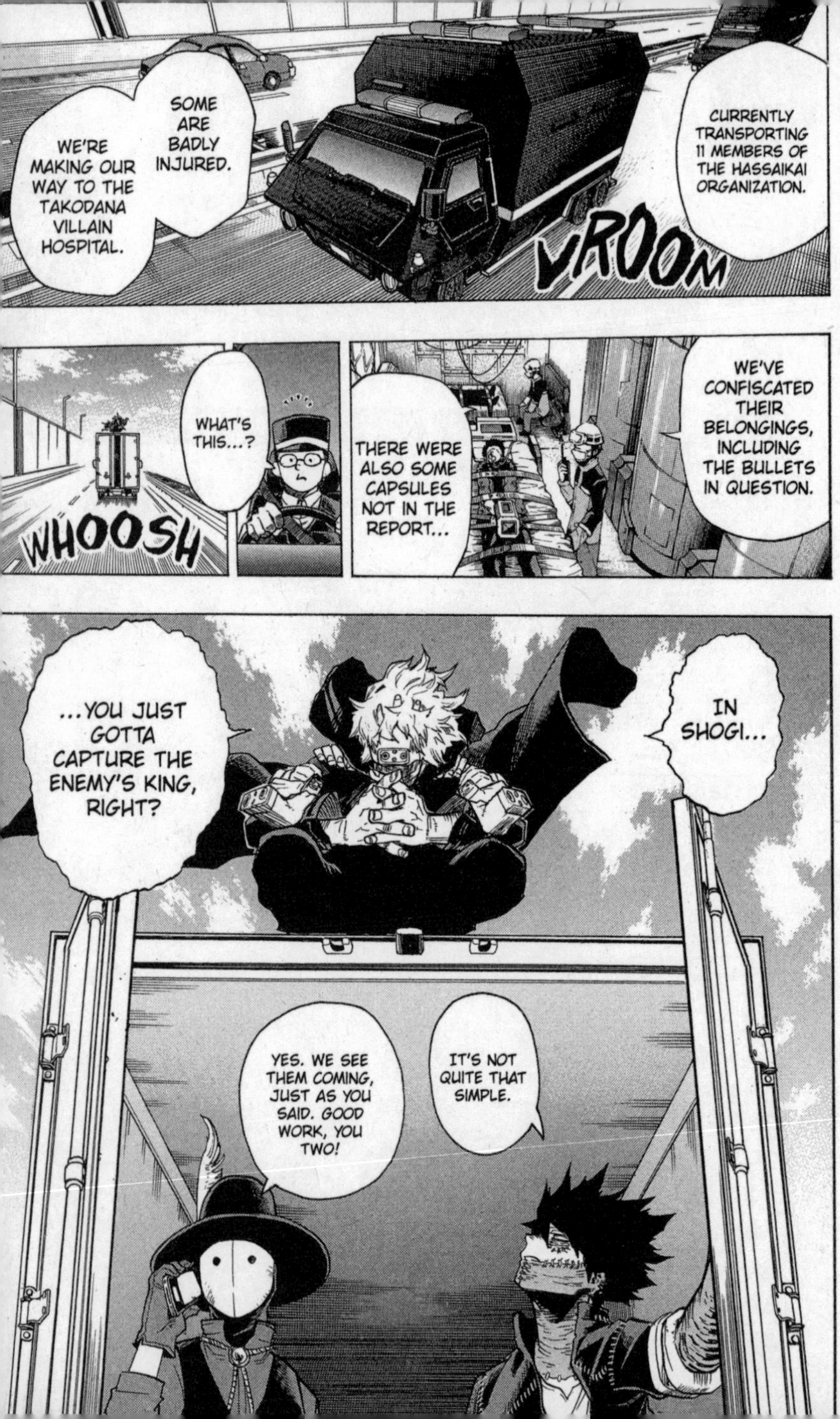
CURRENTLY TRANSPORTING 11 MEMBERS OF THE HASSAIKAI ORGANIZATION.
VROOM
SOME ARE BADLY INJURED.
WE'RE MAKING OUR WAY TO THE TAKODANA VILLAIN HOSPITAL.
WE'VE CONFISCATED THEIR BELONGINGS, INCLUDING THE BULLETS IN QUESTION.
THERE WERE ALSO SOME CAPSULES NOT IN THE REPORT...
WHAT'S THIS...?
WHOOSH
IN SHOGI...
...YOU JUST GOTTA CAPTURE THE ENEMY'S KING, RIGHT?
IT'S NOT QUITE THAT SIMPLE.
YES. WE SEE THEM COMING, JUST AS YOU SAID. GOOD WORK, YOU TWO!

THE POPULARITY POLL!!

Here are the results for the third annual popularity poll.

The top ten have a special display on pages 92 and 93, but the rest–down to 50th place–are listed out here! There were others who got votes too, but we'd be here all day listing out everyone!! Thanks to all who voted!!

RANK	NAME	# OF VOTES
11	Mashirao Ojiro	1,154
12	Best Jeanist	1,078
13	Fumikage Tokoyami	1,018
14	Momo Yaoyorozu	853
15	Tomura Shigaraki	693
16	Present Mic	690
17	Tamaki Amajiki	624
18	Hanta Sero	443
19	Himiko Toga	409
20	Fat Gum	392
21	Endeavor	388
22	Kyoka Jiro	310
23	Tsuyu Asui	286
24	Neito Monoma	240
25	Tetsutetsu Tetsutetsu	229
26	Yuga Aoyama	214
27	Stain	208
28	Mezo Shoji	199
29	Itsuka Kendo	186
30	Seiji Shishikura	173
31	Chisaki (Overhaul)	172
32	Minoru Mineta	156
33	Gang Orca	141
34	Dabi	139
35	Sir Nighteye	131

RANK	NAME	# OF VOTES
36	Mina Ashido	125
37	Cementoss	123
38	Eri	109
39	Mandalay	108
40	Nana Shimura	104
41	Mirio Togata	103
42	Kohei Horikoshi	98
43	Setsuno	94
44	Ingenium	93
45	Koji Koda	86
46	Toru Hagakure	65
47	Mr. Compress	59
48	Mimic	56
49	Mustard	53
50	Curator (Heroes' Battle game)	52

Huhh?

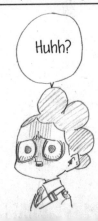

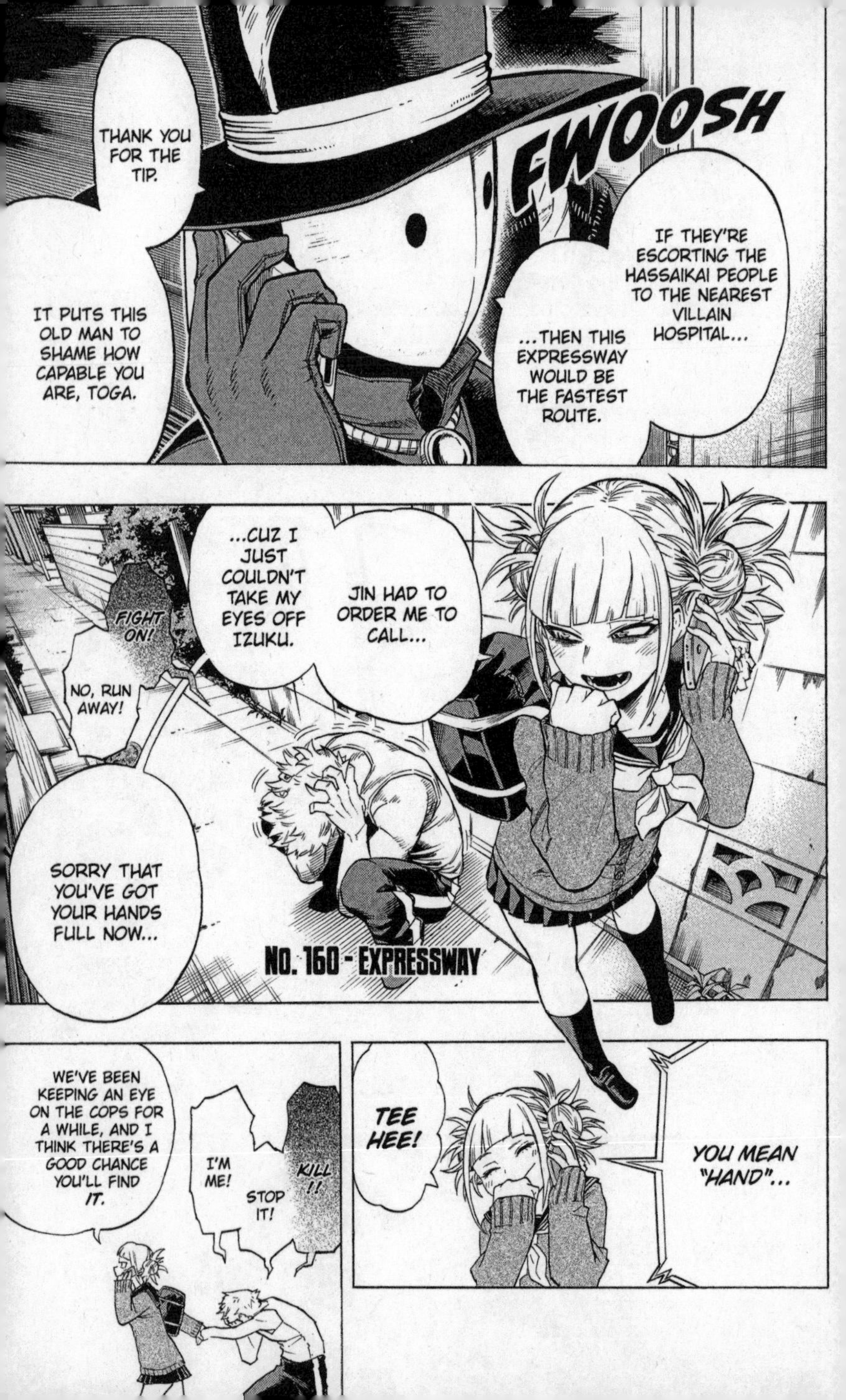
FWOOSH
IF THEY'RE ESCORTING THE HASSAIKAI PEOPLE TO THE NEAREST VILLAIN HOSPITAL...
...THEN THIS EXPRESSWAY WOULD BE THE FASTEST ROUTE.
THANK YOU FOR THE TIP.
IT PUTS THIS OLD MAN TO SHAME HOW CAPABLE YOU ARE, TOGA.
JIN HAD TO ORDER ME TO CALL...
...CUZ I JUST COULDN'T TAKE MY EYES OFF IZUKU.
FIGHT ON!
NO, RUN AWAY!
SORRY THAT YOU'VE GOT YOUR HANDS FULL NOW...
NO. 160 - EXPRESSWAY
YOU MEAN "HAND"...
TEE HEE!
WE'VE BEEN KEEPING AN EYE ON THE COPS FOR A WHILE, AND I THINK THERE'S A GOOD CHANCE YOU'LL FIND *IT*.
KILL!!
STOP IT!
I'M ME!

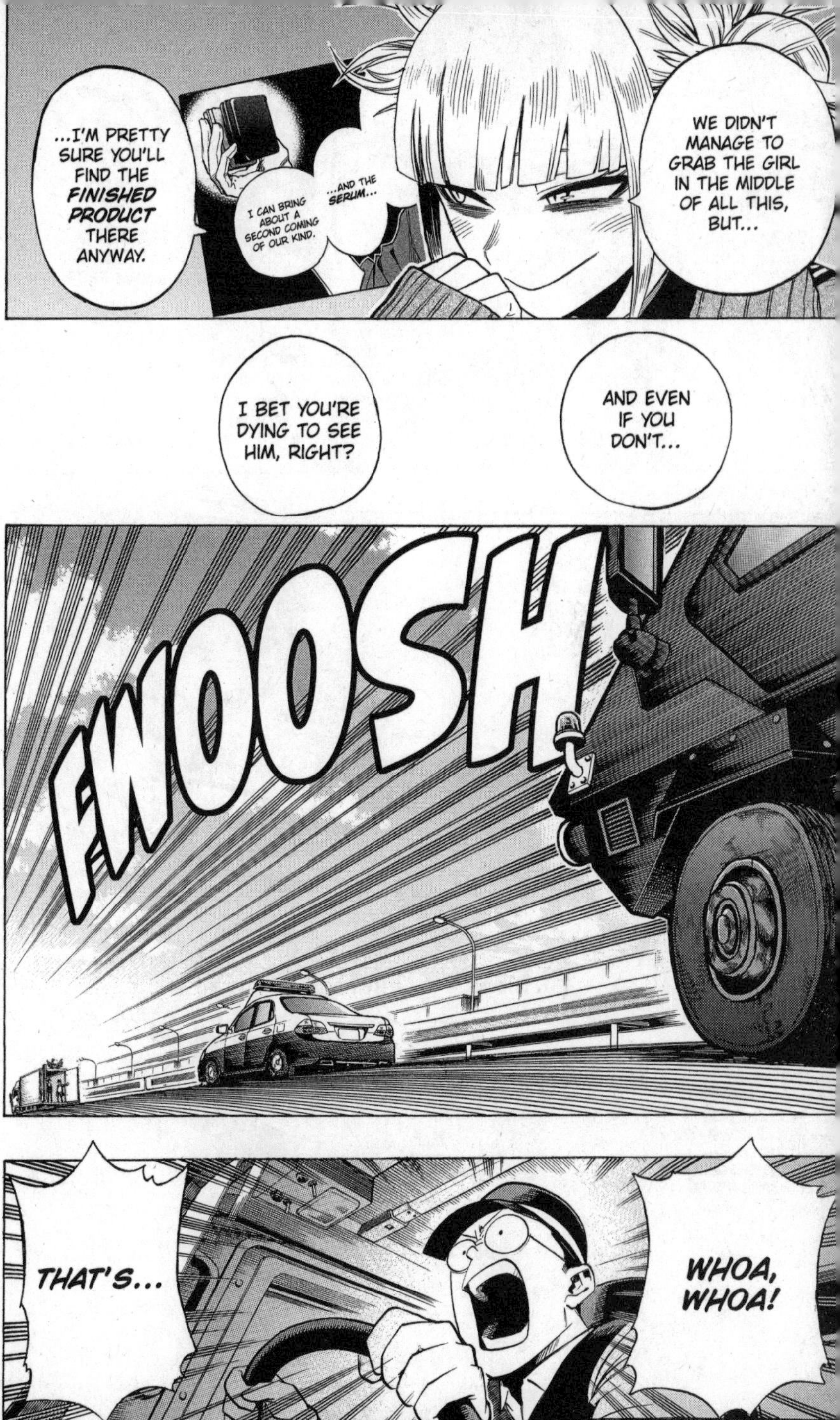
WE DIDN'T MANAGE TO GRAB THE GIRL IN THE MIDDLE OF ALL THIS, BUT...
...AND THE SERUM...
I CAN BRING ABOUT A SECOND COMING OF OUR KIND.
...I'M PRETTY SURE YOU'LL FIND THE FINISHED PRODUCT THERE ANYWAY.
AND EVEN IF YOU DON'T...
I BET YOU'RE DYING TO SEE HIM, RIGHT?
FWOOSH
WHOA, WHOA!
THAT'S...

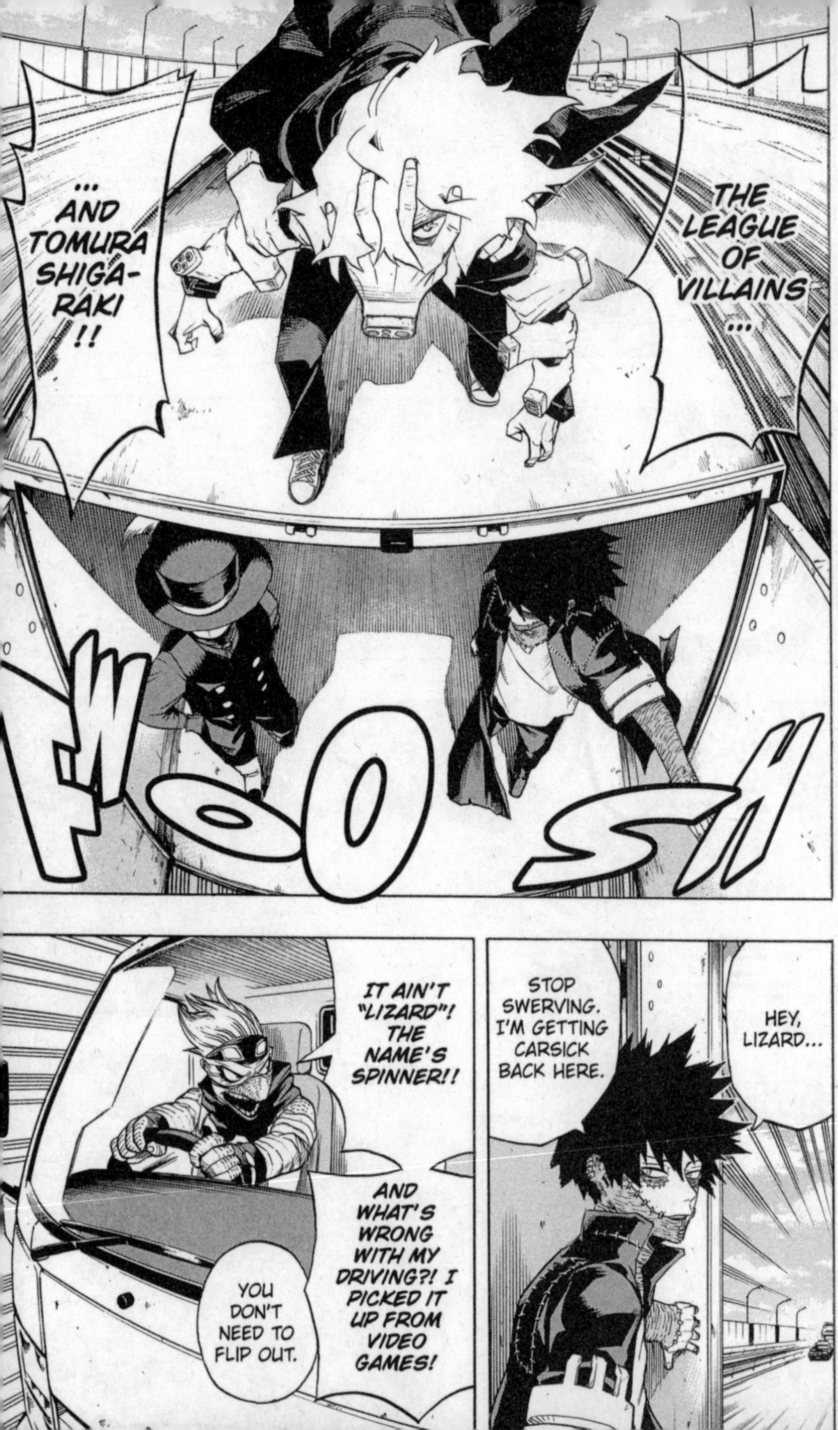
THE LEAGUE OF VILLAINS...
...AND TOMURA SHIGA-RAKI!!
WHOOSH
HEY, LIZARD...
STOP SWERVING. I'M GETTING CARSICK BACK HERE.
IT AIN'T "LIZARD"! THE NAME'S SPINNER!!
AND WHAT'S WRONG WITH MY DRIVING?! I PICKED IT UP FROM VIDEO GAMES!
YOU DON'T NEED TO FLIP OUT.

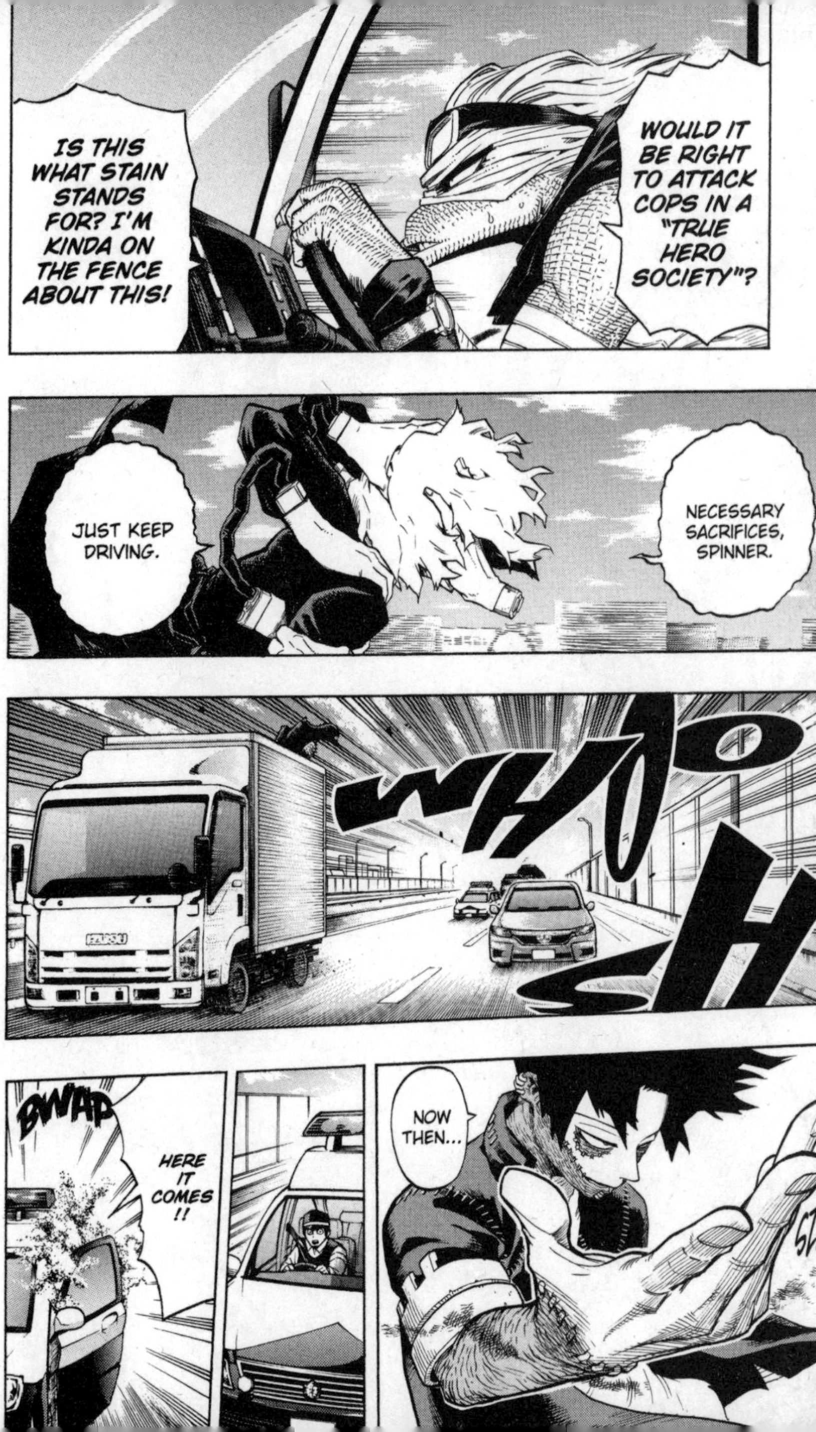
WOULD IT BE RIGHT TO ATTACK COPS IN A "TRUE HERO SOCIETY"?
IS THIS WHAT STAIN STANDS FOR? I'M KINDA ON THE FENCE ABOUT THIS!
NECESSARY SACRIFICES, SPINNER.
JUST KEEP DRIVING.
WHOOSH
NOW THEN...
SZZZ
HERE IT COMES !!
BWAP

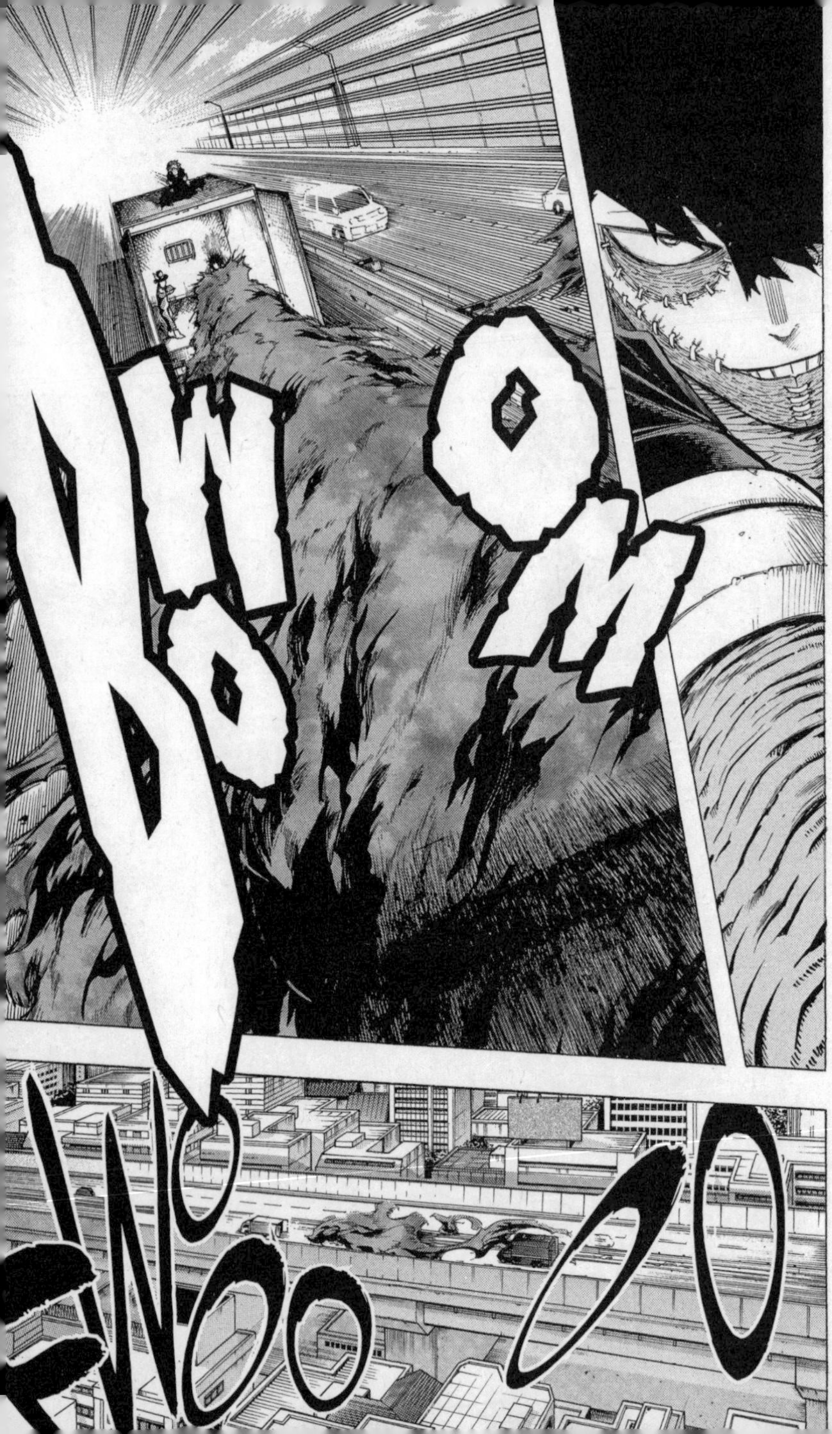

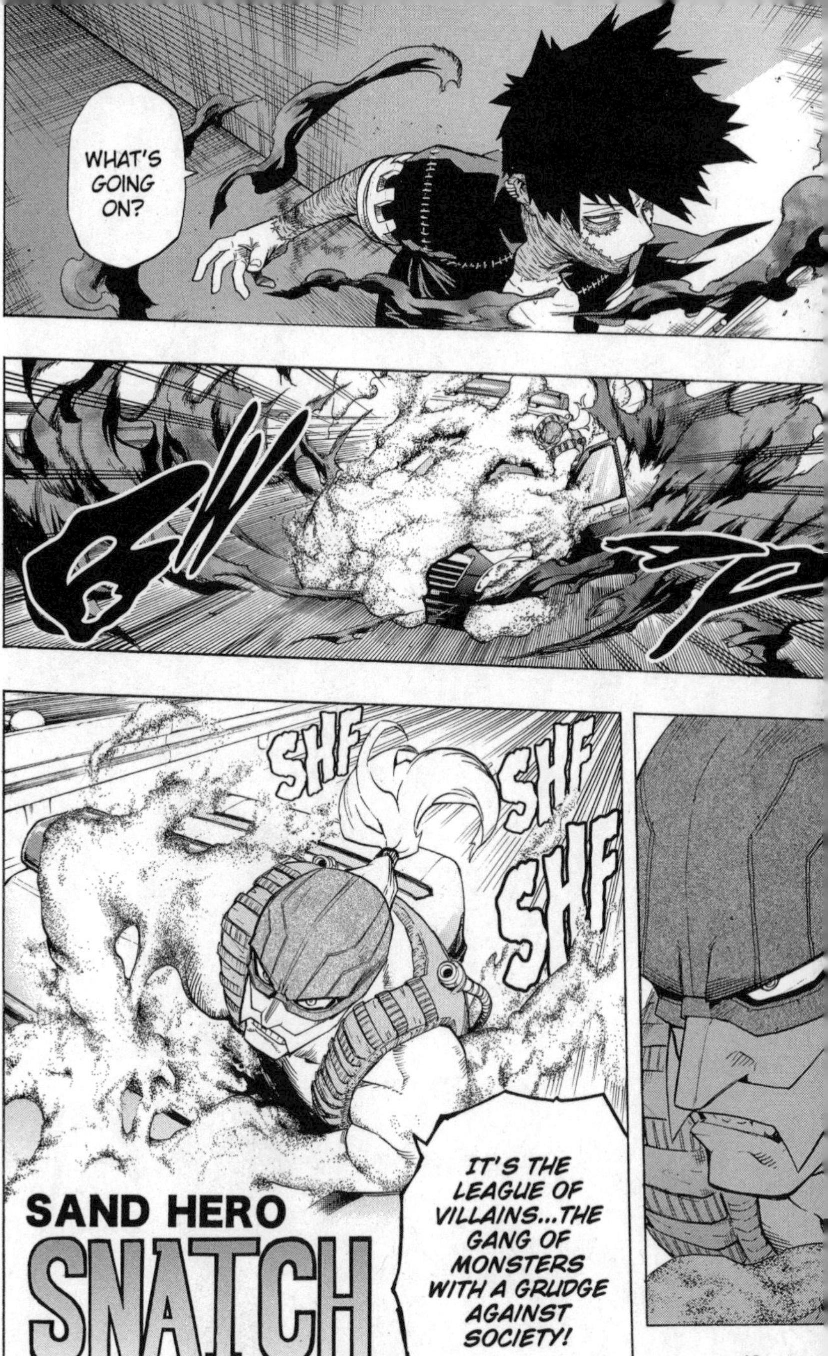

WHAT'S GOING ON?
SHF
SHF
SHF
SHF
IT'S THE LEAGUE OF VILLAINS...THE GANG OF MONSTERS WITH A GRUDGE AGAINST SOCIETY!
SAND HERO
SNATCH

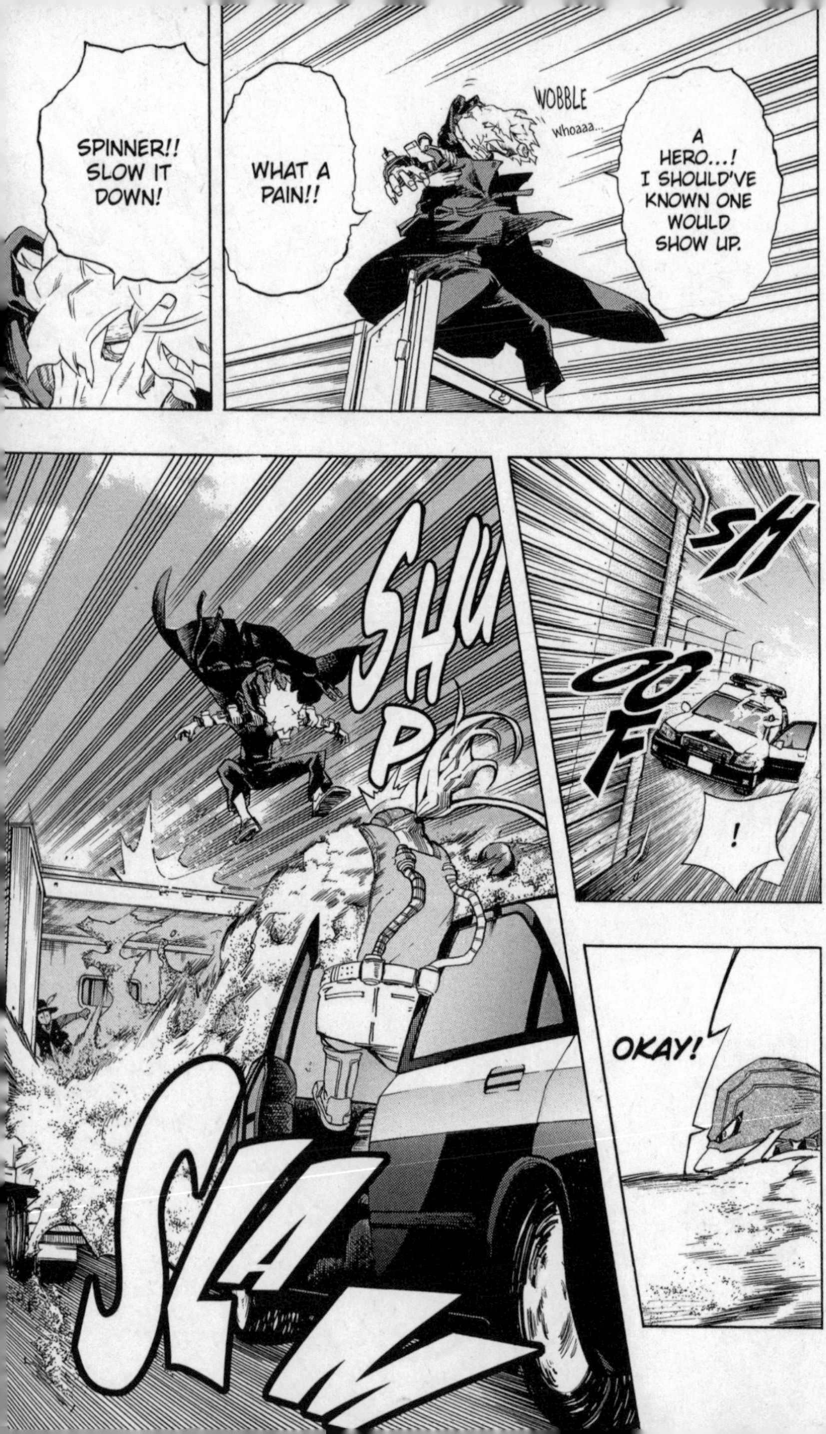
A HERO...! I SHOULD'VE KNOWN ONE WOULD SHOW UP.
WOBBLE
whoaaa...
WHAT A PAIN!!
SPINNER!! SLOW IT DOWN!
SHOOOF
!
OKAY!
SHUP
SLAM

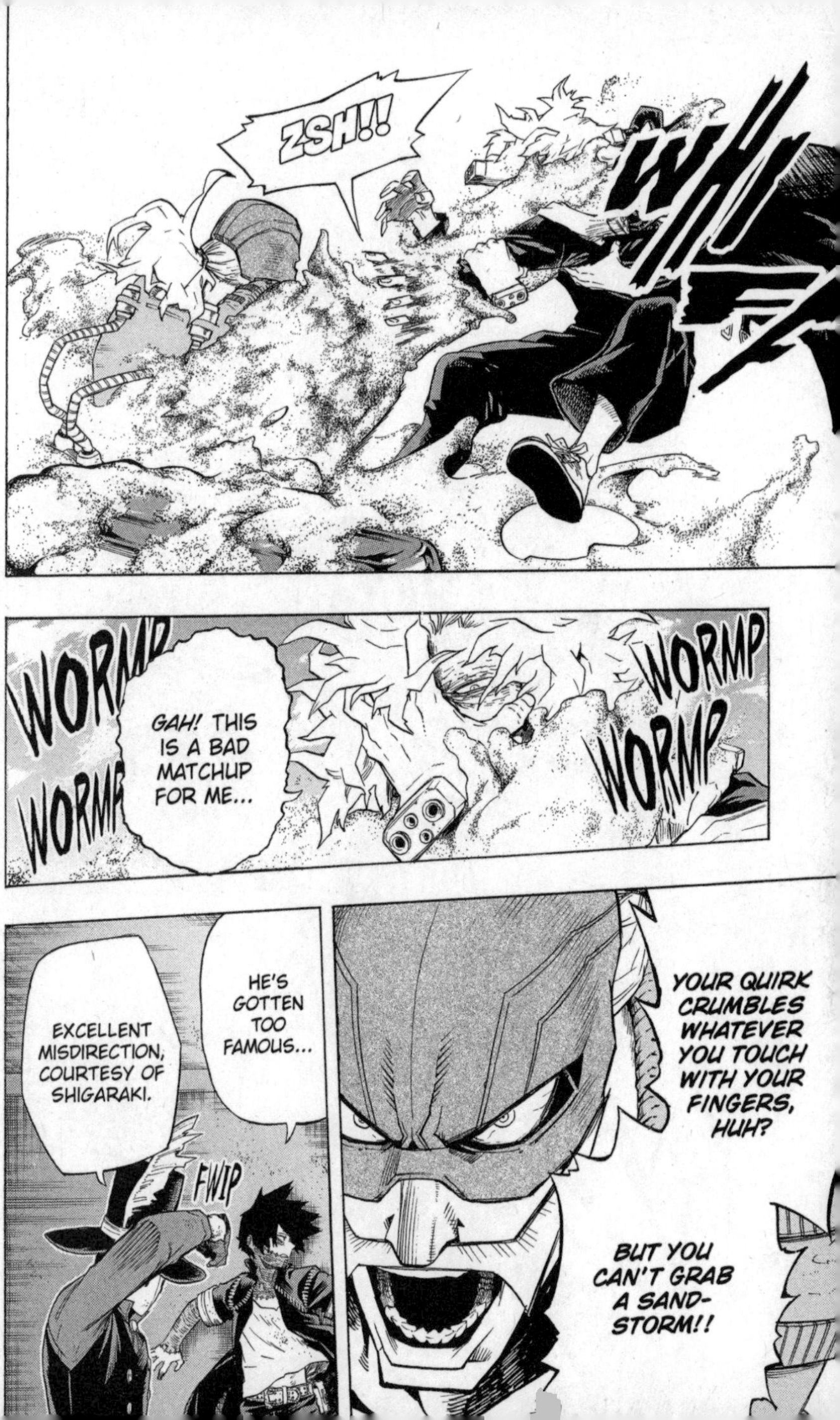
ZSH!!
WORMP
WORMP
GAH! THIS IS A BAD MATCHUP FOR ME...
WORM
WORM
YOUR QUIRK CRUMBLES WHATEVER YOU TOUCH WITH YOUR FINGERS, HUH?
BUT YOU CAN'T GRAB A SAND-STORM!!
HE'S GOTTEN TOO FAMOUS...
EXCELLENT MISDIRECTION, COURTESY OF SHIGARAKI.
FWIP

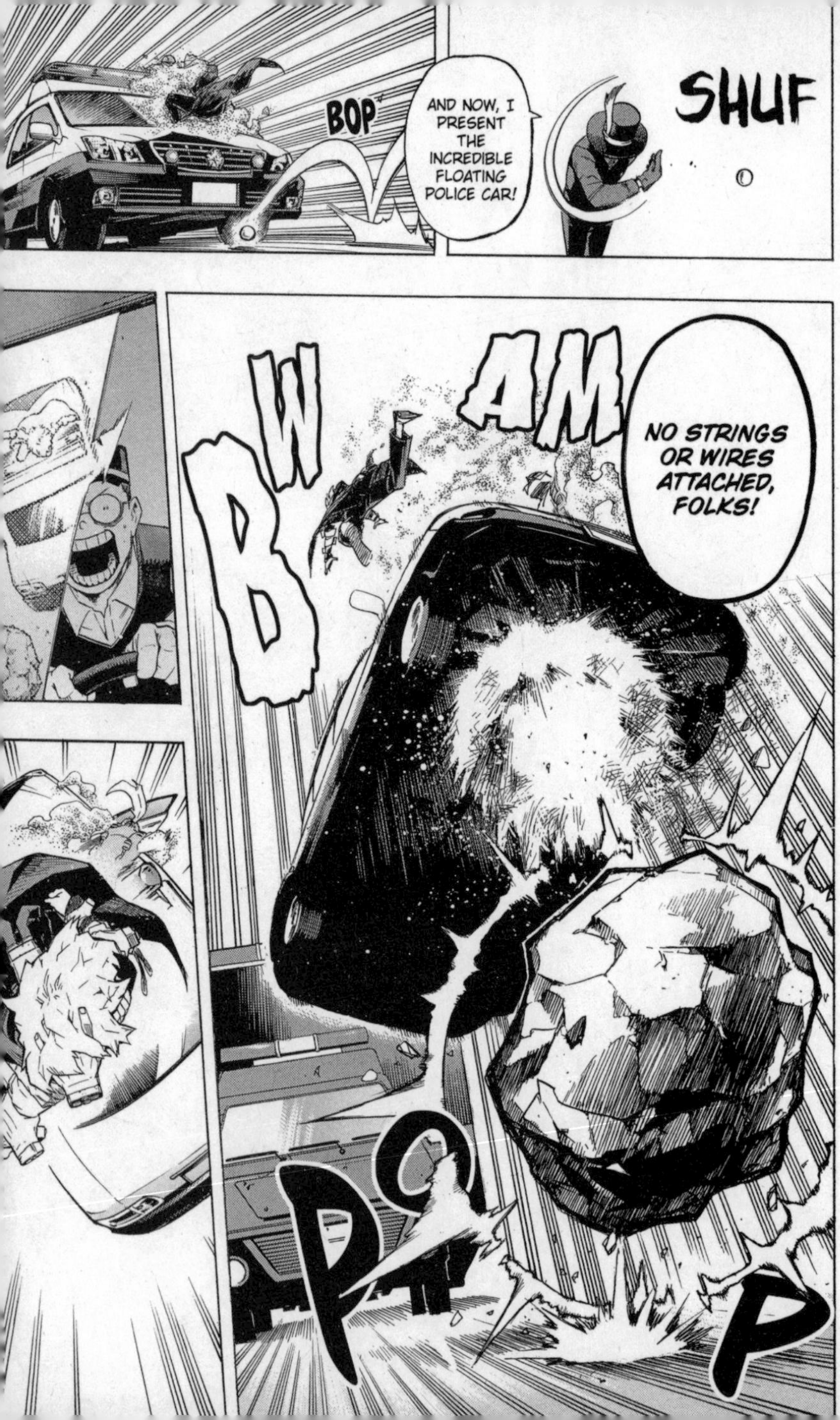
SHUF
AND NOW, I PRESENT THE INCREDIBLE FLOATING POLICE CAR!
BOP
BWAM
NO STRINGS OR WIRES ATTACHED, FOLKS!
POP

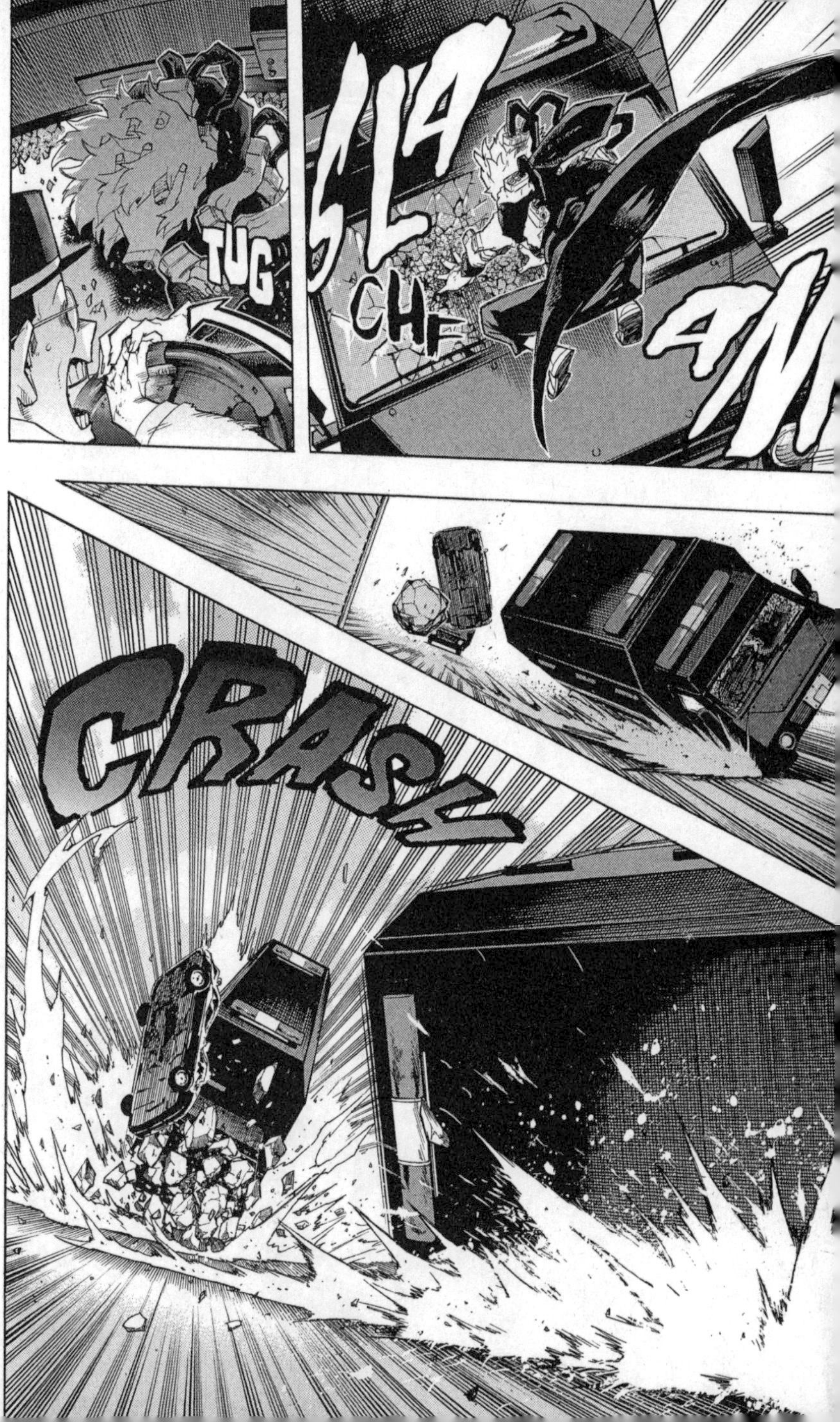
SLAM
CHF
TUG
CRASH

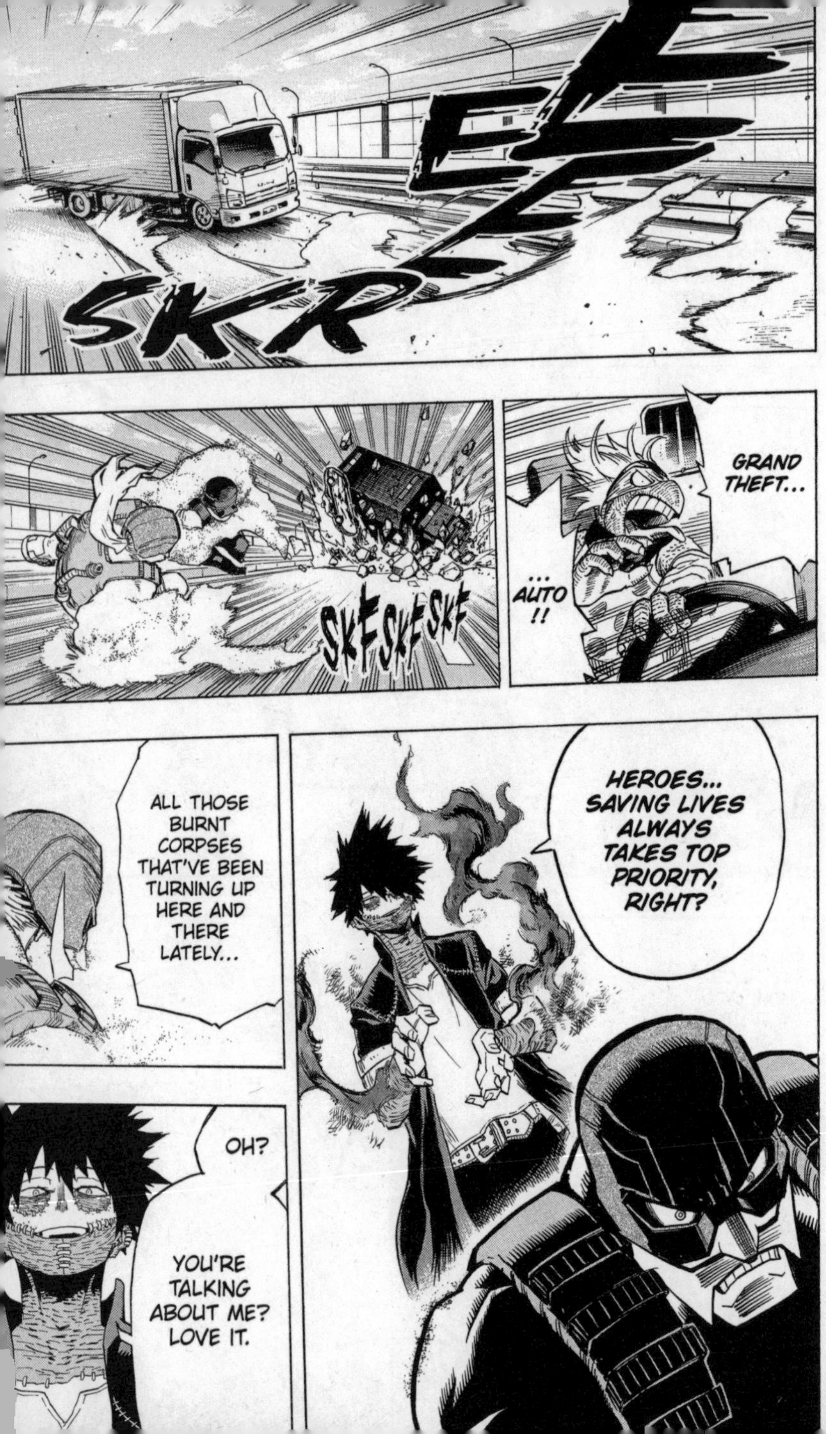
SKREEE
GRAND THEFT...
...AUTO !!
SKFSKFSKF
HEROES... SAVING LIVES ALWAYS TAKES TOP PRIORITY, RIGHT?
ALL THOSE BURNT CORPSES THAT'VE BEEN TURNING UP HERE AND THERE LATELY...
OH?
YOU'RE TALKING ABOUT ME? LOVE IT.

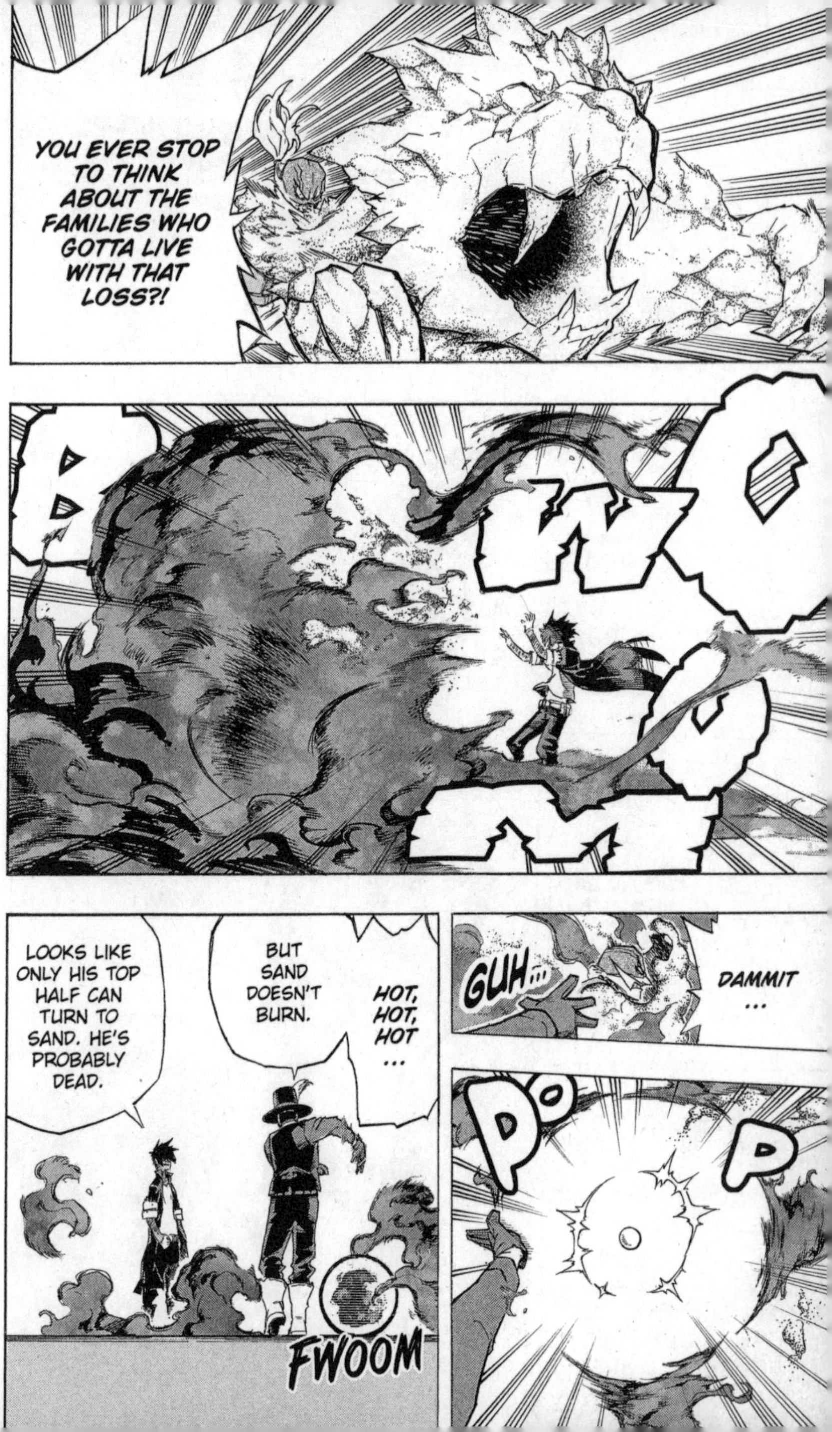
YOU EVER STOP TO THINK ABOUT THE FAMILIES WHO GOTTA LIVE WITH THAT LOSS?!
GUH...
DAMMIT ...
POP
HOT, HOT, HOT ...
BUT SAND DOESN'T BURN.
LOOKS LIKE ONLY HIS TOP HALF CAN TURN TO SAND. HE'S PROBABLY DEAD.
FWOOM

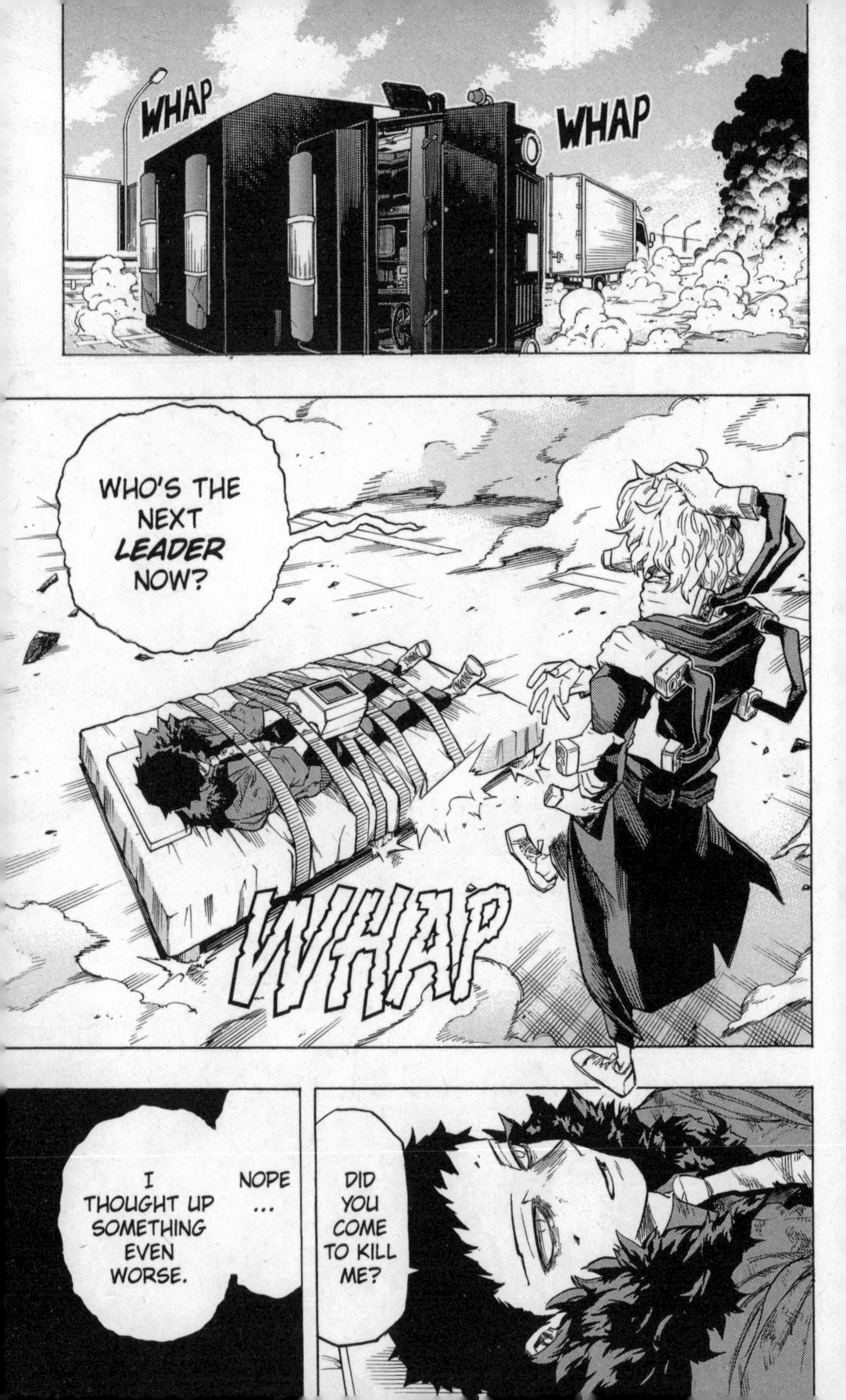
WHAP
WHAP
WHO'S THE NEXT LEADER NOW?
WHAP
DID YOU COME TO KILL ME?
NOPE ...
I THOUGHT UP SOMETHING EVEN WORSE.

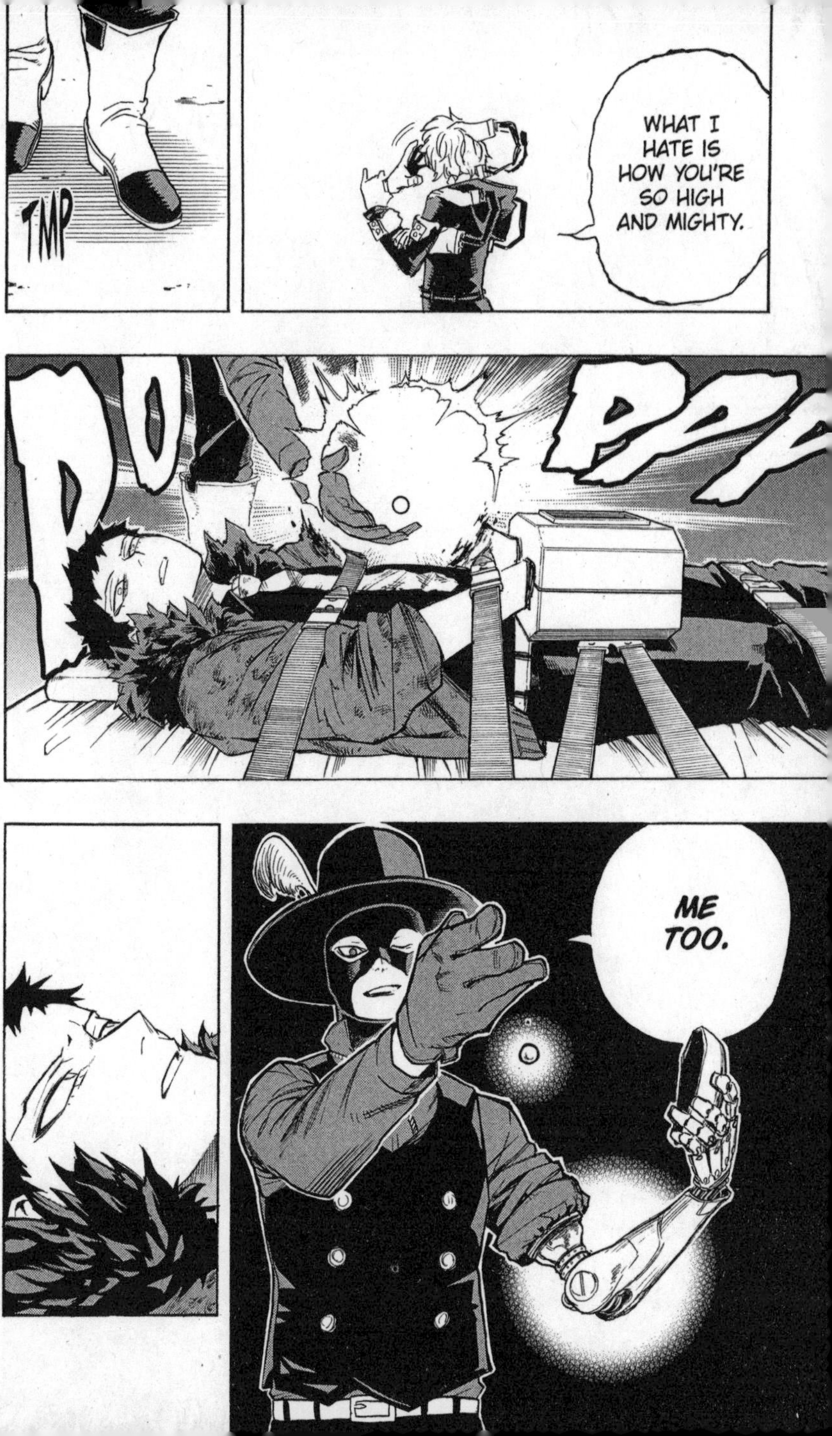
WHAT I HATE IS HOW YOU'RE SO HIGH AND MIGHTY.
TMP
DOPP
ME TOO.

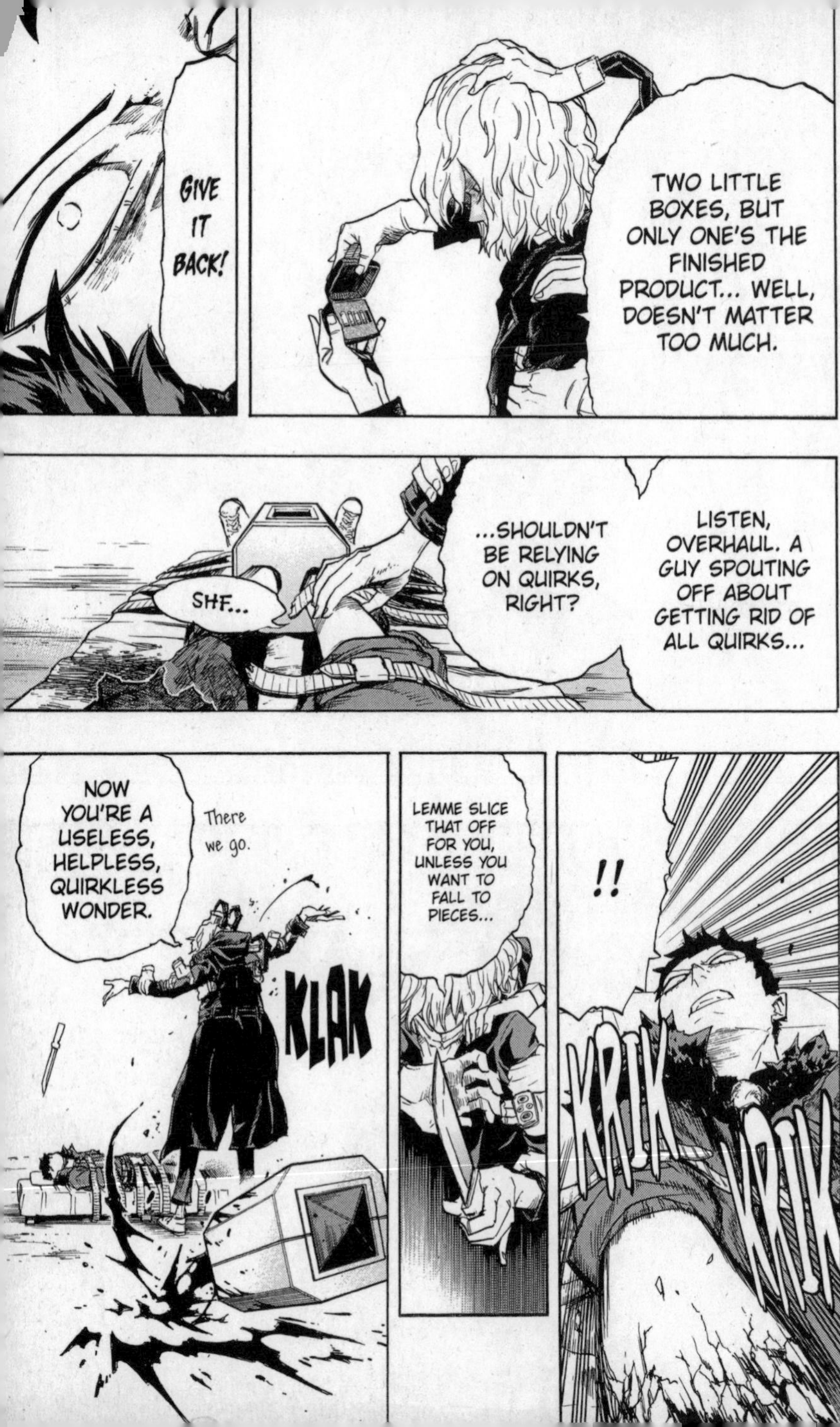
TWO LITTLE BOXES, BUT ONLY ONE'S THE FINISHED PRODUCT... WELL, DOESN'T MATTER TOO MUCH.
GIVE IT BACK!
LISTEN, OVERHAUL. A GUY SPOUTING OFF ABOUT GETTING RID OF ALL QUIRKS...
...SHOULDN'T BE RELYING ON QUIRKS, RIGHT?
SHF...
!!
KRIK
KRIK
LEMME SLICE THAT OFF FOR YOU, UNLESS YOU WANT TO FALL TO PIECES...
There we go.
NOW YOU'RE A USELESS, HELPLESS, QUIRKLESS WONDER.
KLAK

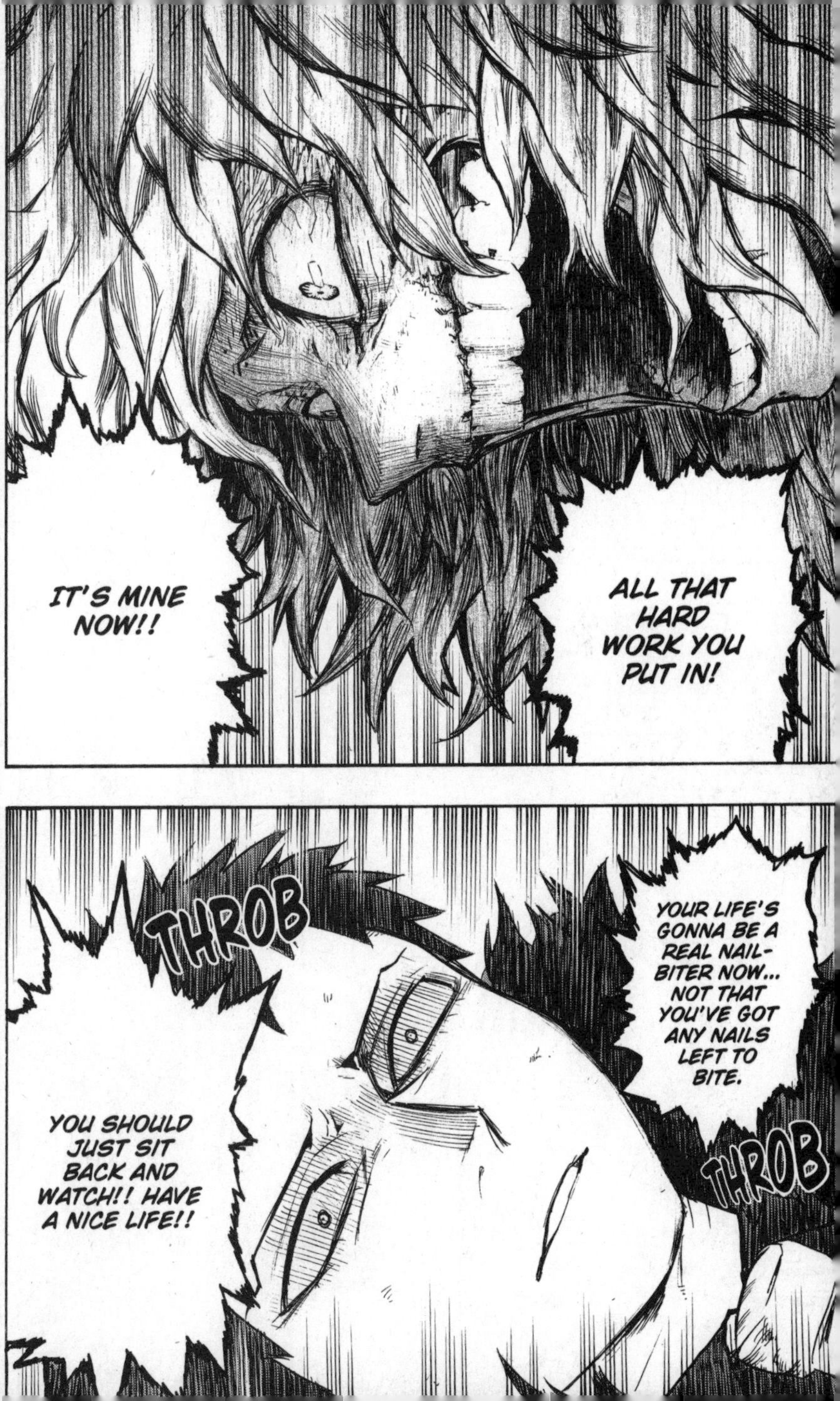
ALL THAT HARD WORK YOU PUT IN!
IT'S MINE NOW!!
YOUR LIFE'S GONNA BE A REAL NAIL-BITER NOW... NOT THAT YOU'VE GOT ANY NAILS LEFT TO BITE.
THROB
THROB
YOU SHOULD JUST SIT BACK AND WATCH!! HAVE A NICE LIFE!!

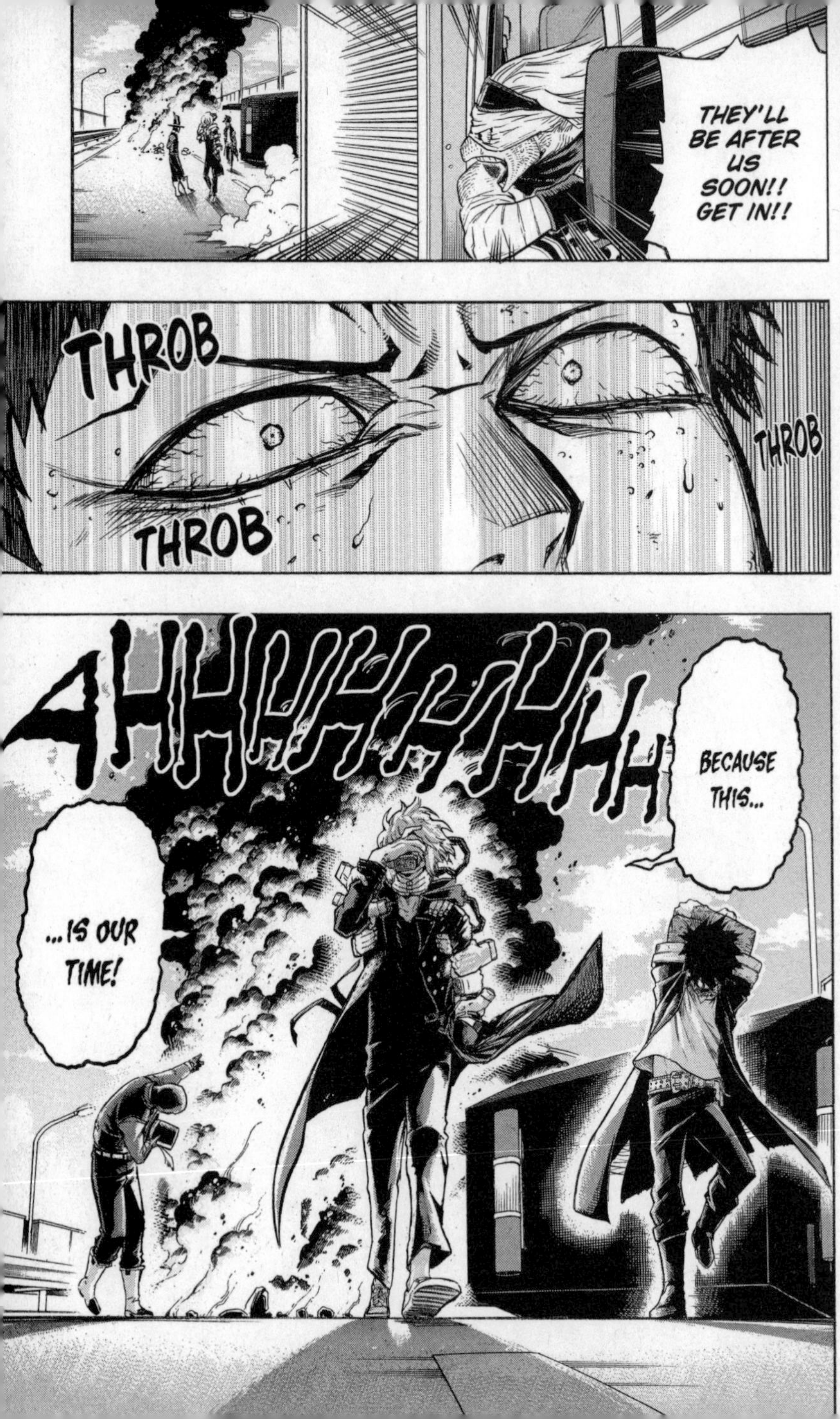
THEY'LL BE AFTER US SOON!! GET IN!!
THROB
THROB
THROB
AHHHHHHHHHH
BECAUSE THIS...
...IS OUR TIME!

STREET CLOTHES

HERO

SNATCH (45)
(SAJIN HIGAWARA)

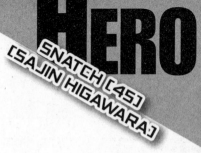

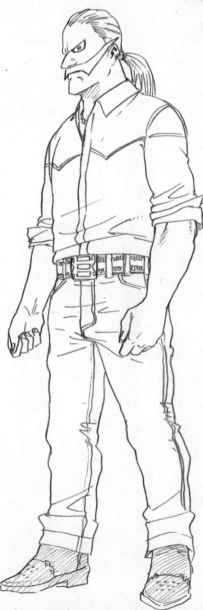

Birthday: 4/14
Height: 180 cm
Favorite Thing: Barbecue

THE SUPPLEMENT

A good-looking middle-aged man who seems pretty strong.

I like this guy, even though he got taken out just like that.

That mustache is so cool.

Facial hair is about to make a comeback.

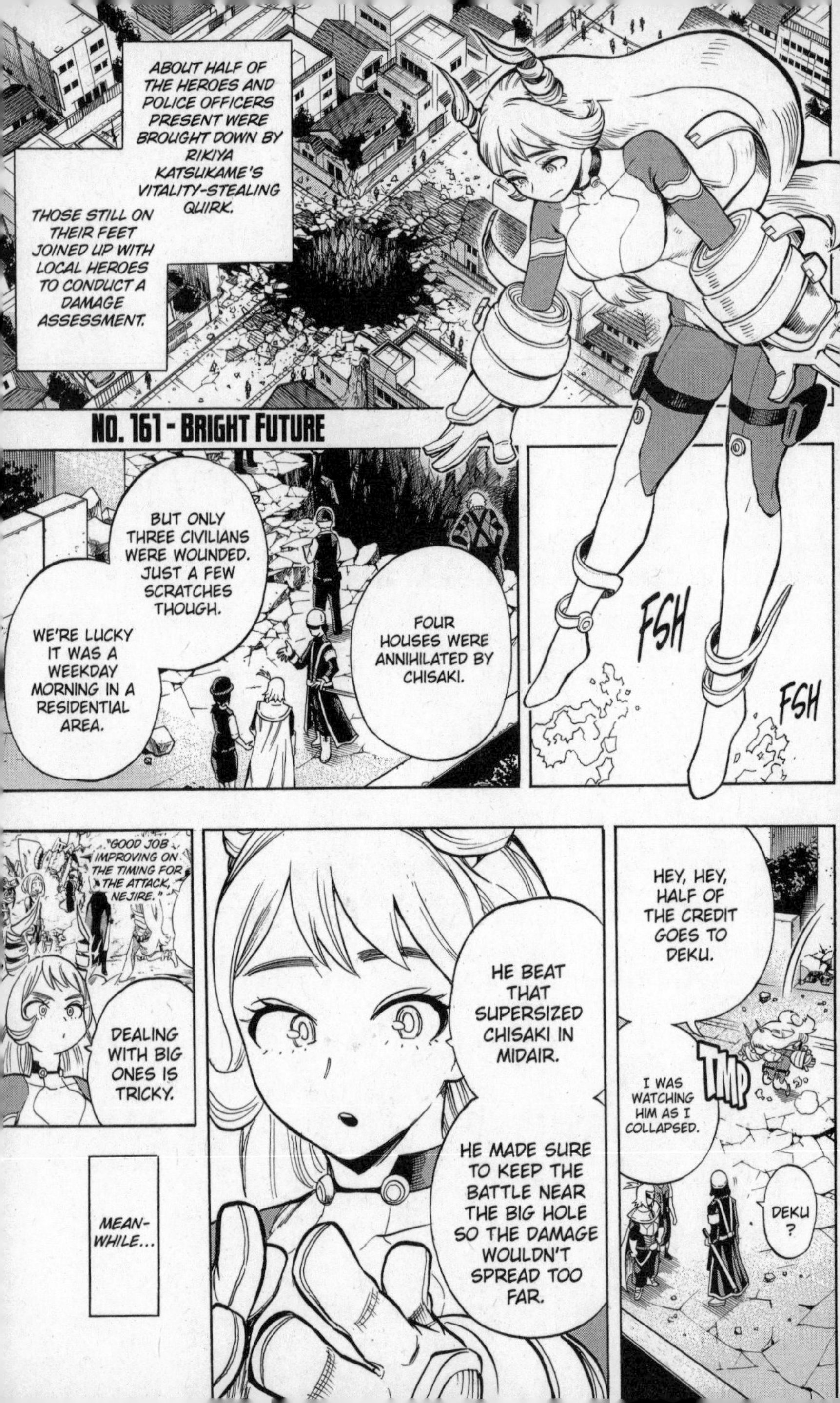
ABOUT HALF OF THE HEROES AND POLICE OFFICERS PRESENT WERE BROUGHT DOWN BY RIKIYA KATSUKAME'S VITALITY-STEALING QUIRK.
THOSE STILL ON THEIR FEET JOINED UP WITH LOCAL HEROES TO CONDUCT A DAMAGE ASSESSMENT.
NO. 161 - BRIGHT FUTURE
FSH
FSH
FOUR HOUSES WERE ANNIHILATED BY CHISAKI.
BUT ONLY THREE CIVILIANS WERE WOUNDED. JUST A FEW SCRATCHES THOUGH.
WE'RE LUCKY IT WAS A WEEKDAY MORNING IN A RESIDENTIAL AREA.
HEY, HEY, HALF OF THE CREDIT GOES TO DEKU.
TMP
I WAS WATCHING HIM AS I COLLAPSED.
DEKU?
HE BEAT THAT SUPERSIZED CHISAKI IN MIDAIR.
HE MADE SURE TO KEEP THE BATTLE NEAR THE BIG HOLE SO THE DAMAGE WOULDN'T SPREAD TOO FAR.
"GOOD JOB IMPROVING ON THE TIMING FOR THE ATTACK, NEJIRE."
DEALING WITH BIG ONES IS TRICKY.
MEAN-WHILE...

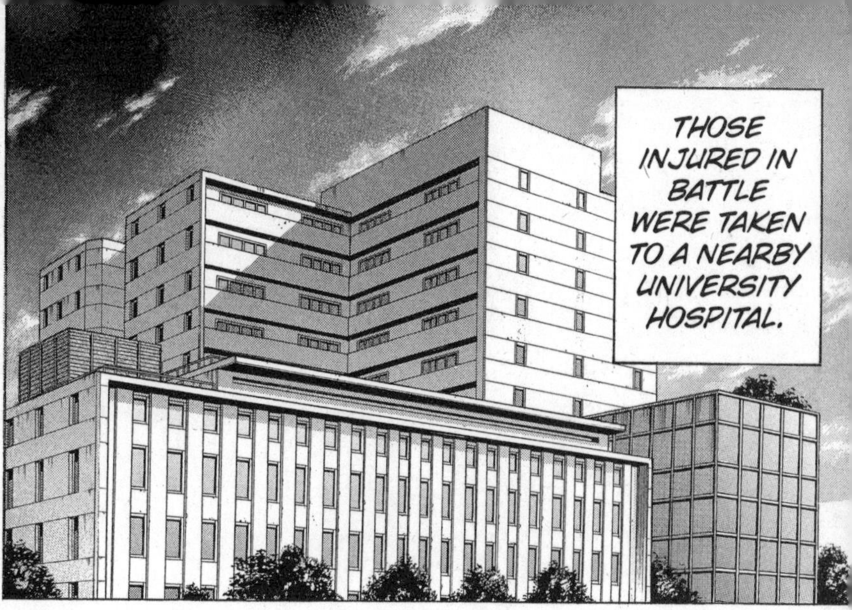
THOSE INJURED IN BATTLE WERE TAKEN TO A NEARBY UNIVERSITY HOSPITAL.

NO. 161 - BRIGHT FUTURE

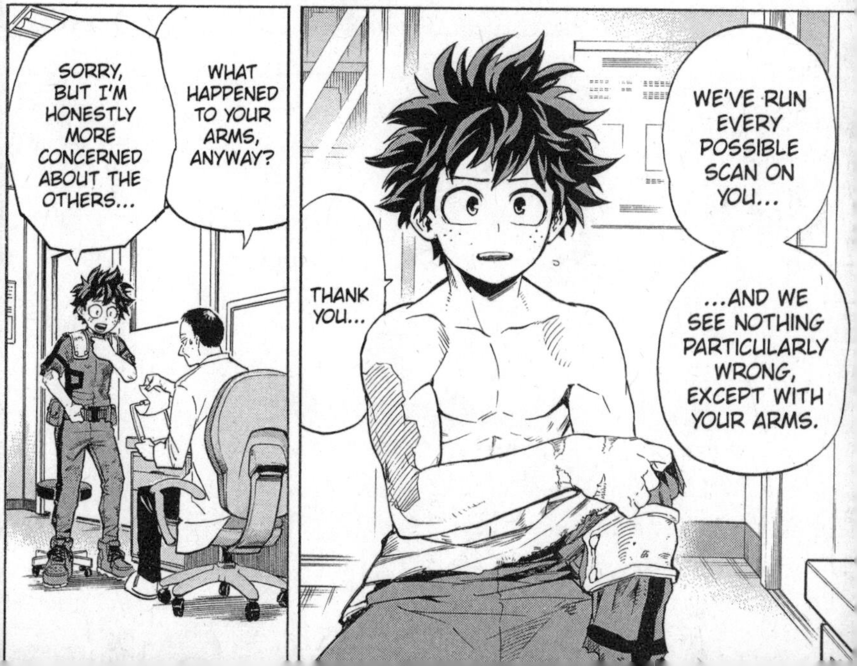
WE'VE RUN EVERY POSSIBLE SCAN ON YOU...
...AND WE SEE NOTHING PARTICULARLY WRONG, EXCEPT WITH YOUR ARMS.
THANK YOU...
WHAT HAPPENED TO YOUR ARMS, ANYWAY?
SORRY, BUT I'M HONESTLY MORE CONCERNED ABOUT THE OTHERS...

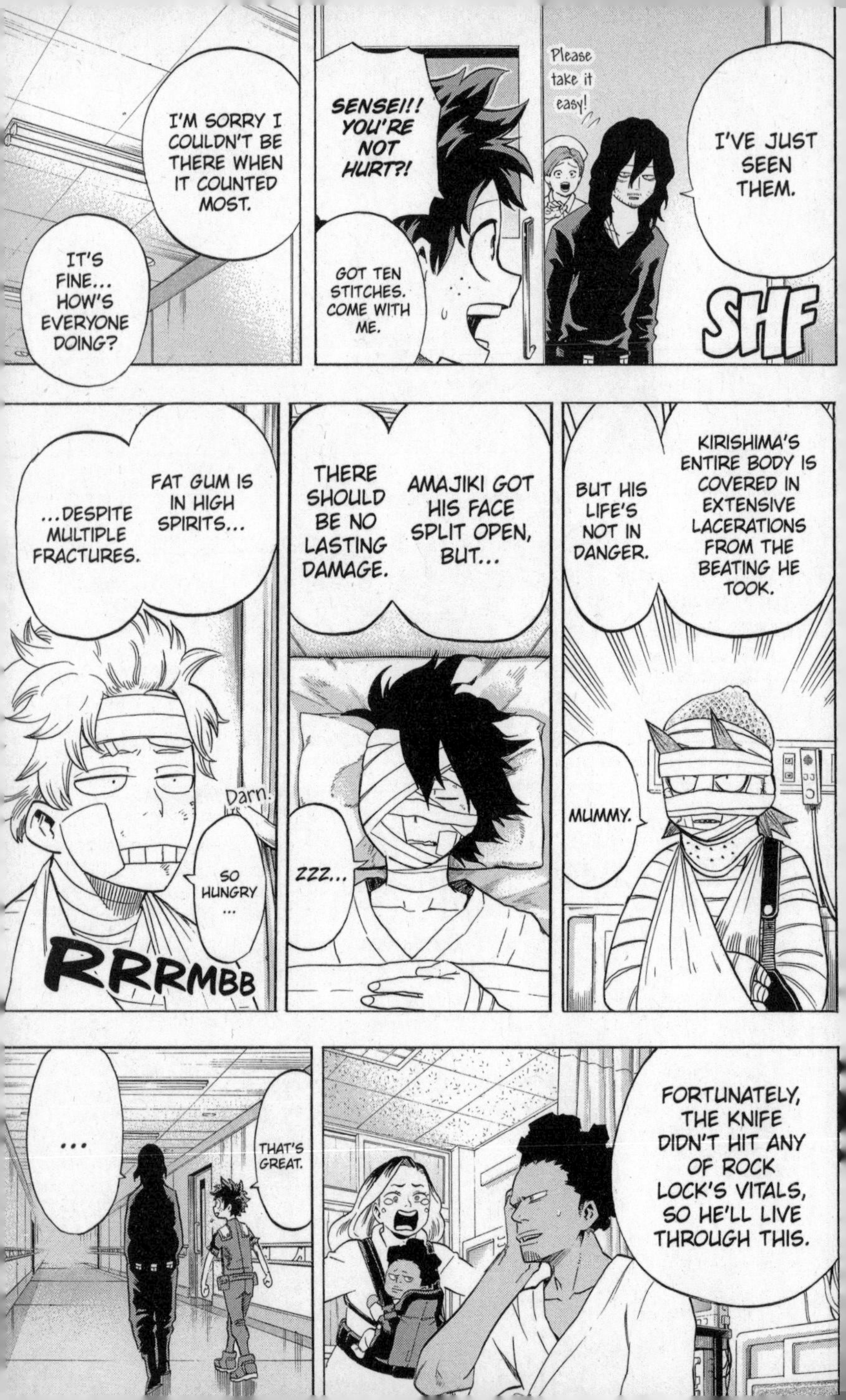
I'VE JUST SEEN THEM.
Please take it easy!
SHF
SENSEI!! YOU'RE NOT HURT?!
GOT TEN STITCHES. COME WITH ME.
I'M SORRY I COULDN'T BE THERE WHEN IT COUNTED MOST.
IT'S FINE... HOW'S EVERYONE DOING?
KIRISHIMA'S ENTIRE BODY IS COVERED IN EXTENSIVE LACERATIONS FROM THE BEATING HE TOOK.
BUT HIS LIFE'S NOT IN DANGER.
MUMMY.
AMAJIKI GOT HIS FACE SPLIT OPEN, BUT...
THERE SHOULD BE NO LASTING DAMAGE.
ZZZ...
FAT GUM IS IN HIGH SPIRITS...
...DESPITE MULTIPLE FRACTURES.
Darn.
SO HUNGRY...
RRRMBB
FORTUNATELY, THE KNIFE DIDN'T HIT ANY OF ROCK LOCK'S VITALS, SO HE'LL LIVE THROUGH THIS.
THAT'S GREAT.
...

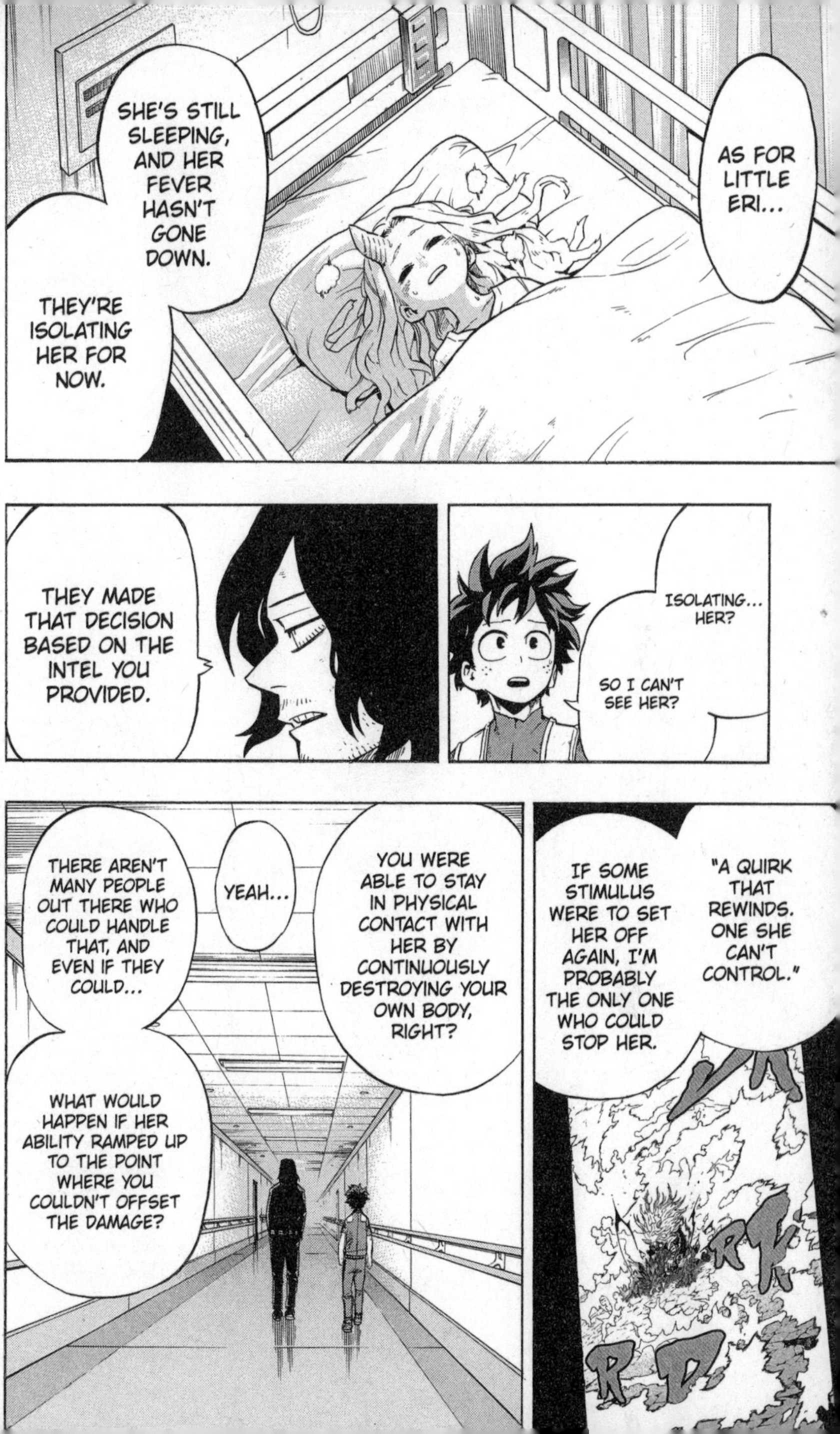
AS FOR LITTLE ERI...
SHE'S STILL SLEEPING, AND HER FEVER HASN'T GONE DOWN.
THEY'RE ISOLATING HER FOR NOW.
ISOLATING... HER?
SO I CAN'T SEE HER?
THEY MADE THAT DECISION BASED ON THE INTEL YOU PROVIDED.
"A QUIRK THAT REWINDS. ONE SHE CAN'T CONTROL."
IF SOME STIMULUS WERE TO SET HER OFF AGAIN, I'M PROBABLY THE ONLY ONE WHO COULD STOP HER.
YOU WERE ABLE TO STAY IN PHYSICAL CONTACT WITH HER BY CONTINUOUSLY DESTROYING YOUR OWN BODY, RIGHT?
YEAH...
THERE AREN'T MANY PEOPLE OUT THERE WHO COULD HANDLE THAT, AND EVEN IF THEY COULD...
WHAT WOULD HAPPEN IF HER ABILITY RAMPED UP TO THE POINT WHERE YOU COULDN'T OFFSET THE DAMAGE?

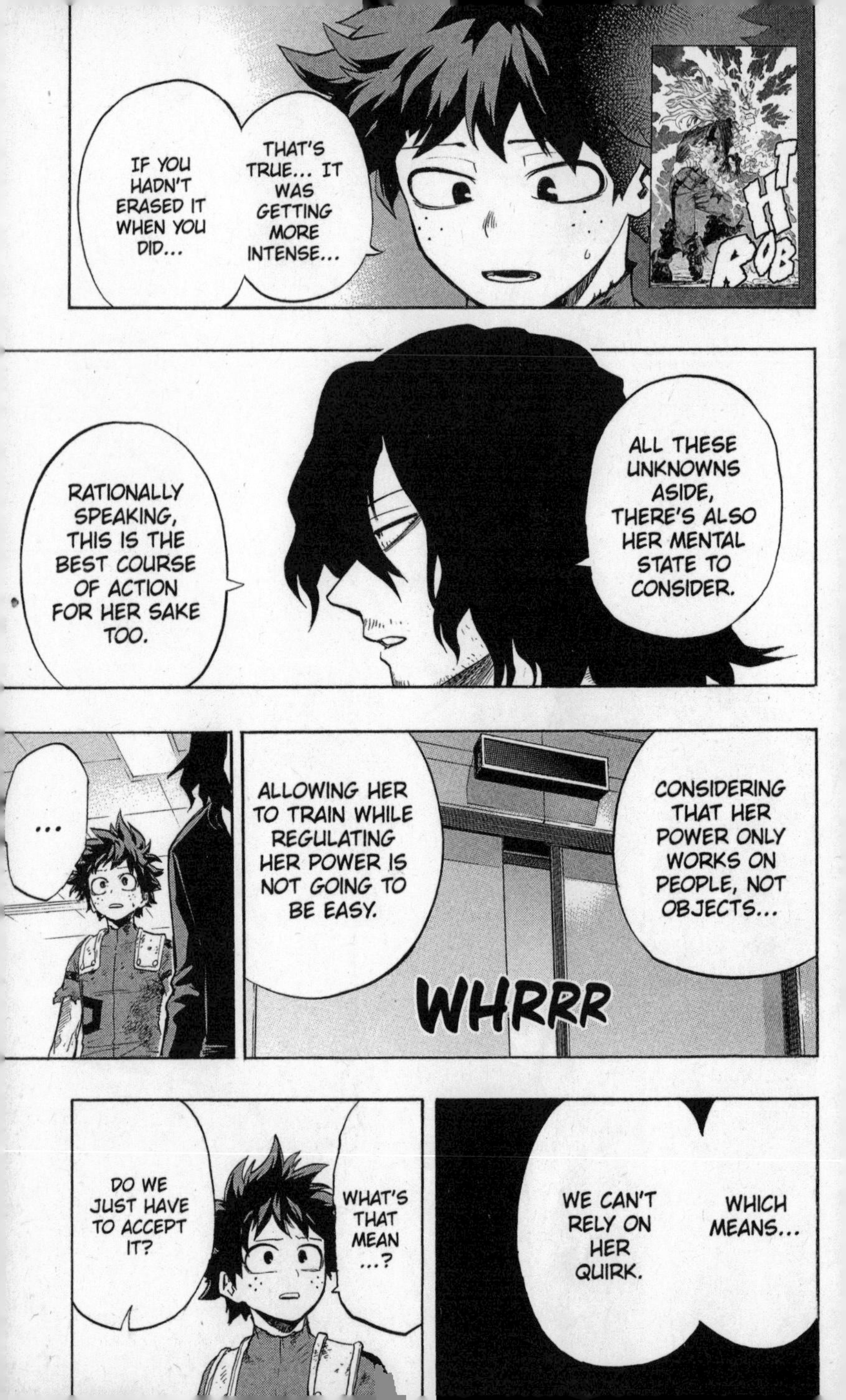

THROB
THAT'S TRUE... IT WAS GETTING MORE INTENSE...
IF YOU HADN'T ERASED IT WHEN YOU DID...
ALL THESE UNKNOWNS ASIDE, THERE'S ALSO HER MENTAL STATE TO CONSIDER.
RATIONALLY SPEAKING, THIS IS THE BEST COURSE OF ACTION FOR HER SAKE TOO.
CONSIDERING THAT HER POWER ONLY WORKS ON PEOPLE, NOT OBJECTS...
ALLOWING HER TO TRAIN WHILE REGULATING HER POWER IS NOT GOING TO BE EASY.
WHRRR
...
WHICH MEANS...
WE CAN'T RELY ON HER QUIRK.
WHAT'S THAT MEAN ...?
DO WE JUST HAVE TO ACCEPT IT?

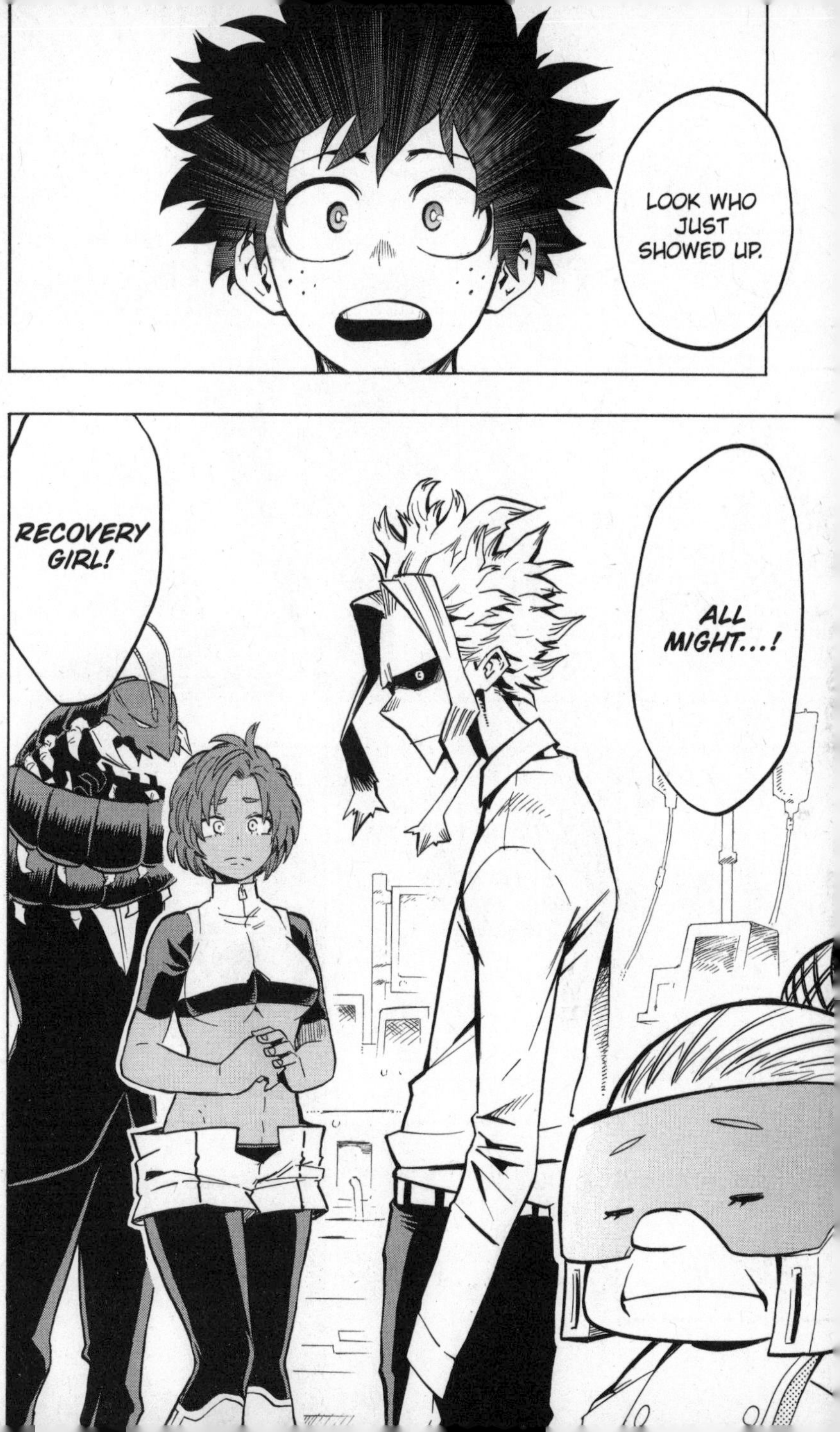
LOOK WHO JUST SHOWED UP.
ALL MIGHT...!
RECOVERY GIRL!

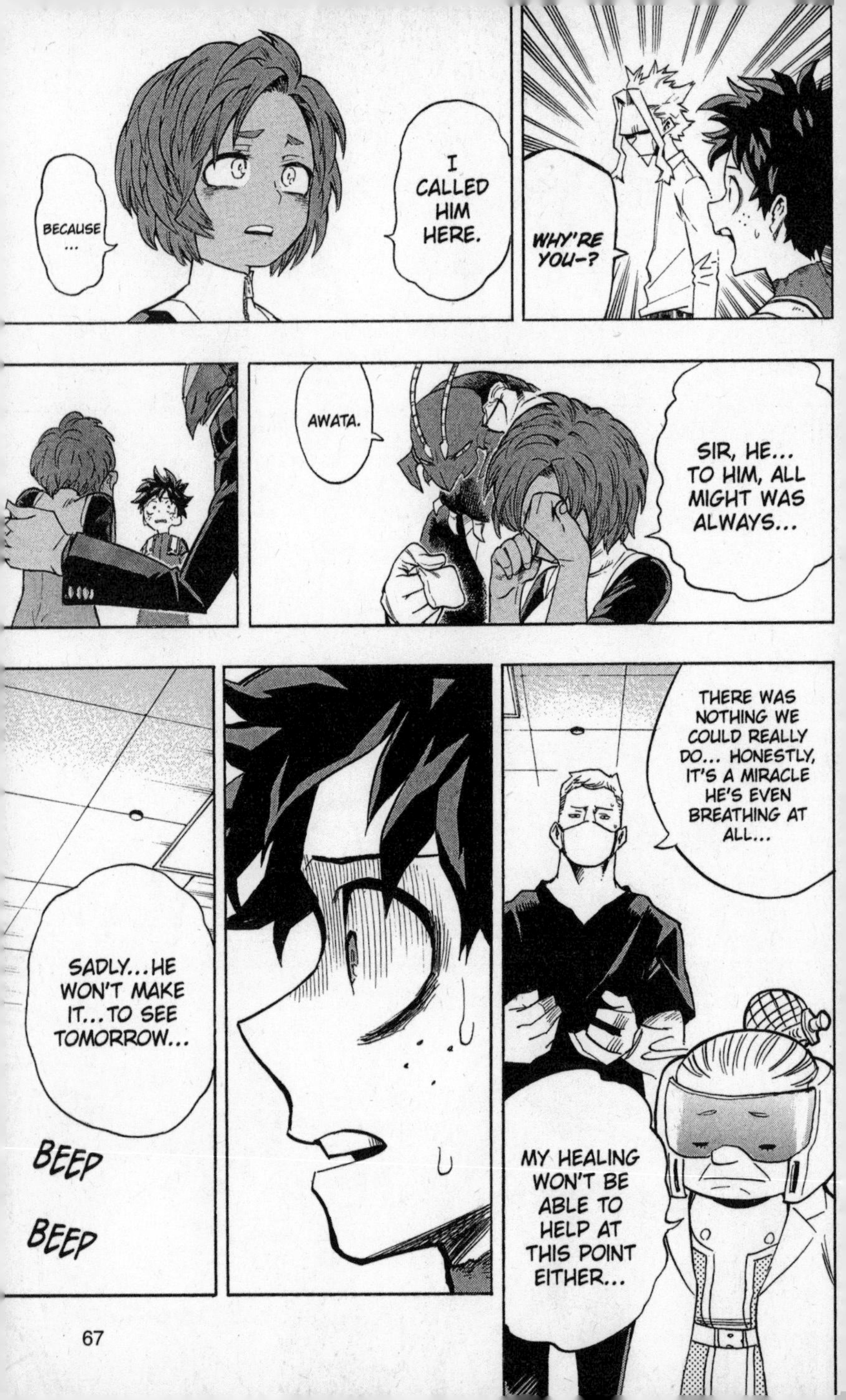
WHY'RE YOU-?
I CALLED HIM HERE.
BECAUSE ...
SIR, HE... TO HIM, ALL MIGHT WAS ALWAYS...
AWATA.
THERE WAS NOTHING WE COULD REALLY DO... HONESTLY, IT'S A MIRACLE HE'S EVEN BREATHING AT ALL...
MY HEALING WON'T BE ABLE TO HELP AT THIS POINT EITHER...
SADLY...HE WON'T MAKE IT...TO SEE TOMORROW...
BEEP
BEEP

BEEP
BEEP
NIGHTEYE ...!!
...

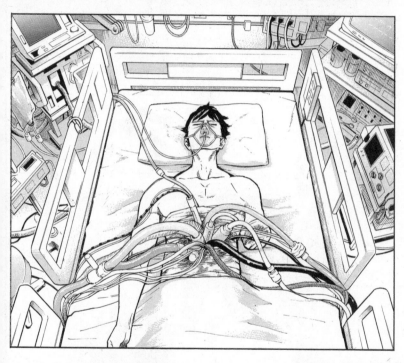

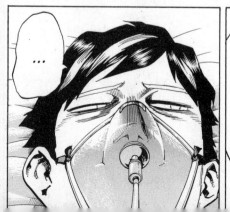

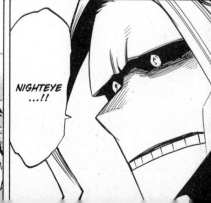

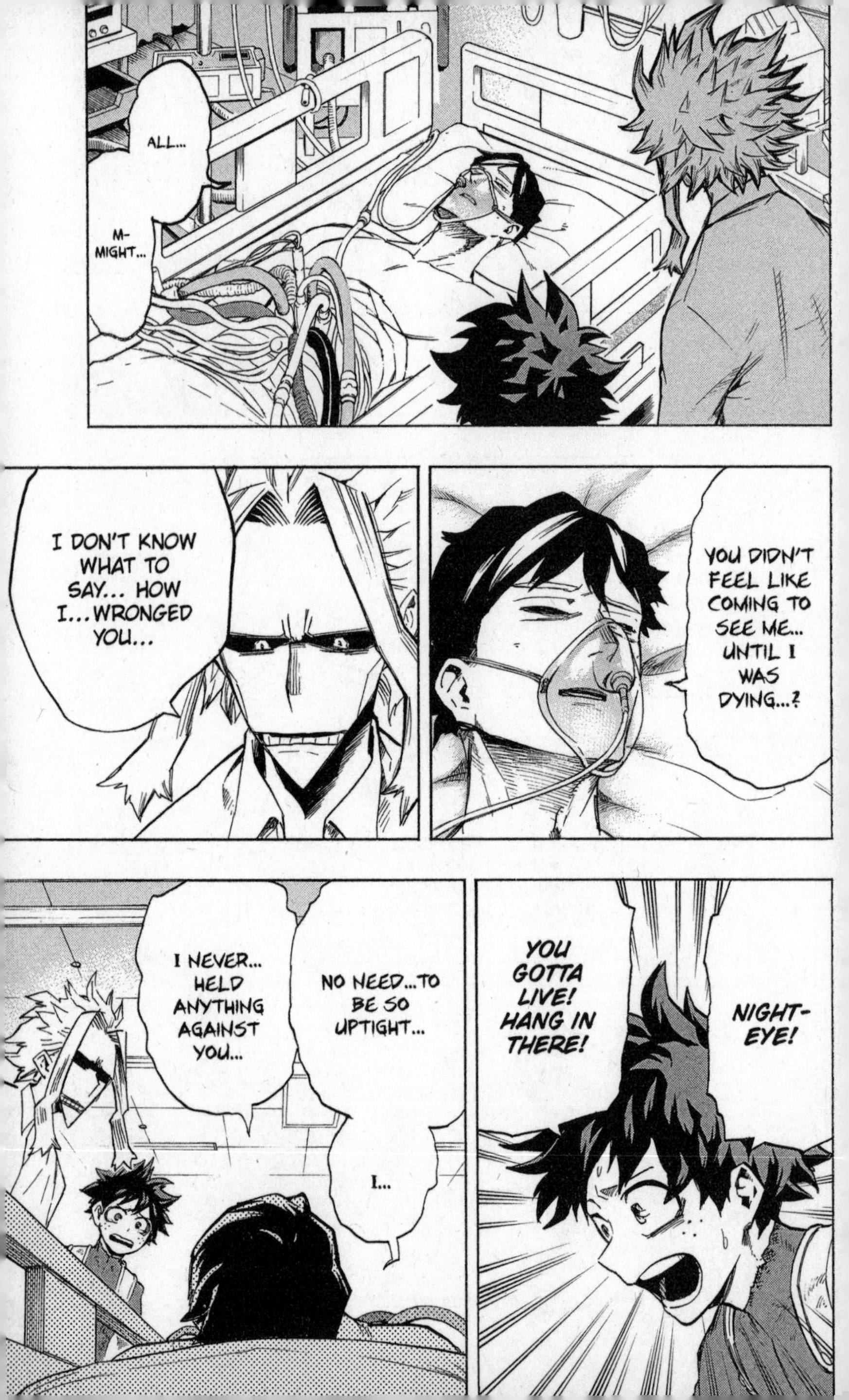
ALL...
M-MIGHT...
YOU DIDN'T FEEL LIKE COMING TO SEE ME... UNTIL I WAS DYING...?
I DON'T KNOW WHAT TO SAY... HOW I...WRONGED YOU...
NIGHT-EYE!
YOU GOTTA LIVE! HANG IN THERE!
NO NEED...TO BE SO UPTIGHT...
I...
I NEVER... HELD ANYTHING AGAINST YOU...

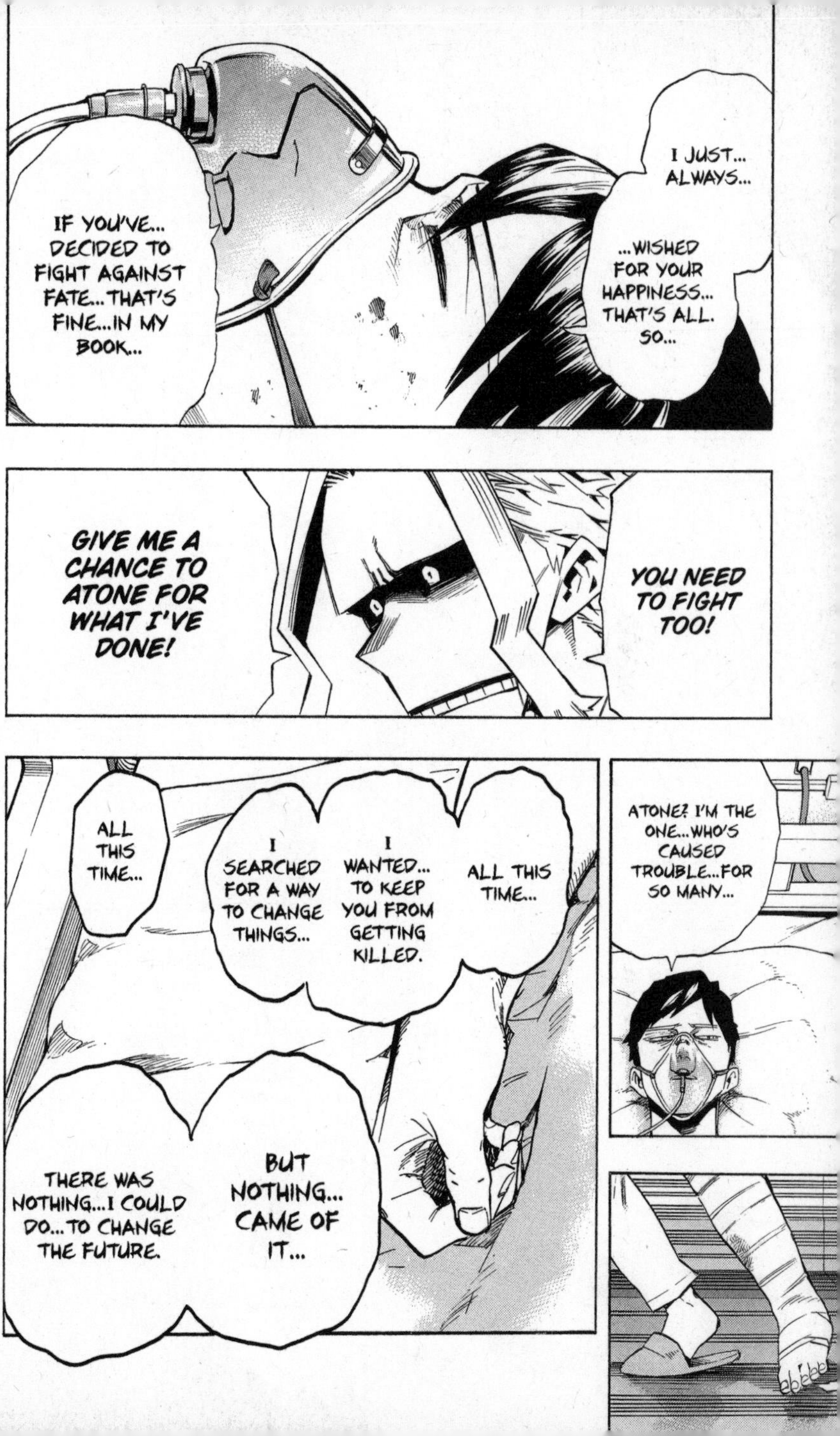
I JUST... ALWAYS...
...WISHED FOR YOUR HAPPINESS... THAT'S ALL. SO...
IF YOU'VE... DECIDED TO FIGHT AGAINST FATE... THAT'S FINE... IN MY BOOK...
YOU NEED TO FIGHT TOO!
GIVE ME A CHANCE TO ATONE FOR WHAT I'VE DONE!
ATONE? I'M THE ONE... WHO'S CAUSED TROUBLE... FOR SO MANY...
ALL THIS TIME...
I WANTED... TO KEEP YOU FROM GETTING KILLED.
I SEARCHED FOR A WAY TO CHANGE THINGS...
ALL THIS TIME...
BUT NOTHING... CAME OF IT...
THERE WAS NOTHING... I COULD DO... TO CHANGE THE FUTURE.

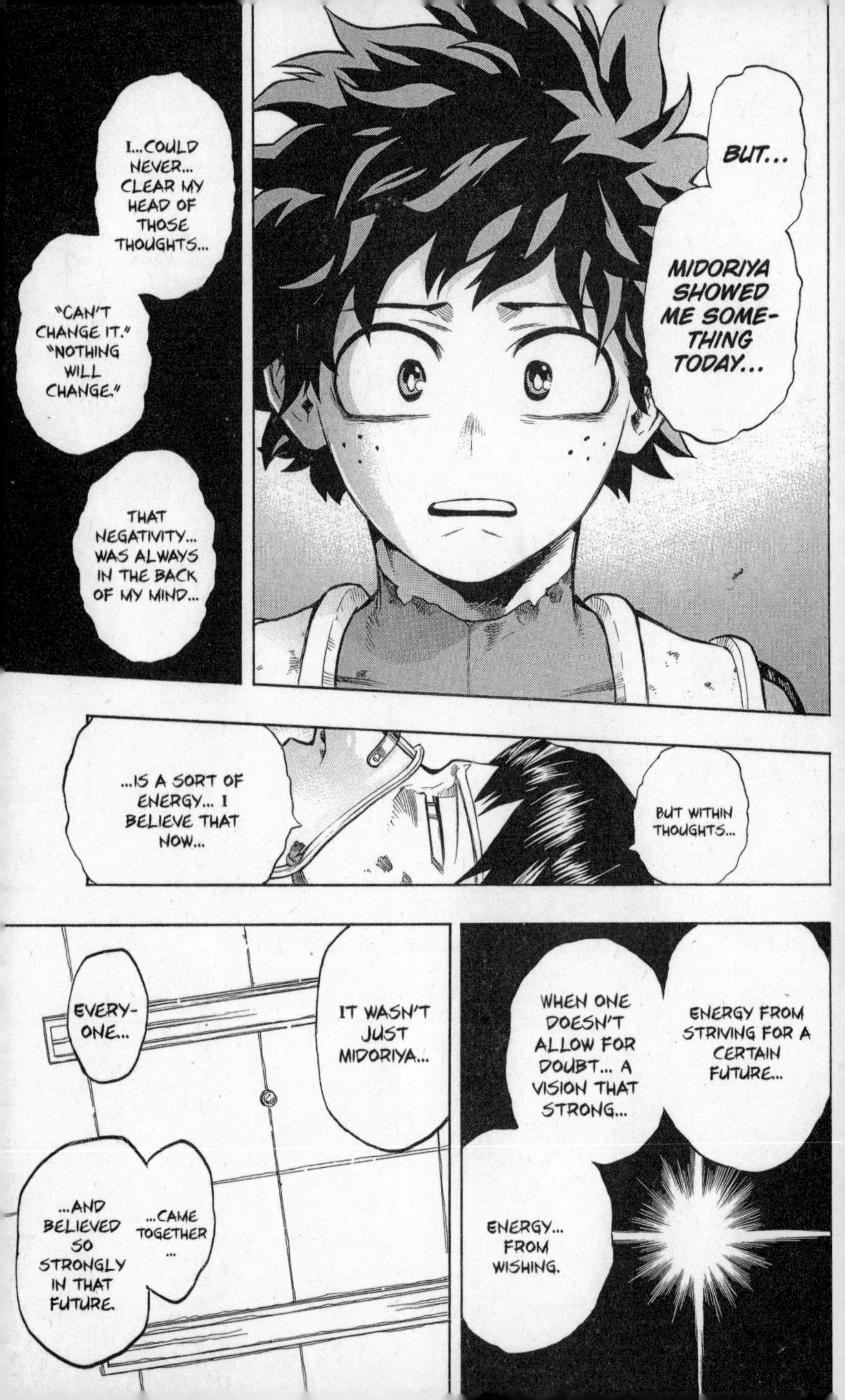
BUT...
MIDORIYA SHOWED ME SOMETHING TODAY...
I...COULD NEVER... CLEAR MY HEAD OF THOSE THOUGHTS...
"CAN'T CHANGE IT." "NOTHING WILL CHANGE."
THAT NEGATIVITY... WAS ALWAYS IN THE BACK OF MY MIND...
BUT WITHIN THOUGHTS...
...IS A SORT OF ENERGY... I BELIEVE THAT NOW...
ENERGY FROM STRIVING FOR A CERTAIN FUTURE...
WHEN ONE DOESN'T ALLOW FOR DOUBT... A VISION THAT STRONG...
ENERGY... FROM WISHING.
IT WASN'T JUST MIDORIYA...
EVERY-ONE...
...CAME TOGETHER...
...AND BELIEVED SO STRONGLY IN THAT FUTURE.

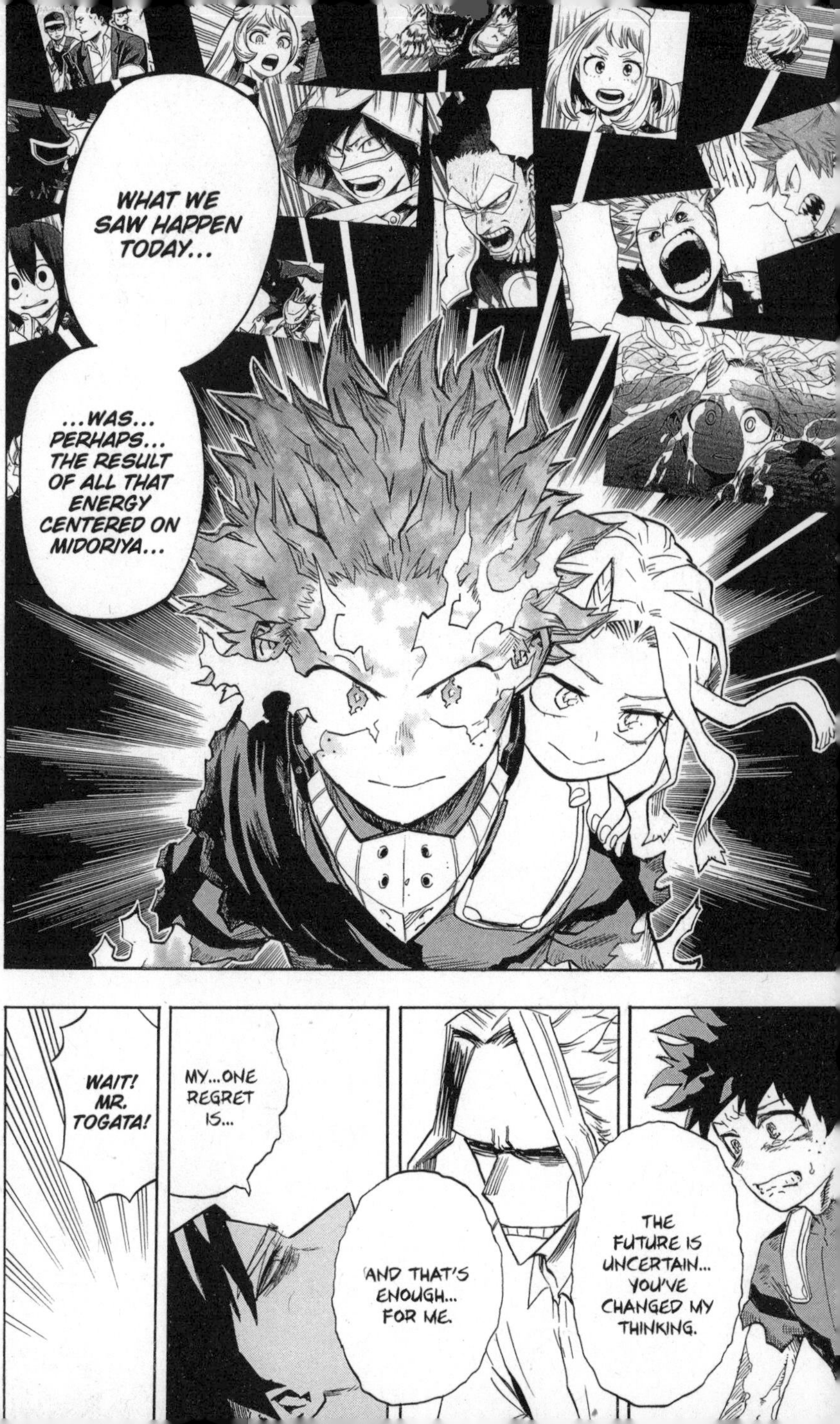
WHAT WE SAW HAPPEN TODAY...
...WAS... PERHAPS... THE RESULT OF ALL THAT ENERGY CENTERED ON MIDORIYA...
THE FUTURE IS UNCERTAIN... YOU'VE CHANGED MY THINKING.
AND THAT'S ENOUGH... FOR ME.
MY...ONE REGRET IS...
WAIT! MR. TOGATA!

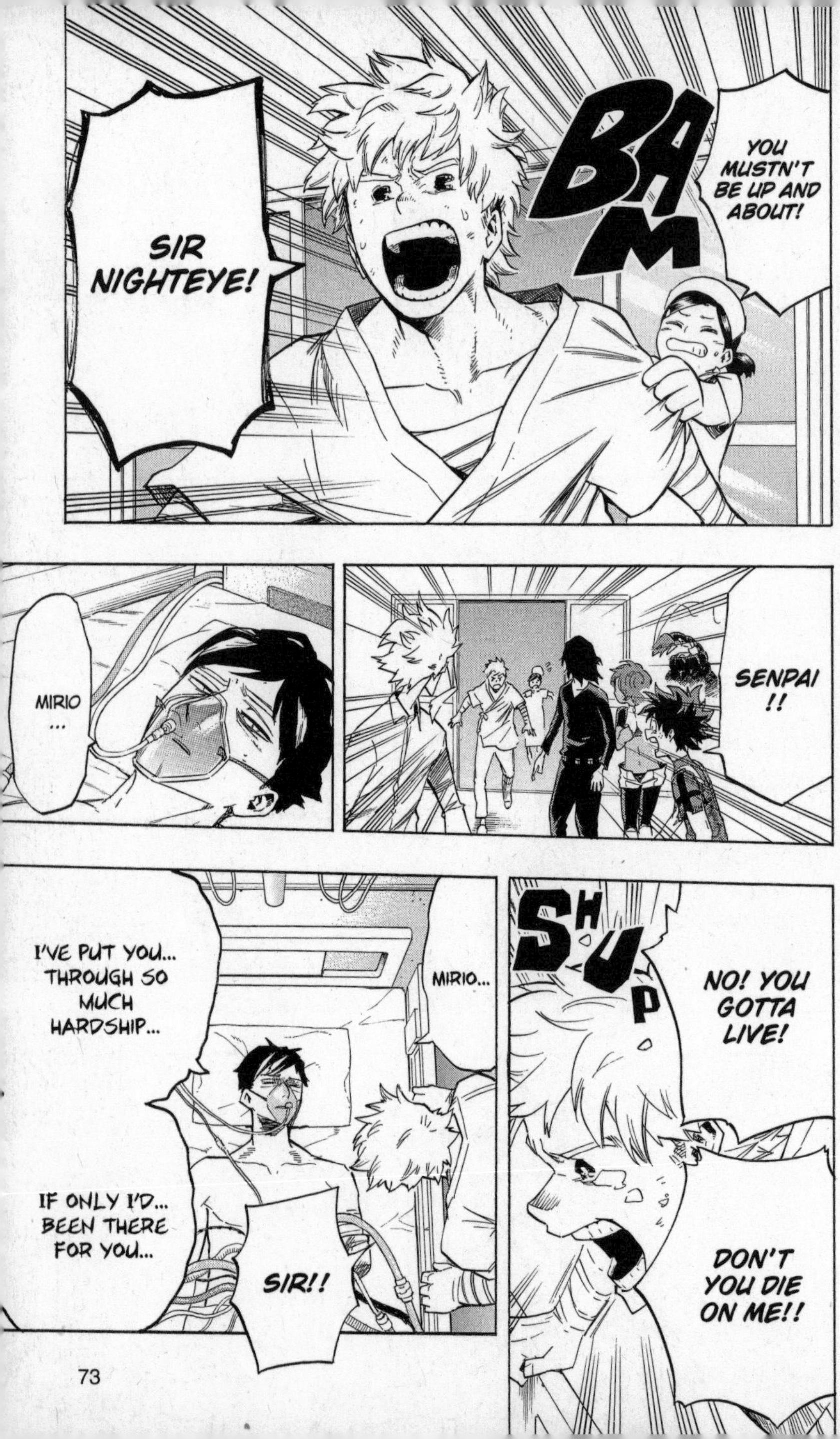
BAM
YOU MUSTN'T BE UP AND ABOUT!
SIR NIGHTEYE!
SENPAI!!
MIRIO...
SHUP
NO! YOU GOTTA LIVE!
DON'T YOU DIE ON ME!!
MIRIO...
I'VE PUT YOU... THROUGH SO MUCH HARDSHIP...
SIR!!
IF ONLY I'D... BEEN THERE FOR YOU...

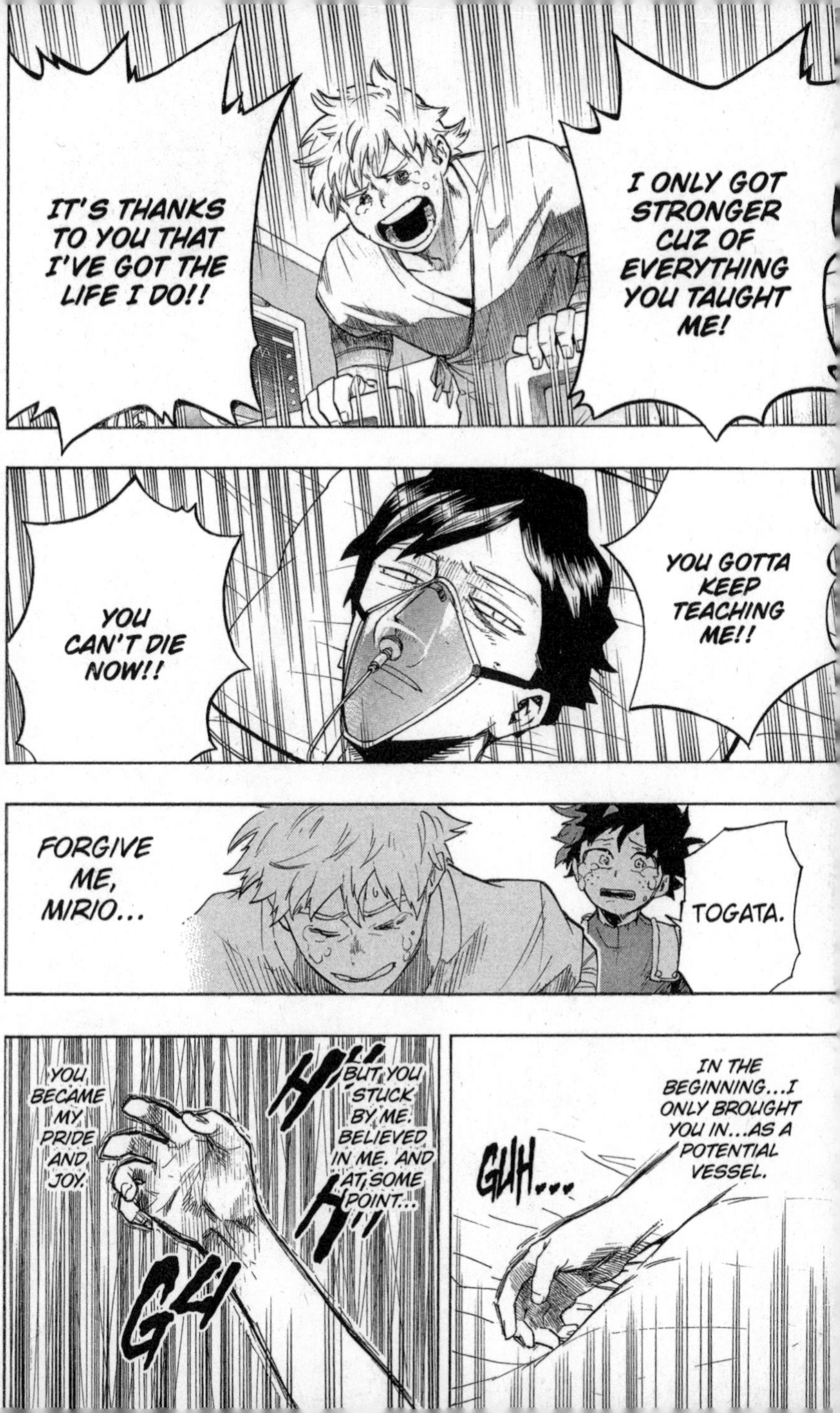
I ONLY GOT STRONGER CUZ OF EVERYTHING YOU TAUGHT ME!
IT'S THANKS TO YOU THAT I'VE GOT THE LIFE I DO!!
YOU GOTTA KEEP TEACHING ME!!
YOU CAN'T DIE NOW!!
TOGATA.
FORGIVE ME, MIRIO...
IN THE BEGINNING...I ONLY BROUGHT YOU IN...AS A POTENTIAL VESSEL.
GUH...
BUT YOU STUCK BY ME. BELIEVED IN ME. AND AT SOME POINT...
YOU BECAME MY PRIDE AND JOY.
GU

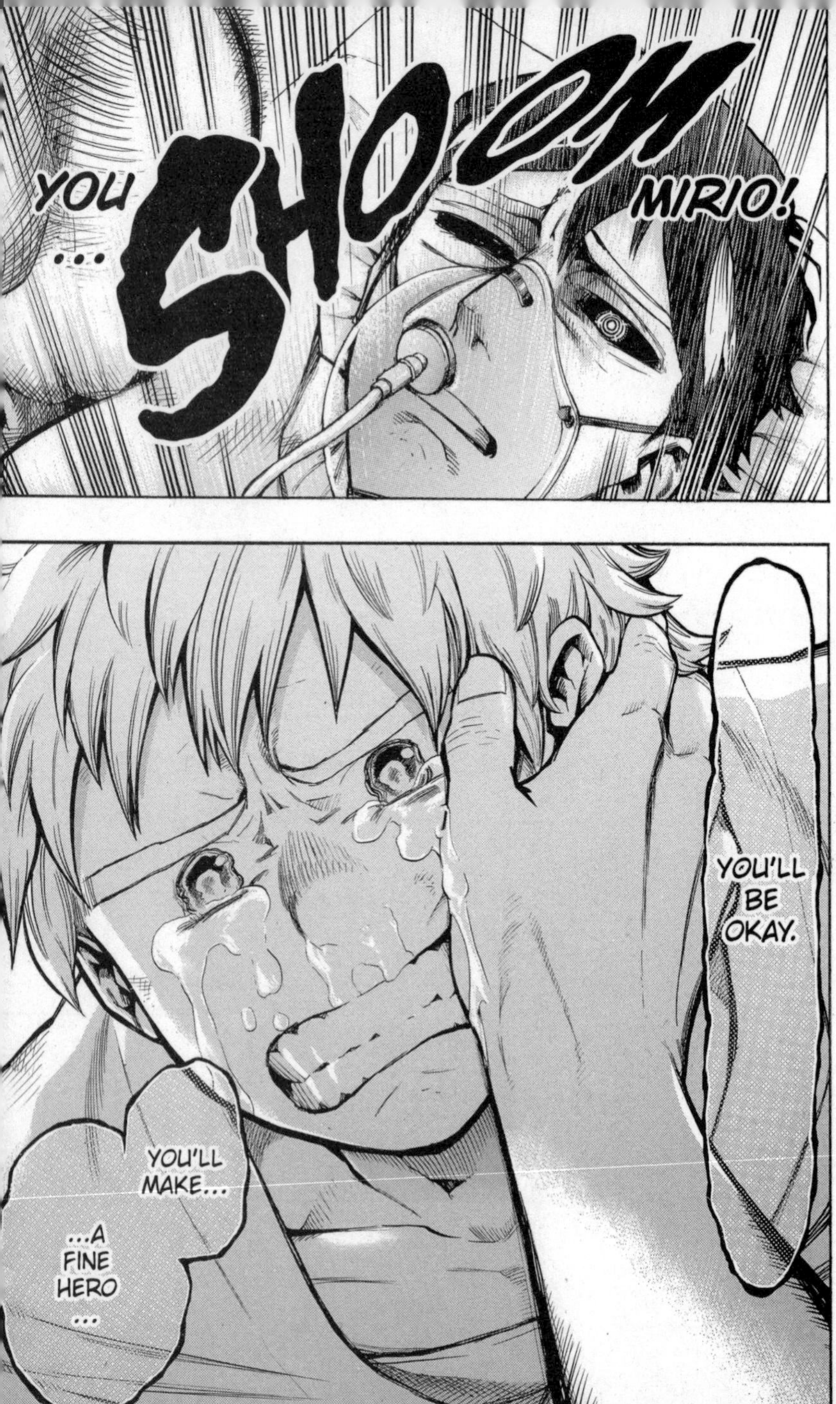
MIRIO!
SHOOM
YOU ...
YOU'LL BE OKAY.
YOU'LL MAKE...
...A FINE HERO ...

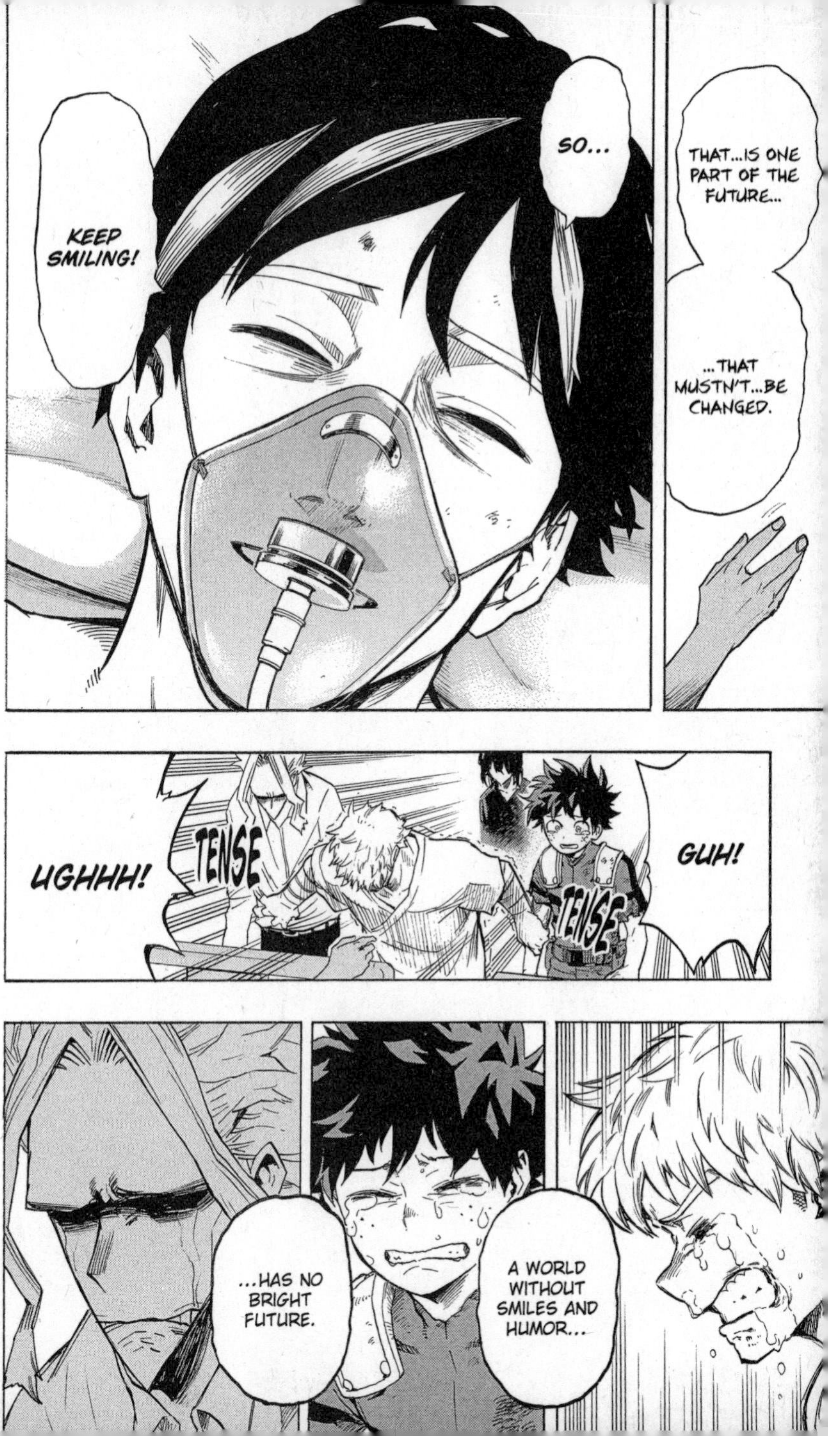
THAT...IS ONE PART OF THE FUTURE...
...THAT MUSTN'T...BE CHANGED.
SO...
KEEP SMILING!
GUH!
TENSE
TENSE
UGHHH!
A WORLD WITHOUT SMILES AND HUMOR...
...HAS NO BRIGHT FUTURE.

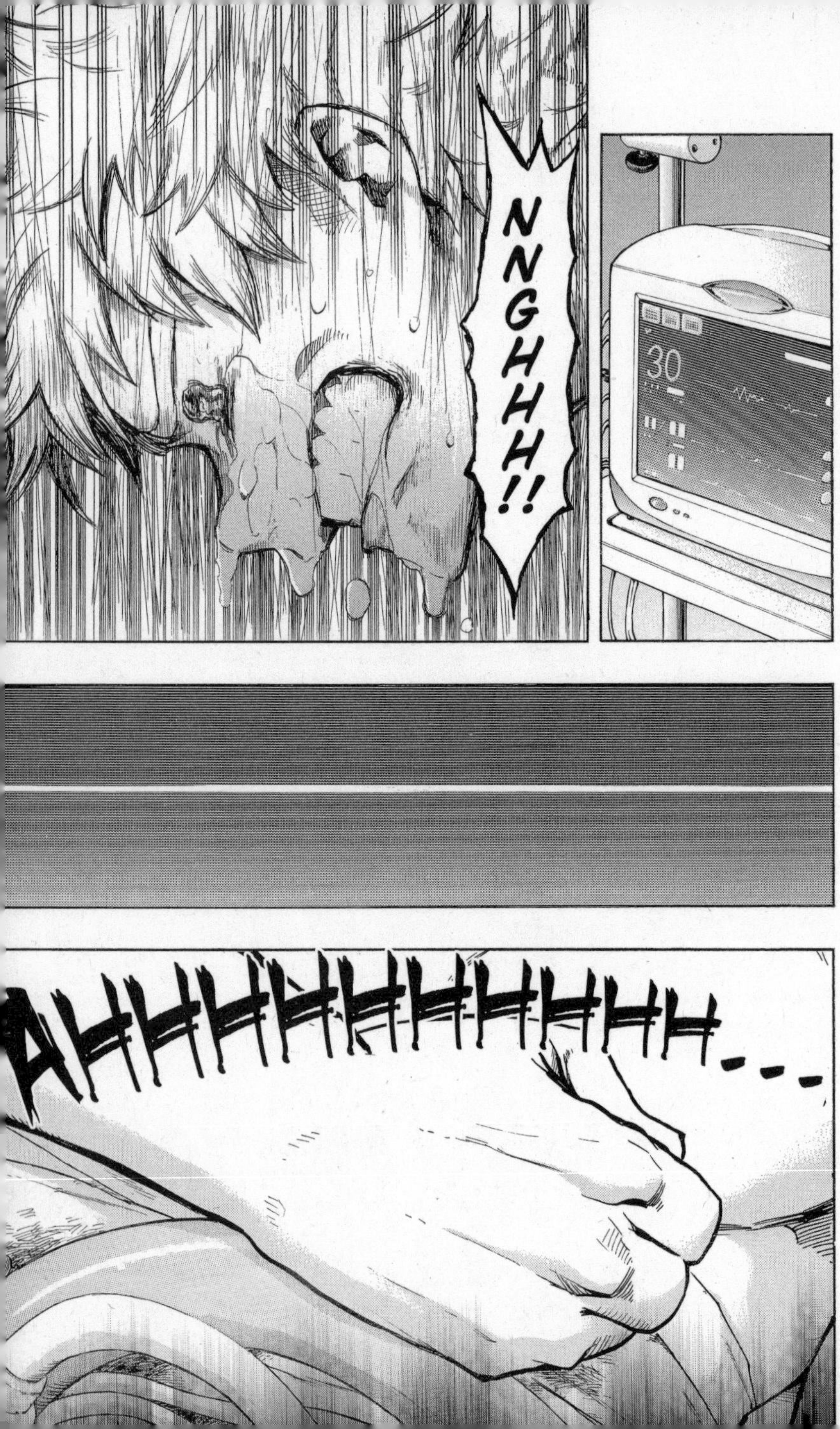
30
NNGHHHH!!
AHHHHHHHHHHH...

MY HERO
ACADEMIA

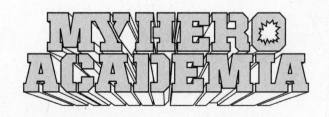

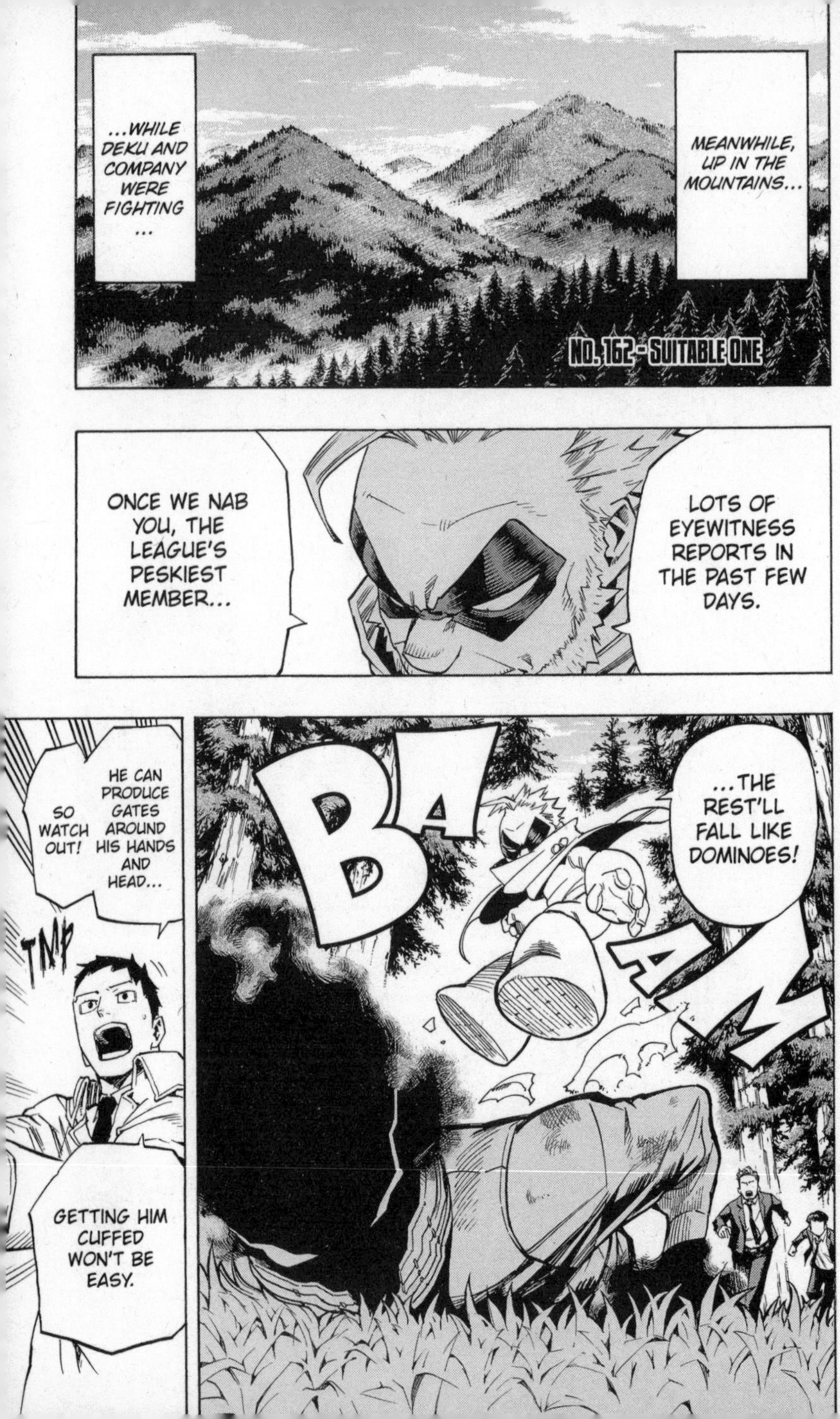
MEANWHILE, UP IN THE MOUNTAINS...
...WHILE DEKU AND COMPANY WERE FIGHTING ...
No. 162 - SUITABLE ONE
LOTS OF EYEWITNESS REPORTS IN THE PAST FEW DAYS.
ONCE WE NAB YOU, THE LEAGUE'S PESKIEST MEMBER...
...THE REST'LL FALL LIKE DOMINOES!
BAM
TMP
HE CAN PRODUCE GATES AROUND HIS HANDS AND HEAD...
SO WATCH OUT!
GETTING HIM CUFFED WON'T BE EASY.

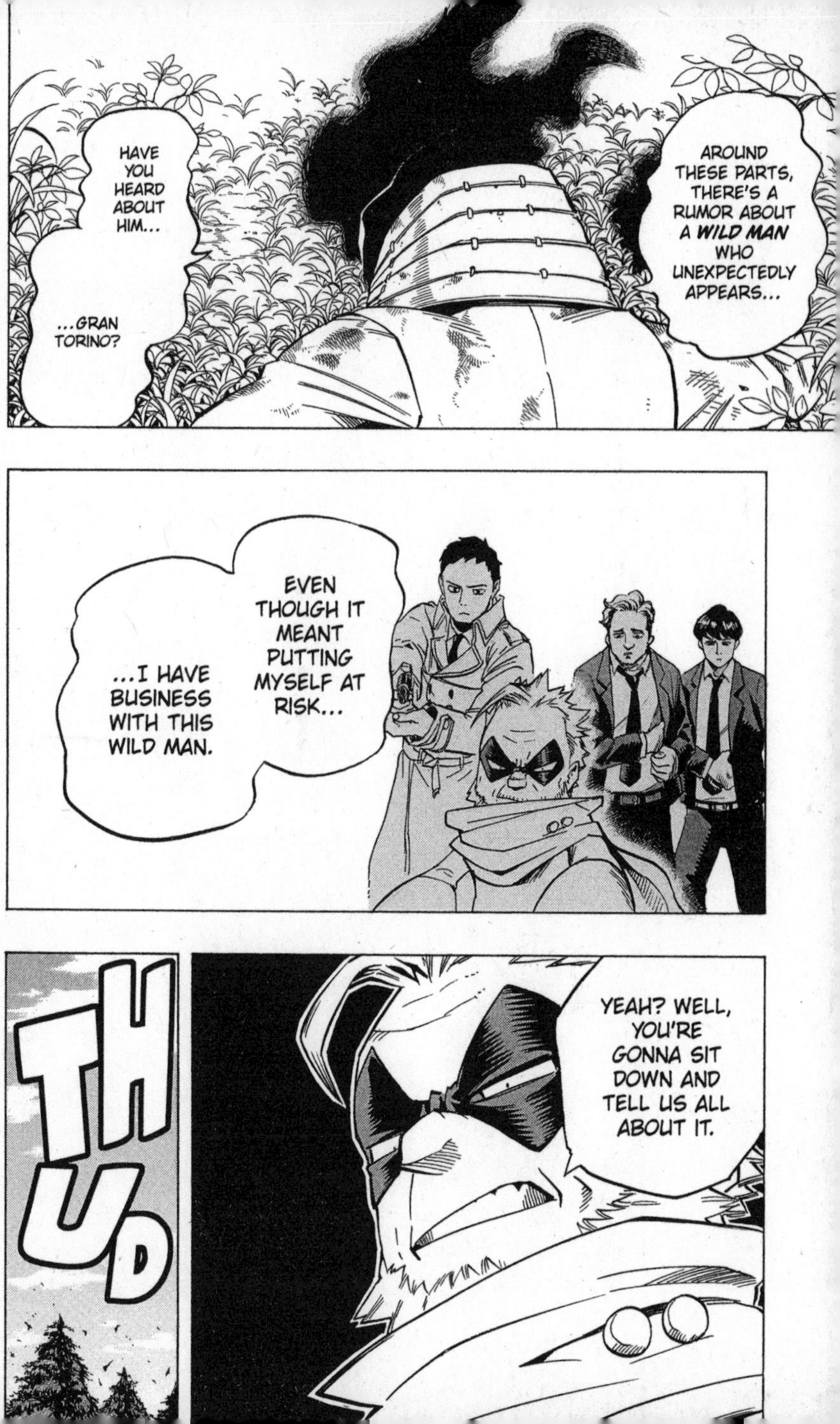
AROUND THESE PARTS, THERE'S A RUMOR ABOUT A **WILD MAN** WHO UNEXPECTEDLY APPEARS...
HAVE YOU HEARD ABOUT HIM...
...GRAN TORINO?
EVEN THOUGH IT MEANT PUTTING MYSELF AT RISK...
...I HAVE BUSINESS WITH THIS WILD MAN.
YEAH? WELL, YOU'RE GONNA SIT DOWN AND TELL US ALL ABOUT IT.
THUD

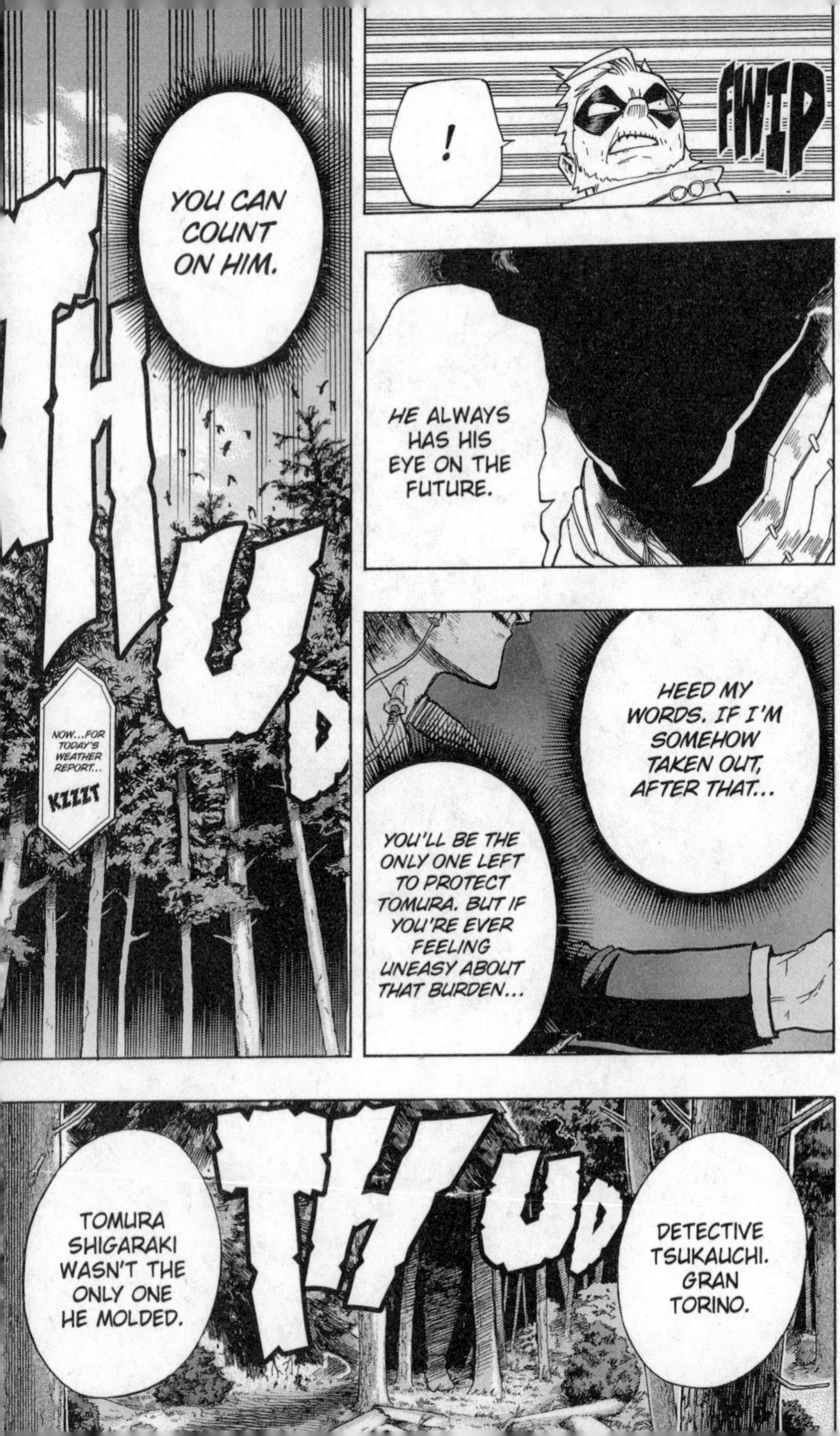
!
FWIP
HE ALWAYS HAS HIS EYE ON THE FUTURE.
HEED MY WORDS. IF I'M SOMEHOW TAKEN OUT, AFTER THAT...
YOU'LL BE THE ONLY ONE LEFT TO PROTECT TOMURA. BUT IF YOU'RE EVER FEELING UNEASY ABOUT THAT BURDEN...
YOU CAN COUNT ON HIM.
THUD
NOW...FOR TODAY'S WEATHER REPORT...
KZZZT
DETECTIVE TSUKAUCHI. GRAN TORINO.
THUD
TOMURA SHIGARAKI WASN'T THE ONLY ONE HE MOLDED.

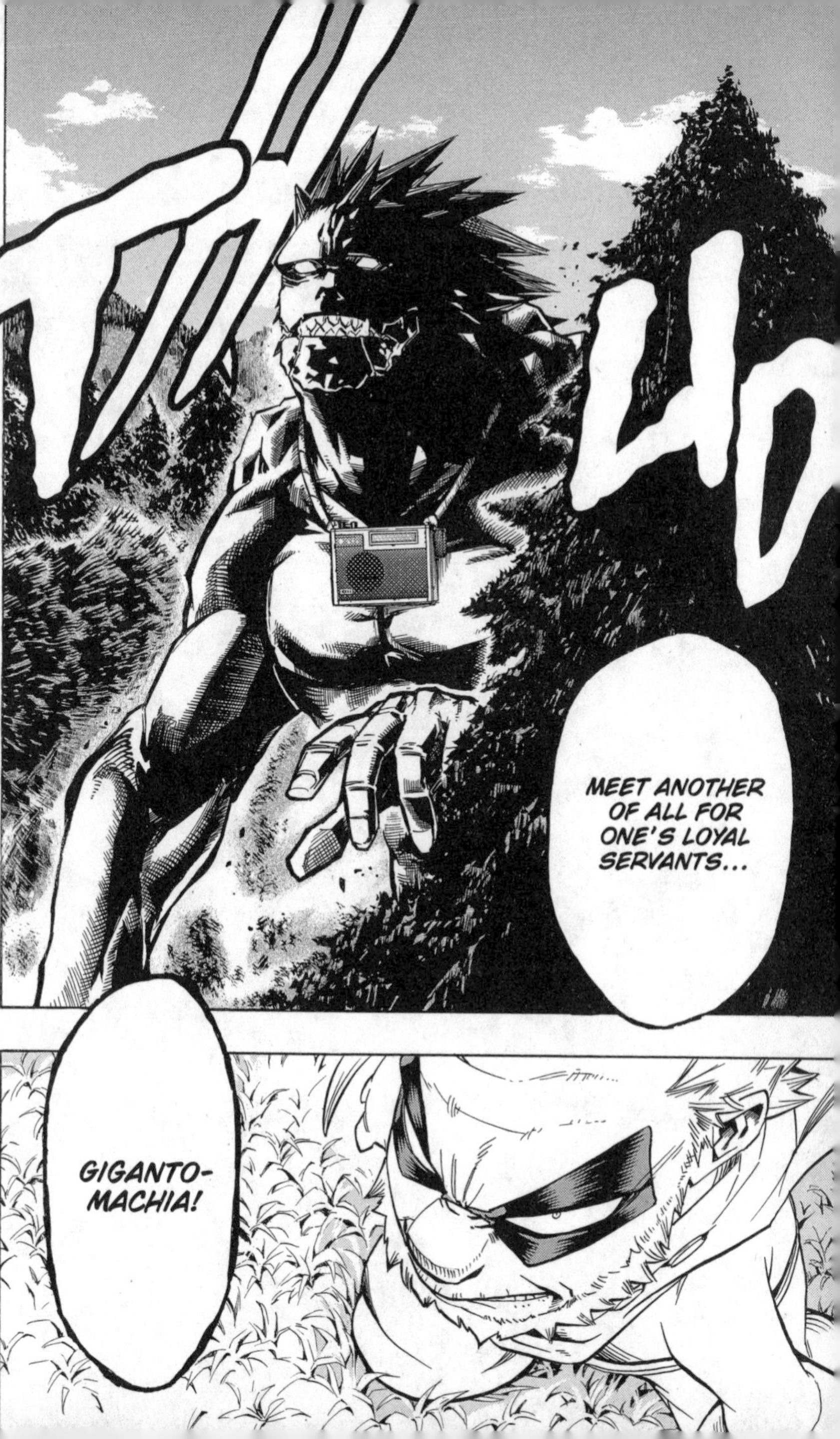
MEET ANOTHER OF ALL FOR ONE'S LOYAL SERVANTS...
GIGANTO-MACHIA!

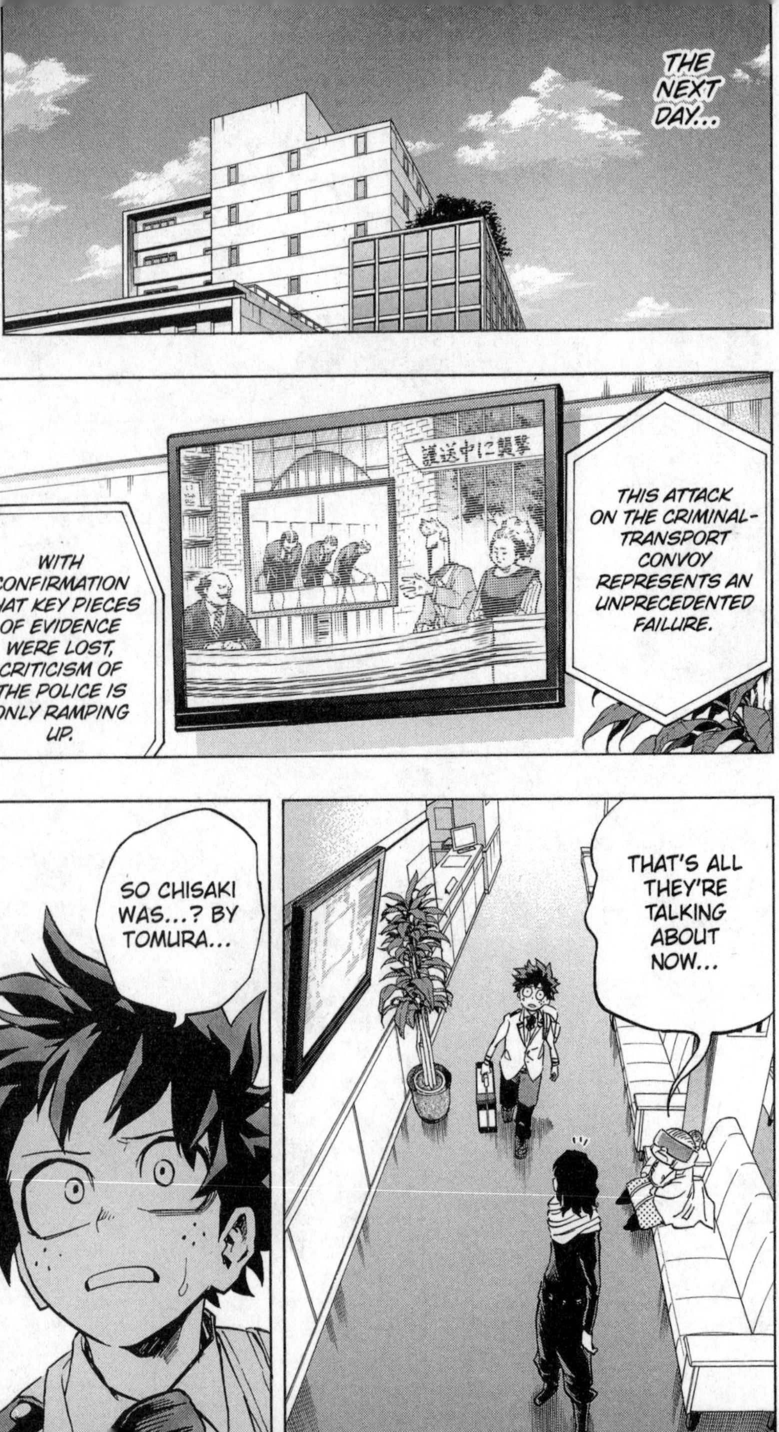
THE NEXT DAY...
護送中に襲撃
THIS ATTACK ON THE CRIMINAL-TRANSPORT CONVOY REPRESENTS AN UNPRECEDENTED FAILURE.
WITH CONFIRMATION THAT KEY PIECES OF EVIDENCE WERE LOST, CRITICISM OF THE POLICE IS ONLY RAMPING UP.
THAT'S ALL THEY'RE TALKING ABOUT NOW...
SO CHISAKI WAS...? BY TOMURA...

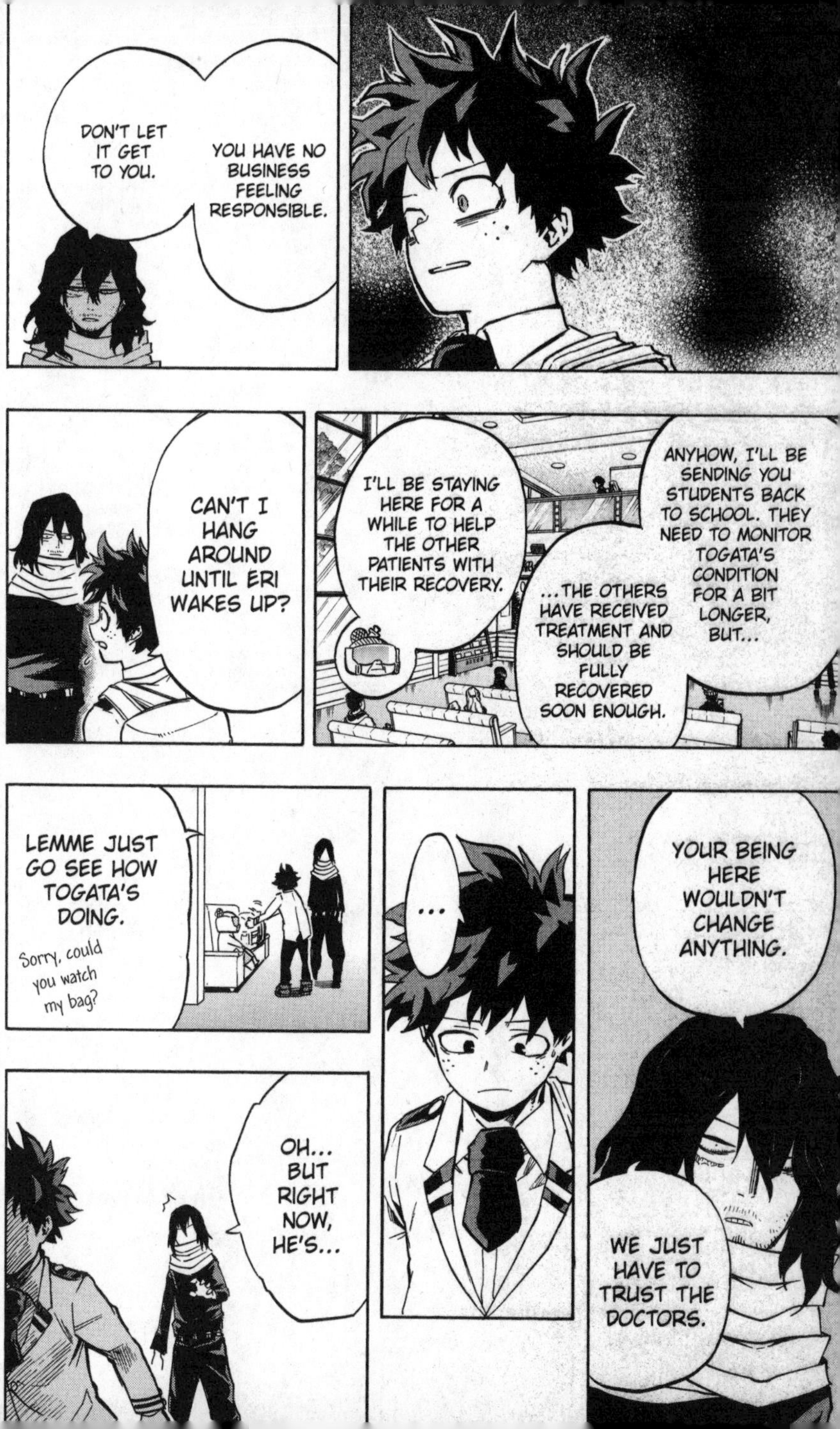

DON'T LET IT GET TO YOU.
YOU HAVE NO BUSINESS FEELING RESPONSIBLE.
ANYHOW, I'LL BE SENDING YOU STUDENTS BACK TO SCHOOL. THEY NEED TO MONITOR TOGATA'S CONDITION FOR A BIT LONGER, BUT...
...THE OTHERS HAVE RECEIVED TREATMENT AND SHOULD BE FULLY RECOVERED SOON ENOUGH.
I'LL BE STAYING HERE FOR A WHILE TO HELP THE OTHER PATIENTS WITH THEIR RECOVERY.
CAN'T I HANG AROUND UNTIL ERI WAKES UP?
YOUR BEING HERE WOULDN'T CHANGE ANYTHING.
WE JUST HAVE TO TRUST THE DOCTORS.
...
LEMME JUST GO SEE HOW TOGATA'S DOING.
Sorry, could you watch my bag?
OH... BUT RIGHT NOW, HE'S...

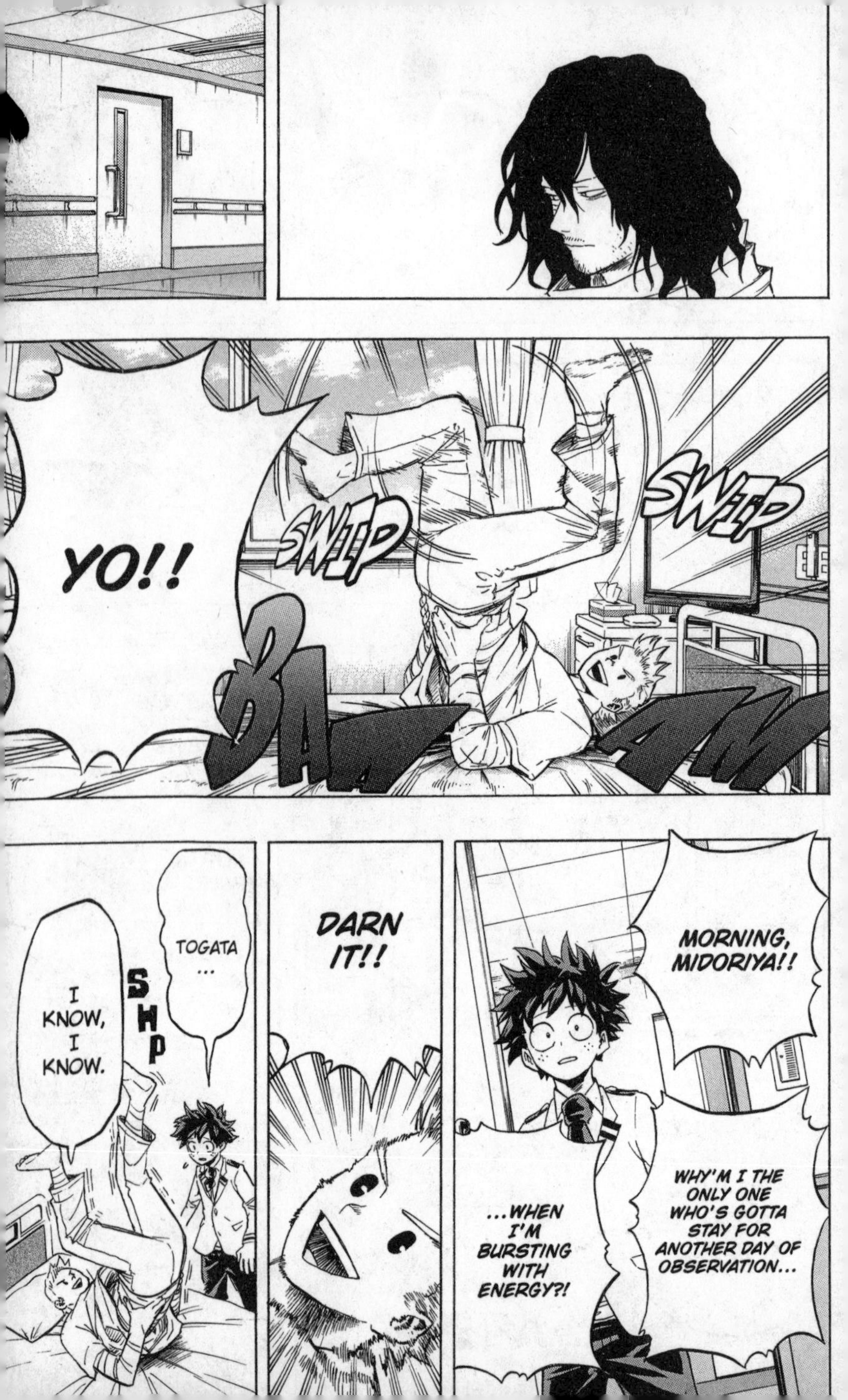
SWIP
SWIP
YO!!
BAAAM
MORNING, MIDORIYA!!
WHY'M I THE ONLY ONE WHO'S GOTTA STAY FOR ANOTHER DAY OF OBSERVATION...
...WHEN I'M BURSTING WITH ENERGY?!
DARN IT!!
TOGATA ...
SHP
I KNOW, I KNOW.

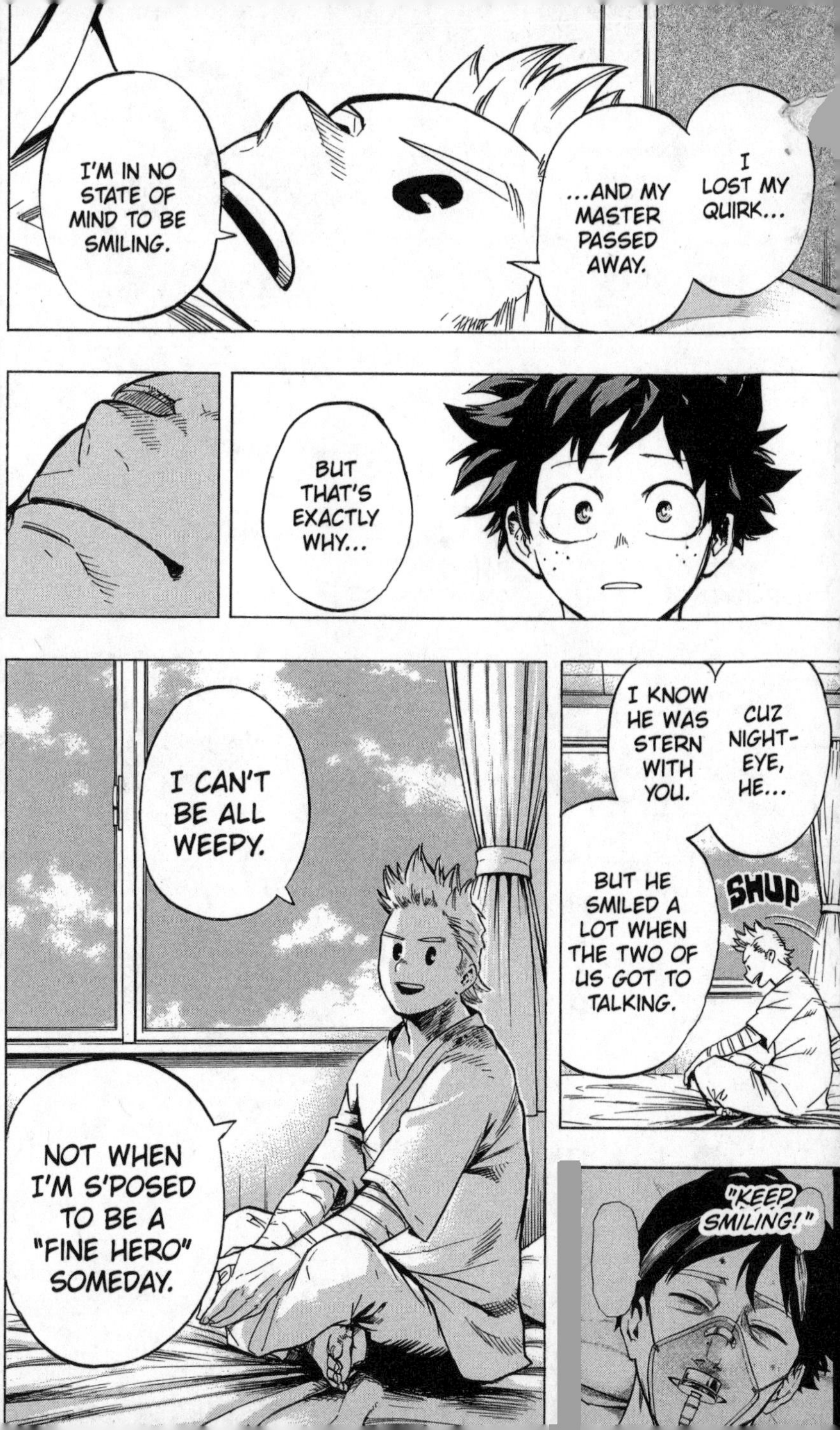
I LOST MY QUIRK...
...AND MY MASTER PASSED AWAY.
I'M IN NO STATE OF MIND TO BE SMILING.
BUT THAT'S EXACTLY WHY...
CUZ NIGHT-EYE, HE...
I KNOW HE WAS STERN WITH YOU.
SHUP
BUT HE SMILED A LOT WHEN THE TWO OF US GOT TO TALKING.
"KEEP SMILING!"
I CAN'T BE ALL WEEPY.
NOT WHEN I'M S'POSED TO BE A "FINE HERO" SOMEDAY.

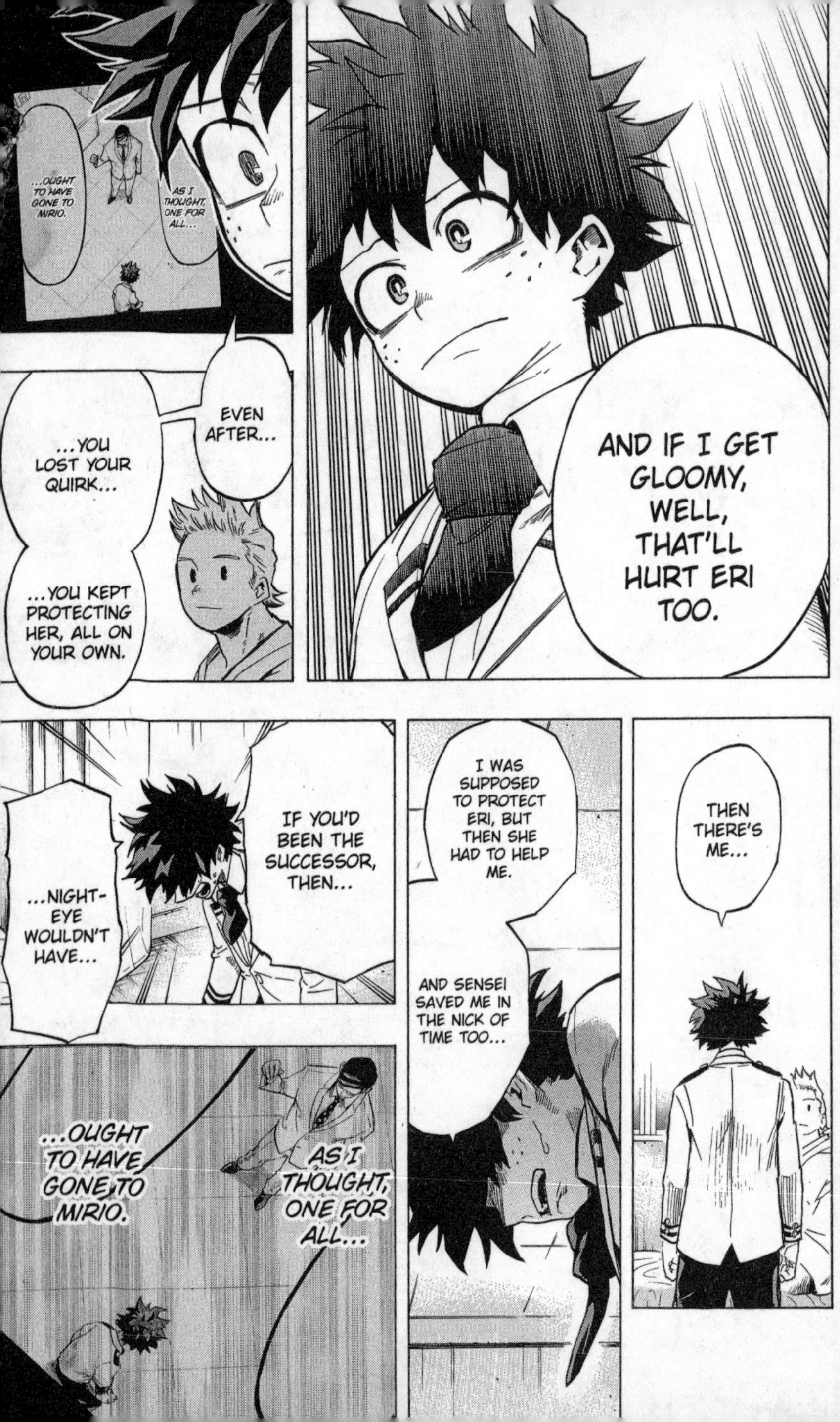

AND IF I GET GLOOMY, WELL, THAT'LL HURT ERI TOO.
AS I THOUGHT, ONE FOR ALL...
...OUGHT TO HAVE GONE TO MIRIO.
EVEN AFTER...
...YOU LOST YOUR QUIRK...
...YOU KEPT PROTECTING HER, ALL ON YOUR OWN.
THEN THERE'S ME...
I WAS SUPPOSED TO PROTECT ERI, BUT THEN SHE HAD TO HELP ME.
AND SENSEI SAVED ME IN THE NICK OF TIME TOO...
IF YOU'D BEEN THE SUCCESSOR, THEN...
...NIGHT-EYE WOULDN'T HAVE...
AS I THOUGHT, ONE FOR ALL...
...OUGHT TO HAVE GONE TO MIRIO.

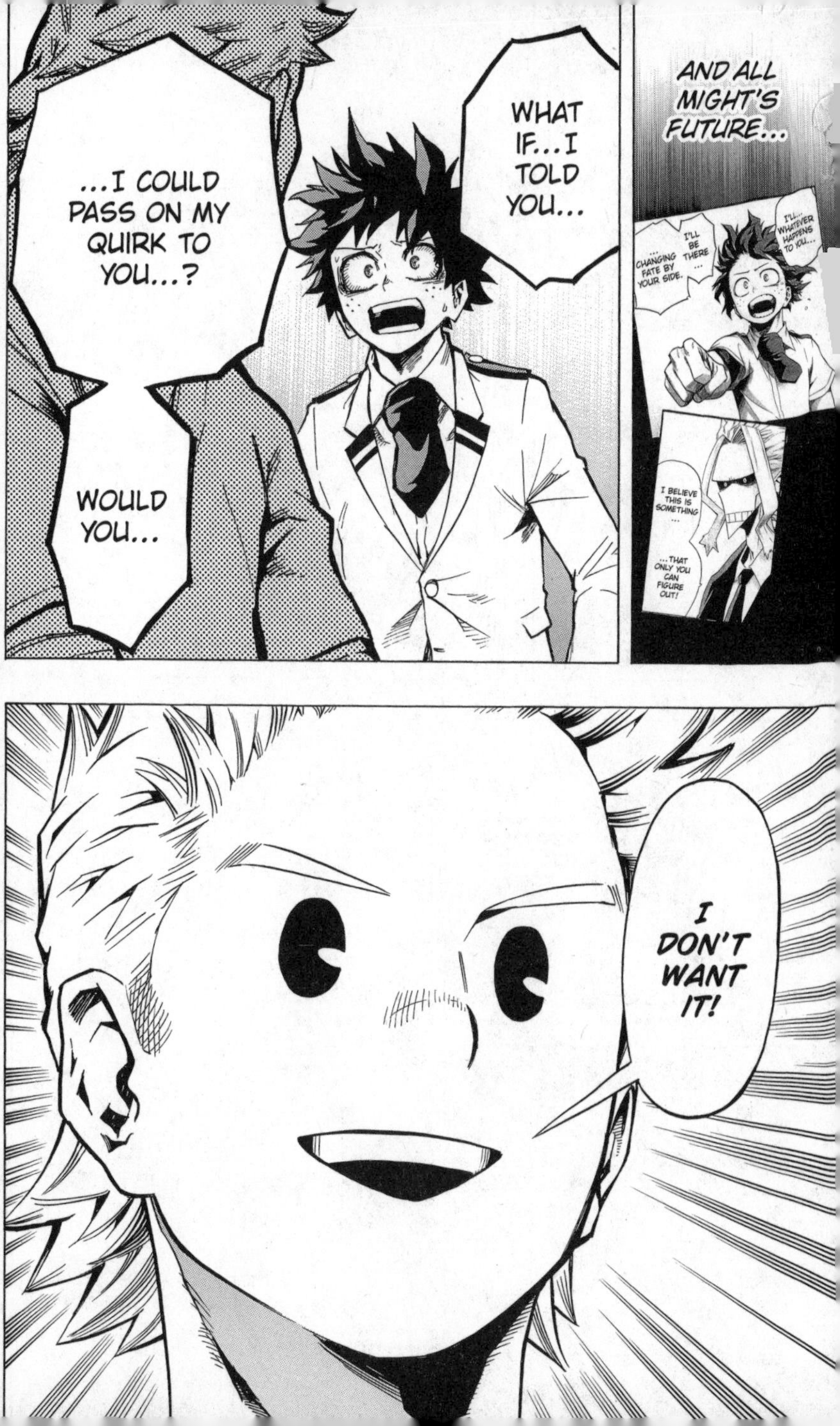
AND ALL MIGHT'S FUTURE...
I'LL... WHATEVER HAPPENS TO YOU...
I'LL BE THERE...
...CHANGING FATE BY YOUR SIDE.
I BELIEVE THIS IS SOMETHING...
...THAT ONLY YOU CAN FIGURE OUT!
WHAT IF...I TOLD YOU...
...I COULD PASS ON MY QUIRK TO YOU...?
WOULD YOU...
I DON'T WANT IT!

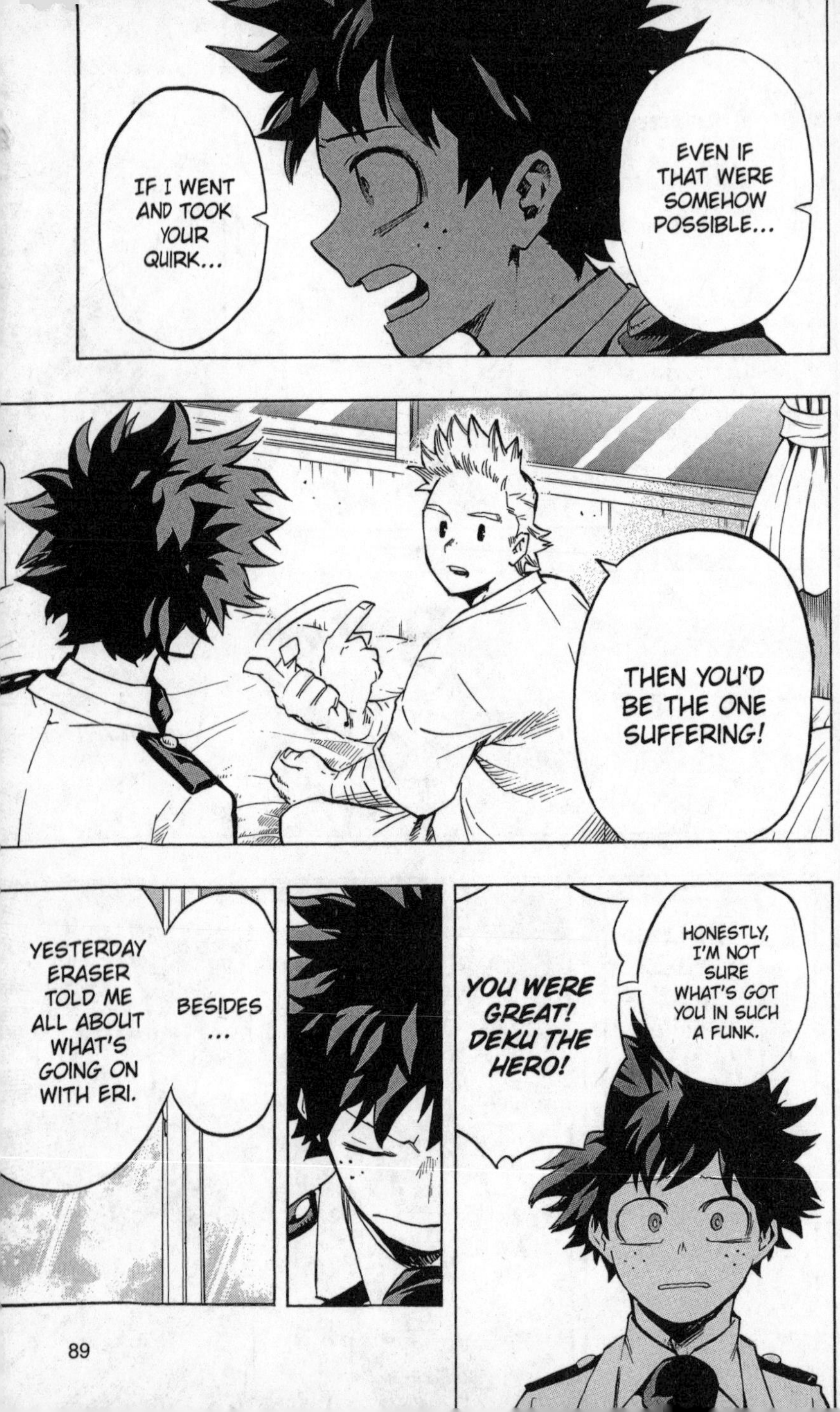
EVEN IF THAT WERE SOMEHOW POSSIBLE...
IF I WENT AND TOOK YOUR QUIRK...
THEN YOU'D BE THE ONE SUFFERING!
HONESTLY, I'M NOT SURE WHAT'S GOT YOU IN SUCH A FUNK.
YOU WERE GREAT! DEKU THE HERO!
BESIDES...
YESTERDAY ERASER TOLD ME ALL ABOUT WHAT'S GOING ON WITH ERI.

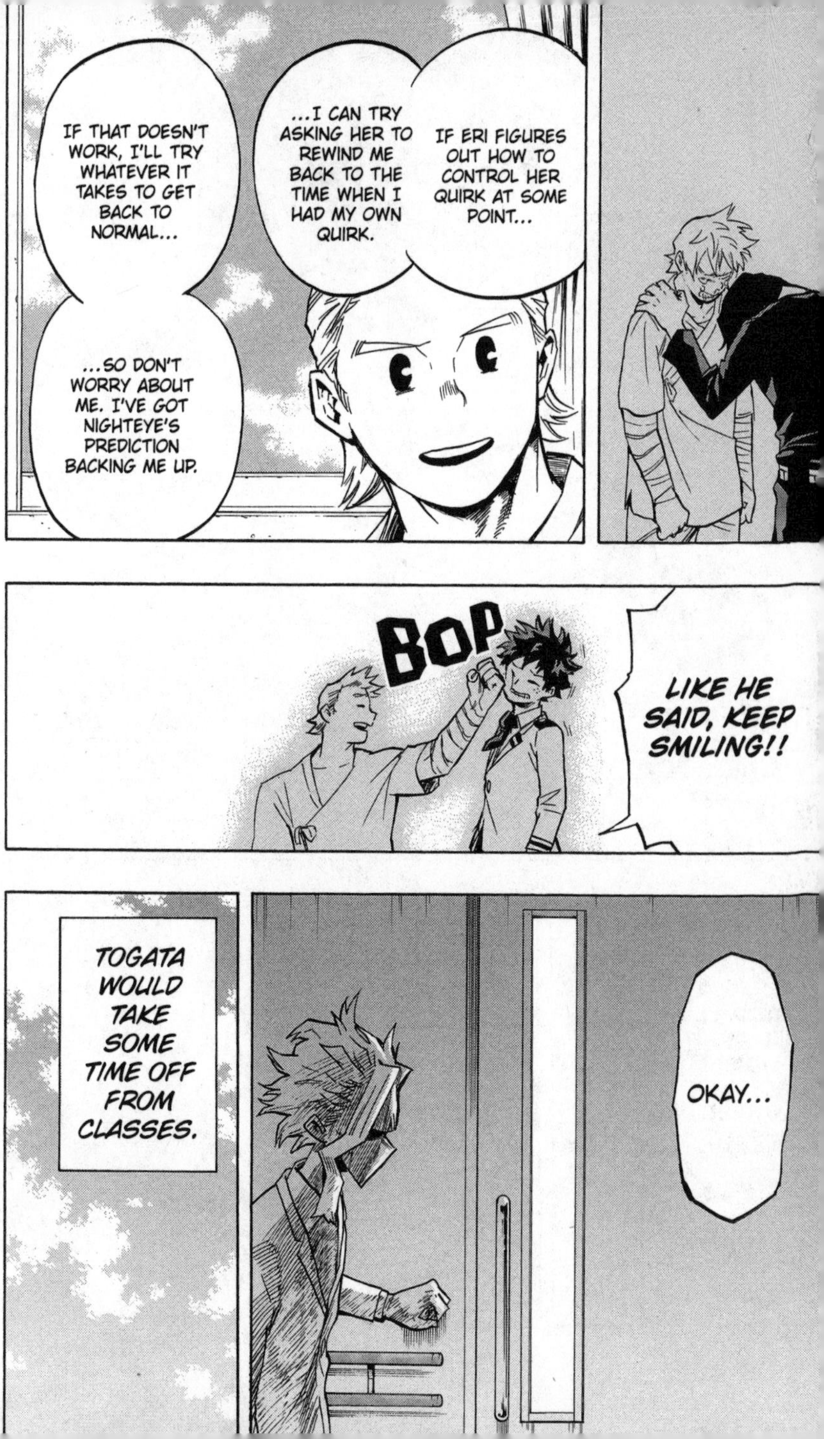
IF ERI FIGURES OUT HOW TO CONTROL HER QUIRK AT SOME POINT...
...I CAN TRY ASKING HER TO REWIND ME BACK TO THE TIME WHEN I HAD MY OWN QUIRK.
IF THAT DOESN'T WORK, I'LL TRY WHATEVER IT TAKES TO GET BACK TO NORMAL...
...SO DON'T WORRY ABOUT ME. I'VE GOT NIGHTEYE'S PREDICTION BACKING ME UP.
LIKE HE SAID, KEEP SMILING!!
BOP
OKAY...
TOGATA WOULD TAKE SOME TIME OFF FROM CLASSES.

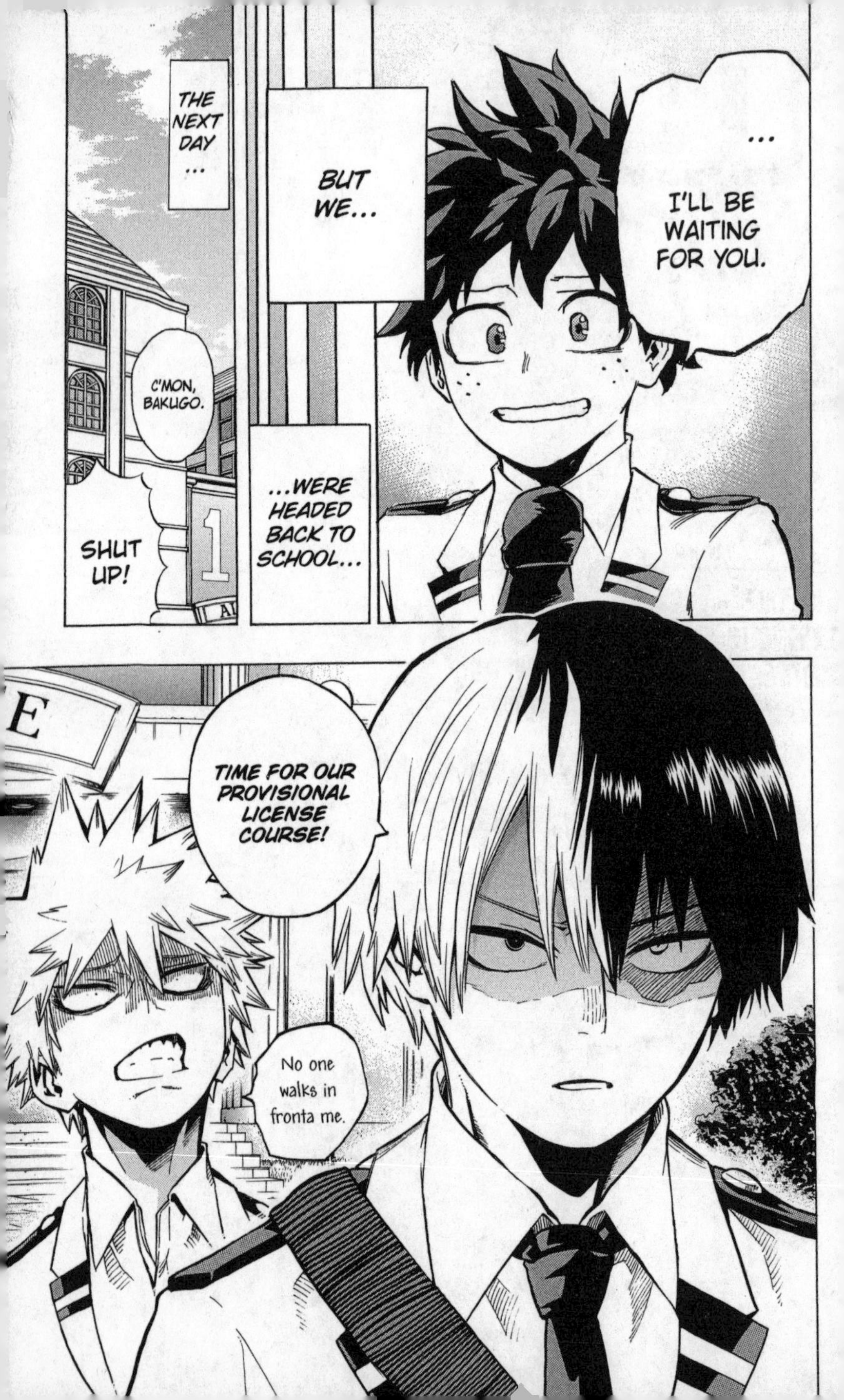
...
I'LL BE WAITING FOR YOU.
BUT WE...
...WERE HEADED BACK TO SCHOOL...
THE NEXT DAY ...
C'MON, BAKUGO.
SHUT UP!
TIME FOR OUR PROVISIONAL LICENSE COURSE!
No one walks in fronta me.

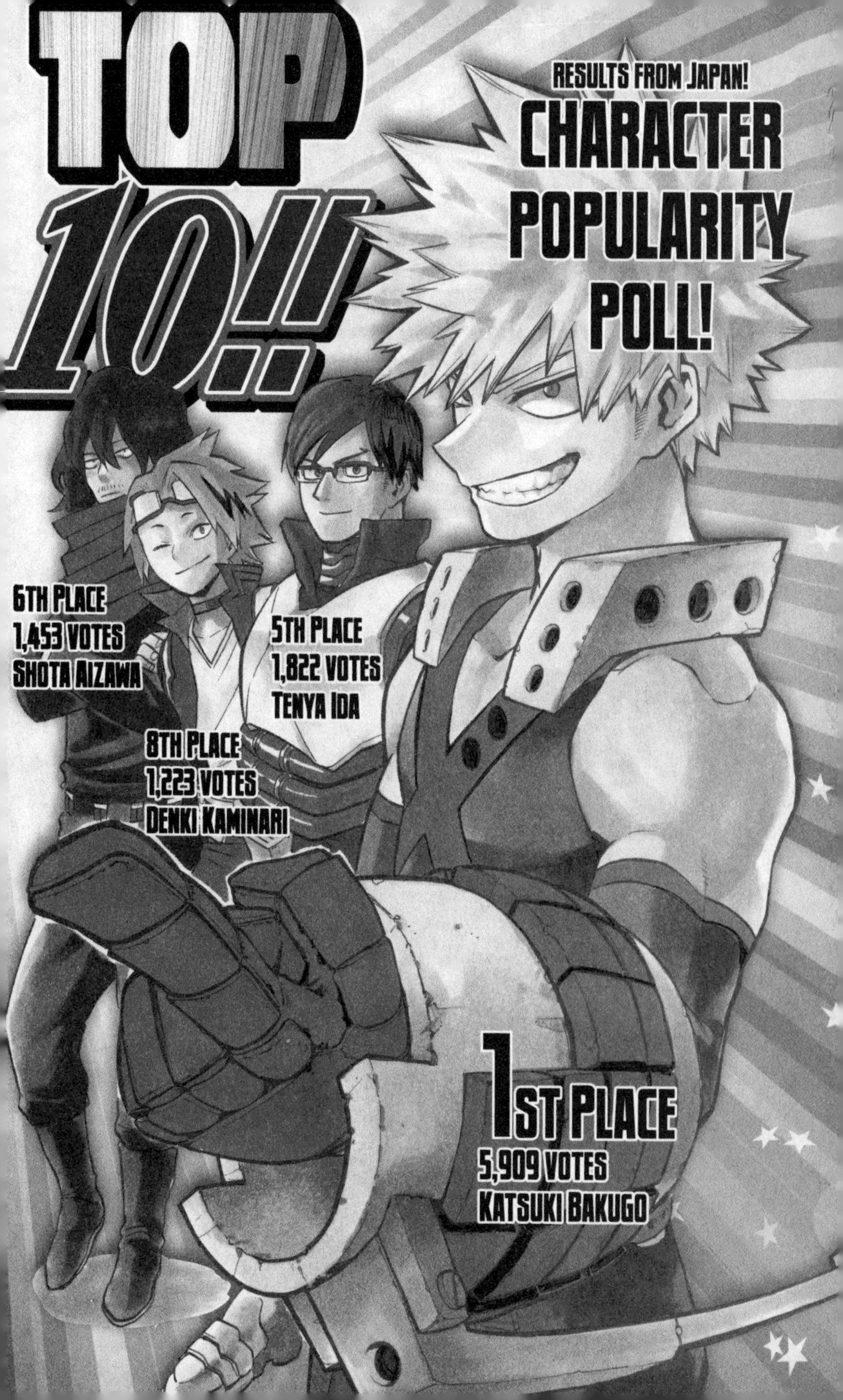
TOP 10!!
RESULTS FROM JAPAN!
CHARACTER POPULARITY POLL!
1ST PLACE
5,909 VOTES
KATSUKI BAKUGO
5TH PLACE
1,822 VOTES
TENYA IDA
6TH PLACE
1,453 VOTES
SHOTA AIZAWA
8TH PLACE
1,223 VOTES
DENKI KAMINARI

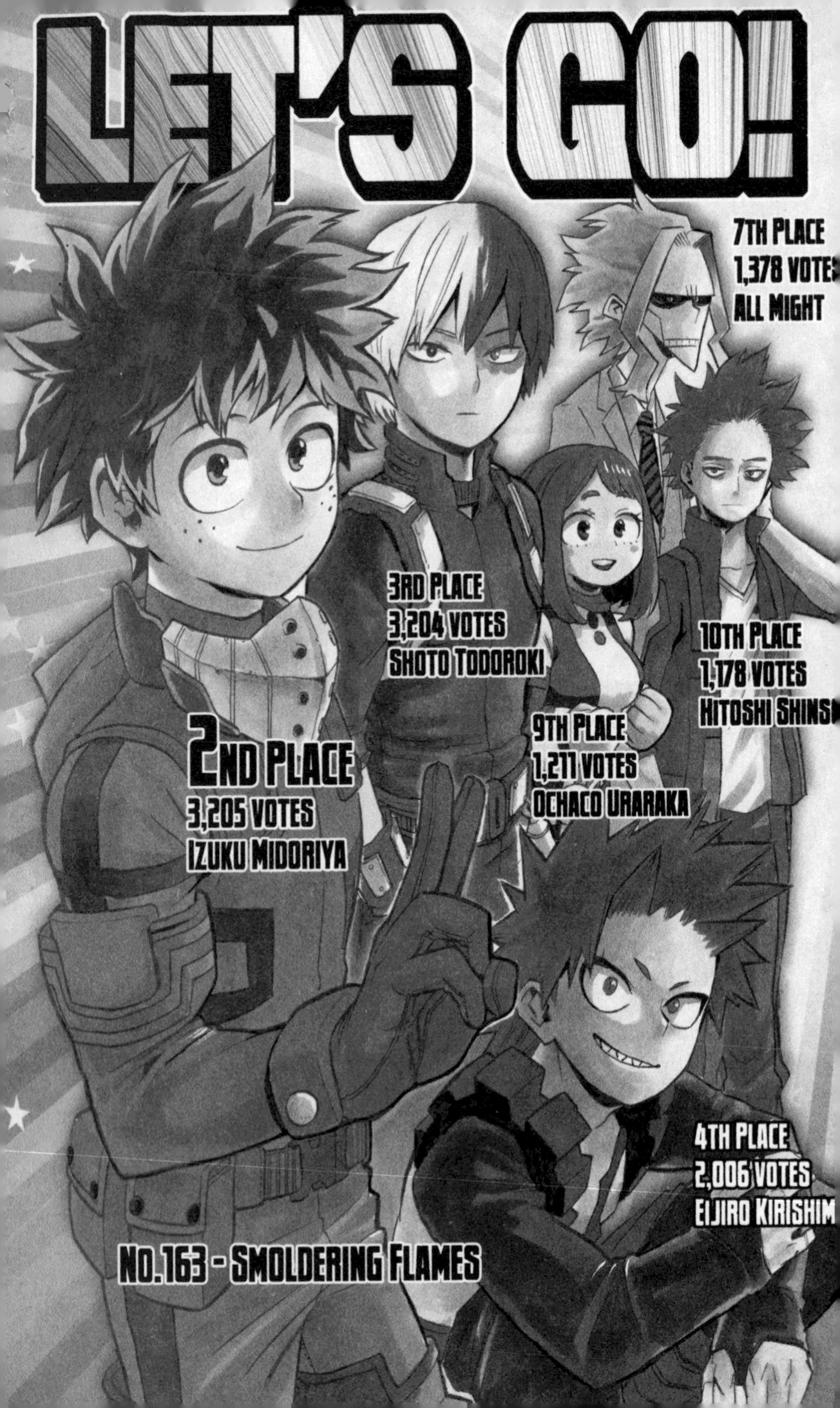
LET'S GO!
7TH PLACE
1,378 VOTES
ALL MIGHT
3RD PLACE
3,204 VOTES
SHOTO TODOROKI
10TH PLACE
1,178 VOTES
HITOSHI SHINSO
2ND PLACE
3,205 VOTES
IZUKU MIDORIYA
9TH PLACE
1,211 VOTES
OCHACO URARAKA
4TH PLACE
2,006 VOTES
EIJIRO KIRISHIMA
NO.163 - SMOLDERING FLAMES

MY HERO ACADEMIA

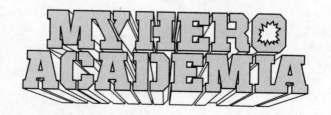

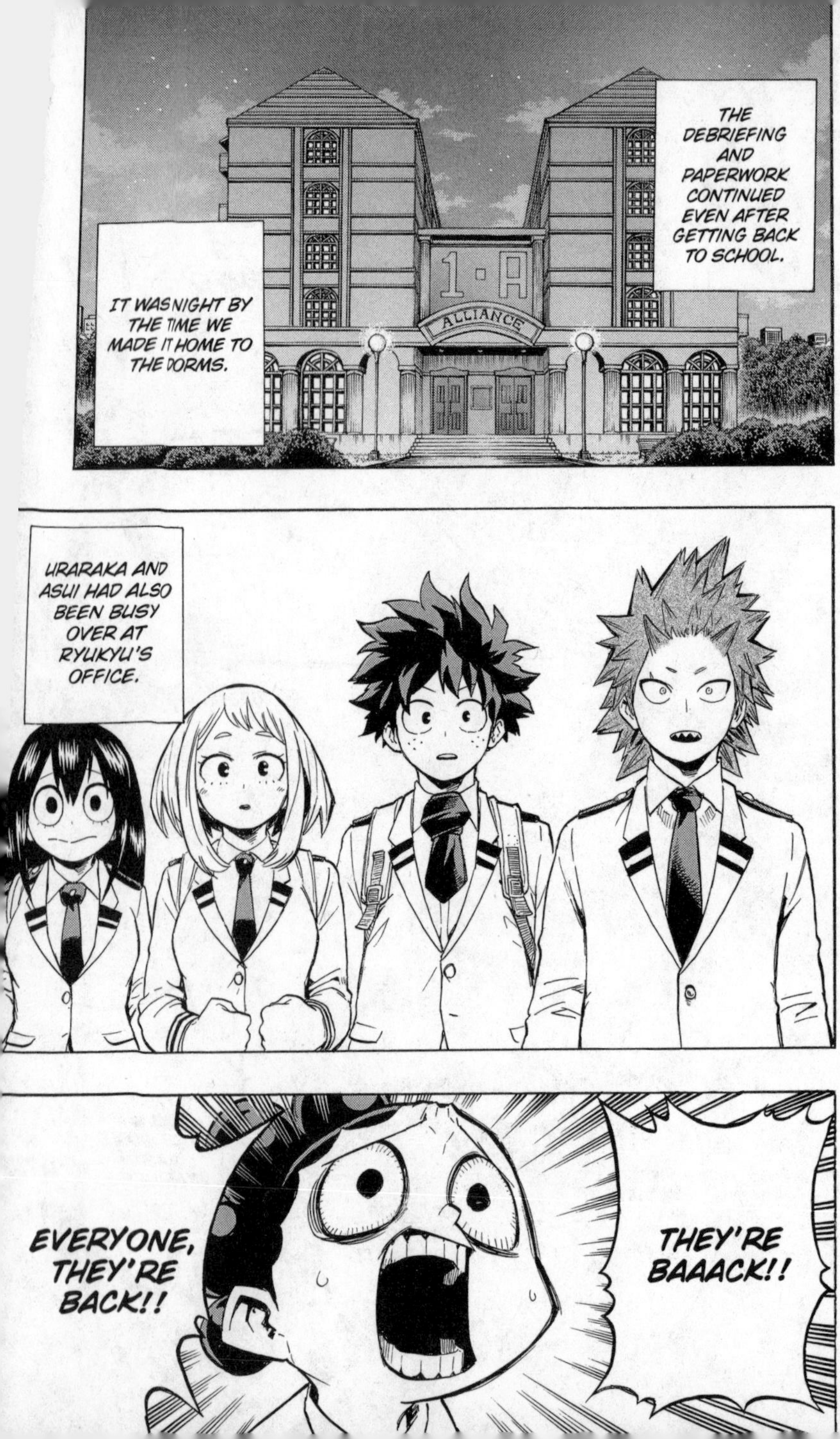
THE DEBRIEFING AND PAPERWORK CONTINUED EVEN AFTER GETTING BACK TO SCHOOL.
IT WAS NIGHT BY THE TIME WE MADE IT HOME TO THE DORMS.
1-A
ALLIANCE
URARAKA AND ASUI HAD ALSO BEEN BUSY OVER AT RYUKYU'S OFFICE.
THEY'RE BAAACK!!
EVERYONE, THEY'RE BACK!!

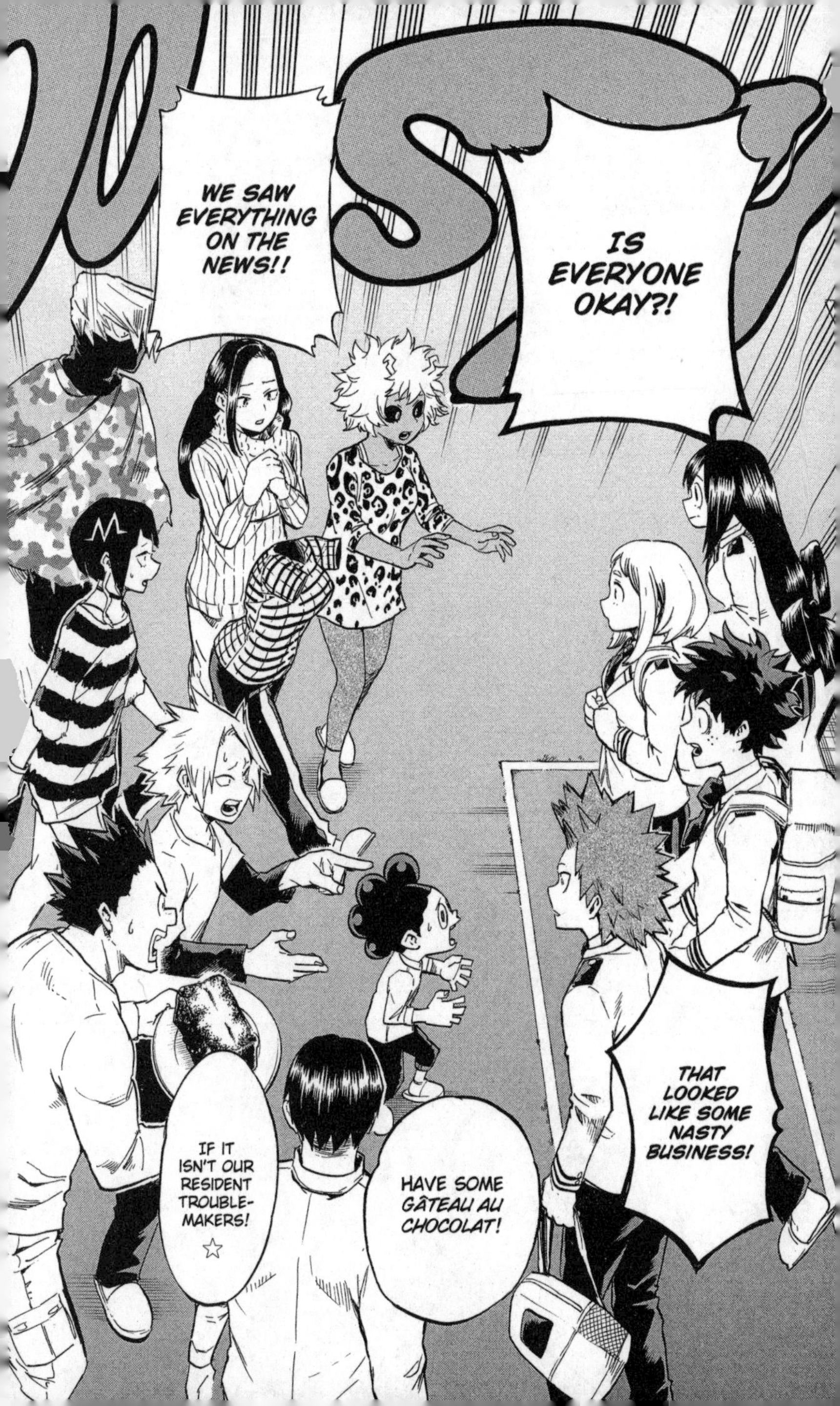
IS EVERYONE OKAY?!
WE SAW EVERYTHING ON THE NEWS!!
THAT LOOKED LIKE SOME NASTY BUSINESS!
HAVE SOME GÂTEAU AU CHOCOLAT!
IF IT ISN'T OUR RESIDENT TROUBLE-MAKERS! ☆

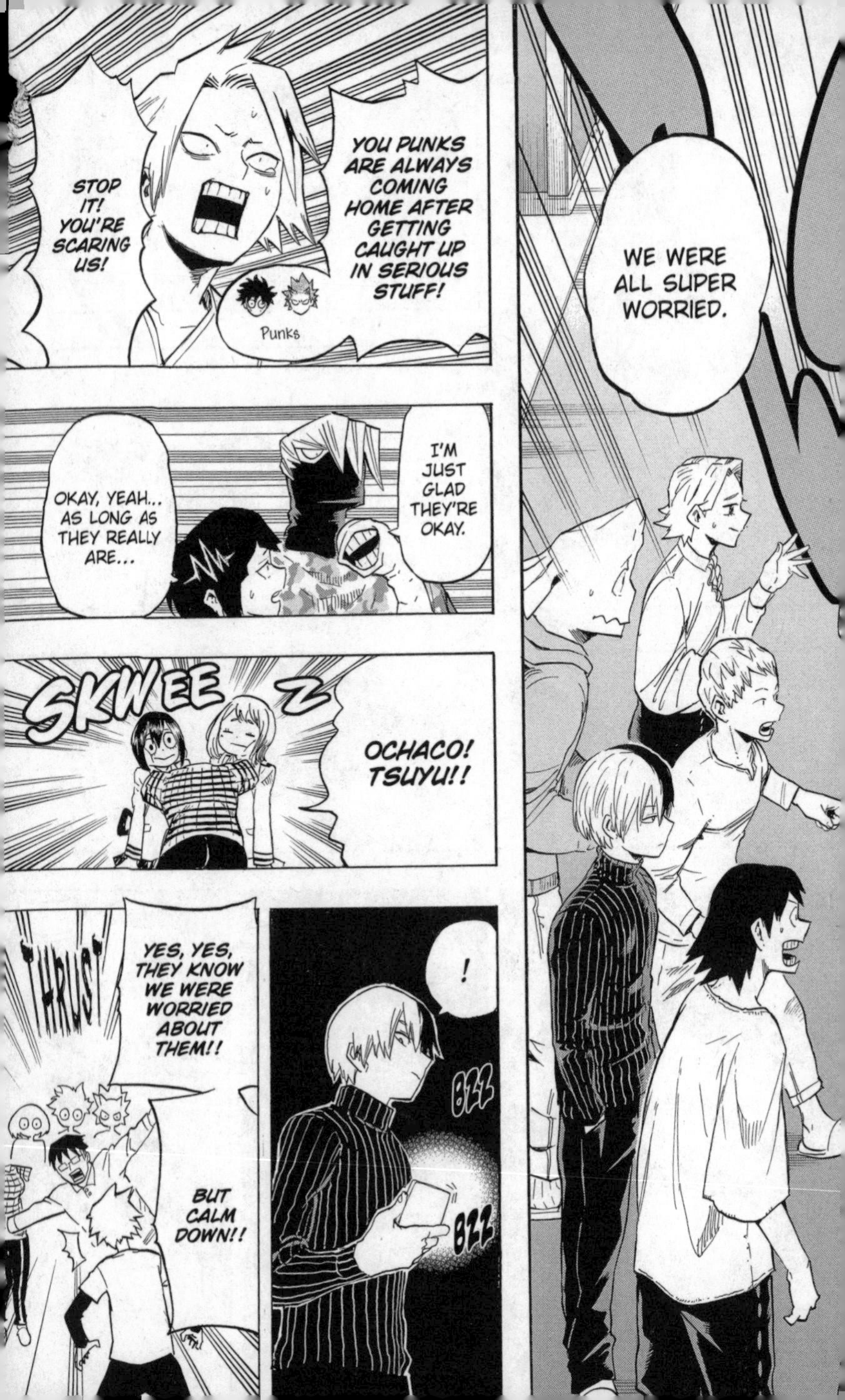
WE WERE ALL SUPER WORRIED.
YOU PUNKS ARE ALWAYS COMING HOME AFTER GETTING CAUGHT UP IN SERIOUS STUFF!
Punks
STOP IT! YOU'RE SCARING US!
I'M JUST GLAD THEY'RE OKAY.
OKAY, YEAH... AS LONG AS THEY REALLY ARE...
OCHACO! TSUYU!!
SKWEEZ
!
BZZ
BZZ
YES, YES, THEY KNOW WE WERE WORRIED ABOUT THEM!!
BUT CALM DOWN!!
THRUST

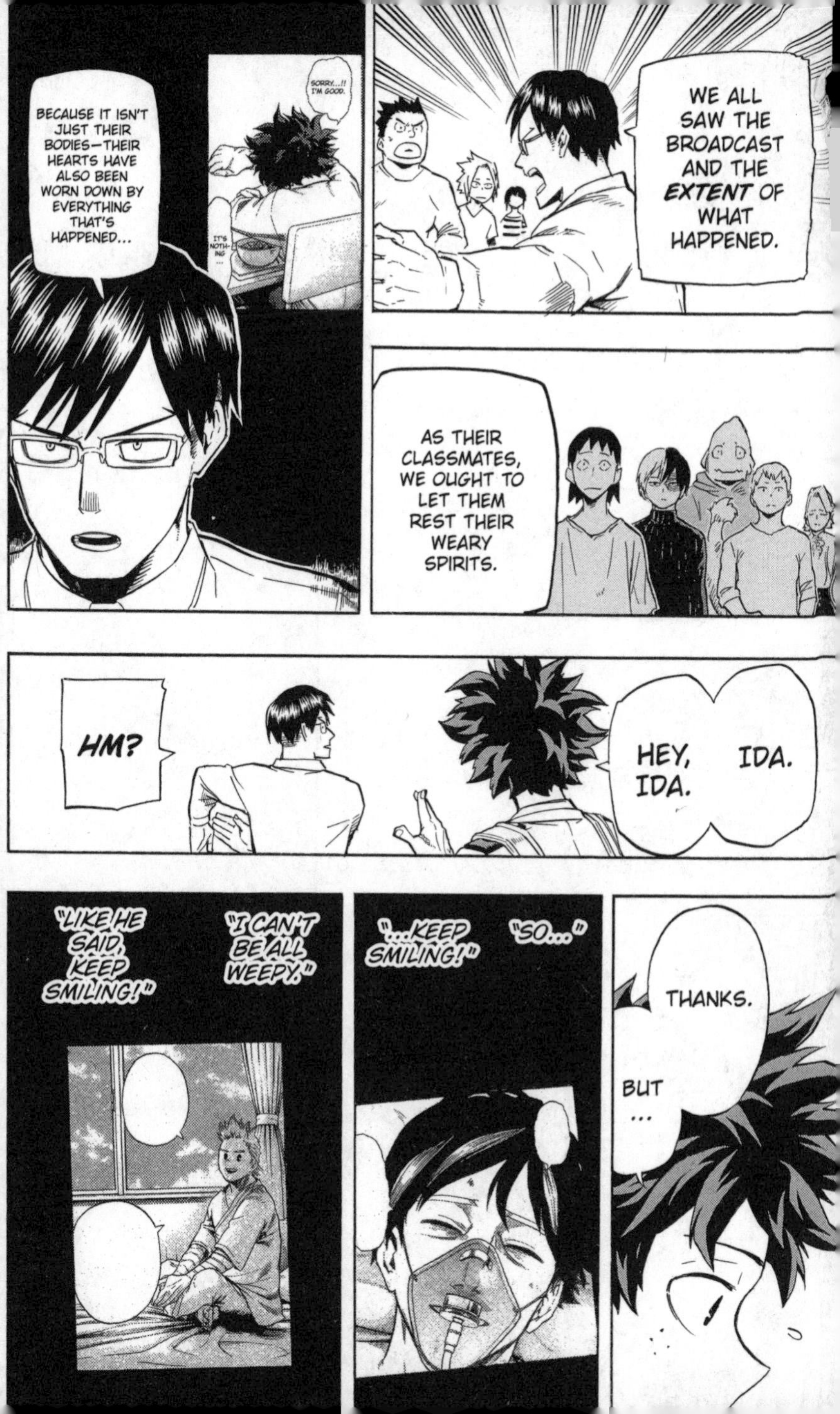
WE ALL SAW THE BROADCAST AND THE *EXTENT* OF WHAT HAPPENED.
AS THEIR CLASSMATES, WE OUGHT TO LET THEM REST THEIR WEARY SPIRITS.
SORRY...!! I'M GOOD.
IT'S NOTHING...
BECAUSE IT ISN'T JUST THEIR BODIES—THEIR HEARTS HAVE ALSO BEEN WORN DOWN BY EVERYTHING THAT'S HAPPENED...
HEY, IDA. IDA.
HM?
THANKS.
BUT...
"SO..."
"...KEEP SMILING!"
"I CAN'T BE ALL WEEPY."
"LIKE HE SAID, KEEP SMILING!"

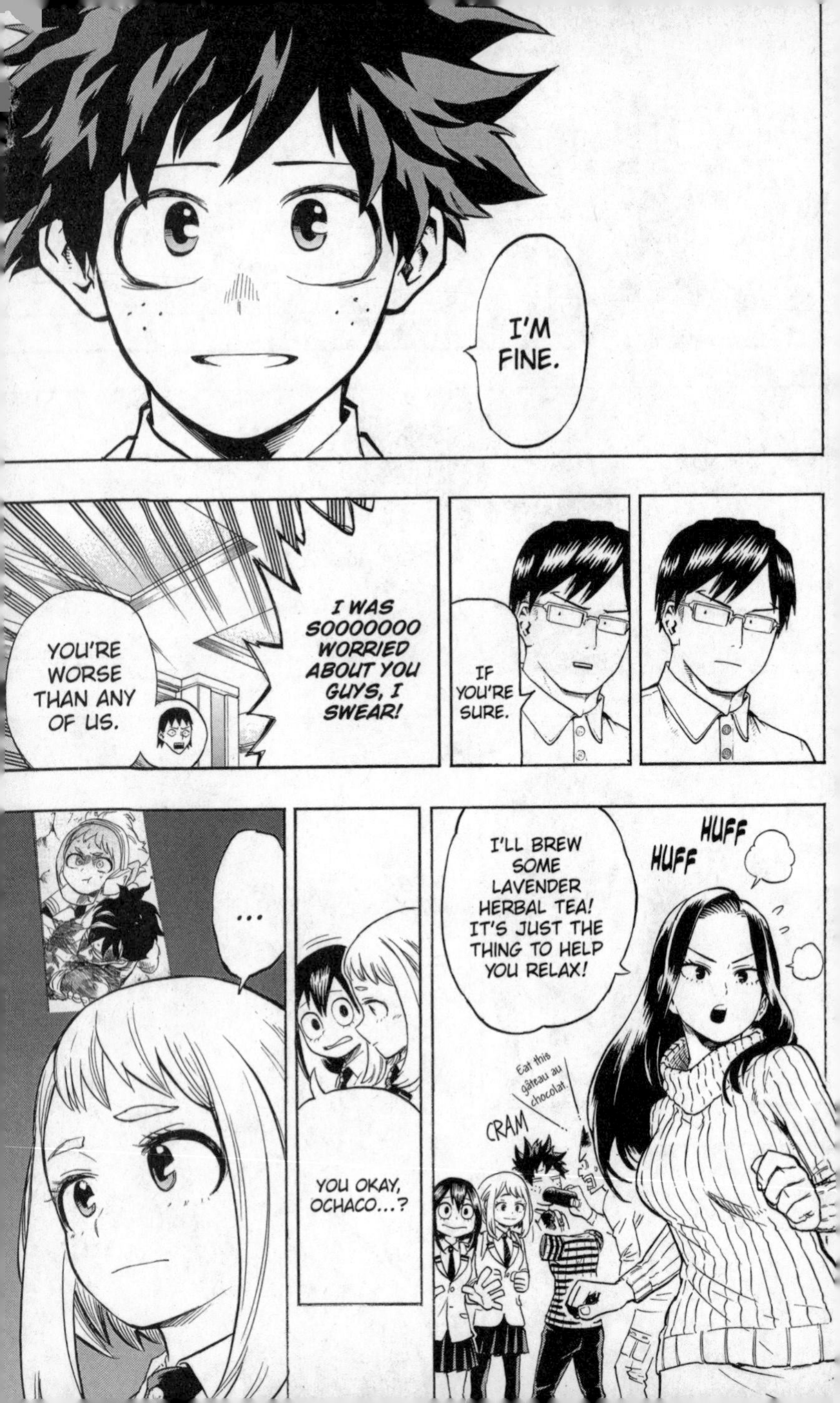
I'M FINE.
IF YOU'RE SURE.
I WAS SOOOOOOO WORRIED ABOUT YOU GUYS, I SWEAR!
YOU'RE WORSE THAN ANY OF US.
HUFF
HUFF
I'LL BREW SOME LAVENDER HERBAL TEA! IT'S JUST THE THING TO HELP YOU RELAX!
Eat this gâteau au chocolat.
CRAM
YOU OKAY, OCHACO...?
...

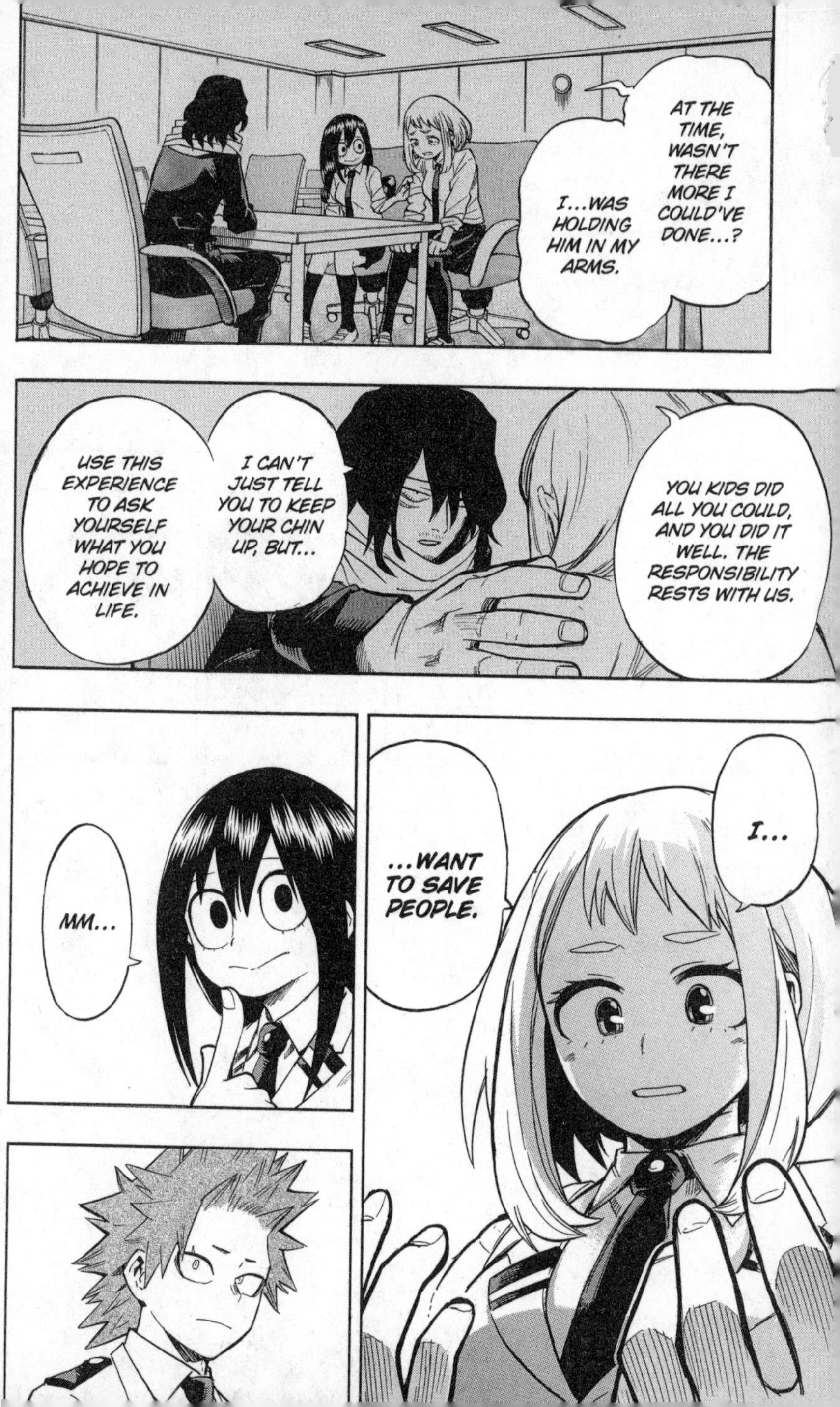
AT THE TIME, WASN'T THERE MORE I COULD'VE DONE...?
I...WAS HOLDING HIM IN MY ARMS.
YOU KIDS DID ALL YOU COULD, AND YOU DID IT WELL. THE RESPONSIBILITY RESTS WITH US.
I CAN'T JUST TELL YOU TO KEEP YOUR CHIN UP, BUT...
USE THIS EXPERIENCE TO ASK YOURSELF WHAT YOU HOPE TO ACHIEVE IN LIFE.
I...
...WANT TO SAVE PEOPLE.
MM...

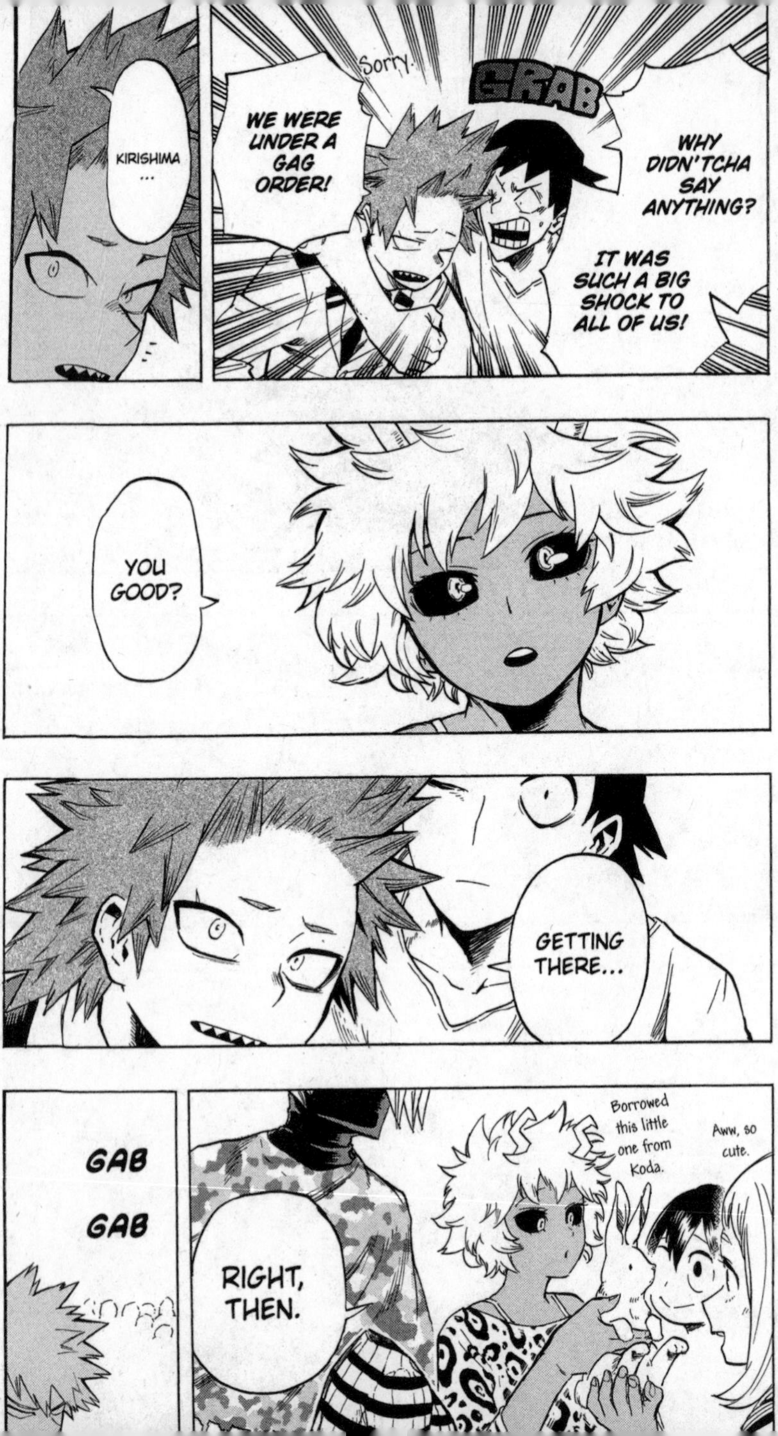
WHY DIDN'TCHA SAY ANYTHING?
IT WAS SUCH A BIG SHOCK TO ALL OF US!
GRAB
Sorry.
WE WERE UNDER A GAG ORDER!
KIRISHIMA...
YOU GOOD?
GETTING THERE...
Aww, so cute.
Borrowed this little one from Koda.
RIGHT, THEN.
GAB
GAB

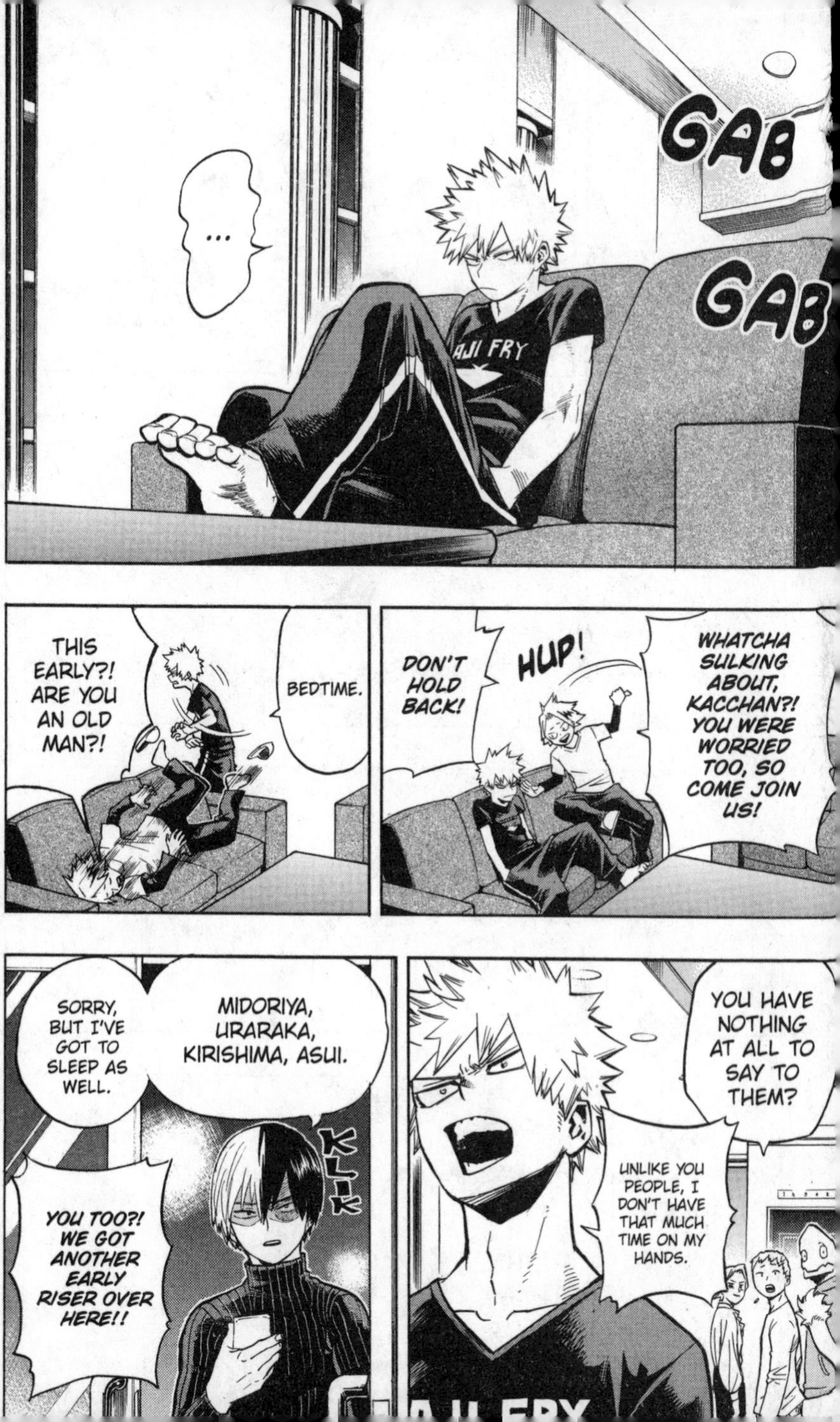
GAB
GAB
...
AJI FRY
WHATCHA SULKING ABOUT, KACCHAN?! YOU WERE WORRIED TOO, SO COME JOIN US!
HUP!
DON'T HOLD BACK!
BEDTIME.
THIS EARLY?! ARE YOU AN OLD MAN?!
YOU HAVE NOTHING AT ALL TO SAY TO THEM?
UNLIKE YOU PEOPLE, I DON'T HAVE THAT MUCH TIME ON MY HANDS.
MIDORIYA, URARAKA, KIRISHIMA, ASUI.
SORRY, BUT I'VE GOT TO SLEEP AS WELL.
KLIK
YOU TOO?! WE GOT ANOTHER EARLY RISER OVER HERE!!

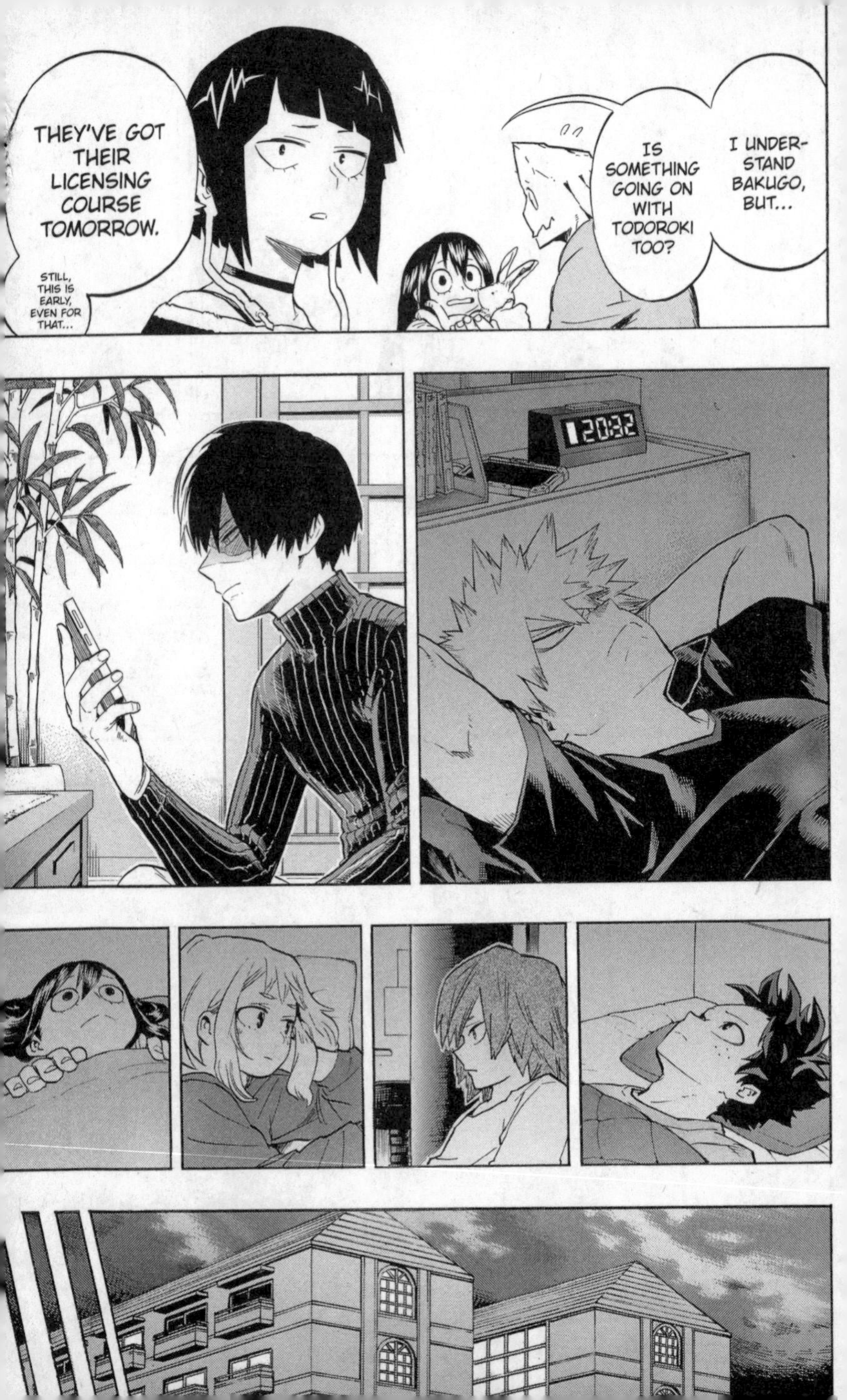
I UNDER-STAND BAKUGO, BUT...
IS SOMETHING GOING ON WITH TODOROKI TOO?
THEY'VE GOT THEIR LICENSING COURSE TOMORROW.
STILL, THIS IS EARLY, EVEN FOR THAT...
20:32

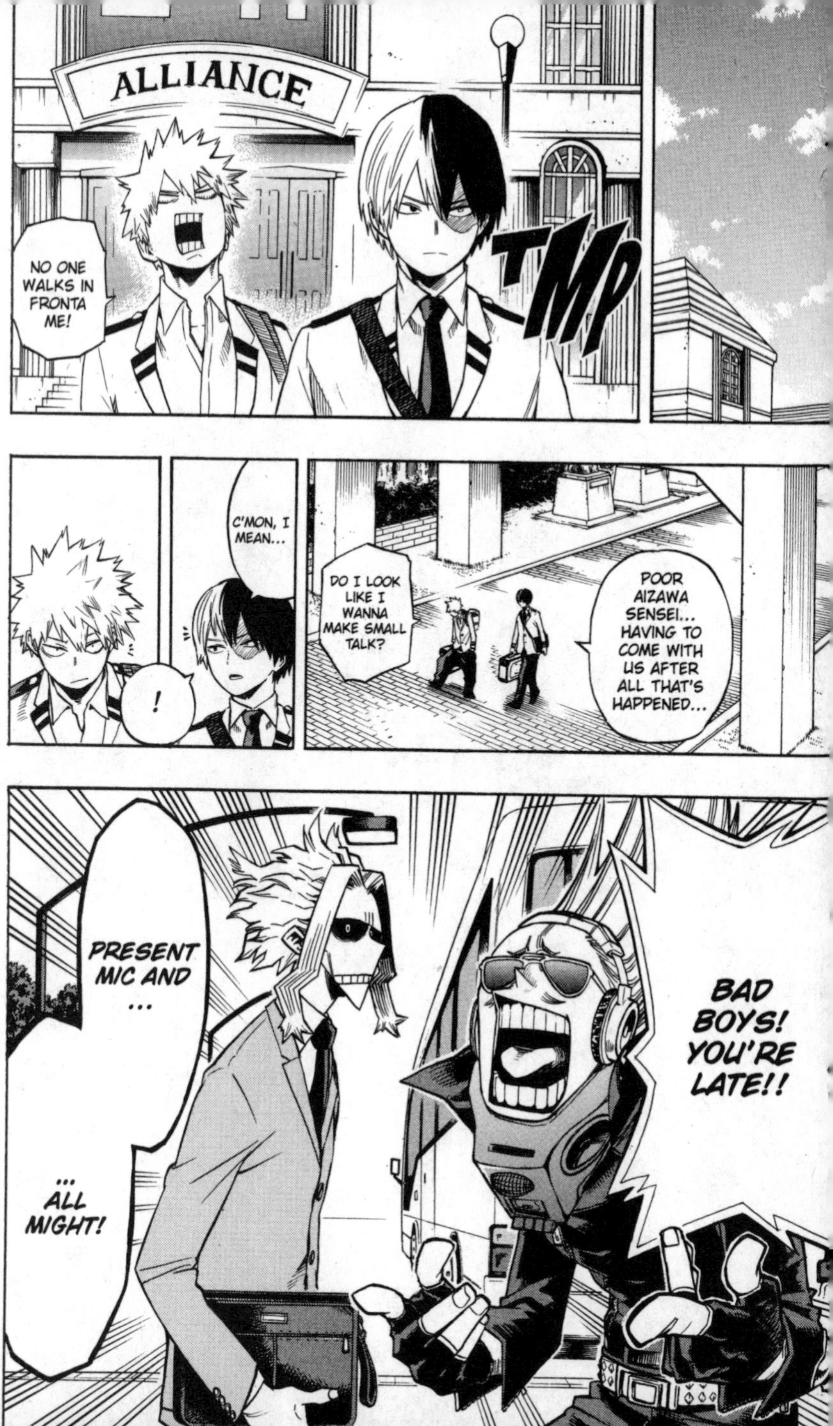
ALLIANCE
TMP
NO ONE WALKS IN FRONTA ME!
POOR AIZAWA SENSEI... HAVING TO COME WITH US AFTER ALL THAT'S HAPPENED...
DO I LOOK LIKE I WANNA MAKE SMALL TALK?
C'MON, I MEAN...
!
BAD BOYS! YOU'RE LATE!!
PRESENT MIC AND ...
... ALL MIGHT!

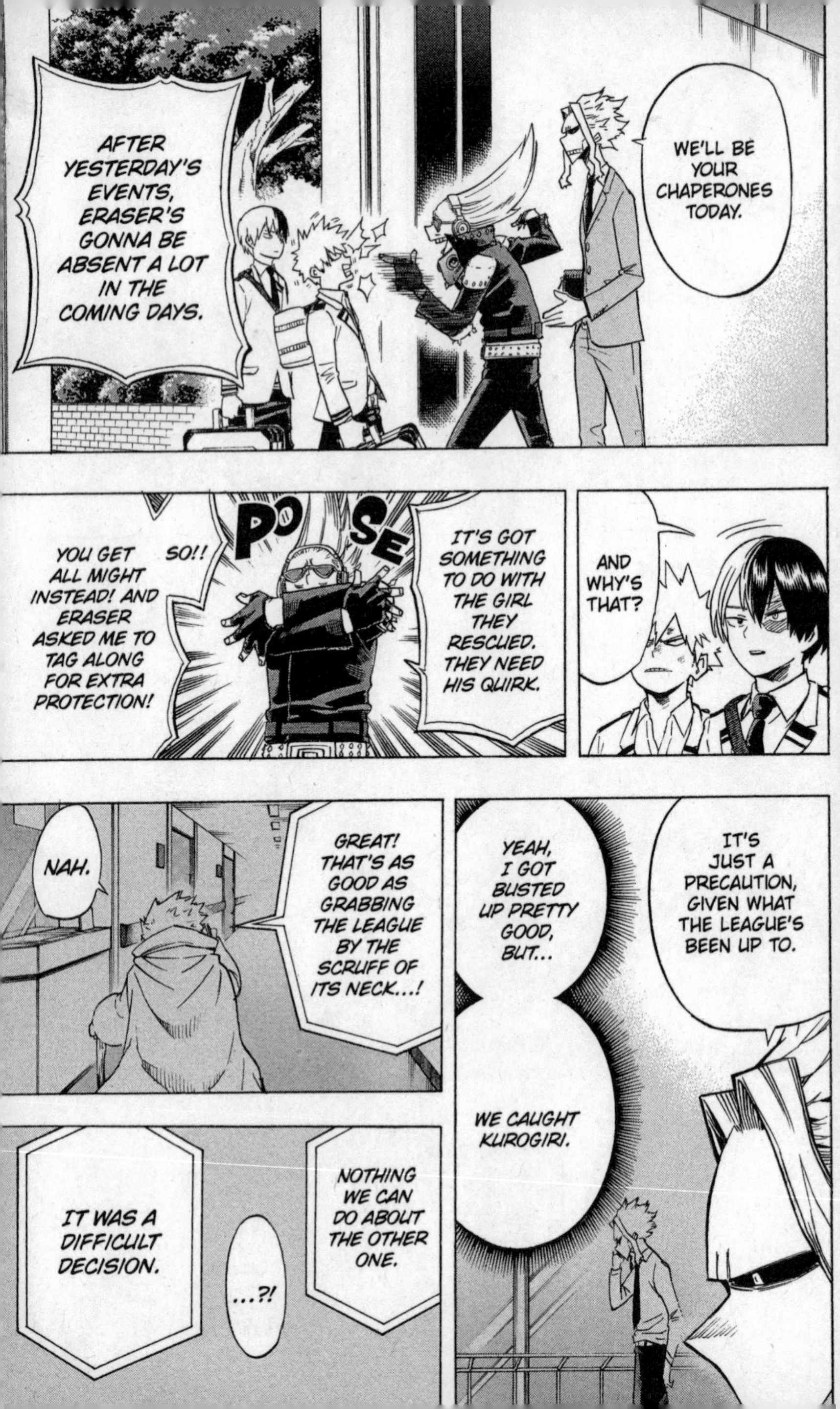
WE'LL BE YOUR CHAPERONES TODAY.
AFTER YESTERDAY'S EVENTS, ERASER'S GONNA BE ABSENT A LOT IN THE COMING DAYS.
AND WHY'S THAT?
IT'S GOT SOMETHING TO DO WITH THE GIRL THEY RESCUED. THEY NEED HIS QUIRK.
POSE
SO!!
YOU GET ALL MIGHT INSTEAD! AND ERASER ASKED ME TO TAG ALONG FOR EXTRA PROTECTION!
IT'S JUST A PRECAUTION, GIVEN WHAT THE LEAGUE'S BEEN UP TO.
YEAH, I GOT BUSTED UP PRETTY GOOD, BUT...
WE CAUGHT KUROGIRI.
GREAT! THAT'S AS GOOD AS GRABBING THE LEAGUE BY THE SCRUFF OF ITS NECK...!
NAH.
NOTHING WE CAN DO ABOUT THE OTHER ONE.
...?!
IT WAS A DIFFICULT DECISION.

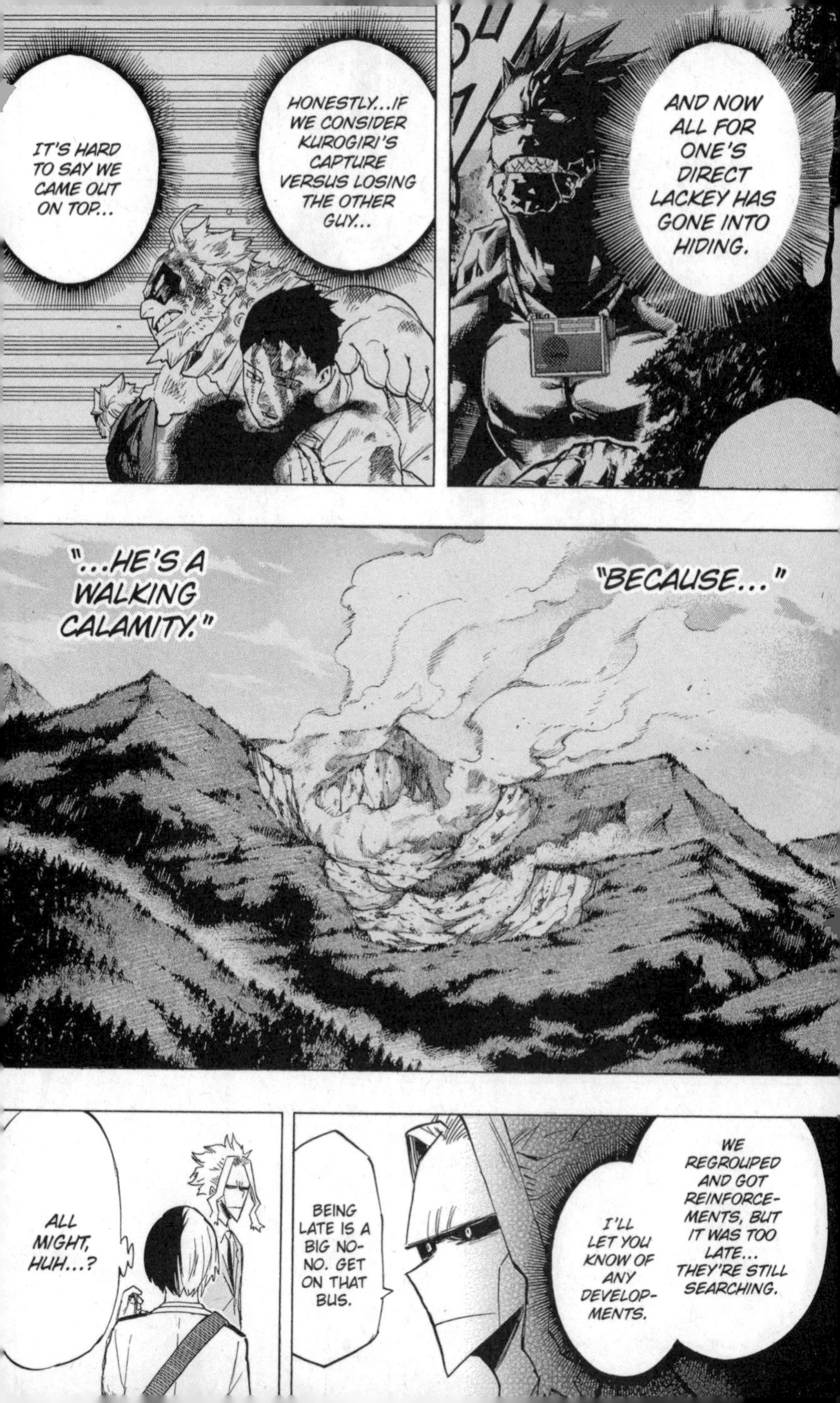
AND NOW ALL FOR ONE'S DIRECT LACKEY HAS GONE INTO HIDING.
HONESTLY...IF WE CONSIDER KUROGIRI'S CAPTURE VERSUS LOSING THE OTHER GUY...
IT'S HARD TO SAY WE CAME OUT ON TOP...
"BECAUSE..."
"...HE'S A WALKING CALAMITY."
WE REGROUPED AND GOT REINFORCE-MENTS, BUT IT WAS TOO LATE... THEY'RE STILL SEARCHING.
I'LL LET YOU KNOW OF ANY DEVELOP-MENTS.
BEING LATE IS A BIG NO-NO. GET ON THAT BUS.
ALL MIGHT, HUH...?

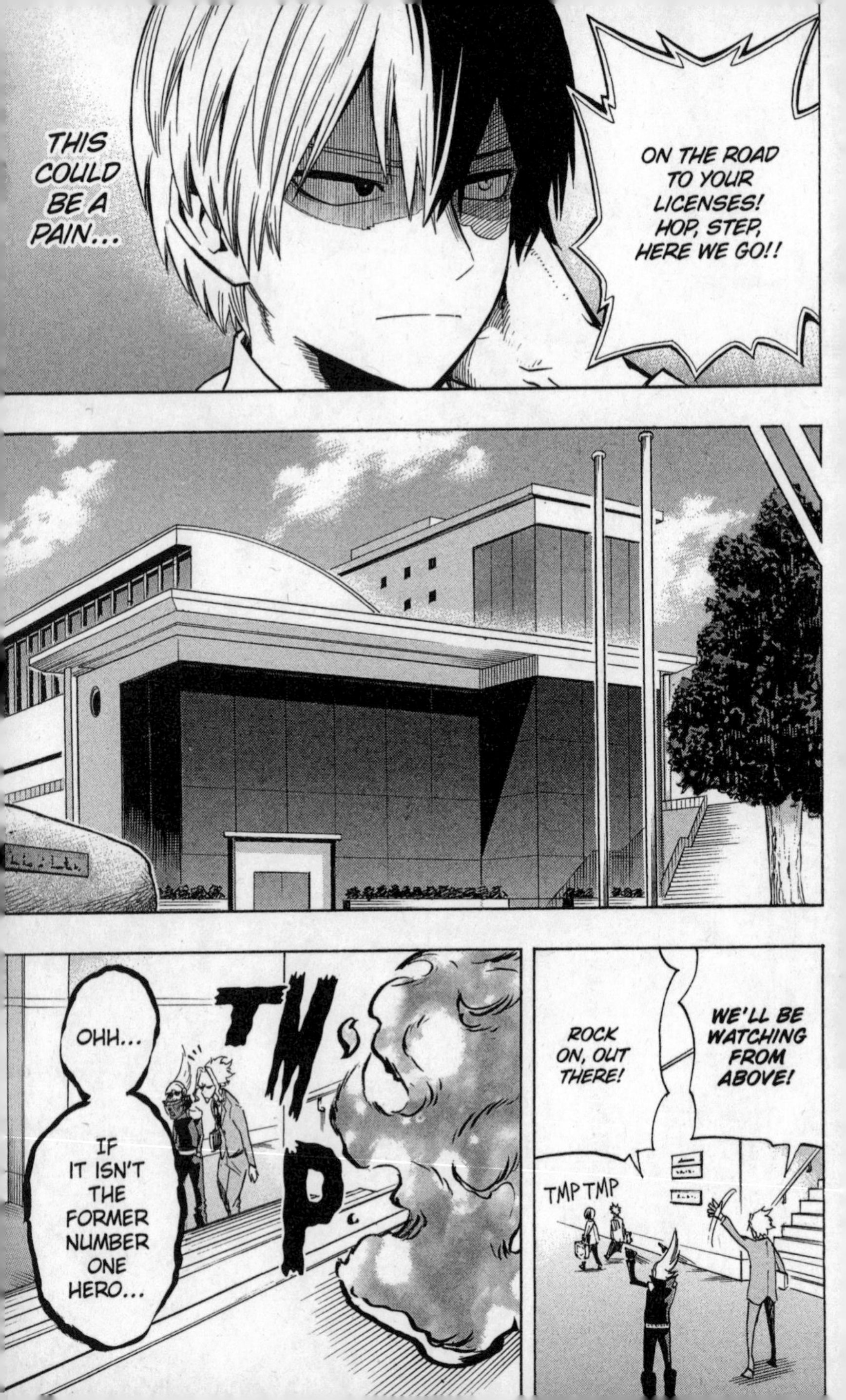
ON THE ROAD TO YOUR LICENSES! HOP, STEP, HERE WE GO!!
THIS COULD BE A PAIN...
WE'LL BE WATCHING FROM ABOVE!
ROCK ON, OUT THERE!
TMP TMP
TMP
OHH...
IF IT ISN'T THE FORMER NUMBER ONE HERO...

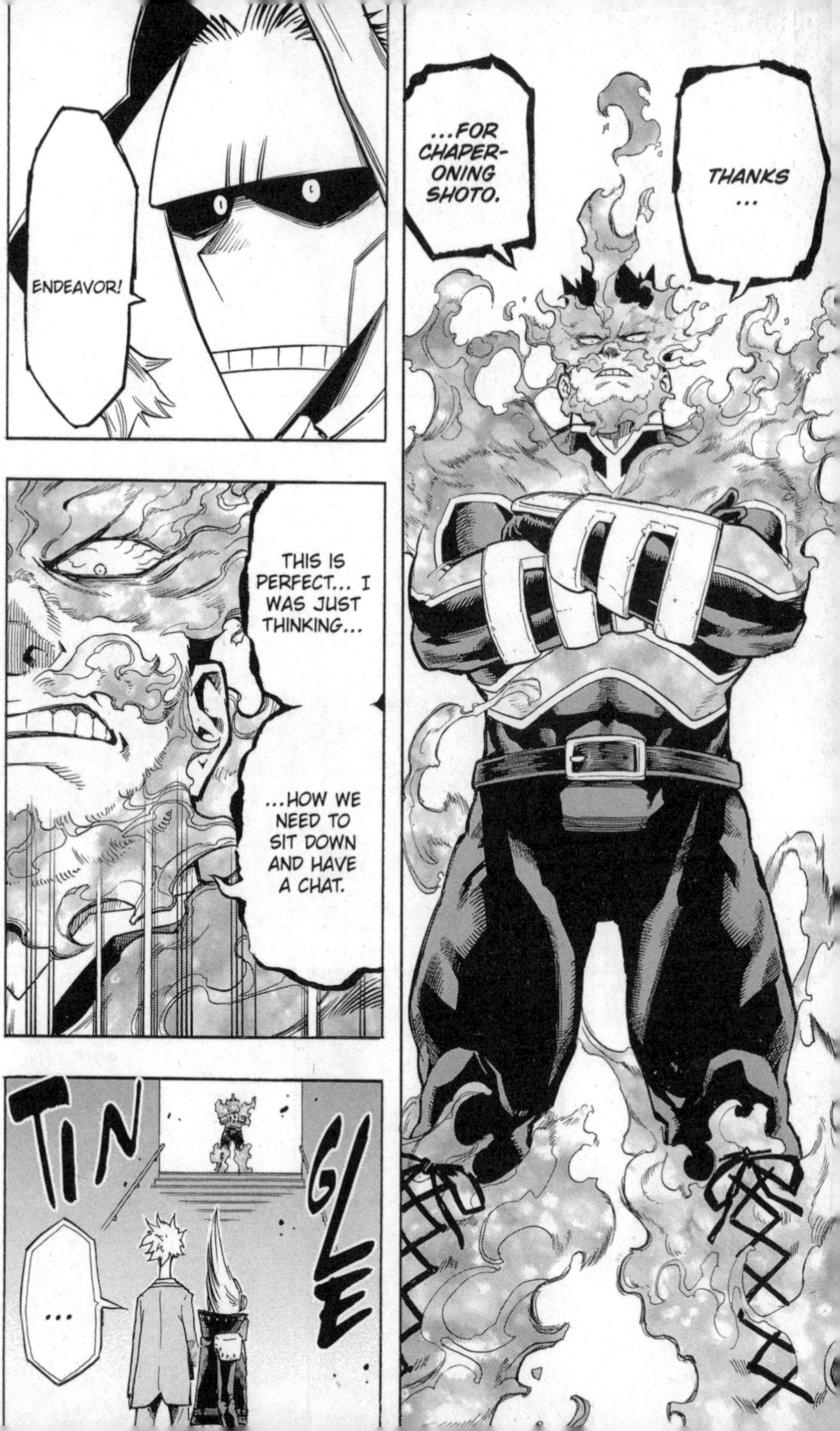
THANKS...
...FOR CHAPER-ONING SHOTO.
ENDEAVOR!
THIS IS PERFECT... I WAS JUST THINKING...
...HOW WE NEED TO SIT DOWN AND HAVE A CHAT.
TINGLE
...

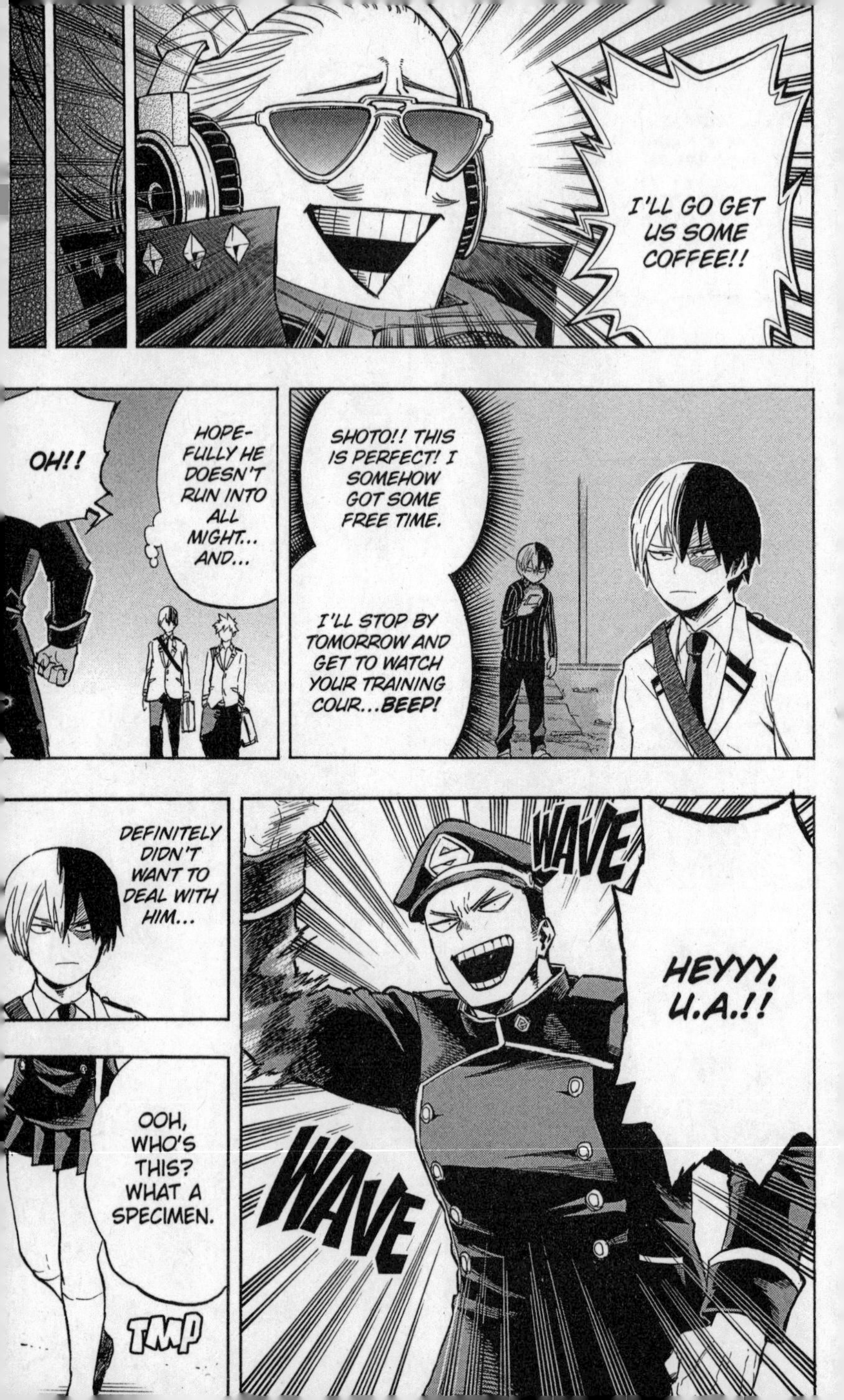
I'LL GO GET US SOME COFFEE!!
SHOTO!! THIS IS PERFECT! I SOMEHOW GOT SOME FREE TIME.
I'LL STOP BY TOMORROW AND GET TO WATCH YOUR TRAINING COUR...BEEP!
HOPEFULLY HE DOESN'T RUN INTO ALL MIGHT... AND...
OH!!
WAVE
HEYYY, U.A.!!
WAVE
DEFINITELY DIDN'T WANT TO DEAL WITH HIM...
OOH, WHO'S THIS? WHAT A SPECIMEN.
TMP

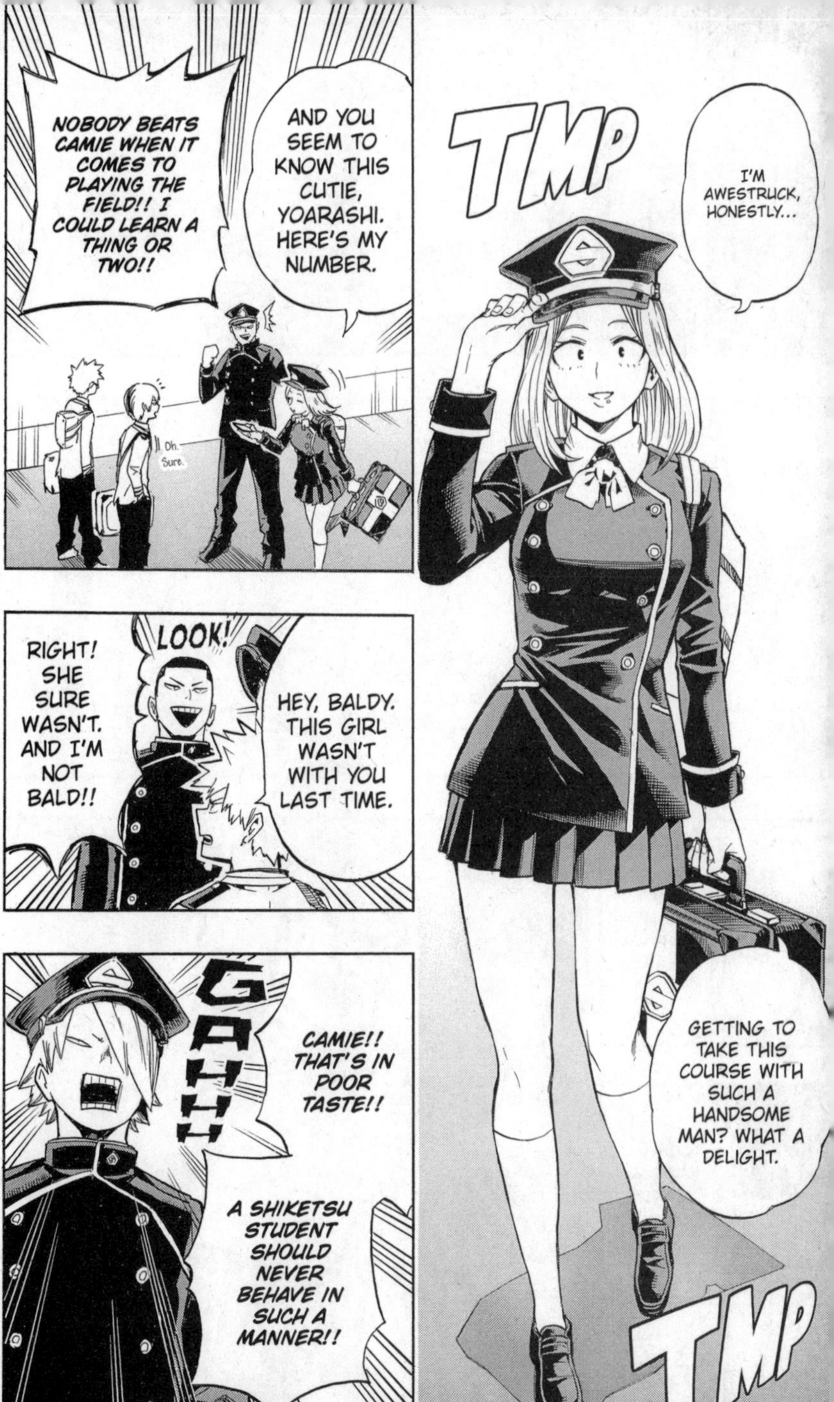
TMP
I'M AWESTRUCK, HONESTLY...
GETTING TO TAKE THIS COURSE WITH SUCH A HANDSOME MAN? WHAT A DELIGHT.
TMP
AND YOU SEEM TO KNOW THIS CUTIE, YOARASHI. HERE'S MY NUMBER.
NOBODY BEATS CAMIE WHEN IT COMES TO PLAYING THE FIELD!! I COULD LEARN A THING OR TWO!!
Oh. Sure.
HEY, BALDY. THIS GIRL WASN'T WITH YOU LAST TIME.
LOOK!
RIGHT! SHE SURE WASN'T. AND I'M NOT BALD!!
GAHHH
CAMIE!! THAT'S IN POOR TASTE!!
A SHIKETSU STUDENT SHOULD NEVER BEHAVE IN SUCH A MANNER!!

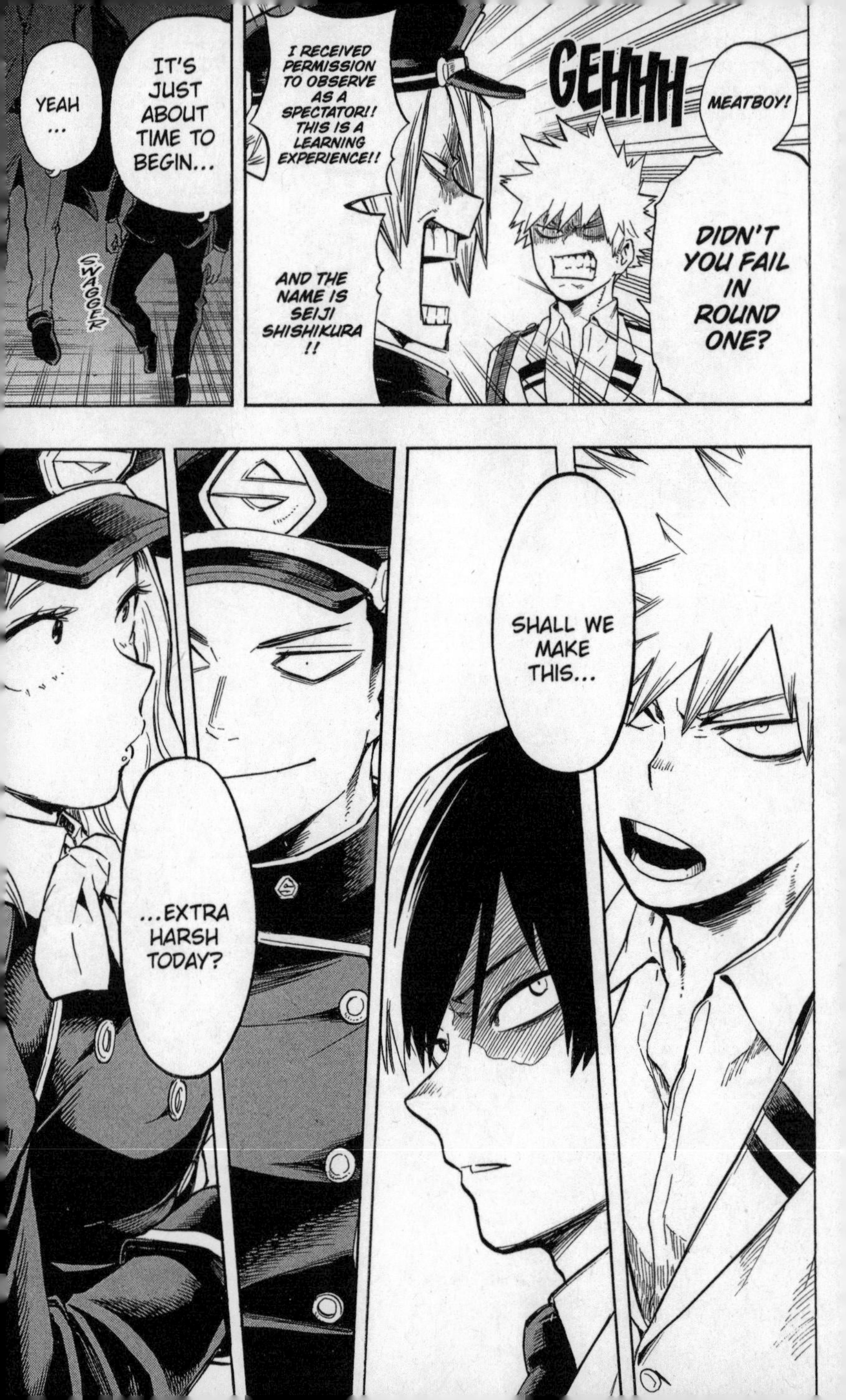
MEATBOY!
GEHHH
I RECEIVED PERMISSION TO OBSERVE AS A SPECTATOR!! THIS IS A LEARNING EXPERIENCE!!
DIDN'T YOU FAIL IN ROUND ONE?
AND THE NAME IS SEIJI SHISHIKURA!!
IT'S JUST ABOUT TIME TO BEGIN...
YEAH...
SWAGGER
SHALL WE MAKE THIS...
...EXTRA HARSH TODAY?

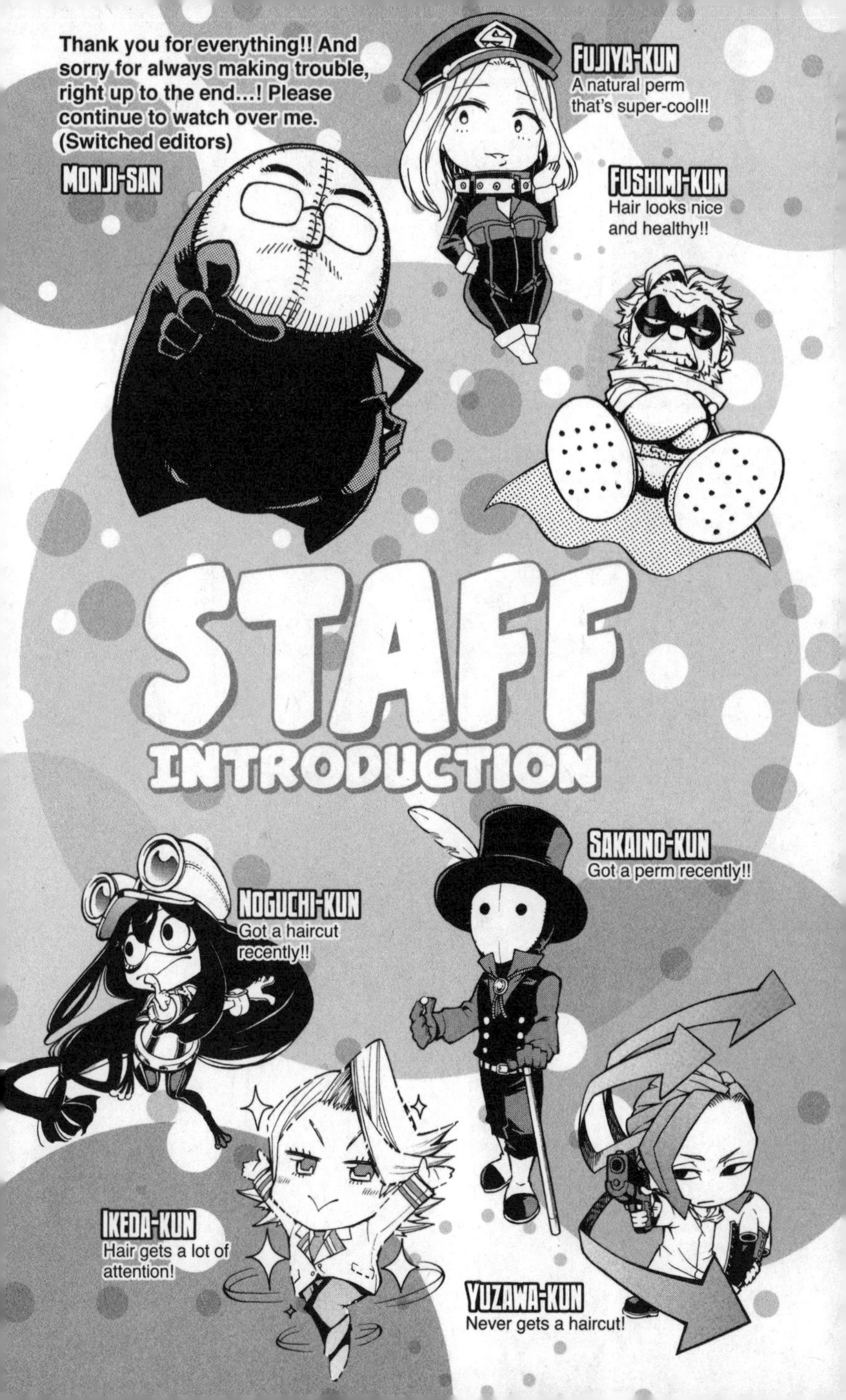

Fujiya-kun
A natural perm that's super-cool!!
Thank you for everything!! And sorry for always making trouble, right up to the end...! Please continue to watch over me. (Switched editors)
Monji-san
Fushimi-kun
Hair looks nice and healthy!!
STAFF INTRODUCTION
Sakaino-kun
Got a perm recently!!
Noguchi-kun
Got a haircut recently!!
Yuzawa-kun
Never gets a haircut!
Ikeda-kun
Hair gets a lot of attention!

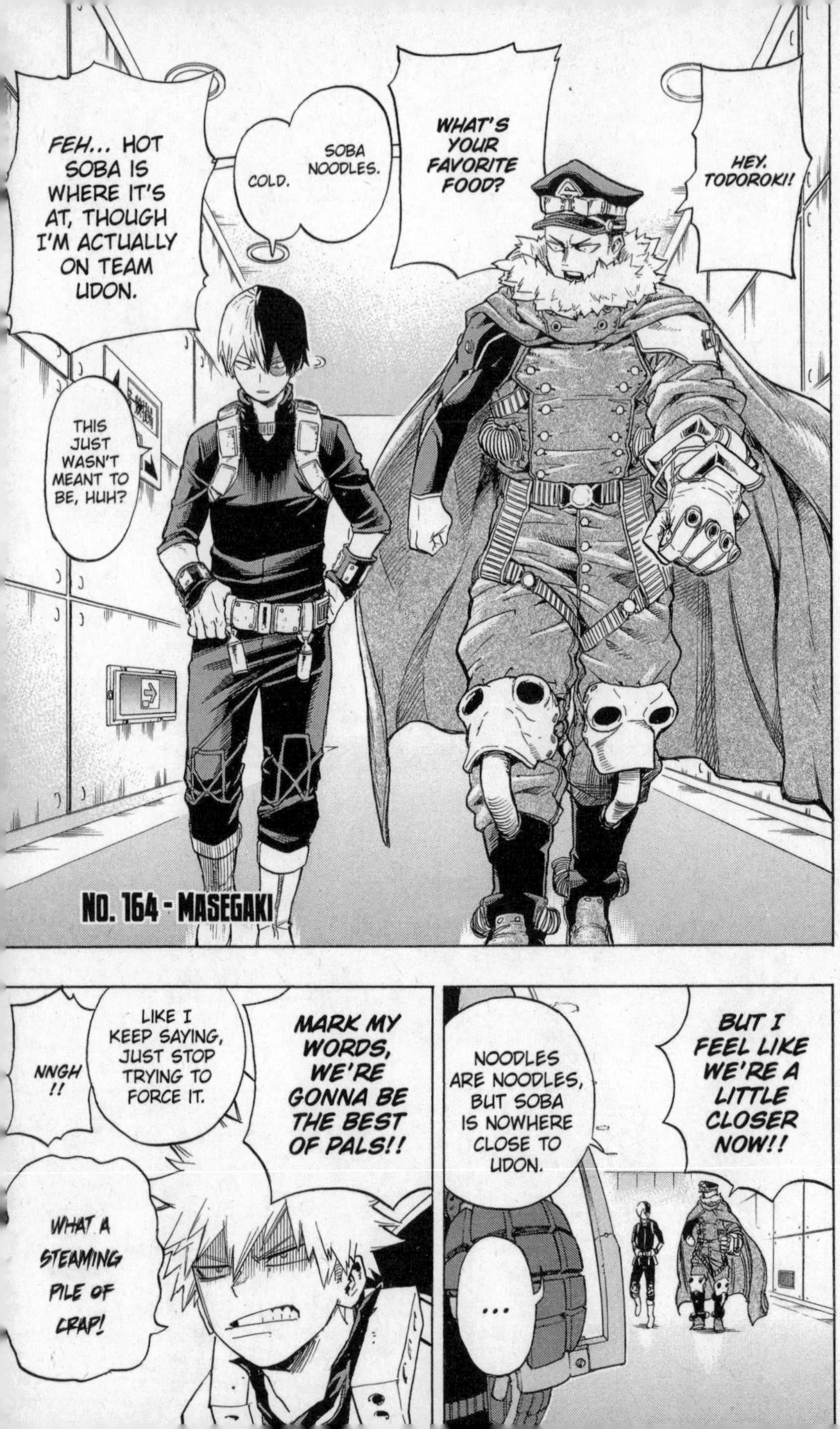
HEY. TODOROKI!
WHAT'S YOUR FAVORITE FOOD?
SOBA NOODLES.
COLD.
FEH... HOT SOBA IS WHERE IT'S AT, THOUGH I'M ACTUALLY ON TEAM UDON.
THIS JUST WASN'T MEANT TO BE, HUH?
NO. 164 - MASEGAKI
BUT I FEEL LIKE WE'RE A LITTLE CLOSER NOW!!
NOODLES ARE NOODLES, BUT SOBA IS NOWHERE CLOSE TO UDON.
...
MARK MY WORDS, WE'RE GONNA BE THE BEST OF PALS!!
LIKE I KEEP SAYING, JUST STOP TRYING TO FORCE IT.
NNGH!!
WHAT A STEAMING PILE OF CRAP!

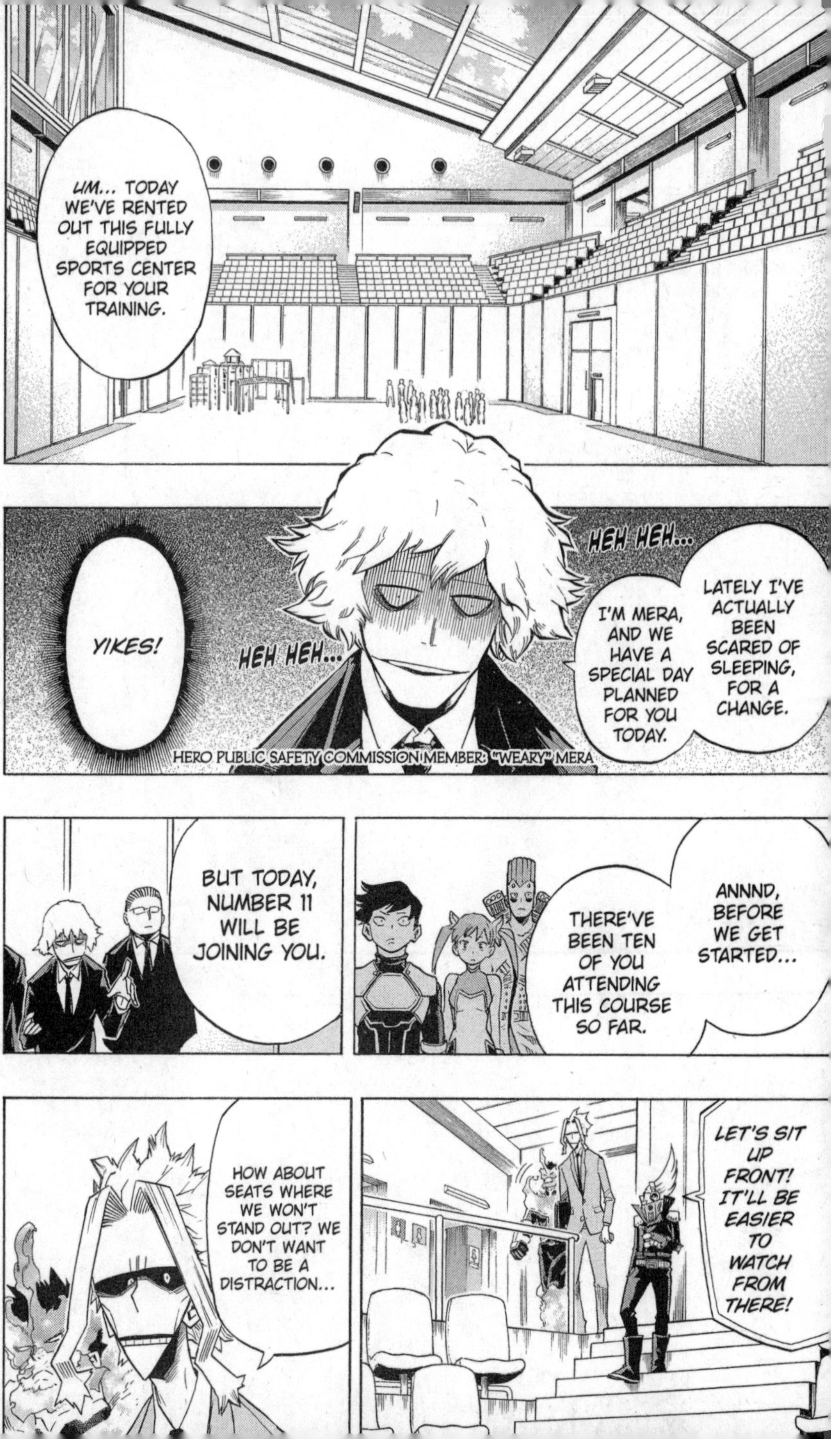
UM... TODAY WE'VE RENTED OUT THIS FULLY EQUIPPED SPORTS CENTER FOR YOUR TRAINING.
LATELY I'VE ACTUALLY BEEN SCARED OF SLEEPING, FOR A CHANGE.
HEH HEH...
I'M MERA, AND WE HAVE A SPECIAL DAY PLANNED FOR YOU TODAY.
HEH HEH...
YIKES!
HERO PUBLIC SAFETY COMMISSION MEMBER: "WEARY" MERA
ANNND, BEFORE WE GET STARTED...
THERE'VE BEEN TEN OF YOU ATTENDING THIS COURSE SO FAR.
BUT TODAY, NUMBER 11 WILL BE JOINING YOU.
LET'S SIT UP FRONT! IT'LL BE EASIER TO WATCH FROM THERE!
HOW ABOUT SEATS WHERE WE WON'T STAND OUT? WE DON'T WANT TO BE A DISTRACTION...

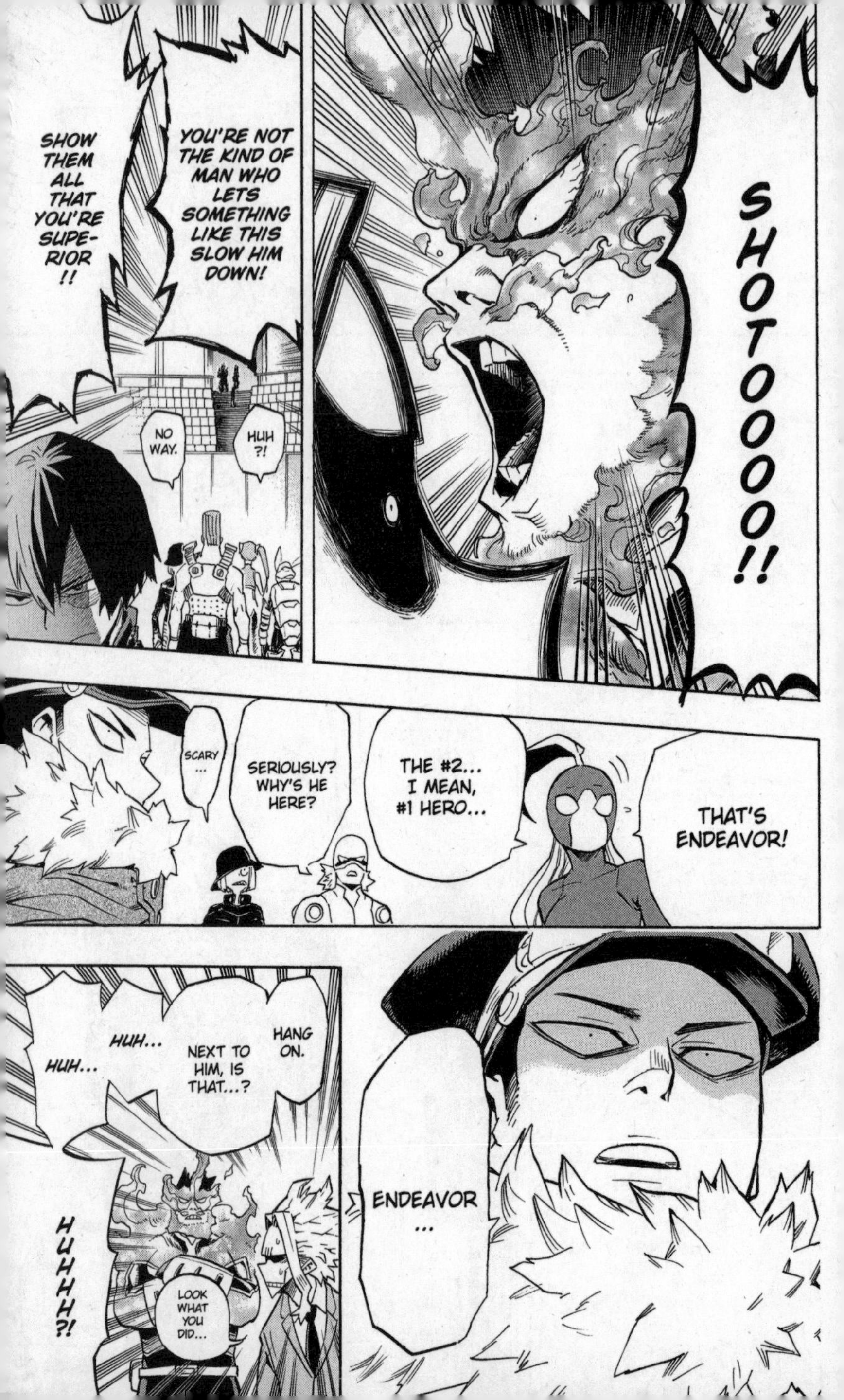
SHOTOOOOO!!
YOU'RE NOT THE KIND OF MAN WHO LETS SOMETHING LIKE THIS SLOW HIM DOWN!
SHOW THEM ALL THAT YOU'RE SUPERIOR!!
HUH?!
NO WAY.
THAT'S ENDEAVOR!
THE #2... I MEAN, #1 HERO...
SERIOUSLY? WHY'S HE HERE?
SCARY...
ENDEAVOR...
HANG ON.
NEXT TO HIM, IS THAT...?
HUH...
HUH...
HUHHH?!
LOOK WHAT YOU DID...

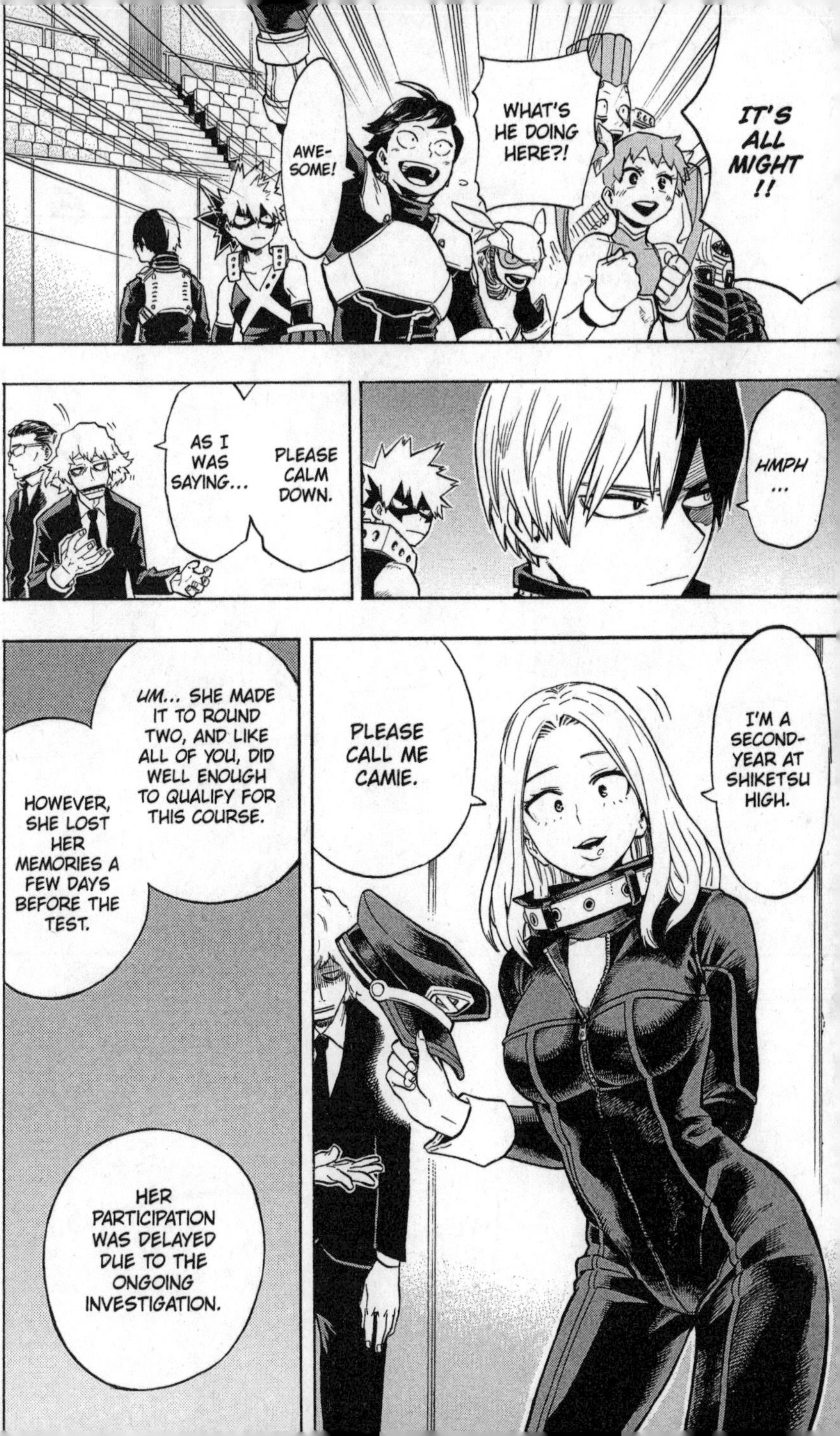
IT'S ALL MIGHT!!
WHAT'S HE DOING HERE?!
AWE-SOME!
HMPH...
PLEASE CALM DOWN.
AS I WAS SAYING...
I'M A SECOND-YEAR AT SHIKETSU HIGH.
PLEASE CALL ME CAMIE.
UM... SHE MADE IT TO ROUND TWO, AND LIKE ALL OF YOU, DID WELL ENOUGH TO QUALIFY FOR THIS COURSE.
HOWEVER, SHE LOST HER MEMORIES A FEW DAYS BEFORE THE TEST.
HER PARTICIPATION WAS DELAYED DUE TO THE ONGOING INVESTIGATION.

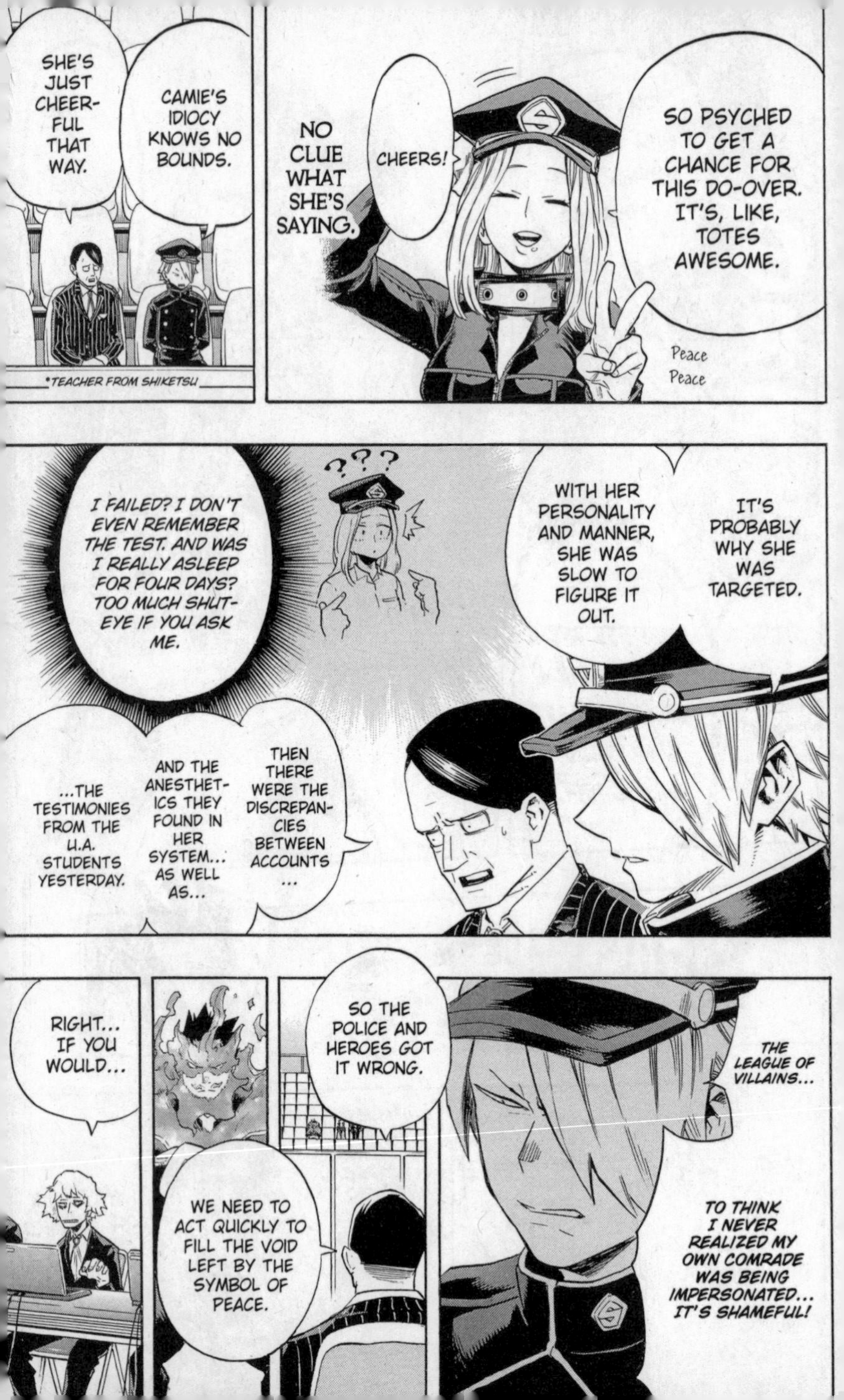
SO PSYCHED TO GET A CHANCE FOR THIS DO-OVER. IT'S, LIKE, TOTES AWESOME.
Peace Peace
CHEERS!
NO CLUE WHAT SHE'S SAYING.
CAMIE'S IDIOCY KNOWS NO BOUNDS.
SHE'S JUST CHEERFUL THAT WAY.
*TEACHER FROM SHIKETSU
IT'S PROBABLY WHY SHE WAS TARGETED.
WITH HER PERSONALITY AND MANNER, SHE WAS SLOW TO FIGURE IT OUT.
???
I FAILED? I DON'T EVEN REMEMBER THE TEST. AND WAS I REALLY ASLEEP FOR FOUR DAYS? TOO MUCH SHUT-EYE IF YOU ASK ME.
THEN THERE WERE THE DISCREPANCIES BETWEEN ACCOUNTS...
AND THE ANESTHETICS THEY FOUND IN HER SYSTEM... AS WELL AS...
...THE TESTIMONIES FROM THE U.A. STUDENTS YESTERDAY.
THE LEAGUE OF VILLAINS...
TO THINK I NEVER REALIZED MY OWN COMRADE WAS BEING IMPERSONATED... IT'S SHAMEFUL!
SO THE POLICE AND HEROES GOT IT WRONG.
WE NEED TO ACT QUICKLY TO FILL THE VOID LEFT BY THE SYMBOL OF PEACE.
RIGHT... IF YOU WOULD...

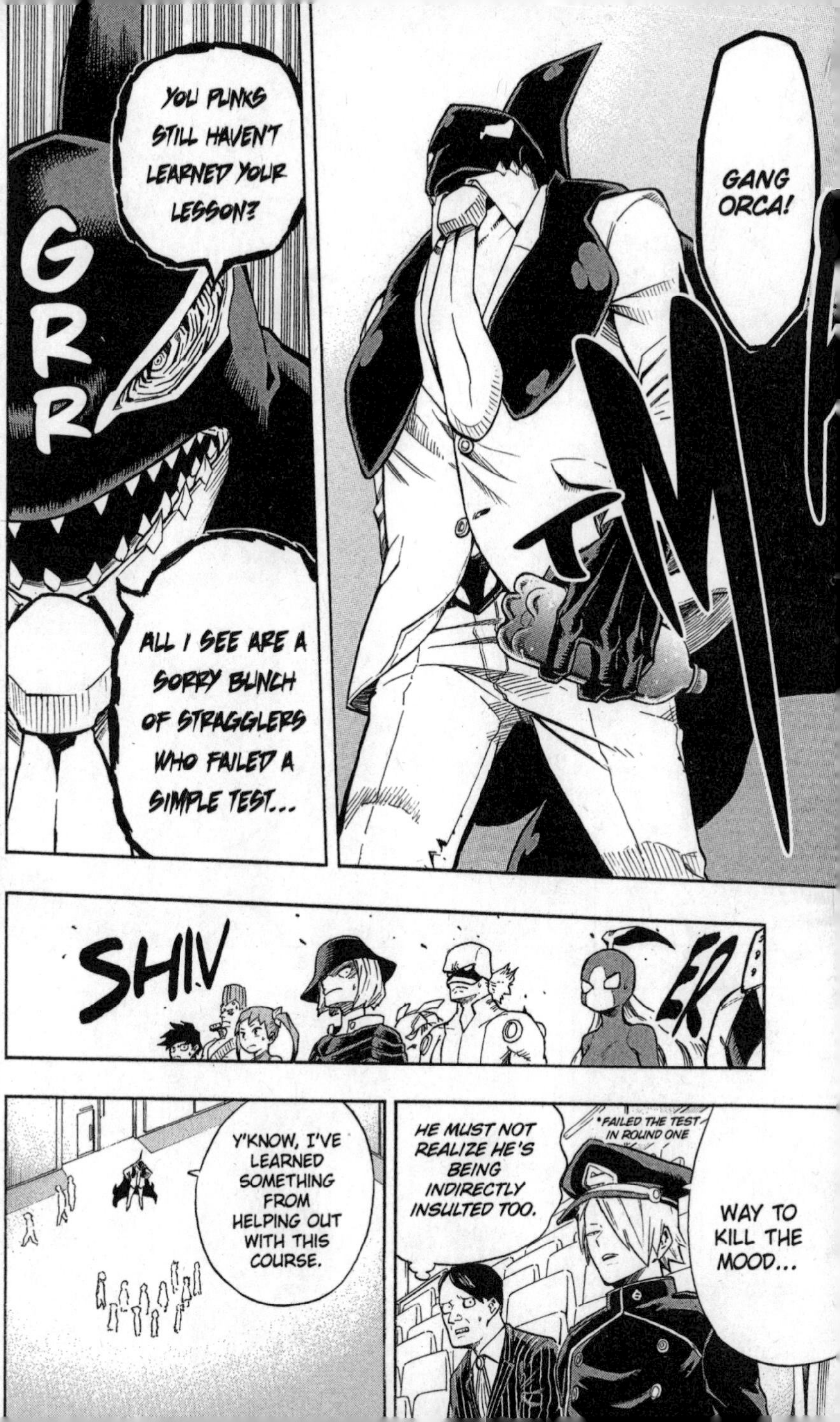
GANG ORCA!
YOU PUNKS STILL HAVEN'T LEARNED YOUR LESSON?
GRR
ALL I SEE ARE A SORRY BUNCH OF STRAGGLERS WHO FAILED A SIMPLE TEST...
SHIV
ER
WAY TO KILL THE MOOD...
*FAILED THE TEST IN ROUND ONE
HE MUST NOT REALIZE HE'S BEING INDIRECTLY INSULTED TOO.
Y'KNOW, I'VE LEARNED SOMETHING FROM HELPING OUT WITH THIS COURSE.

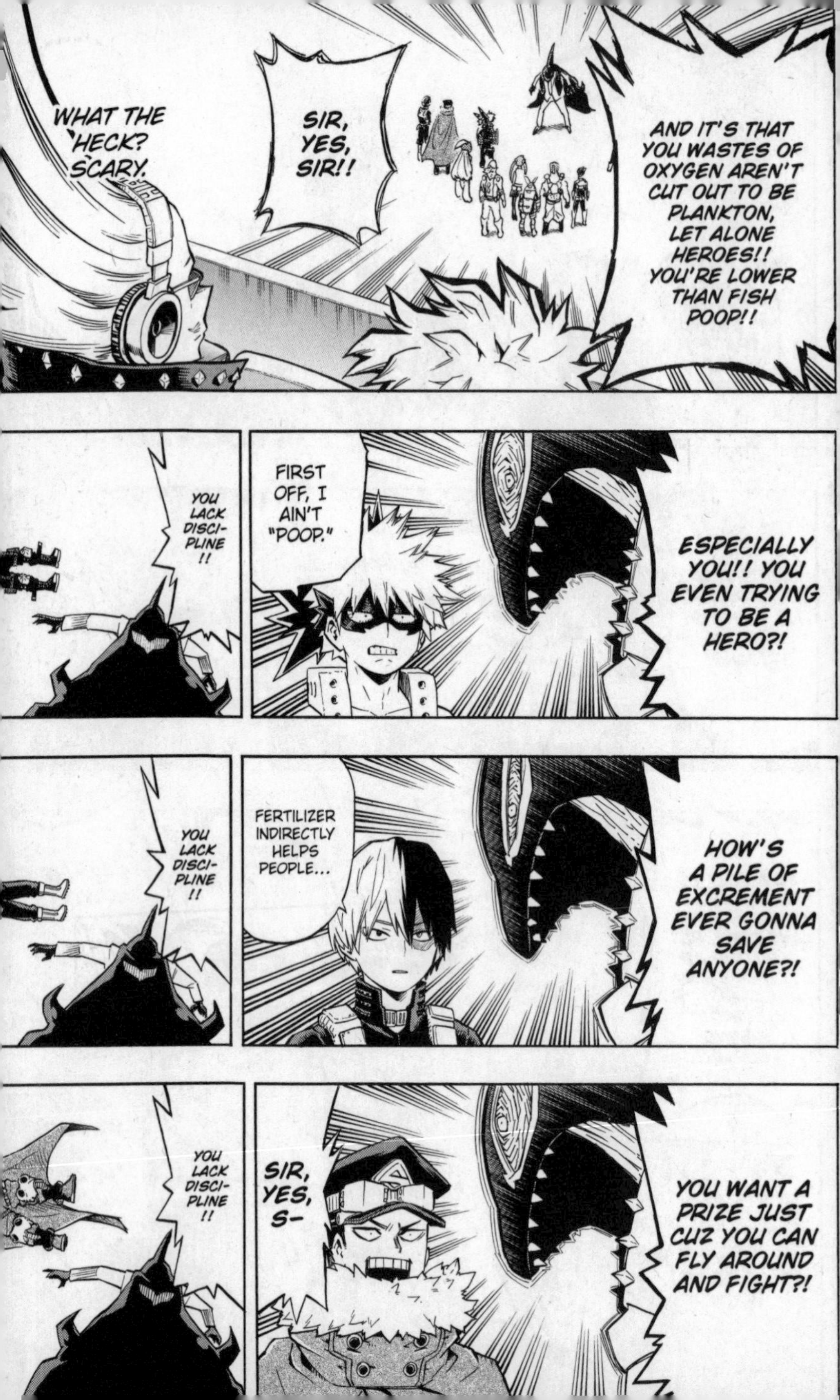
AND IT'S THAT YOU WASTES OF OXYGEN AREN'T CUT OUT TO BE PLANKTON, LET ALONE HEROES!! YOU'RE LOWER THAN FISH POOP!!
SIR, YES, SIR!!
WHAT THE HECK? SCARY.
ESPECIALLY YOU!! YOU EVEN TRYING TO BE A HERO?!
FIRST OFF, I AIN'T "POOP."
YOU LACK DISCI-PLINE !!
HOW'S A PILE OF EXCREMENT EVER GONNA SAVE ANYONE?!
FERTILIZER INDIRECTLY HELPS PEOPLE...
YOU LACK DISCI-PLINE !!
YOU WANT A PRIZE JUST CUZ YOU CAN FLY AROUND AND FIGHT?!
SIR, YES, S-
YOU LACK DISCI-PLINE !!

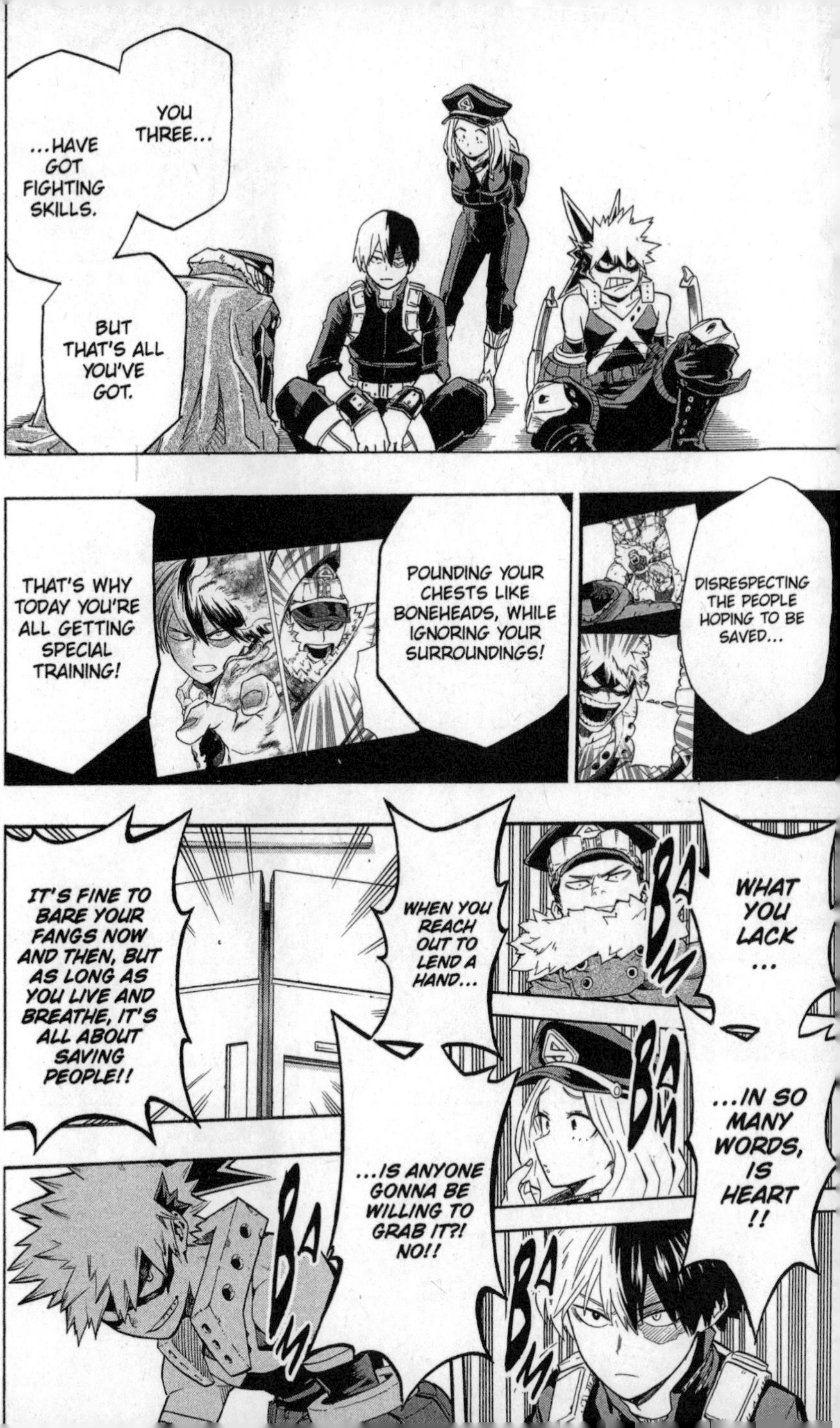
YOU THREE...
...HAVE GOT FIGHTING SKILLS.
BUT THAT'S ALL YOU'VE GOT.
DISRESPECTING THE PEOPLE HOPING TO BE SAVED...
POUNDING YOUR CHESTS LIKE BONEHEADS, WHILE IGNORING YOUR SURROUNDINGS!
THAT'S WHY TODAY YOU'RE ALL GETTING SPECIAL TRAINING!
IT'S FINE TO BARE YOUR FANGS NOW AND THEN, BUT AS LONG AS YOU LIVE AND BREATHE, IT'S ALL ABOUT SAVING PEOPLE!!
WHEN YOU REACH OUT TO LEND A HAND...
...IS ANYONE GONNA BE WILLING TO GRAB IT?! NO!!
WHAT YOU LACK ...
BAM
BAM
...IN SO MANY WORDS, IS HEART !!
BAM
BAM

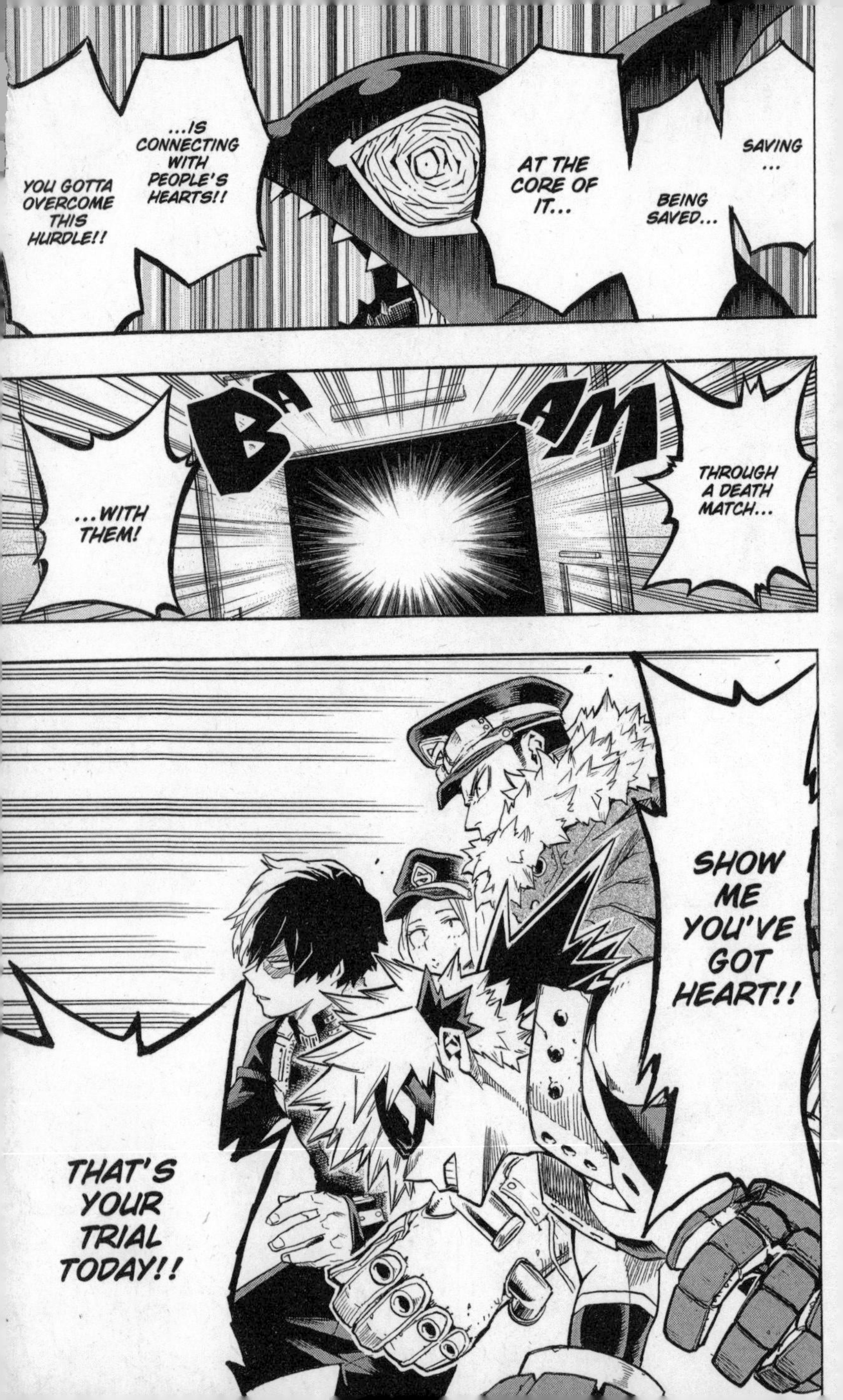
SAVING ...
BEING SAVED...
AT THE CORE OF IT...
...IS CONNECTING WITH PEOPLE'S HEARTS!!
YOU GOTTA OVERCOME THIS HURDLE!!
THROUGH A DEATH MATCH...
BAAM
...WITH THEM!
SHOW ME YOU'VE GOT HEART!!
THAT'S YOUR TRIAL TODAY!!

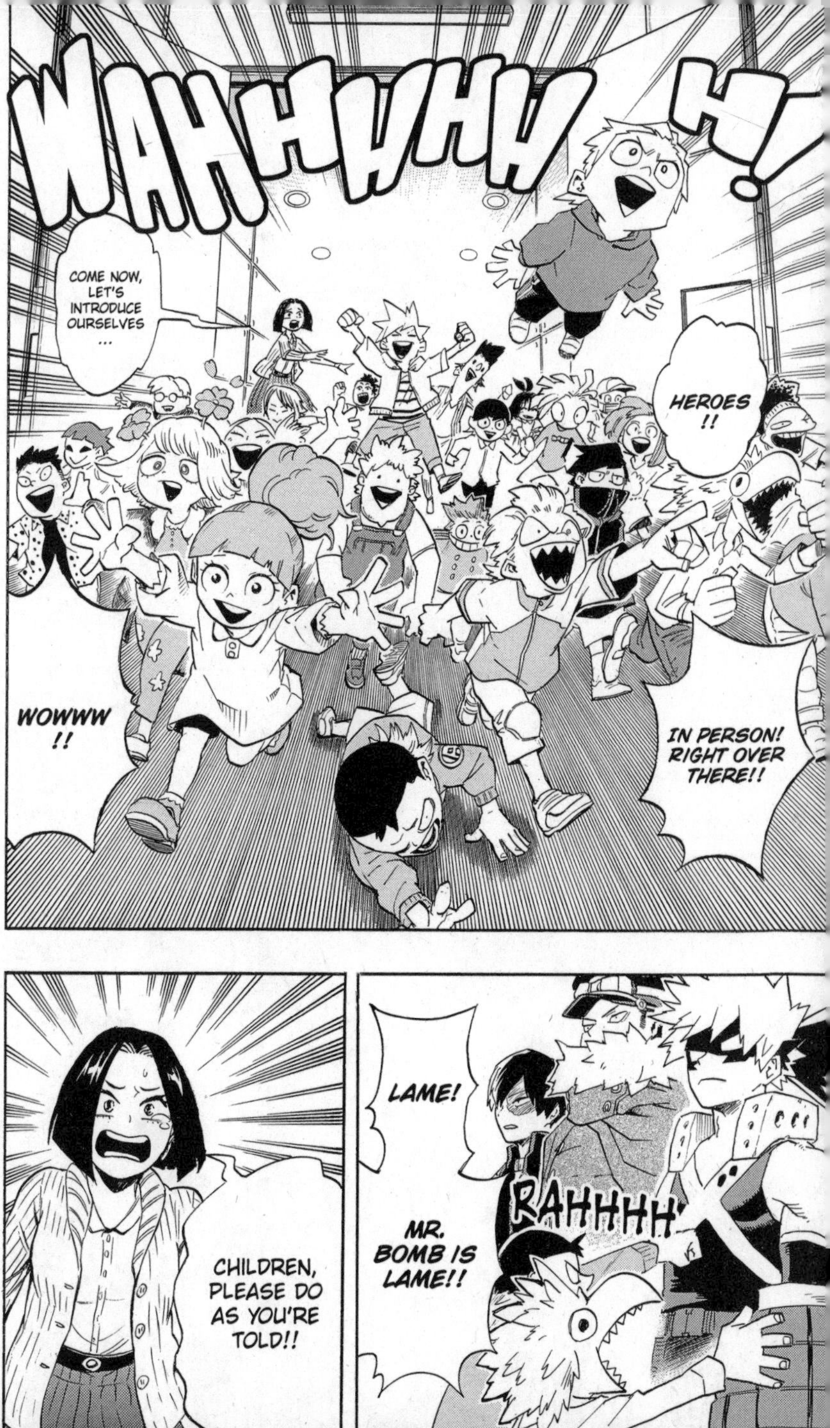
WAHHHHHH!
HEROES !!
COME NOW, LET'S INTRODUCE OURSELVES ...
IN PERSON! RIGHT OVER THERE!!
WOWWW !!
LAME!
RAHHHH
MR. BOMB IS LAME!!
CHILDREN, PLEASE DO AS YOU'RE TOLD!!

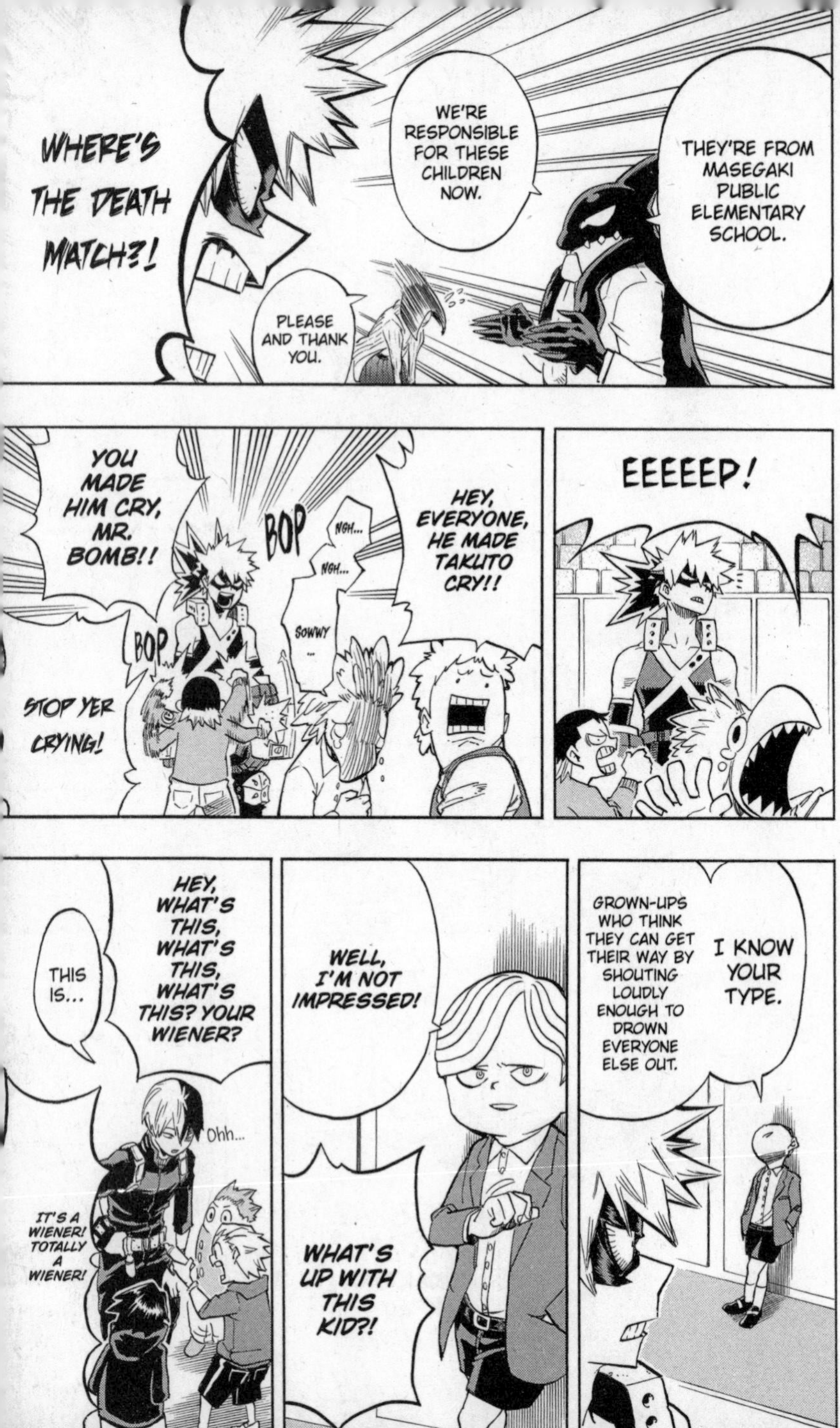
THEY'RE FROM MASEGAKI PUBLIC ELEMENTARY SCHOOL.
WE'RE RESPONSIBLE FOR THESE CHILDREN NOW.
PLEASE AND THANK YOU.
WHERE'S THE DEATH MATCH?!
EEEEEP!
HEY, EVERYONE, HE MADE TAKUTO CRY!!
NGH...
NGH...
SOWWY...
BOP
YOU MADE HIM CRY, MR. BOMB!!
BOP
STOP YER CRYING!
I KNOW YOUR TYPE.
GROWN-UPS WHO THINK THEY CAN GET THEIR WAY BY SHOUTING LOUDLY ENOUGH TO DROWN EVERYONE ELSE OUT.
WELL, I'M NOT IMPRESSED!
WHAT'S UP WITH THIS KID?!
HEY, WHAT'S THIS, WHAT'S THIS, WHAT'S THIS? YOUR WIENER?
THIS IS...
Ohh...
IT'S A WIENER! TOTALLY A WIENER!

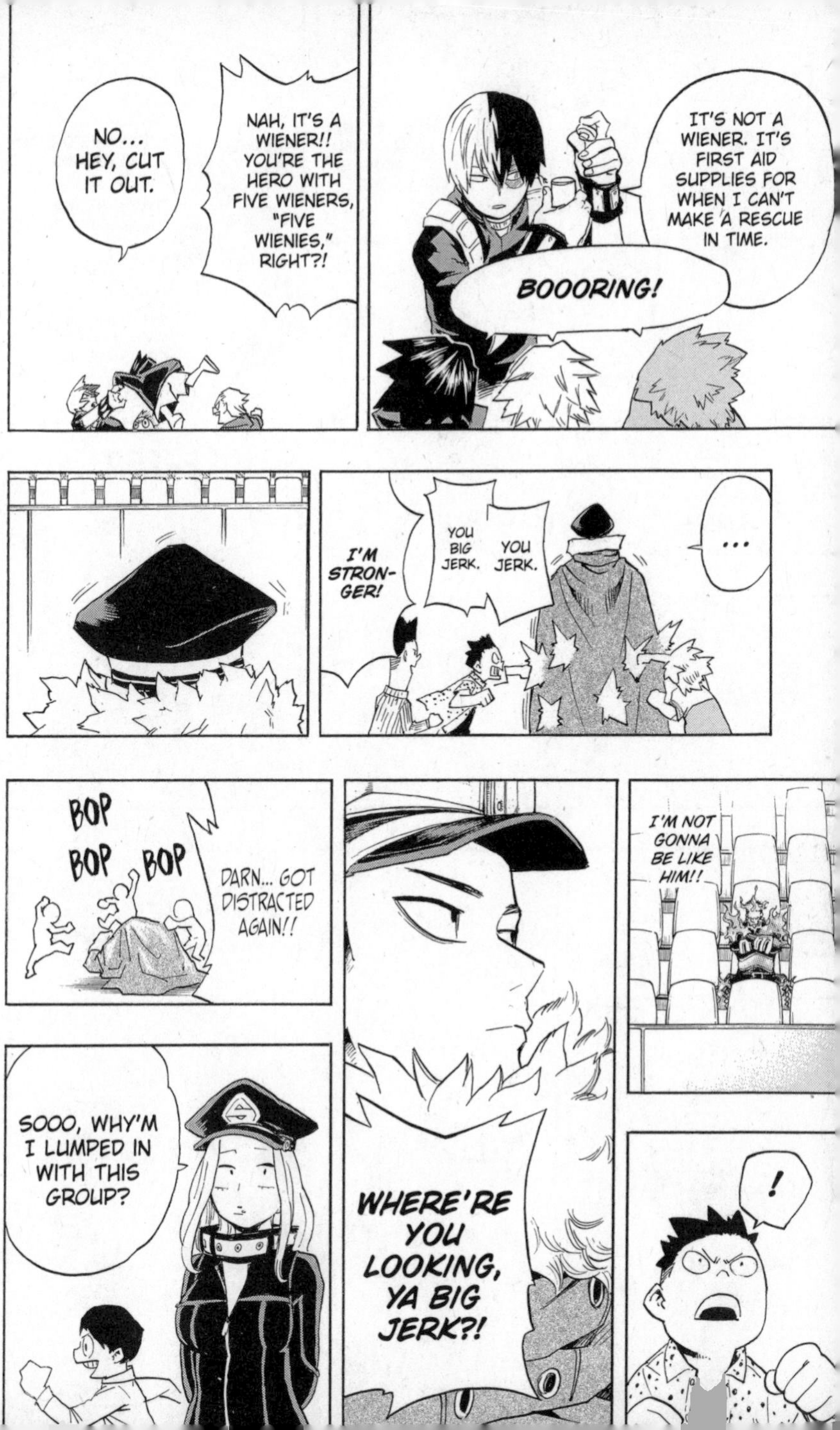
IT'S NOT A WIENER. IT'S FIRST AID SUPPLIES FOR WHEN I CAN'T MAKE A RESCUE IN TIME.
BOOORING!
NAH, IT'S A WIENER!! YOU'RE THE HERO WITH FIVE WIENERS, "FIVE WIENIES," RIGHT?!
NO... HEY, CUT IT OUT.
...
YOU JERK.
YOU BIG JERK.
I'M STRONGER!
I'M NOT GONNA BE LIKE HIM!!
!
WHERE'RE YOU LOOKING, YA BIG JERK?!
DARN... GOT DISTRACTED AGAIN!!
BOP
BOP BOP
SOOO, WHY'M I LUMPED IN WITH THIS GROUP?

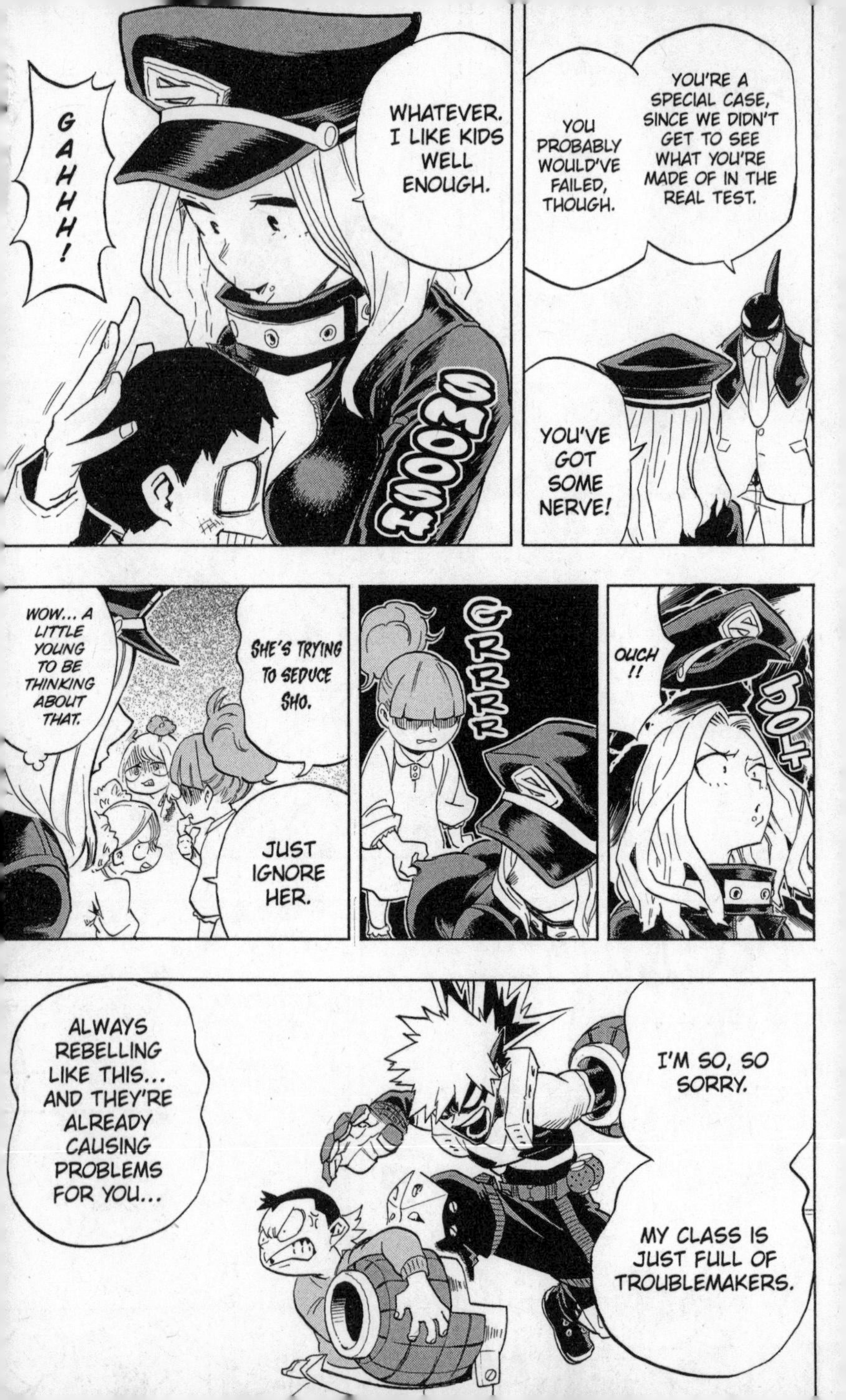
YOU'RE A SPECIAL CASE, SINCE WE DIDN'T GET TO SEE WHAT YOU'RE MADE OF IN THE REAL TEST.
YOU PROBABLY WOULD'VE FAILED, THOUGH.
YOU'VE GOT SOME NERVE!
WHATEVER. I LIKE KIDS WELL ENOUGH.
GAHHH!
SMOOSH
OUCH!!
JOLT
GRRRR
SHE'S TRYING TO SEDUCE SHO.
WOW... A LITTLE YOUNG TO BE THINKING ABOUT THAT.
JUST IGNORE HER.
I'M SO, SO SORRY.
MY CLASS IS JUST FULL OF TROUBLEMAKERS.
ALWAYS REBELLING LIKE THIS... AND THEY'RE ALREADY CAUSING PROBLEMS FOR YOU...

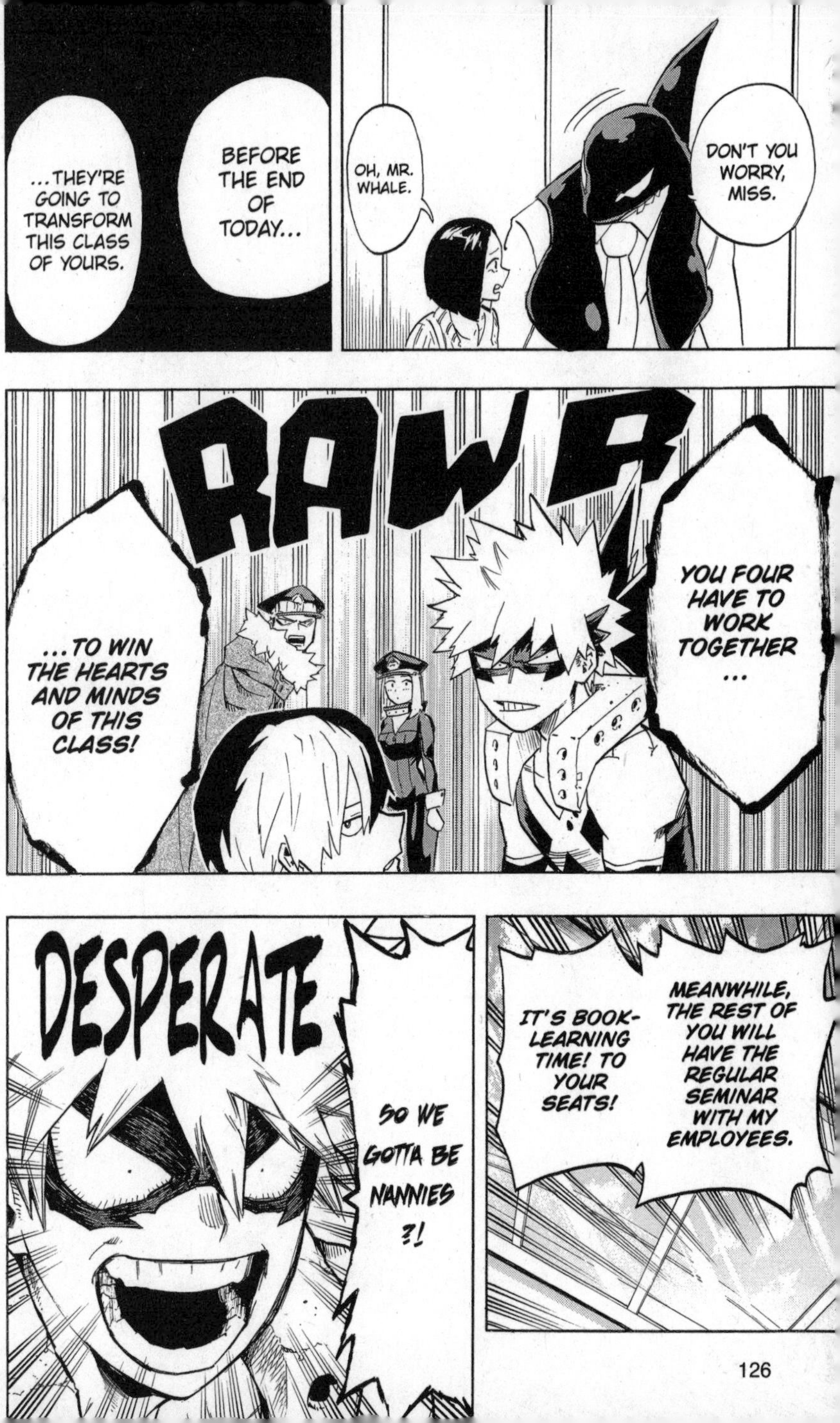
DON'T YOU WORRY, MISS.
OH, MR. WHALE.
BEFORE THE END OF TODAY...
...THEY'RE GOING TO TRANSFORM THIS CLASS OF YOURS.
RAWR
YOU FOUR HAVE TO WORK TOGETHER ...
...TO WIN THE HEARTS AND MINDS OF THIS CLASS!
MEANWHILE, THE REST OF YOU WILL HAVE THE REGULAR SEMINAR WITH MY EMPLOYEES.
IT'S BOOK-LEARNING TIME! TO YOUR SEATS!
DESPERATE
SO WE GOTTA BE NANNIES ?!

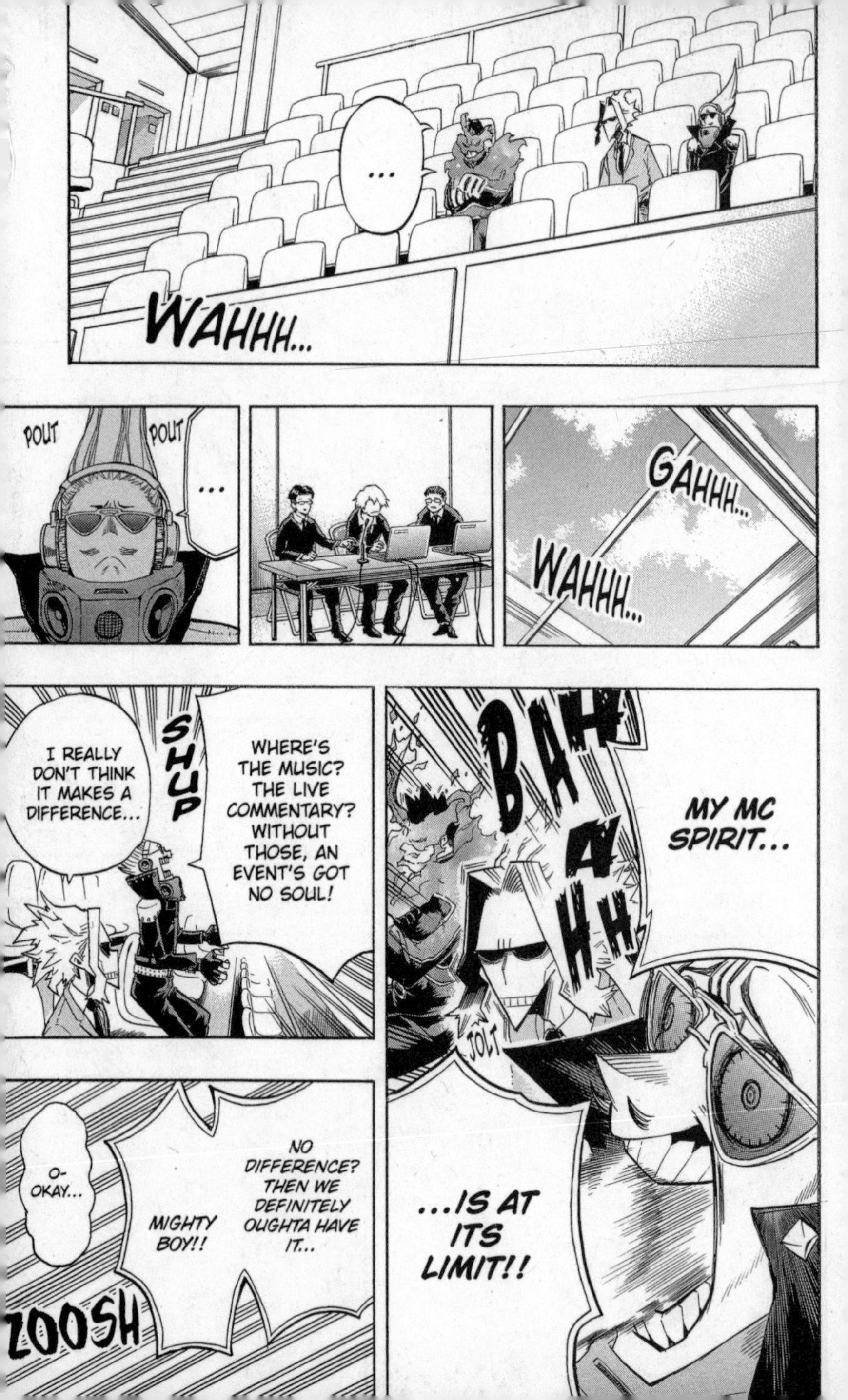
...
WAHHH...
GAHHH...
WAHHH...
POUT
POUT
...
BAHAHHH
MY MC SPIRIT...
JOLT
...IS AT ITS LIMIT!!
WHERE'S THE MUSIC? THE LIVE COMMENTARY? WITHOUT THOSE, AN EVENT'S GOT NO SOUL!
SHUP
I REALLY DON'T THINK IT MAKES A DIFFERENCE...
NO DIFFERENCE? THEN WE DEFINITELY OUGHTA HAVE IT...
MIGHTY BOY!!
O-OKAY...
ZOOSH

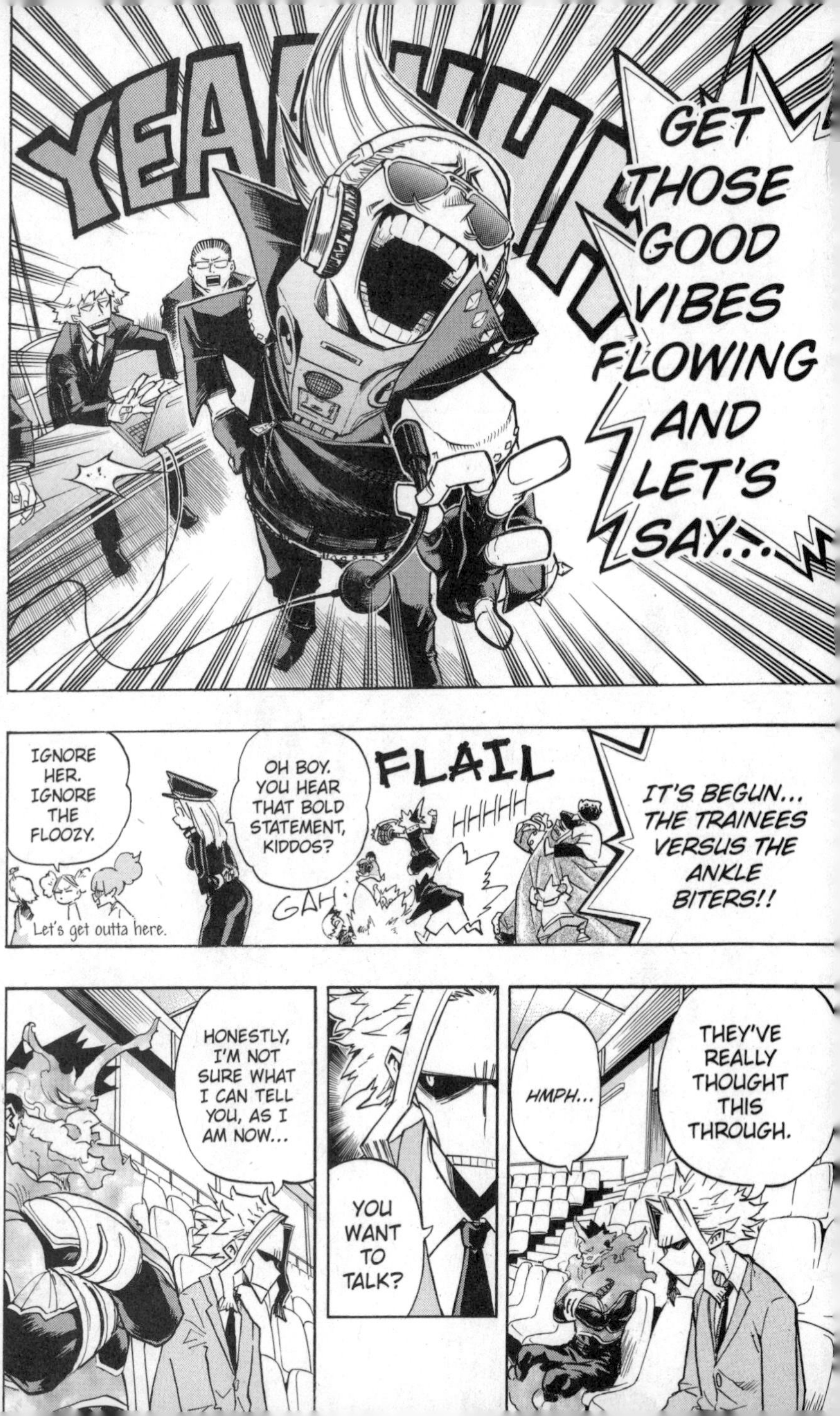
GET THOSE GOOD VIBES FLOWING AND LET'S SAY...
IT'S BEGUN... THE TRAINEES VERSUS THE ANKLE BITERS!!
HHHHH
FLAIL
GAH
OH BOY. YOU HEAR THAT BOLD STATEMENT, KIDDOS?
IGNORE HER. IGNORE THE FLOOZY.
Let's get outta here.
THEY'VE REALLY THOUGHT THIS THROUGH.
HMPH...
YOU WANT TO TALK?
HONESTLY, I'M NOT SURE WHAT I CAN TELL YOU, AS I AM NOW...

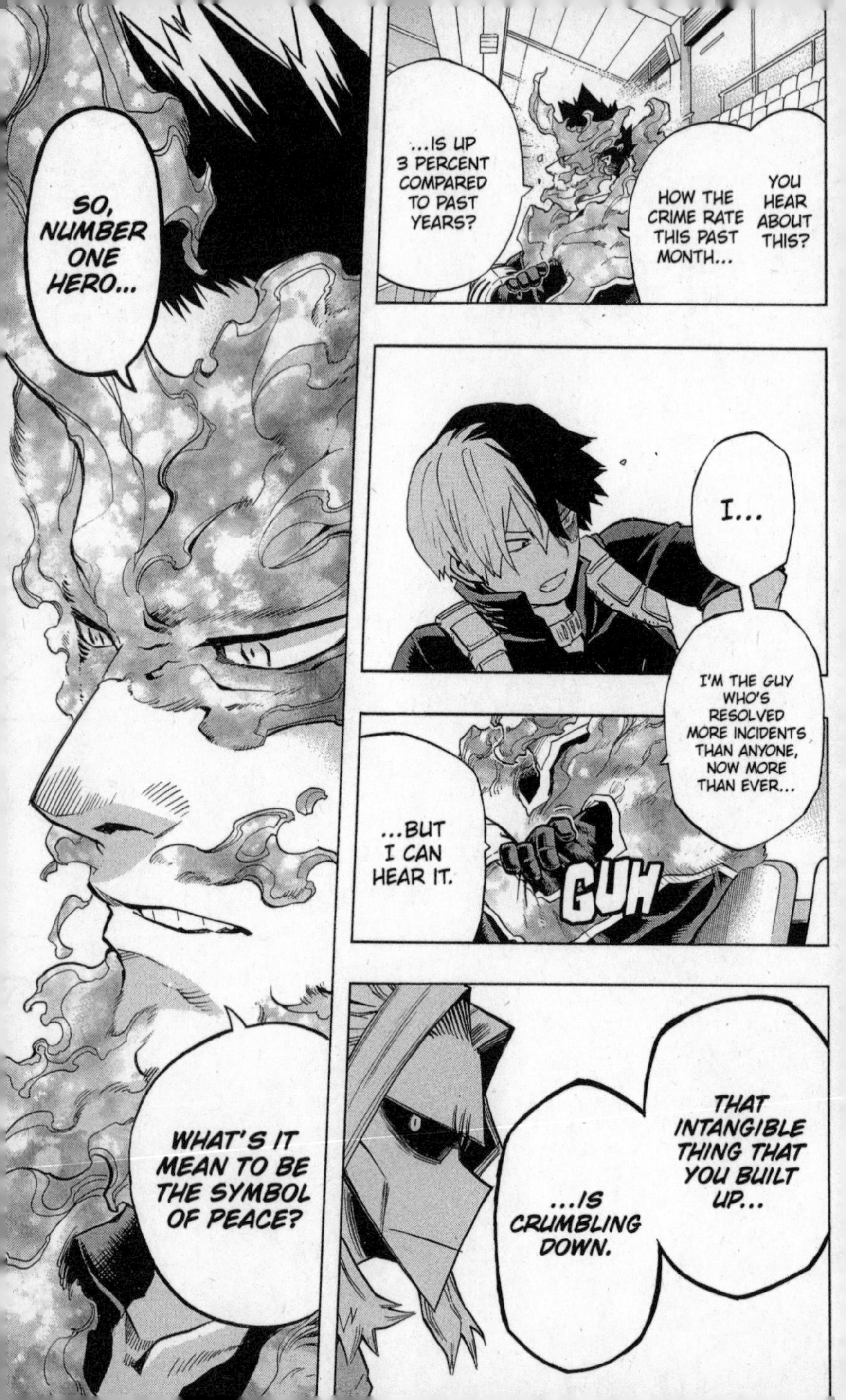
YOU HEAR ABOUT THIS?
HOW THE CRIME RATE THIS PAST MONTH...
...IS UP 3 PERCENT COMPARED TO PAST YEARS?
I...
I'M THE GUY WHO'S RESOLVED MORE INCIDENTS THAN ANYONE, NOW MORE THAN EVER...
...BUT I CAN HEAR IT.
GUH
THAT INTANGIBLE THING THAT YOU BUILT UP...
...IS CRUMBLING DOWN.
SO, NUMBER ONE HERO...
WHAT'S IT MEAN TO BE THE SYMBOL OF PEACE?

KOMARI IKOMA [23]

MASEGAKI
ELEMENTARY
SCHOOL
TEACHER
MASEGAKI
ELEMENTARY
SCHOOL

THE TEACHER

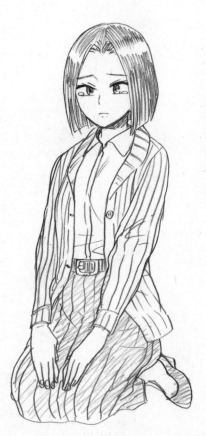

Birthday: 11/26
Height: 157 cm
Favorite Thing: Beer

THE TEACHER
A new teacher with a meek
personality.

She's cute.

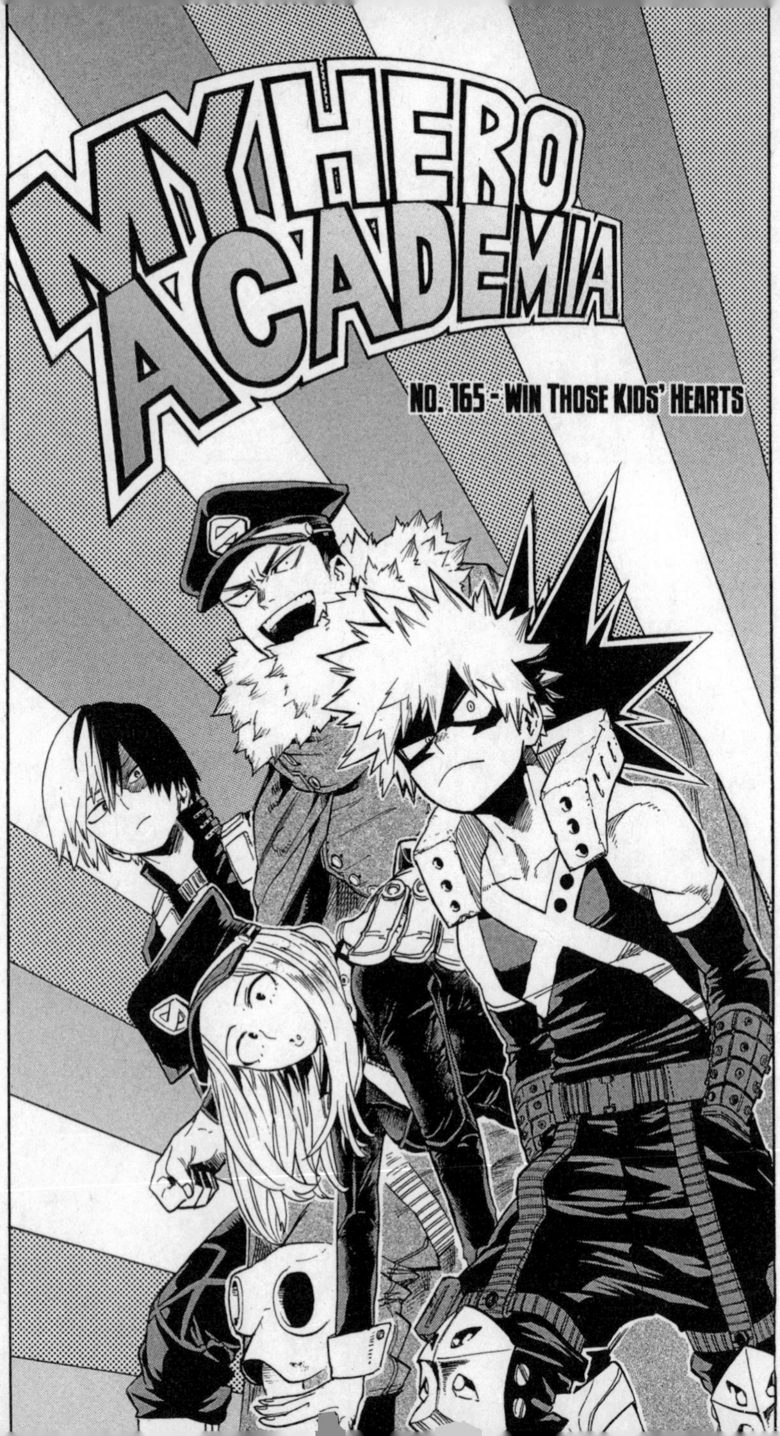
MY HERO ACADEMIA
No. 165 - Win Those Kids' Hearts

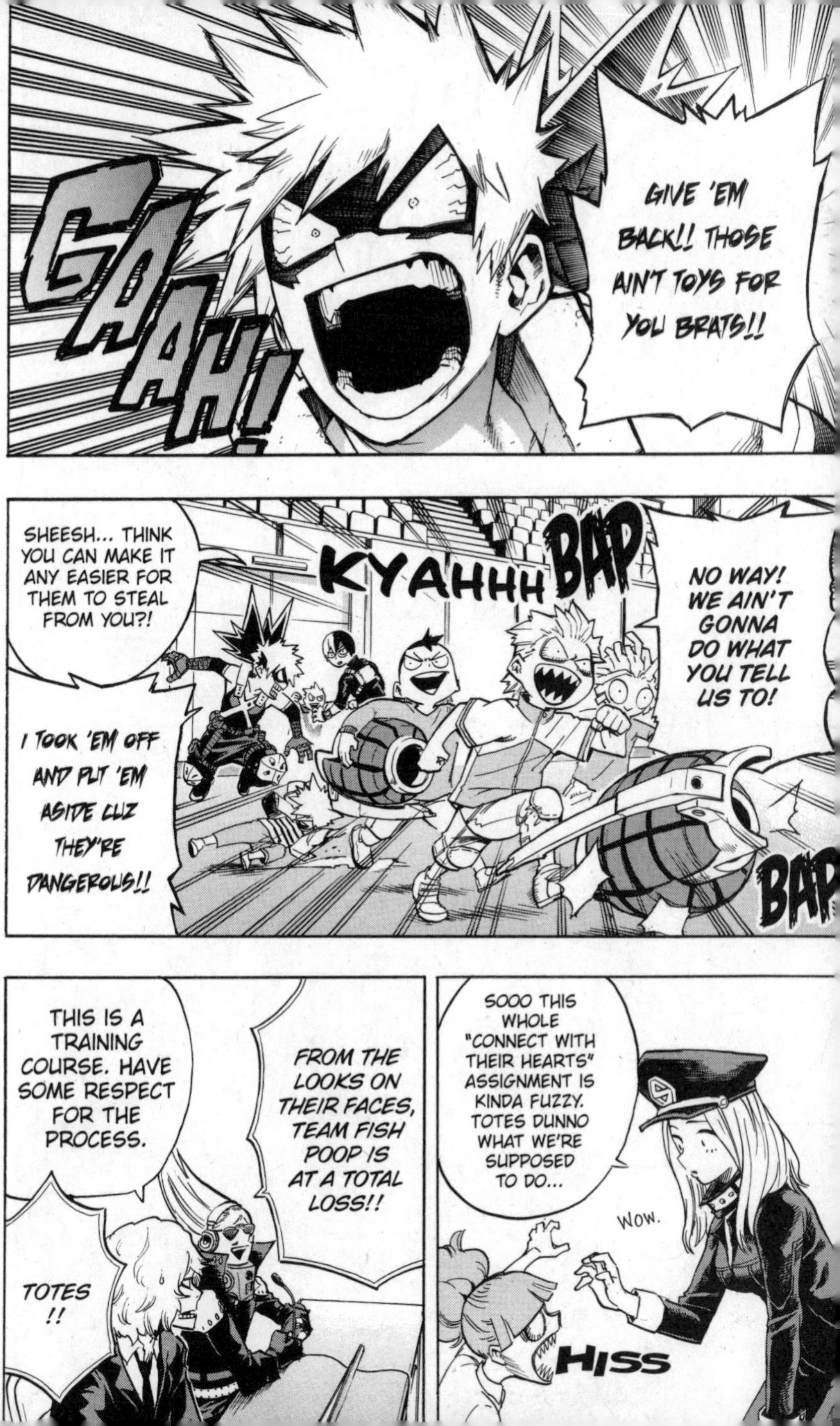
GIVE 'EM BACK!! THOSE AIN'T TOYS FOR YOU BRATS!!
GAAH!
NO WAY! WE AIN'T GONNA DO WHAT YOU TELL US TO!
BAP
KYAHHH
SHEESH... THINK YOU CAN MAKE IT ANY EASIER FOR THEM TO STEAL FROM YOU?!
I TOOK 'EM OFF AND PUT 'EM ASIDE CUZ THEY'RE DANGEROUS!!
BAP
SOOO THIS WHOLE "CONNECT WITH THEIR HEARTS" ASSIGNMENT IS KINDA FUZZY. TOTES DUNNO WHAT WE'RE SUPPOSED TO DO...
WOW.
HISS
FROM THE LOOKS ON THEIR FACES, TEAM FISH POOP IS AT A TOTAL LOSS!!
THIS IS A TRAINING COURSE. HAVE SOME RESPECT FOR THE PROCESS.
TOTES !!

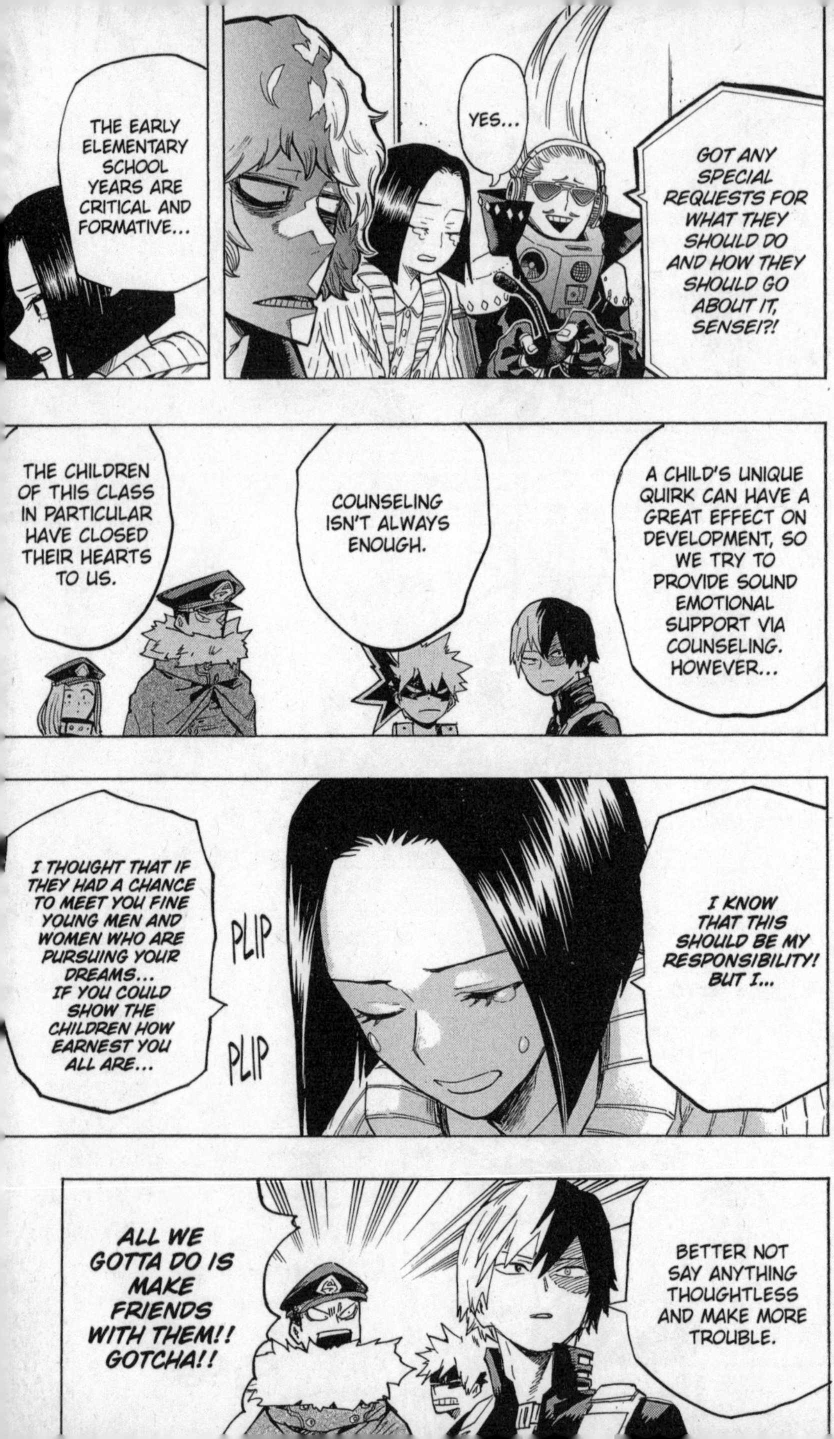
GOT ANY SPECIAL REQUESTS FOR WHAT THEY SHOULD DO AND HOW THEY SHOULD GO ABOUT IT, SENSEI?!
YES...
THE EARLY ELEMENTARY SCHOOL YEARS ARE CRITICAL AND FORMATIVE...
A CHILD'S UNIQUE QUIRK CAN HAVE A GREAT EFFECT ON DEVELOPMENT, SO WE TRY TO PROVIDE SOUND EMOTIONAL SUPPORT VIA COUNSELING. HOWEVER...
COUNSELING ISN'T ALWAYS ENOUGH.
THE CHILDREN OF THIS CLASS IN PARTICULAR HAVE CLOSED THEIR HEARTS TO US.
I KNOW THAT THIS SHOULD BE MY RESPONSIBILITY! BUT I...
PLIP
PLIP
I THOUGHT THAT IF THEY HAD A CHANCE TO MEET YOU FINE YOUNG MEN AND WOMEN WHO ARE PURSUING YOUR DREAMS... IF YOU COULD SHOW THE CHILDREN HOW EARNEST YOU ALL ARE...
BETTER NOT SAY ANYTHING THOUGHTLESS AND MAKE MORE TROUBLE.
ALL WE GOTTA DO IS MAKE FRIENDS WITH THEM!! GOTCHA!!

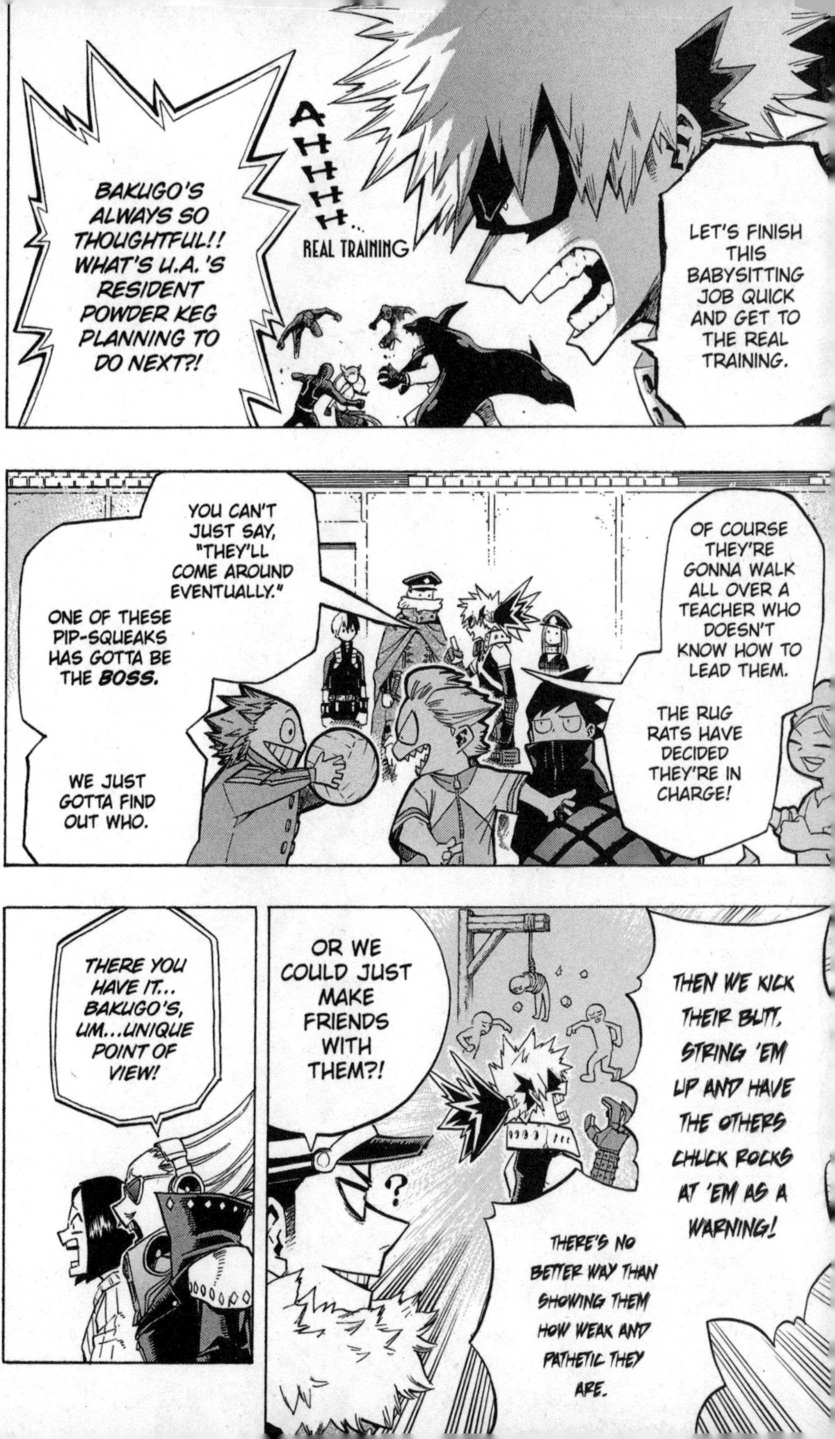
LET'S FINISH THIS BABYSITTING JOB QUICK AND GET TO THE REAL TRAINING.
AHHHH...
REAL TRAINING
BAKUGO'S ALWAYS SO THOUGHTFUL!! WHAT'S U.A.'S RESIDENT POWDER KEG PLANNING TO DO NEXT?!
OF COURSE THEY'RE GONNA WALK ALL OVER A TEACHER WHO DOESN'T KNOW HOW TO LEAD THEM.
THE RUG RATS HAVE DECIDED THEY'RE IN CHARGE!
YOU CAN'T JUST SAY, "THEY'LL COME AROUND EVENTUALLY."
ONE OF THESE PIP-SQUEAKS HAS GOTTA BE THE BOSS.
WE JUST GOTTA FIND OUT WHO.
THEN WE KICK THEIR BUTT, STRING 'EM UP AND HAVE THE OTHERS CHUCK ROCKS AT 'EM AS A WARNING!
THERE'S NO BETTER WAY THAN SHOWING THEM HOW WEAK AND PATHETIC THEY ARE.
OR WE COULD JUST MAKE FRIENDS WITH THEM?!
?
THERE YOU HAVE IT... BAKUGO'S, UM...UNIQUE POINT OF VIEW!

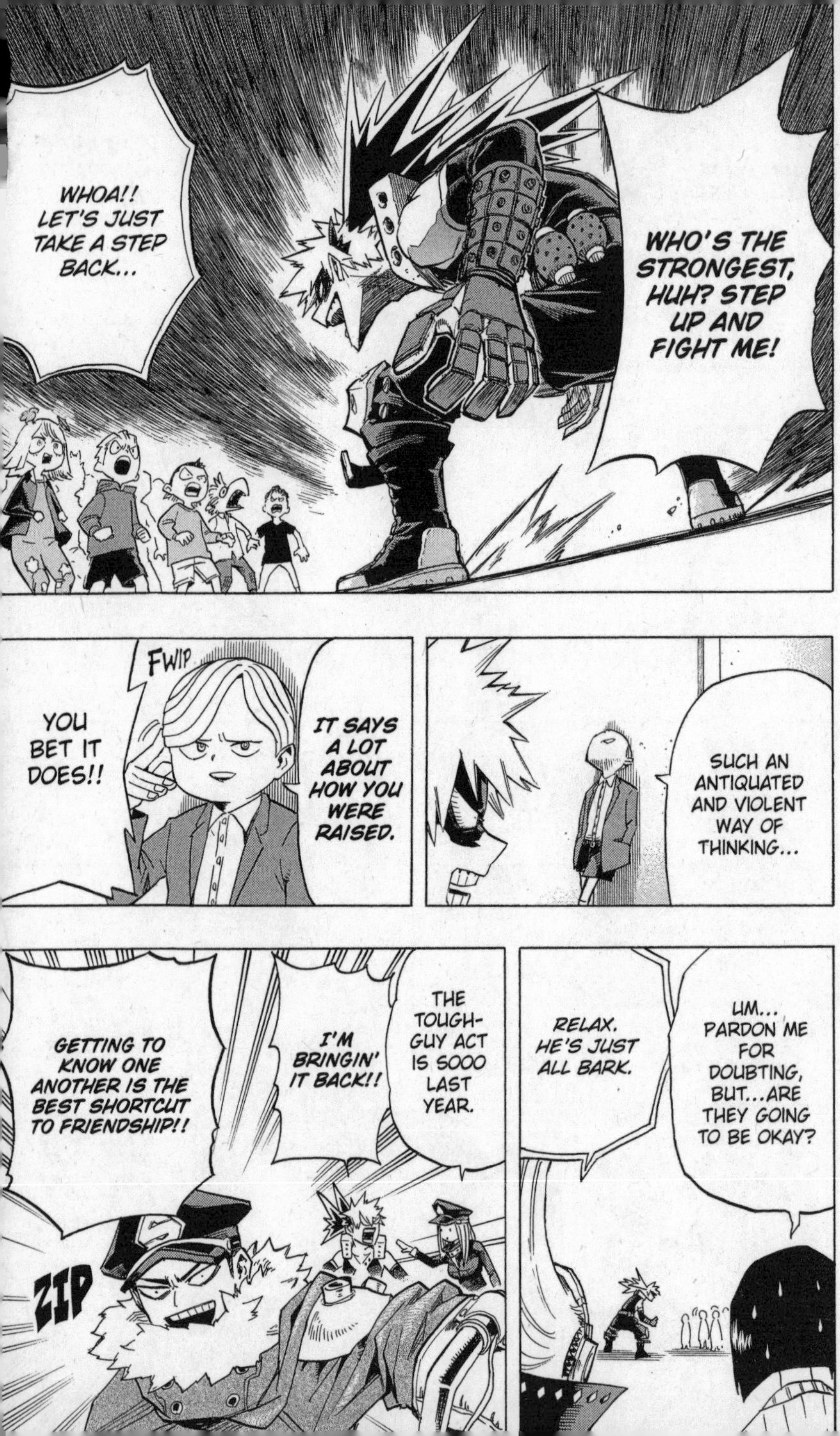
WHO'S THE STRONGEST, HUH? STEP UP AND FIGHT ME!
WHOA!! LET'S JUST TAKE A STEP BACK...
SUCH AN ANTIQUATED AND VIOLENT WAY OF THINKING...
IT SAYS A LOT ABOUT HOW YOU WERE RAISED.
FWIP
YOU BET IT DOES!!
UM... PARDON ME FOR DOUBTING, BUT...ARE THEY GOING TO BE OKAY?
RELAX. HE'S JUST ALL BARK.
THE TOUGH-GUY ACT IS SOOO LAST YEAR.
I'M BRINGIN' IT BACK!!
GETTING TO KNOW ONE ANOTHER IS THE BEST SHORTCUT TO FRIENDSHIP!!
ZIP

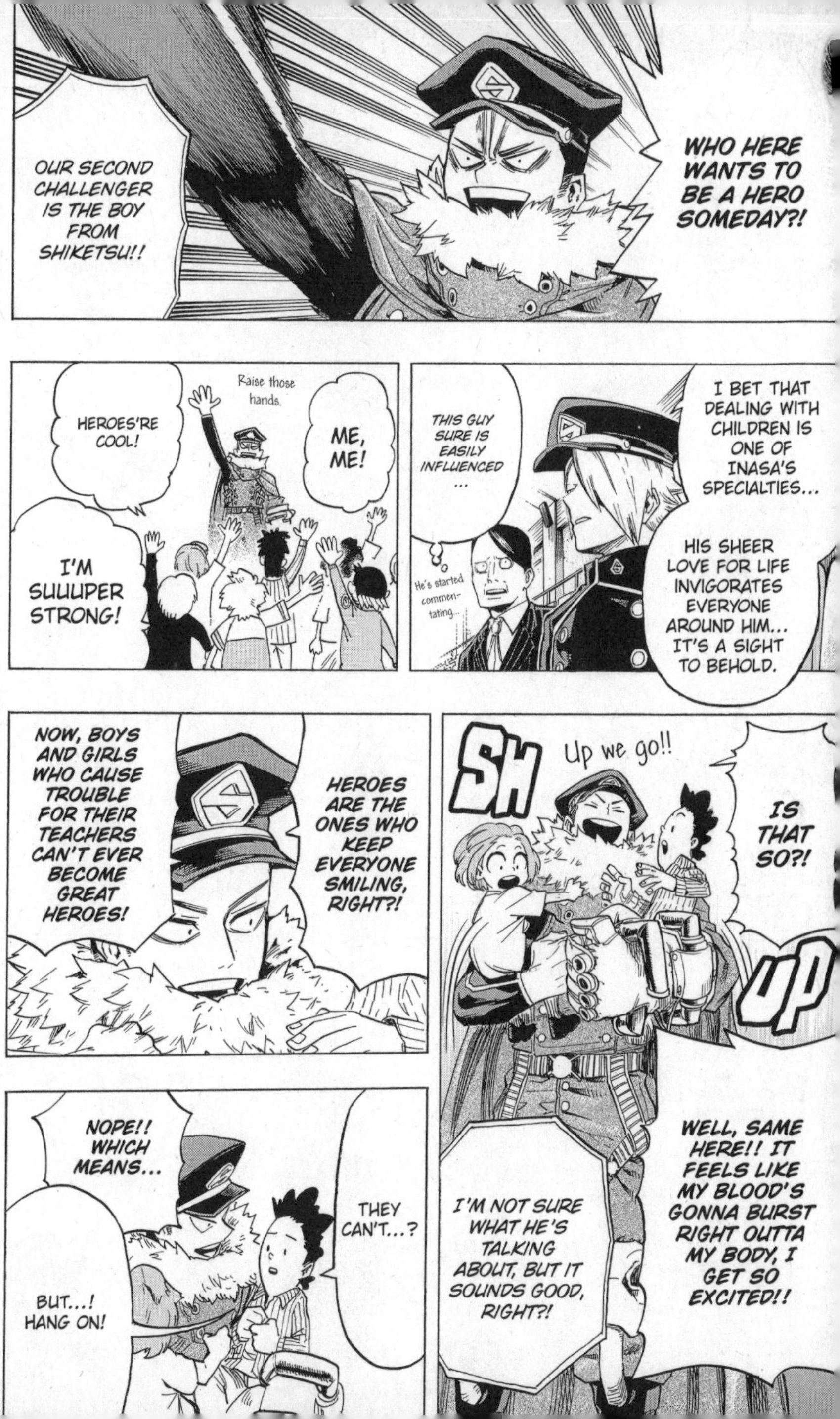

WHO HERE WANTS TO BE A HERO SOMEDAY?!
OUR SECOND CHALLENGER IS THE BOY FROM SHIKETSU!!
I BET THAT DEALING WITH CHILDREN IS ONE OF INASA'S SPECIALTIES...
HIS SHEER LOVE FOR LIFE INVIGORATES EVERYONE AROUND HIM... IT'S A SIGHT TO BEHOLD.
THIS GUY SURE IS EASILY INFLUENCED ...
He's started commentating...
Raise those hands.
ME, ME!
HEROES'RE COOL!
I'M SUUUPER STRONG!
IS THAT SO?!
Up we go!!
SH
UP
WELL, SAME HERE!! IT FEELS LIKE MY BLOOD'S GONNA BURST RIGHT OUTTA MY BODY, I GET SO EXCITED!!
I'M NOT SURE WHAT HE'S TALKING ABOUT, BUT IT SOUNDS GOOD, RIGHT?!
HEROES ARE THE ONES WHO KEEP EVERYONE SMILING, RIGHT?!
NOW, BOYS AND GIRLS WHO CAUSE TROUBLE FOR THEIR TEACHERS CAN'T EVER BECOME GREAT HEROES!
THEY CAN'T...?
NOPE!! WHICH MEANS...
BUT...! HANG ON!

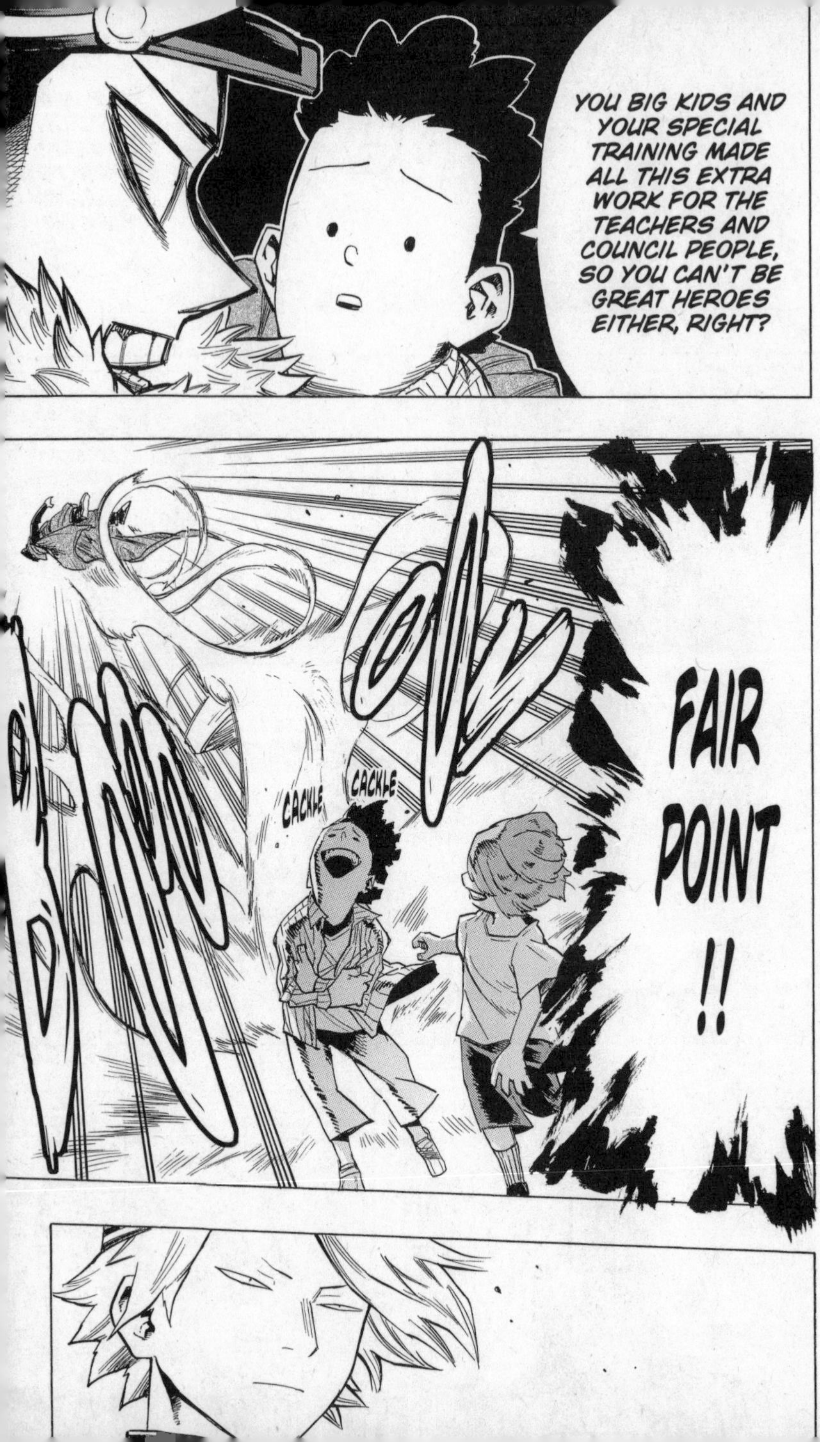
YOU BIG KIDS AND YOUR SPECIAL TRAINING MADE ALL THIS EXTRA WORK FOR THE TEACHERS AND COUNCIL PEOPLE, SO YOU CAN'T BE GREAT HEROES EITHER, RIGHT?
FAIR POINT !!
CACKLE
CACKLE

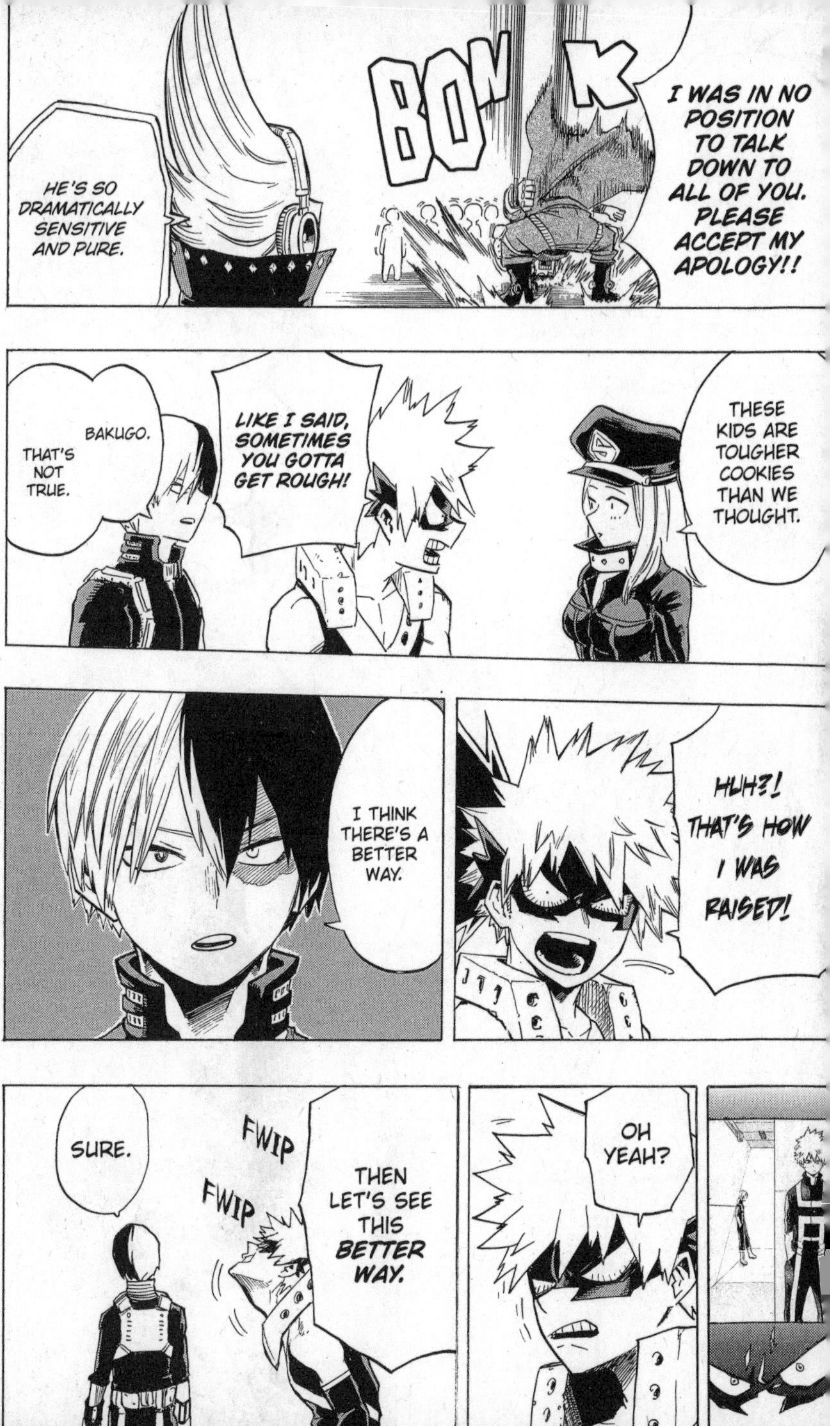
BONK
I WAS IN NO POSITION TO TALK DOWN TO ALL OF YOU. PLEASE ACCEPT MY APOLOGY!!
HE'S SO DRAMATICALLY SENSITIVE AND PURE.
THESE KIDS ARE TOUGHER COOKIES THAN WE THOUGHT.
LIKE I SAID, SOMETIMES YOU GOTTA GET ROUGH!
BAKUGO.
THAT'S NOT TRUE.
HUH?! THAT'S HOW I WAS RAISED!
I THINK THERE'S A BETTER WAY.
OH YEAH?
THEN LET'S SEE THIS BETTER WAY.
FWIP
FWIP
SURE.

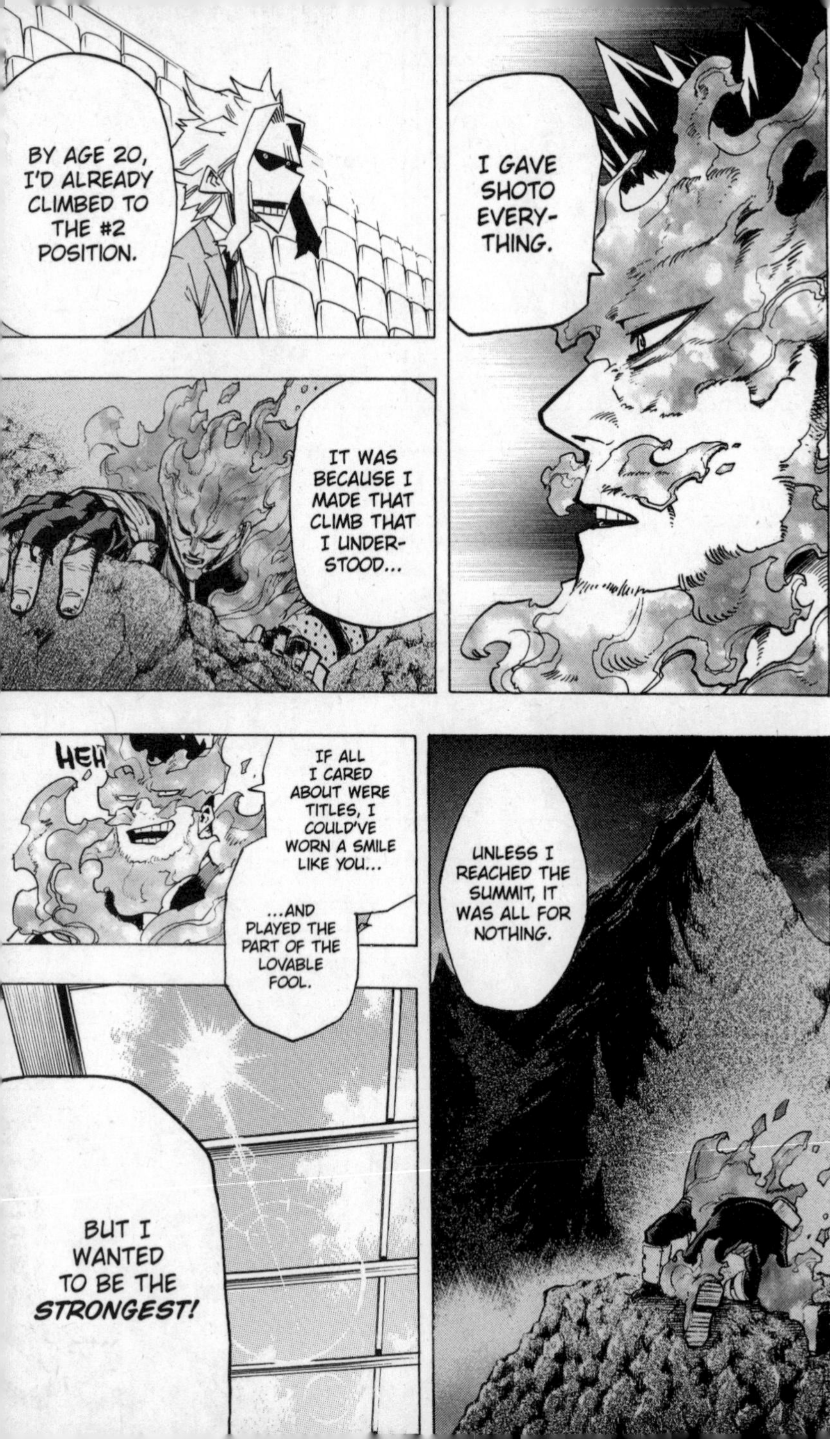
I GAVE SHOTO EVERY-THING.
BY AGE 20, I'D ALREADY CLIMBED TO THE #2 POSITION.
IT WAS BECAUSE I MADE THAT CLIMB THAT I UNDER-STOOD...
UNLESS I REACHED THE SUMMIT, IT WAS ALL FOR NOTHING.
HEH
IF ALL I CARED ABOUT WERE TITLES, I COULD'VE WORN A SMILE LIKE YOU...
...AND PLAYED THE PART OF THE LOVABLE FOOL.
BUT I WANTED TO BE THE *STRONGEST!*

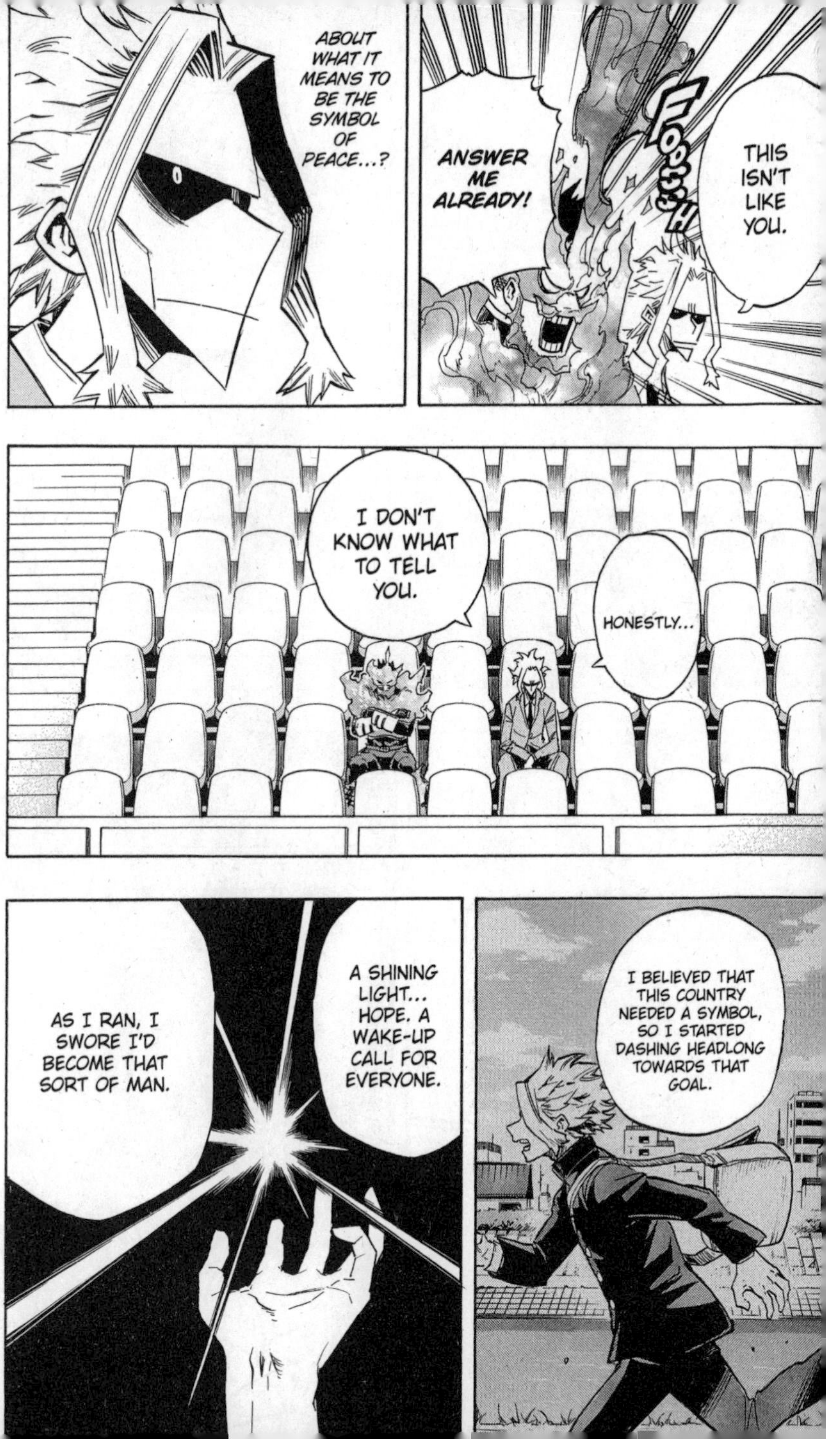
THIS ISN'T LIKE YOU.
FOOSH
ANSWER ME ALREADY!
ABOUT WHAT IT MEANS TO BE THE SYMBOL OF PEACE...?
HONESTLY...
I DON'T KNOW WHAT TO TELL YOU.
I BELIEVED THAT THIS COUNTRY NEEDED A SYMBOL, SO I STARTED DASHING HEADLONG TOWARDS THAT GOAL.
A SHINING LIGHT... HOPE. A WAKE-UP CALL FOR EVERYONE.
AS I RAN, I SWORE I'D BECOME THAT SORT OF MAN.

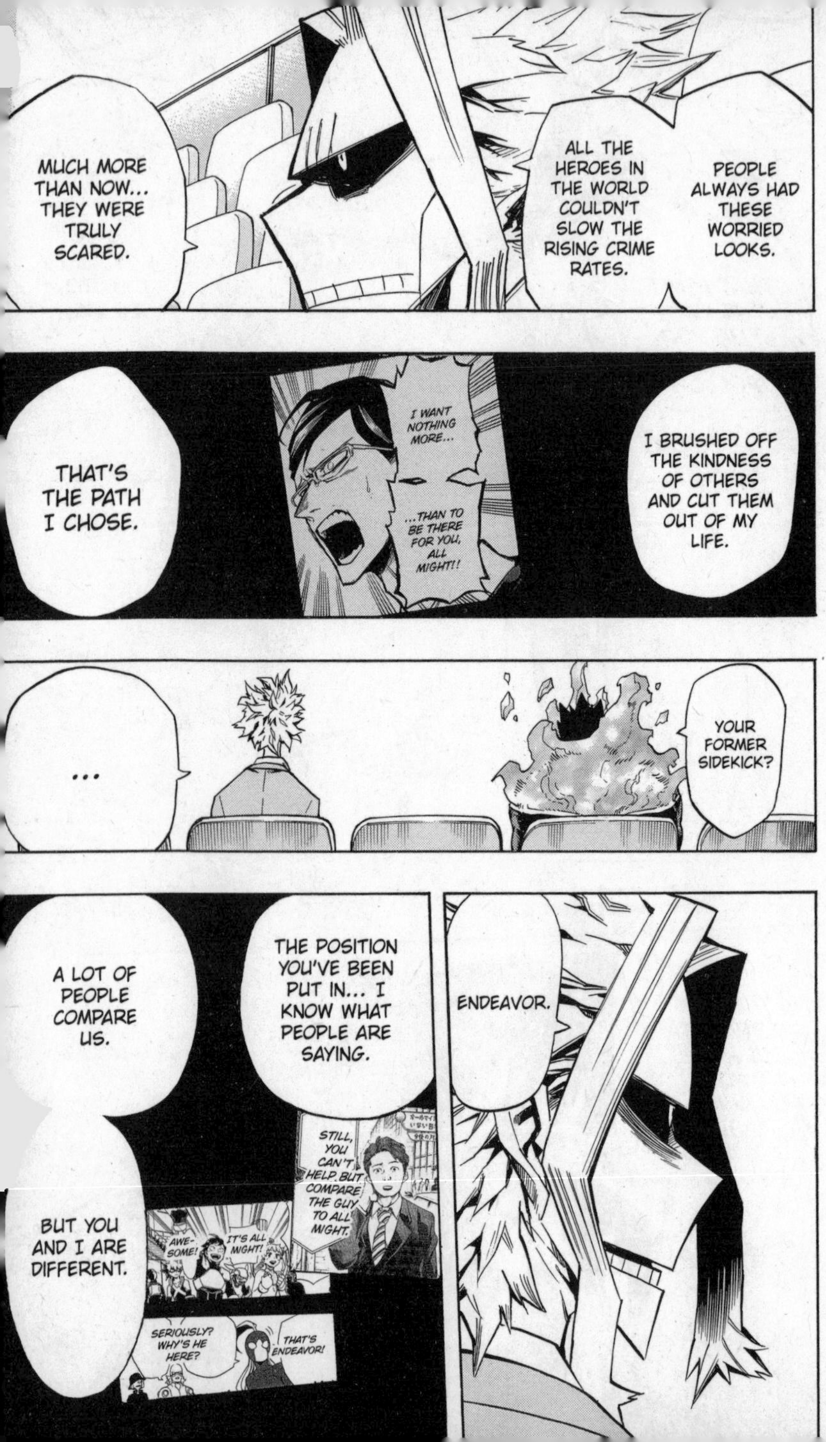
PEOPLE ALWAYS HAD THESE WORRIED LOOKS.
ALL THE HEROES IN THE WORLD COULDN'T SLOW THE RISING CRIME RATES.
MUCH MORE THAN NOW... THEY WERE TRULY SCARED.
I BRUSHED OFF THE KINDNESS OF OTHERS AND CUT THEM OUT OF MY LIFE.
I WANT NOTHING MORE...
...THAN TO BE THERE FOR YOU, ALL MIGHT!!
THAT'S THE PATH I CHOSE.
YOUR FORMER SIDEKICK?
...
ENDEAVOR.
THE POSITION YOU'VE BEEN PUT IN... I KNOW WHAT PEOPLE ARE SAYING.
A LOT OF PEOPLE COMPARE US.
STILL, YOU CAN'T HELP BUT COMPARE THE GUY TO ALL MIGHT.
IT'S ALL MIGHT!
AWE-SOME!
BUT YOU AND I ARE DIFFERENT.
THAT'S ENDEAVOR!
SERIOUSLY? WHY'S HE HERE?

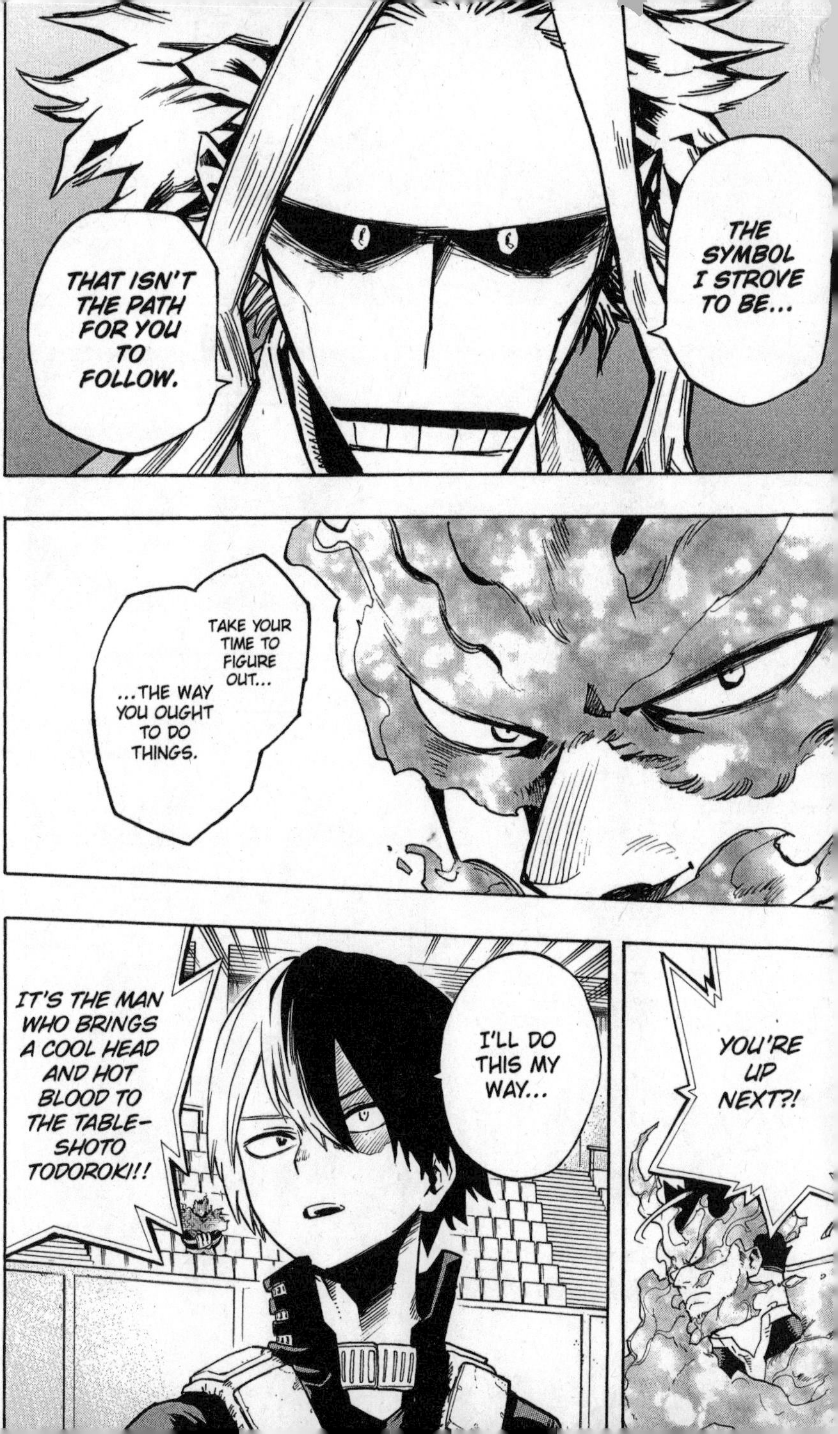
THE SYMBOL I STROVE TO BE...
THAT ISN'T THE PATH FOR YOU TO FOLLOW.
TAKE YOUR TIME TO FIGURE OUT...
...THE WAY YOU OUGHT TO DO THINGS.
YOU'RE UP NEXT?!
I'LL DO THIS MY WAY...
IT'S THE MAN WHO BRINGS A COOL HEAD AND HOT BLOOD TO THE TABLE—SHOTO TODOROKI!!

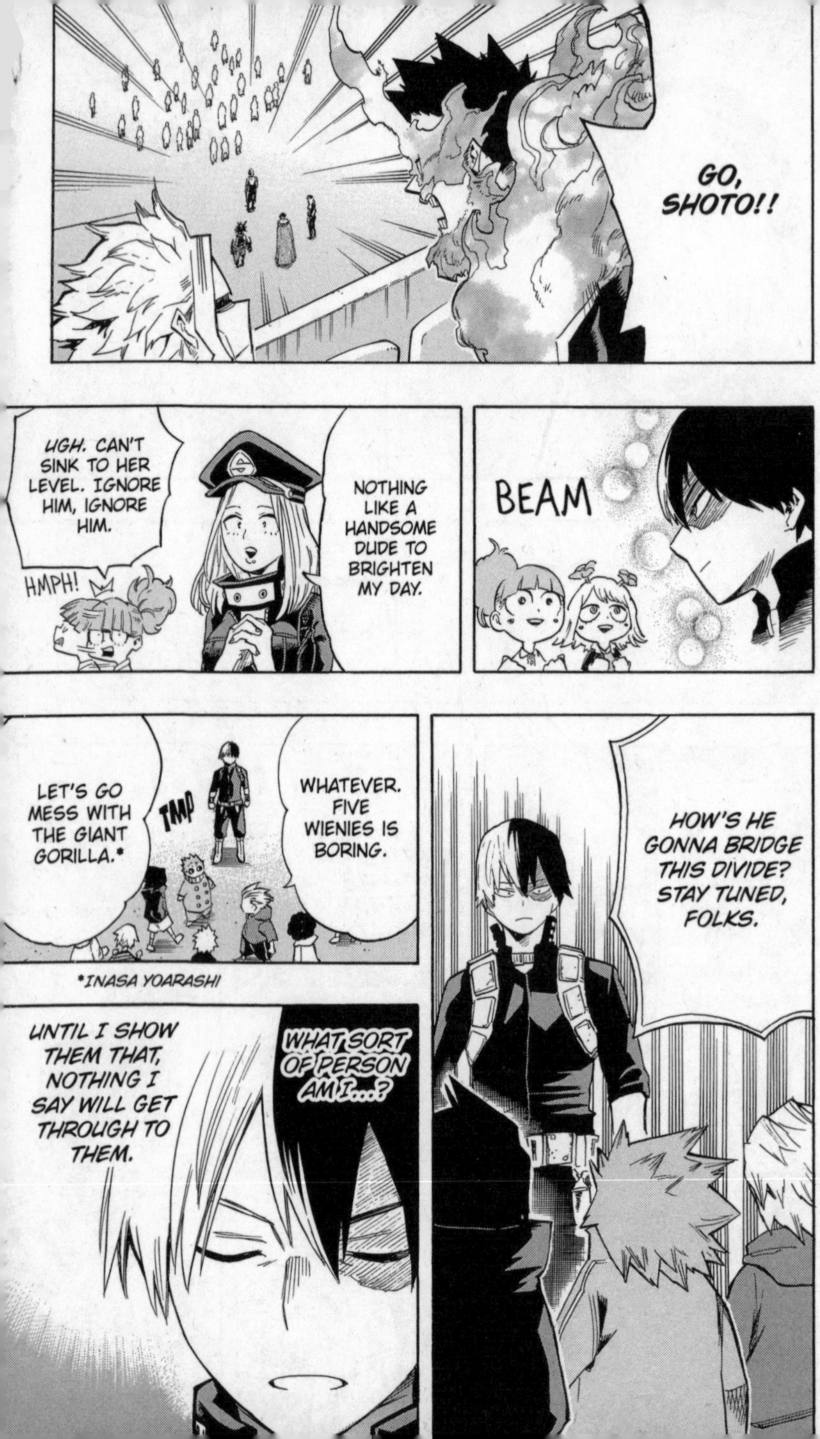
GO, SHOTO!!
BEAM
NOTHING LIKE A HANDSOME DUDE TO BRIGHTEN MY DAY.
UGH. CAN'T SINK TO HER LEVEL. IGNORE HIM, IGNORE HIM.
HMPH!
HOW'S HE GONNA BRIDGE THIS DIVIDE? STAY TUNED, FOLKS.
WHATEVER. FIVE WIENIES IS BORING.
TMP
LET'S GO MESS WITH THE GIANT GORILLA.*
*INASA YOARASHI
WHAT SORT OF PERSON AM I...?
UNTIL I SHOW THEM THAT, NOTHING I SAY WILL GET THROUGH TO THEM.

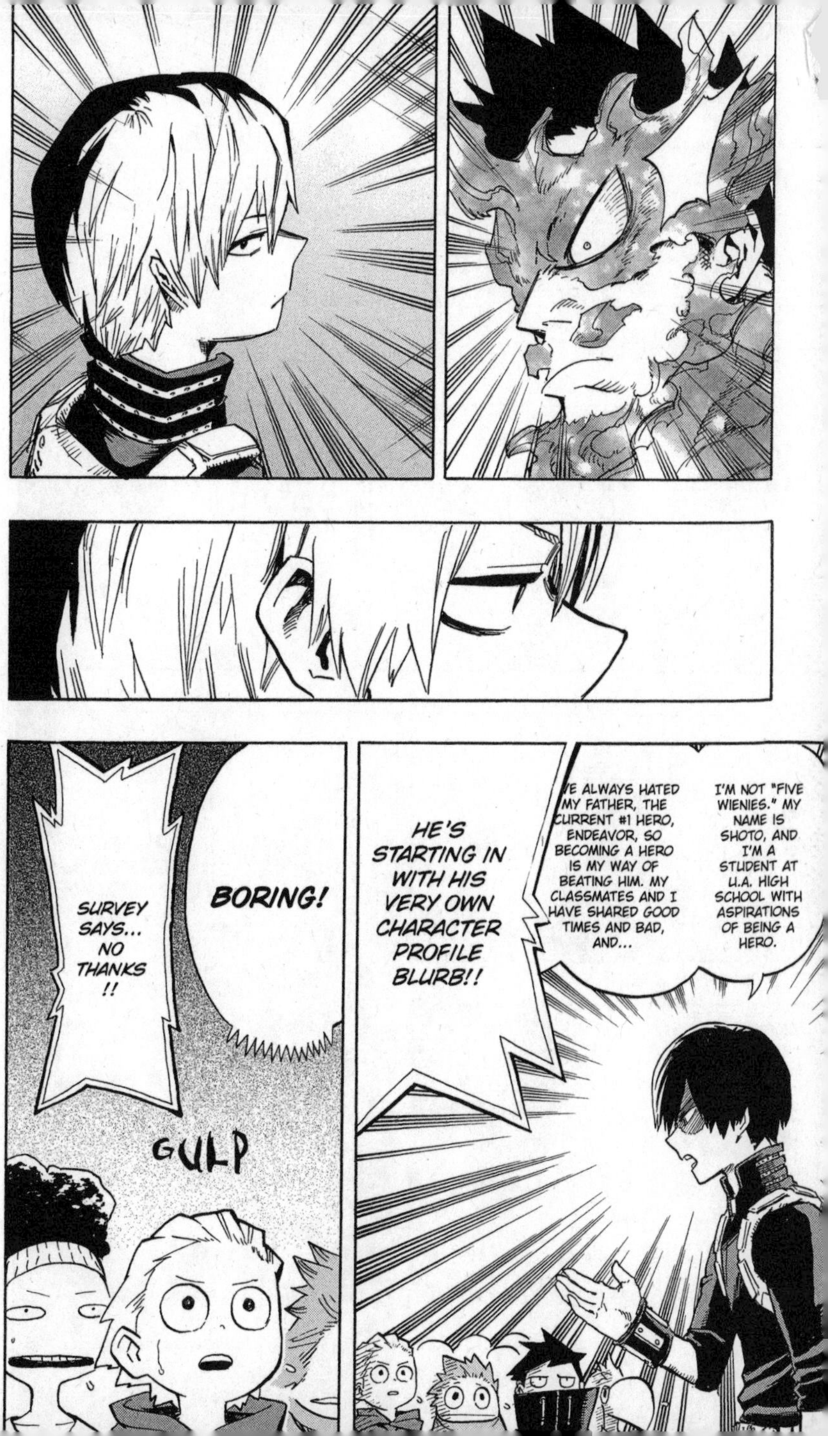

I'M NOT "FIVE WIENIES." MY NAME IS SHOTO, AND I'M A STUDENT AT U.A. HIGH SCHOOL WITH ASPIRATIONS OF BEING A HERO.
VE ALWAYS HATED MY FATHER, THE CURRENT #1 HERO, ENDEAVOR, SO BECOMING A HERO IS MY WAY OF BEATING HIM. MY CLASSMATES AND I HAVE SHARED GOOD TIMES AND BAD, AND...
HE'S STARTING IN WITH HIS VERY OWN CHARACTER PROFILE BLURB!!
BORING!
SURVEY SAYS... NO THANKS !!
GULP

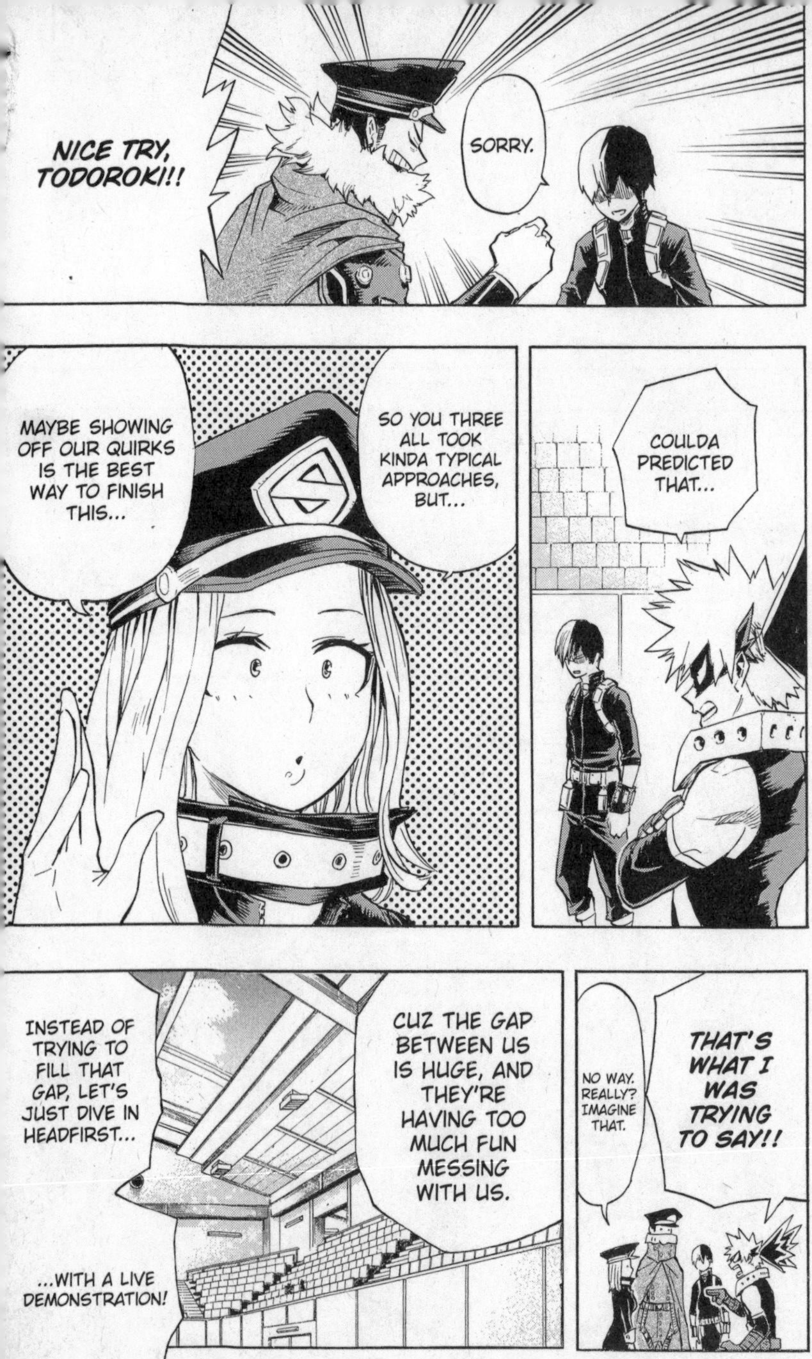
SORRY.
NICE TRY, TODOROKI!!
COULDA PREDICTED THAT...
SO YOU THREE ALL TOOK KINDA TYPICAL APPROACHES, BUT...
MAYBE SHOWING OFF OUR QUIRKS IS THE BEST WAY TO FINISH THIS...
THAT'S WHAT I WAS TRYING TO SAY!!
NO WAY. REALLY? IMAGINE THAT.
CUZ THE GAP BETWEEN US IS HUGE, AND THEY'RE HAVING TOO MUCH FUN MESSING WITH US.
INSTEAD OF TRYING TO FILL THAT GAP, LET'S JUST DIVE IN HEADFIRST...
...WITH A LIVE DEMONSTRATION!

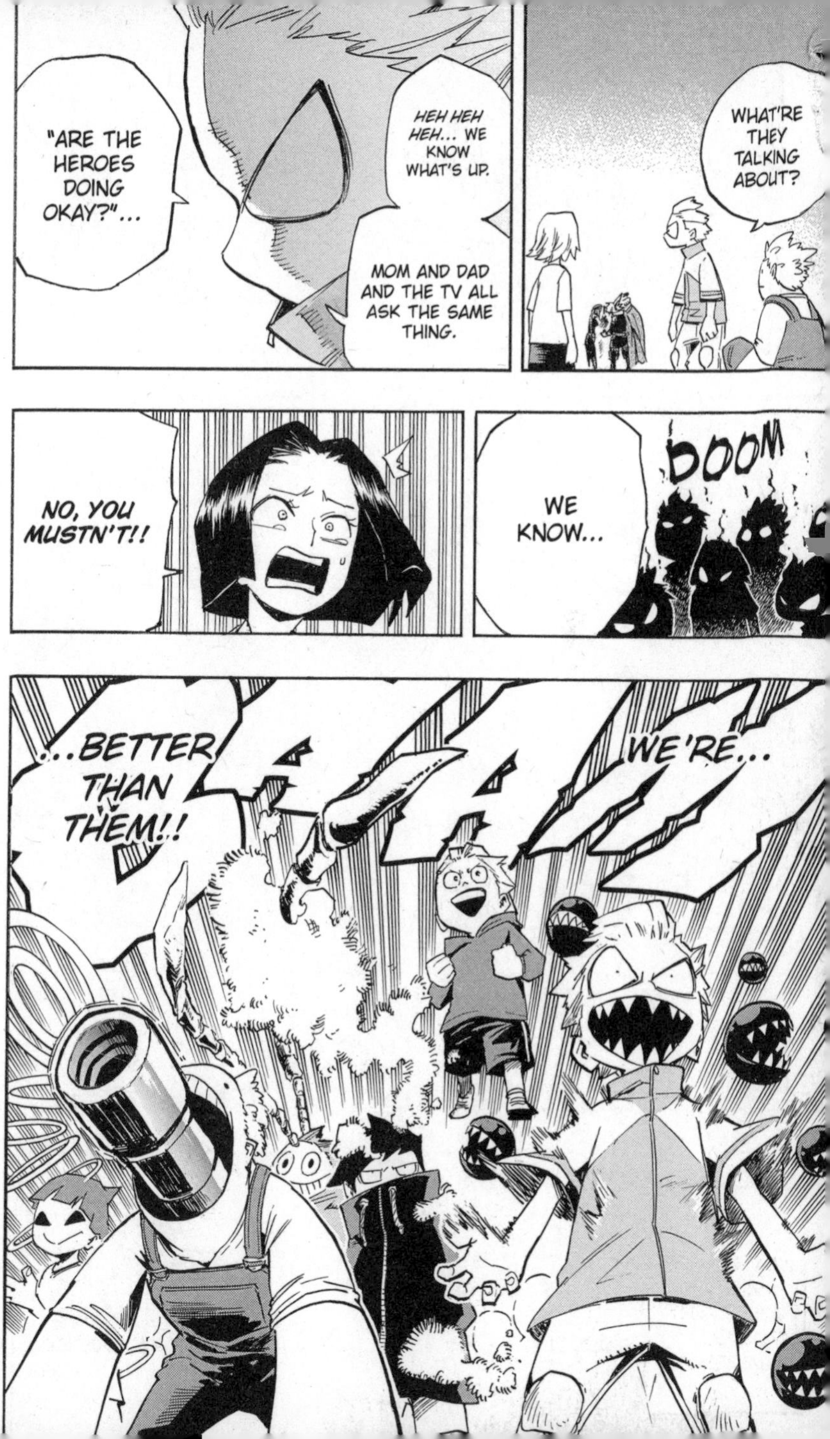
WHAT'RE THEY TALKING ABOUT?
HEH HEH HEH... WE KNOW WHAT'S UP.
MOM AND DAD AND THE TV ALL ASK THE SAME THING.
"ARE THE HEROES DOING OKAY?"...
WE KNOW...
DOOM
NO, YOU MUSTN'T!!
WE'RE...
...BETTER THAN THEM!!

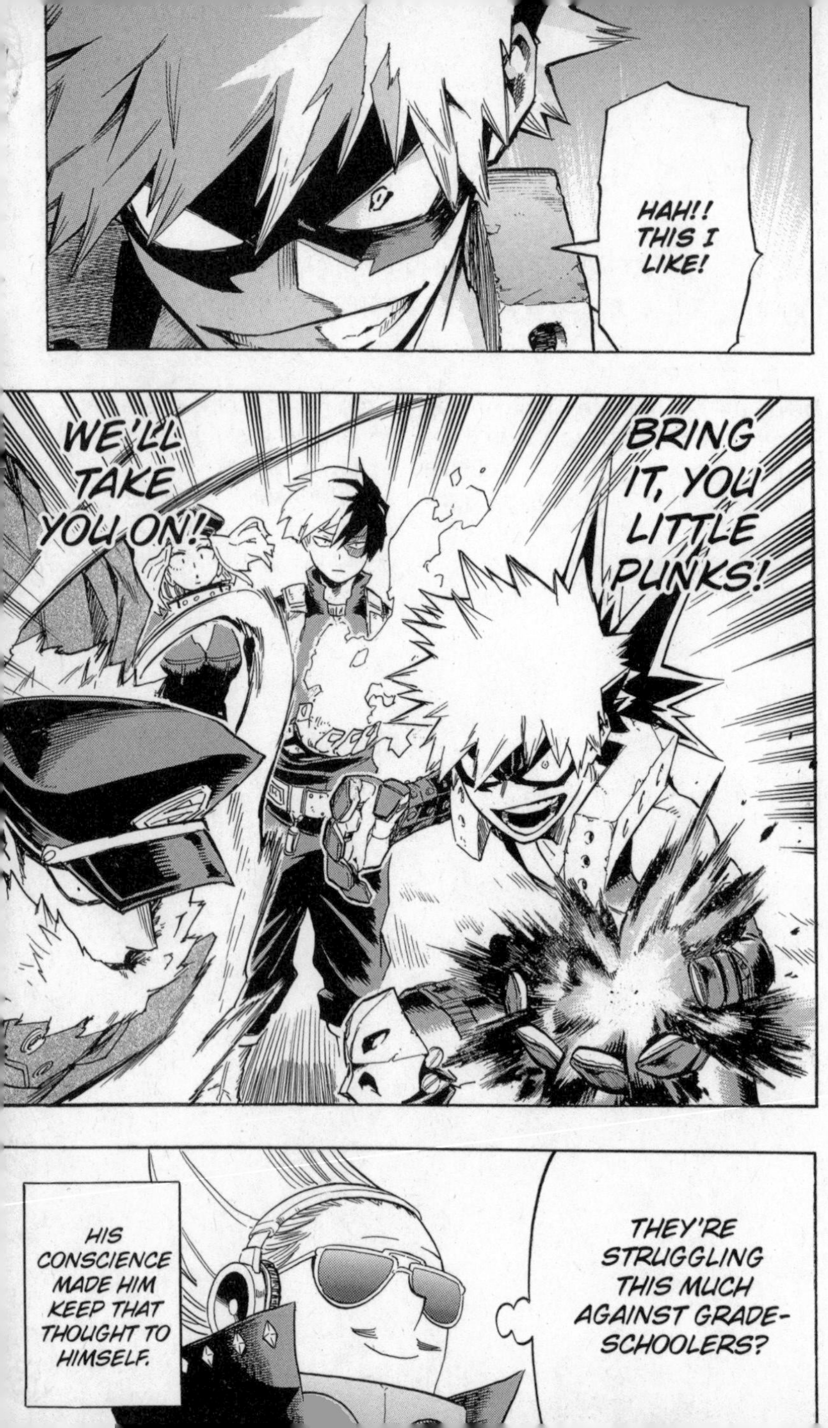
HAH!! THIS I LIKE!
BRING IT, YOU LITTLE PUNKS!
WE'LL TAKE YOU ON!!
THEY'RE STRUGGLING THIS MUCH AGAINST GRADE-SCHOOLERS?
HIS CONSCIENCE MADE HIM KEEP THAT THOUGHT TO HIMSELF.

IS THIS BECOMING A TRADITION?!

THE "I GOT GIFTED AN ILLUSTRATION" CORNER!! + THE AFTERWORD, A BIT EARLY

Volume 4 of *Vigilantes* is out in Japan, and it's got some exciting developments! The story's only getting more interesting, so be sure to check it out!! Also, I received another piece of commemorative art, so thank you, Betten Sensei!!

Back in our department, volume 19 will see the start of the school festival, so get hyped!!

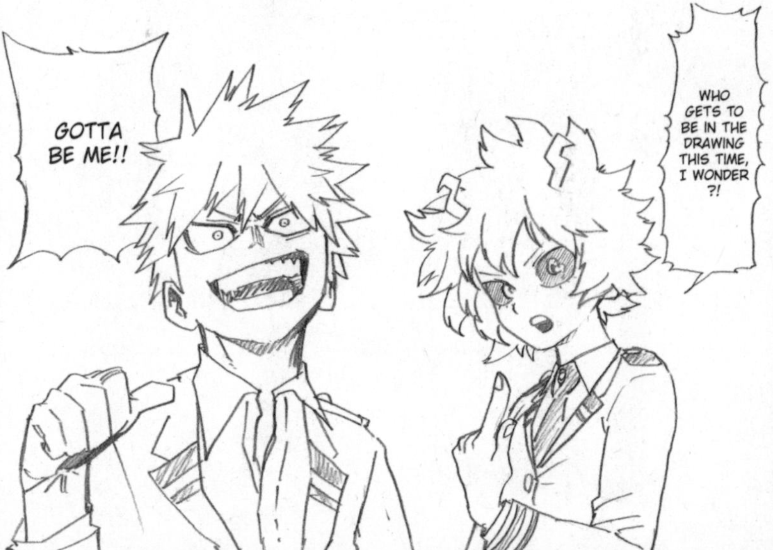
WHO GETS TO BE IN THE DRAWING THIS TIME, I WONDER ?!
GOTTA BE ME!!

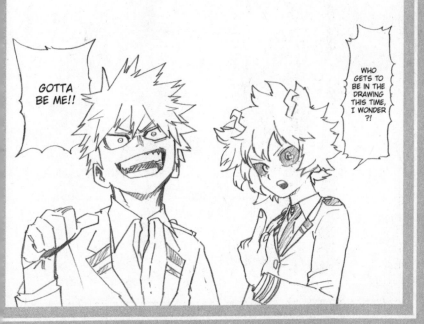

No. 166 - Be Proud, License Trainees

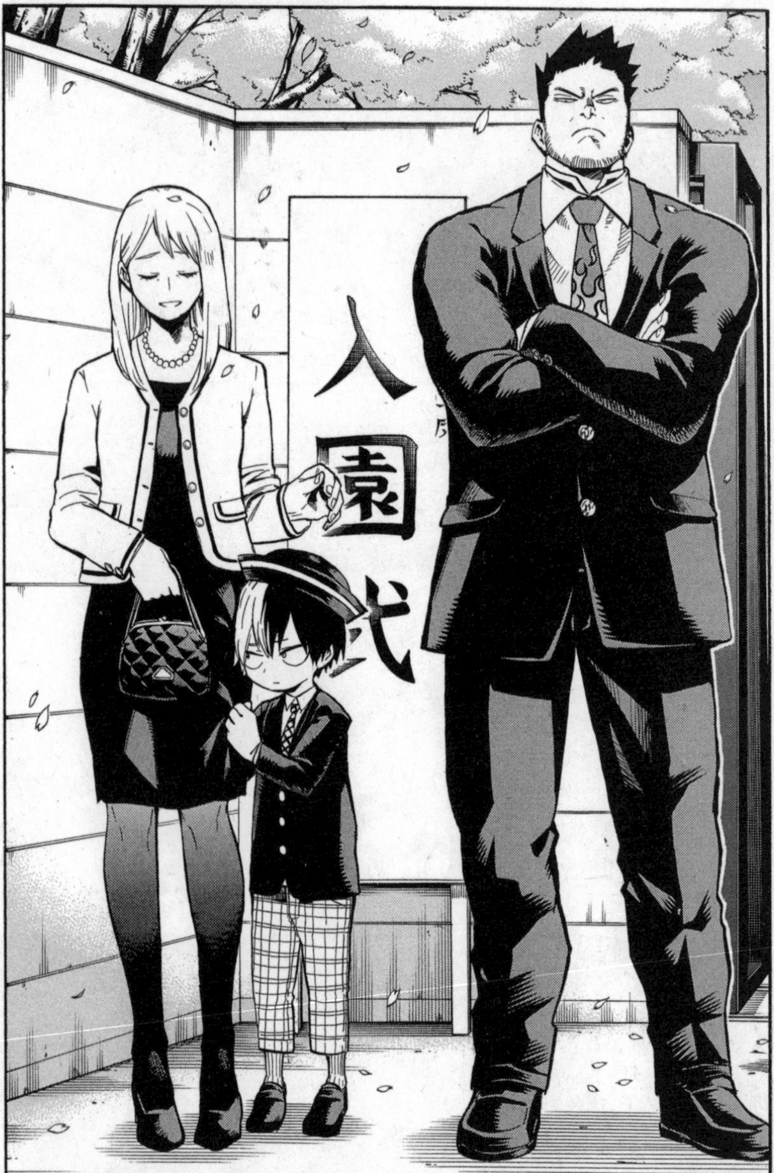
入園式

*SIGN: KINDERGARTEN ENTRANCE CEREMONY

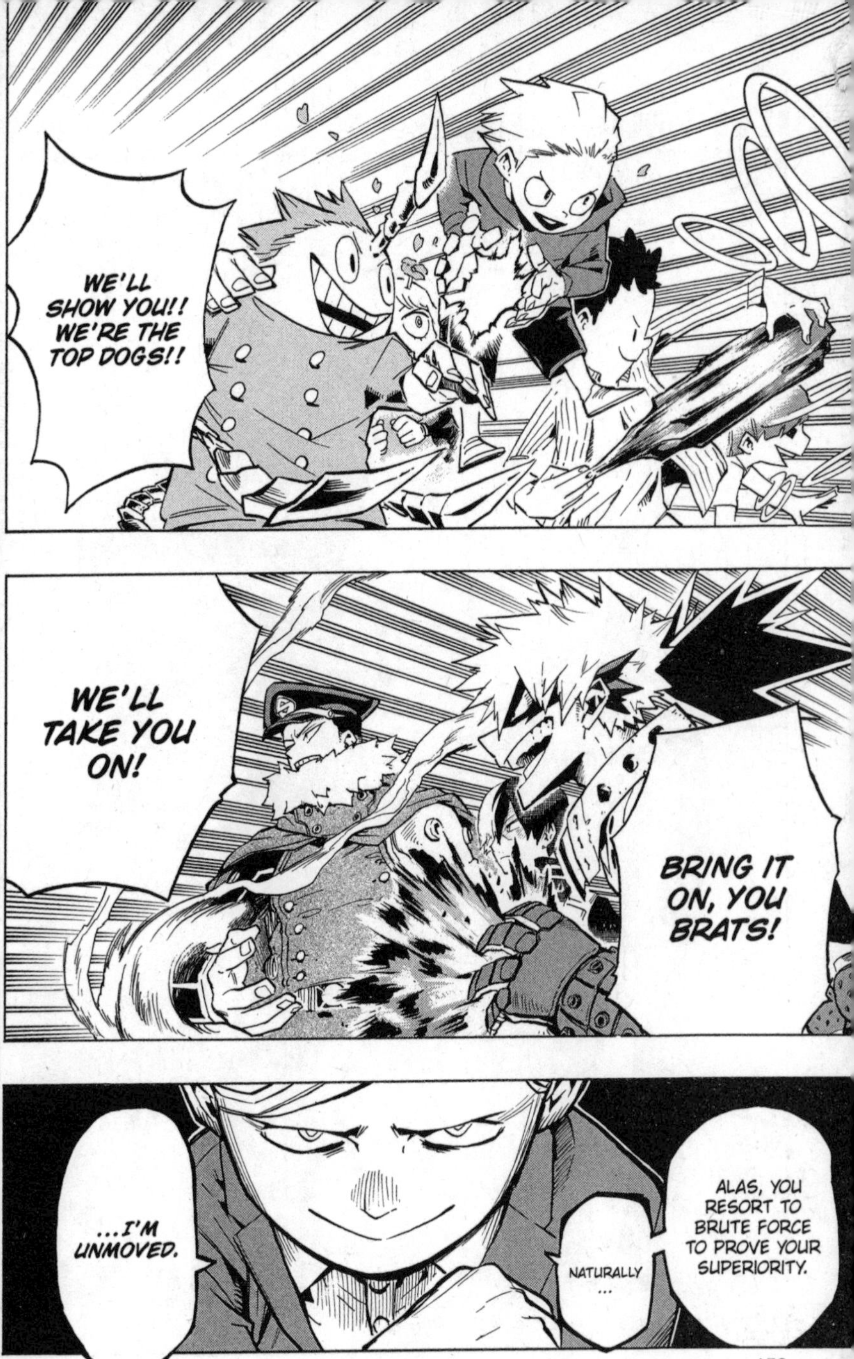
WE'LL SHOW YOU!! WE'RE THE TOP DOGS!!
BRING IT ON, YOU BRATS!
WE'LL TAKE YOU ON!
ALAS, YOU RESORT TO BRUTE FORCE TO PROVE YOUR SUPERIORITY.
NATURALLY...
...I'M UNMOVED.

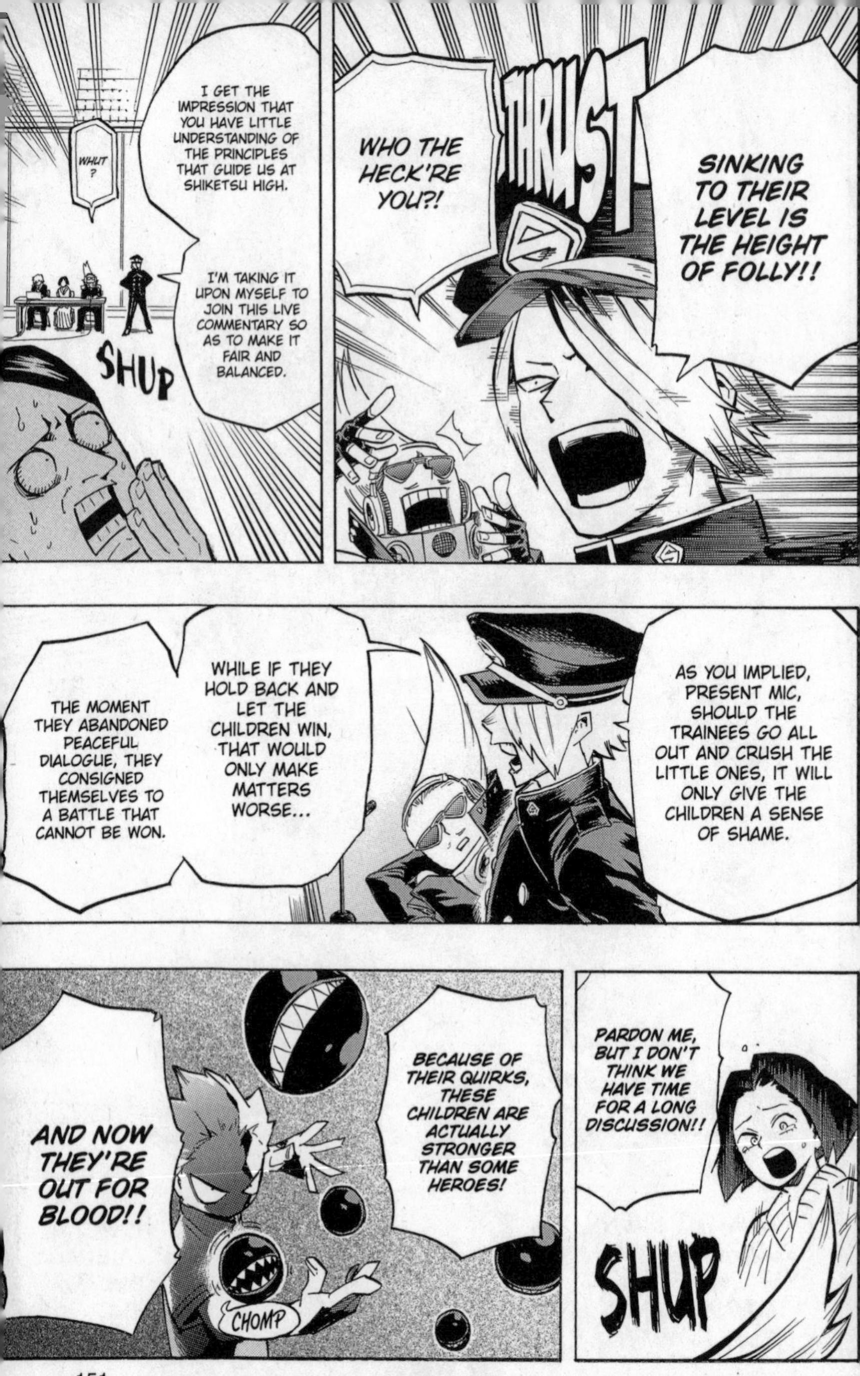
SINKING TO THEIR LEVEL IS THE HEIGHT OF FOLLY!!
THRUST
WHO THE HECK'RE YOU?!
I GET THE IMPRESSION THAT YOU HAVE LITTLE UNDERSTANDING OF THE PRINCIPLES THAT GUIDE US AT SHIKETSU HIGH.
WHUT ?
I'M TAKING IT UPON MYSELF TO JOIN THIS LIVE COMMENTARY SO AS TO MAKE IT FAIR AND BALANCED.
SHUP
AS YOU IMPLIED, PRESENT MIC, SHOULD THE TRAINEES GO ALL OUT AND CRUSH THE LITTLE ONES, IT WILL ONLY GIVE THE CHILDREN A SENSE OF SHAME.
WHILE IF THEY HOLD BACK AND LET THE CHILDREN WIN, THAT WOULD ONLY MAKE MATTERS WORSE...
THE MOMENT THEY ABANDONED PEACEFUL DIALOGUE, THEY CONSIGNED THEMSELVES TO A BATTLE THAT CANNOT BE WON.
PARDON ME, BUT I DON'T THINK WE HAVE TIME FOR A LONG DISCUSSION!!
SHUP
BECAUSE OF THEIR QUIRKS, THESE CHILDREN ARE ACTUALLY STRONGER THAN SOME HEROES!
AND NOW THEY'RE OUT FOR BLOOD!!
CHOMP

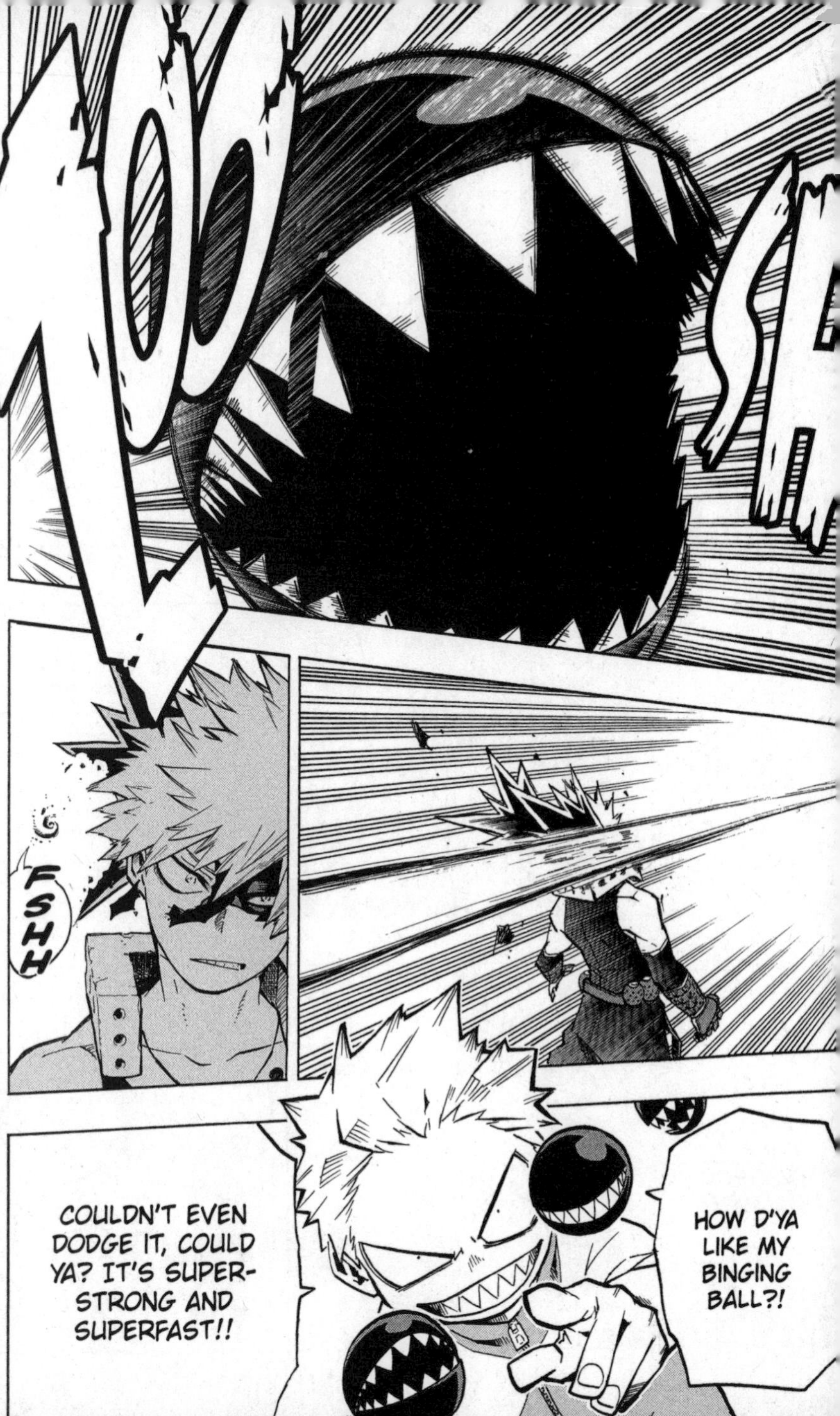
FSHH
HOW D'YA LIKE MY BINGING BALL?!
COULDN'T EVEN DODGE IT, COULD YA? IT'S SUPER-STRONG AND SUPERFAST!!

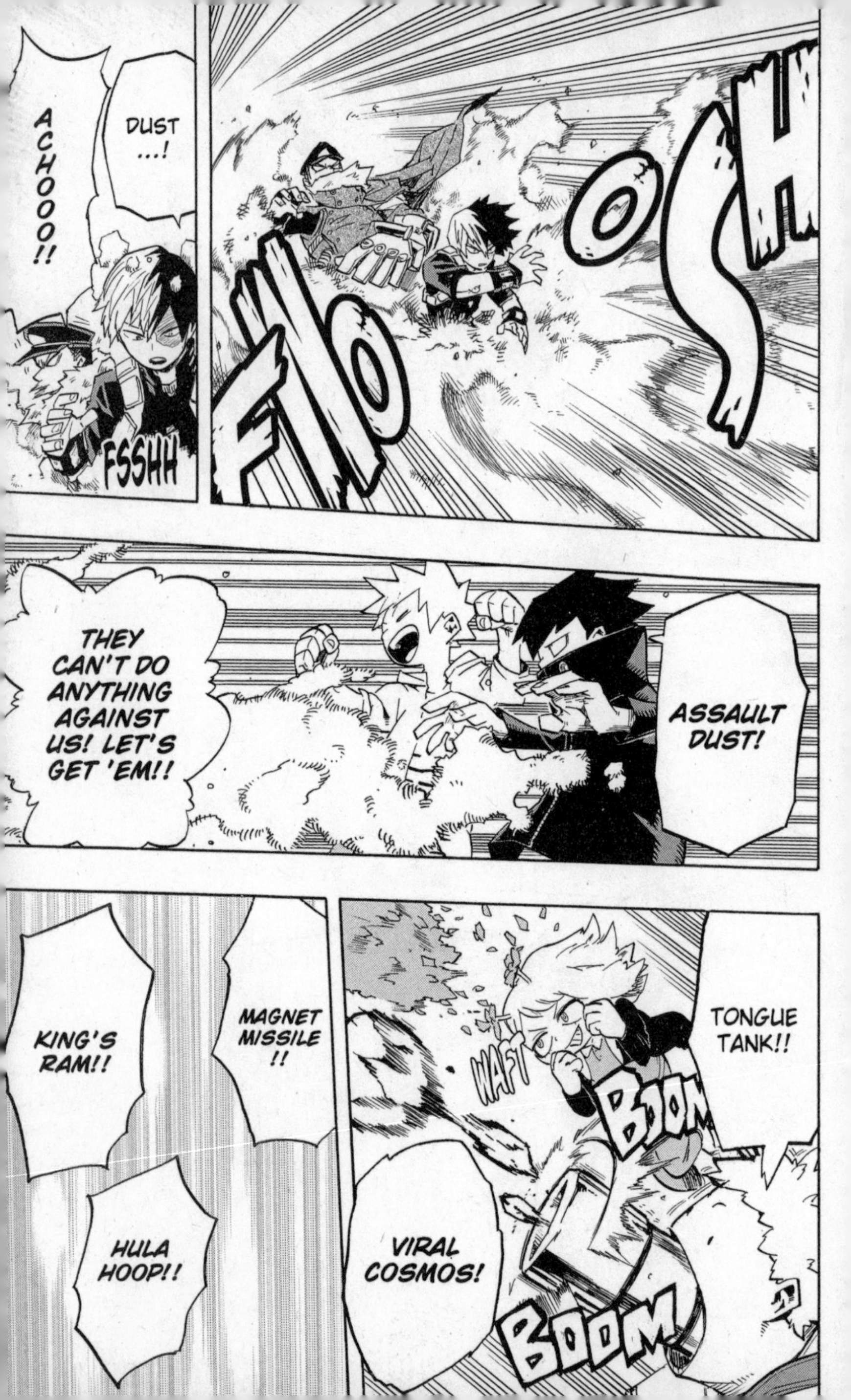
DUST ...!
ACHOOOO!!
FSSHH
ASSAULT DUST!
THEY CAN'T DO ANYTHING AGAINST US! LET'S GET 'EM!!
TONGUE TANK!!
WAFT
BOOM
VIRAL COSMOS!
BOOM
MAGNET MISSILE !!
KING'S RAM!!
HULA HOOP!!

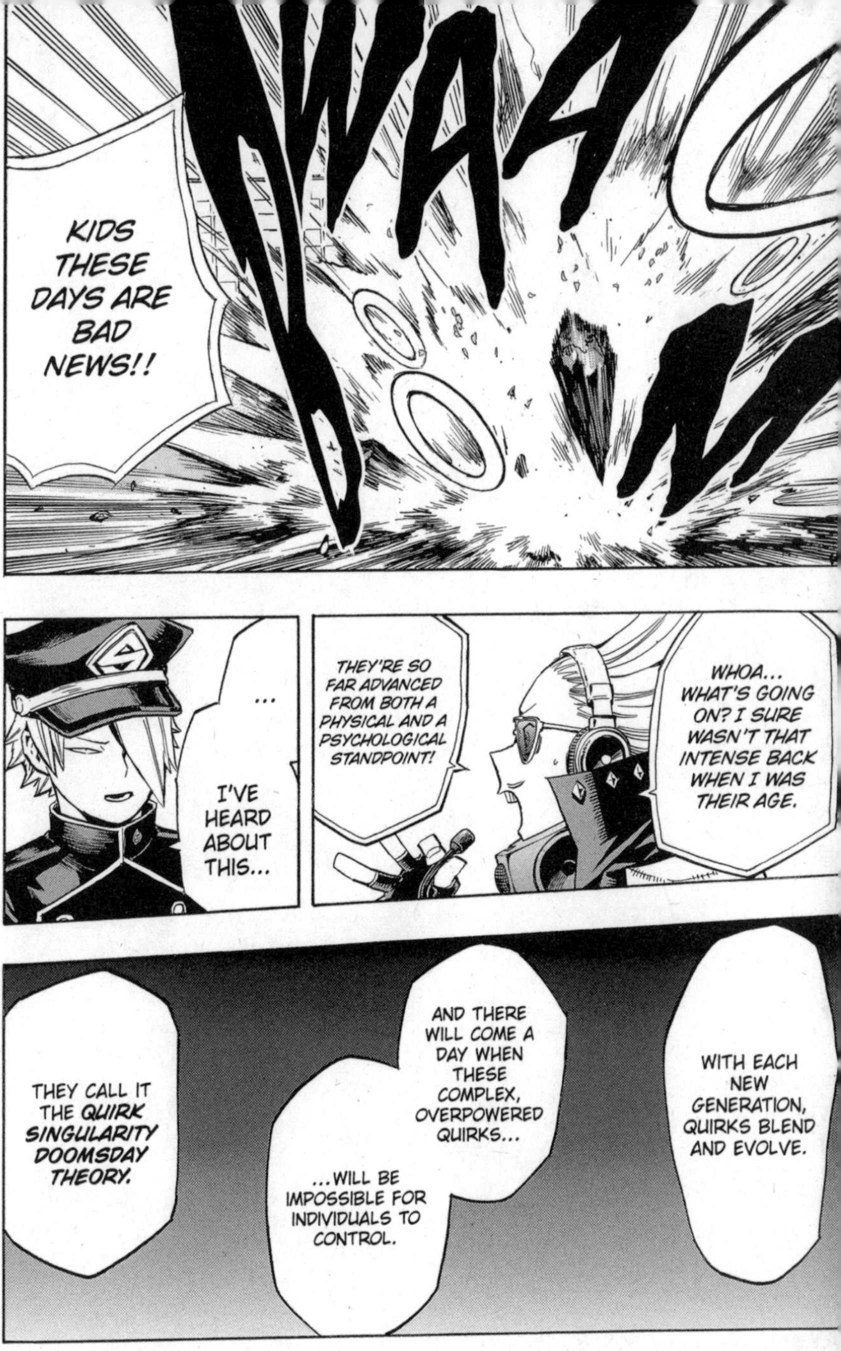
KIDS THESE DAYS ARE BAD NEWS!!
WHOA... WHAT'S GOING ON? I SURE WASN'T THAT INTENSE BACK WHEN I WAS THEIR AGE.
THEY'RE SO FAR ADVANCED FROM BOTH A PHYSICAL AND A PSYCHOLOGICAL STANDPOINT!
...
I'VE HEARD ABOUT THIS...
WITH EACH NEW GENERATION, QUIRKS BLEND AND EVOLVE.
AND THERE WILL COME A DAY WHEN THESE COMPLEX, OVERPOWERED QUIRKS...
...WILL BE IMPOSSIBLE FOR INDIVIDUALS TO CONTROL.
THEY CALL IT THE QUIRK SINGULARITY DOOMSDAY THEORY.

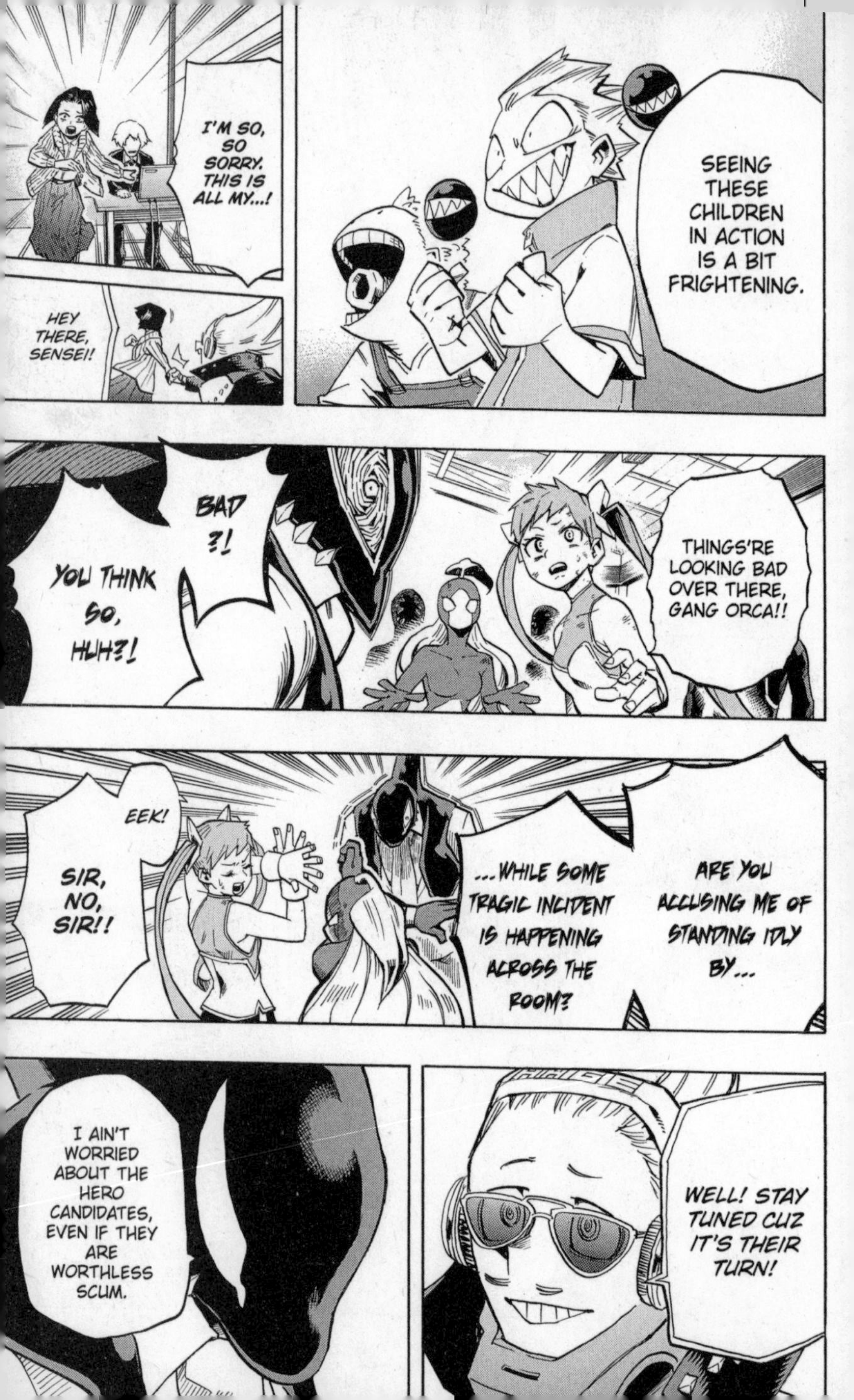
SEEING THESE CHILDREN IN ACTION IS A BIT FRIGHTENING.
I'M SO, SO SORRY. THIS IS ALL MY...!
HEY THERE, SENSEI!
THINGS'RE LOOKING BAD OVER THERE, GANG ORCA!!
BAD ?!
YOU THINK SO, HUH?!
ARE YOU ACCUSING ME OF STANDING IDLY BY...
...WHILE SOME TRAGIC INCIDENT IS HAPPENING ACROSS THE ROOM?
EEK!
SIR, NO, SIR!!
WELL! STAY TUNED CUZ IT'S THEIR TURN!
I AIN'T WORRIED ABOUT THE HERO CANDIDATES, EVEN IF THEY ARE WORTHLESS SCUM.

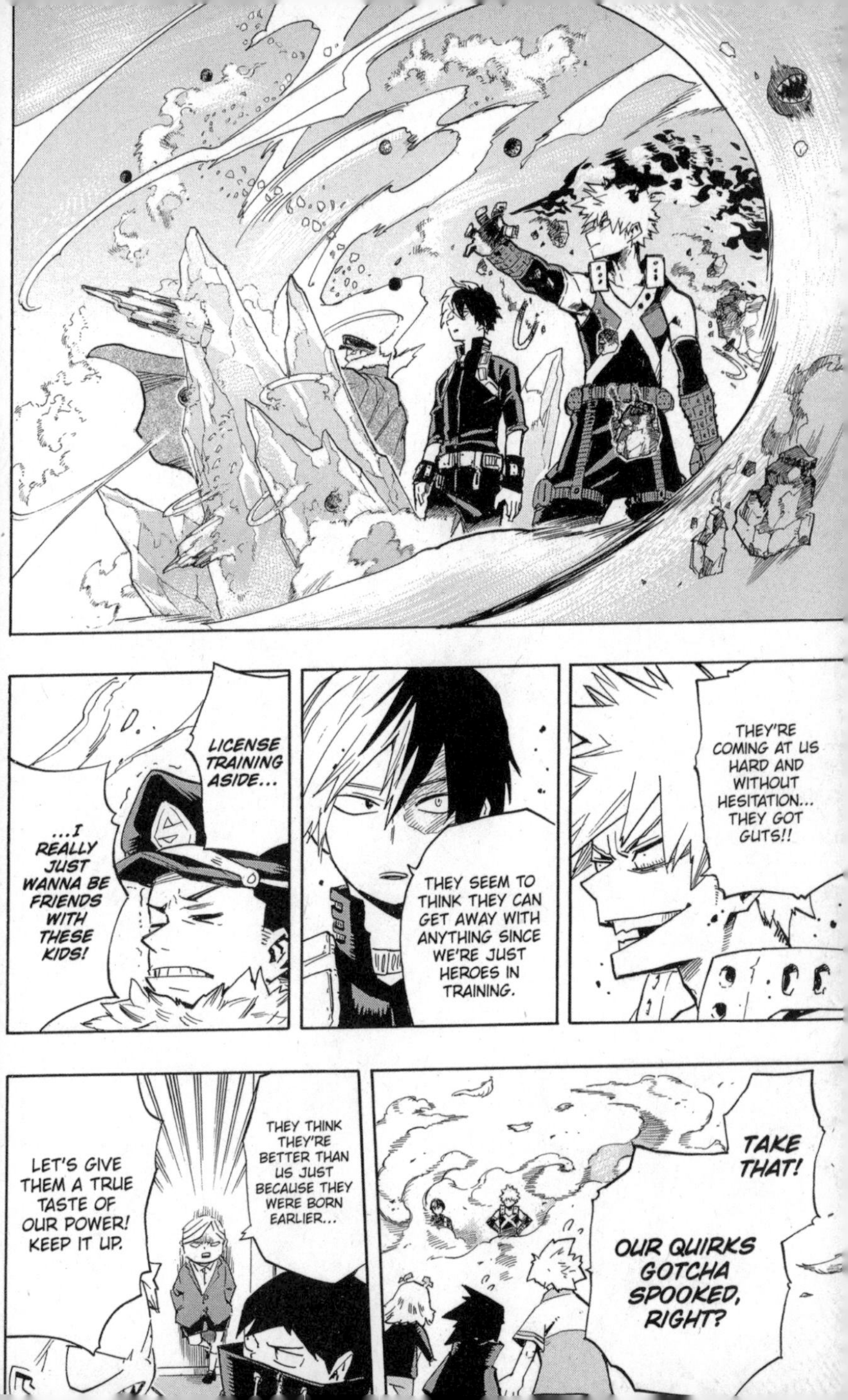
THEY'RE COMING AT US HARD AND WITHOUT HESITATION... THEY GOT GUTS!!
THEY SEEM TO THINK THEY CAN GET AWAY WITH ANYTHING SINCE WE'RE JUST HEROES IN TRAINING.
LICENSE TRAINING ASIDE...
...I REALLY JUST WANNA BE FRIENDS WITH THESE KIDS!
TAKE THAT!
OUR QUIRKS GOTCHA SPOOKED, RIGHT?
THEY THINK THEY'RE BETTER THAN US JUST BECAUSE THEY WERE BORN EARLIER...
LET'S GIVE THEM A TRUE TASTE OF OUR POWER! KEEP IT UP.

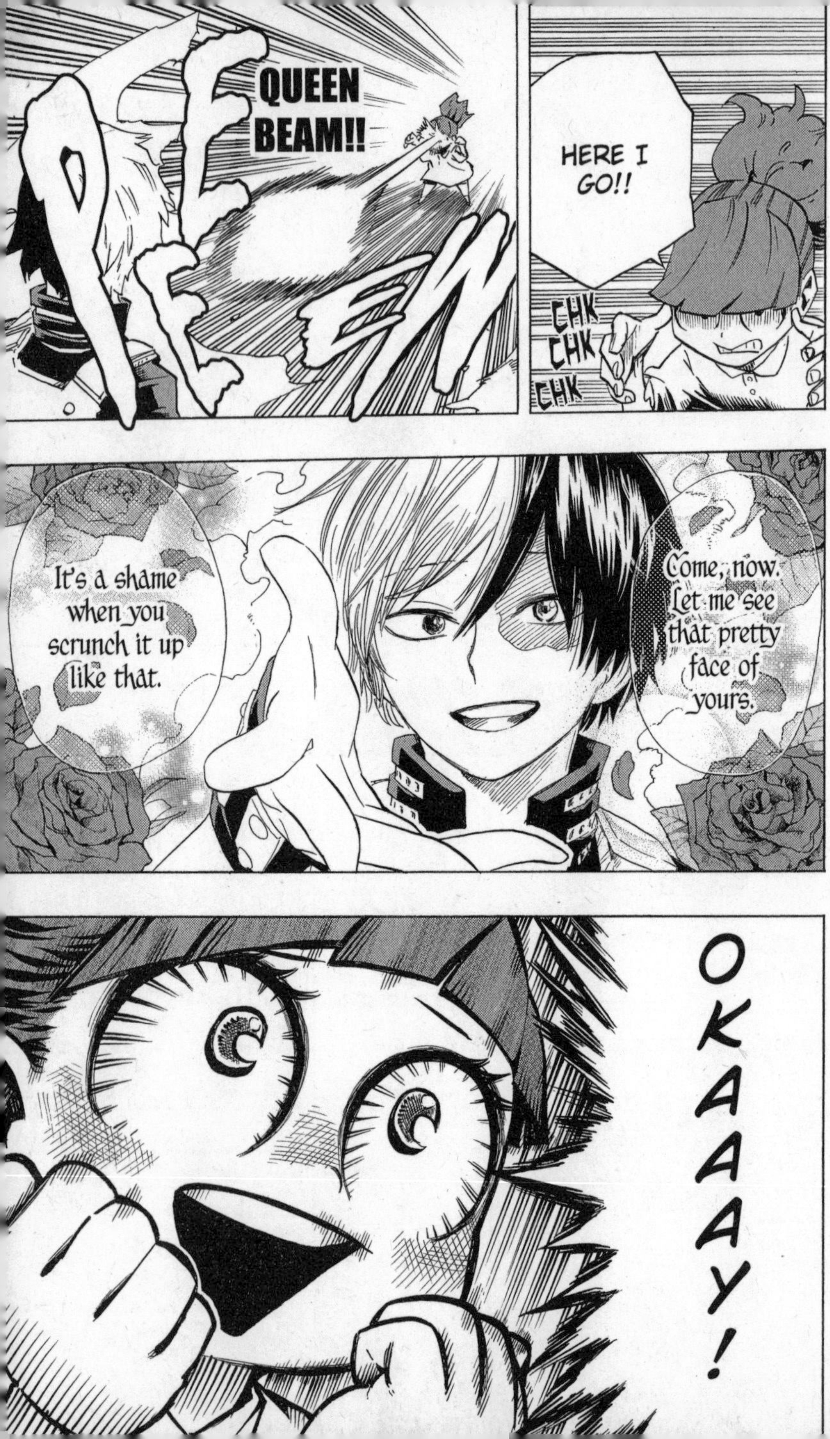
HERE I GO!!
CHK CHK CHK
QUEEN BEAM!!
Come, now. Let me see that pretty face of yours.
It's a shame when you scrunch it up like that.
OKAAAAY!

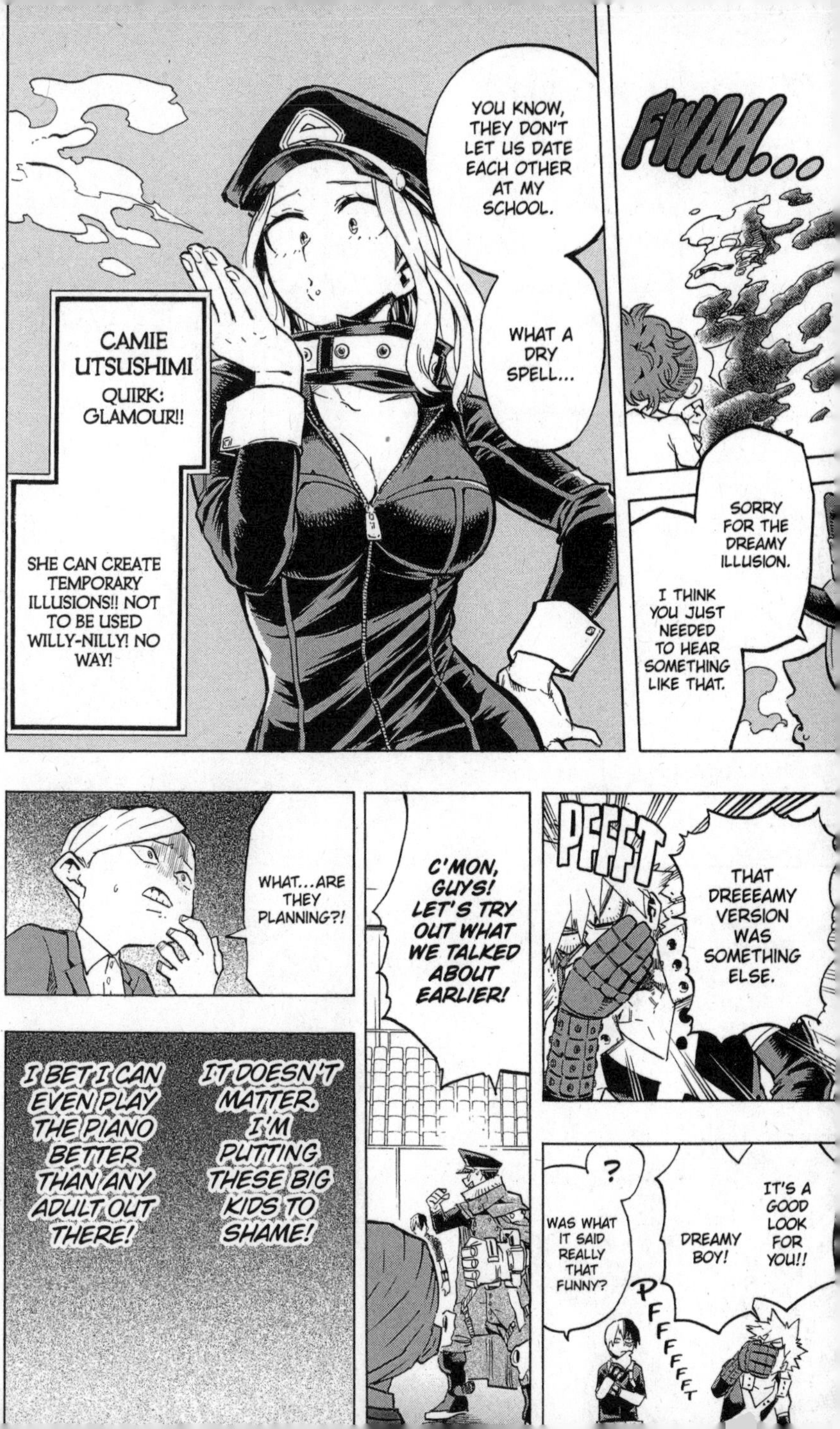
FWAH...
SORRY FOR THE DREAMY ILLUSION.
I THINK YOU JUST NEEDED TO HEAR SOMETHING LIKE THAT.
YOU KNOW, THEY DON'T LET US DATE EACH OTHER AT MY SCHOOL.
WHAT A DRY SPELL...
CAMIE UTSUSHIMI
QUIRK: GLAMOUR!!
SHE CAN CREATE TEMPORARY ILLUSIONS!! NOT TO BE USED WILLY-NILLY! NO WAY!
PFFFT
THAT DREEEAMY VERSION WAS SOMETHING ELSE.
IT'S A GOOD LOOK FOR YOU!!
DREAMY BOY!
PFFFFFFT
?
WAS WHAT IT SAID REALLY THAT FUNNY?
C'MON, GUYS! LET'S TRY OUT WHAT WE TALKED ABOUT EARLIER!
WHAT...ARE THEY PLANNING?!
IT DOESN'T MATTER. I'M PUTTING THESE BIG KIDS TO SHAME!
I BET I CAN EVEN PLAY THE PIANO BETTER THAN ANY ADULT OUT THERE!

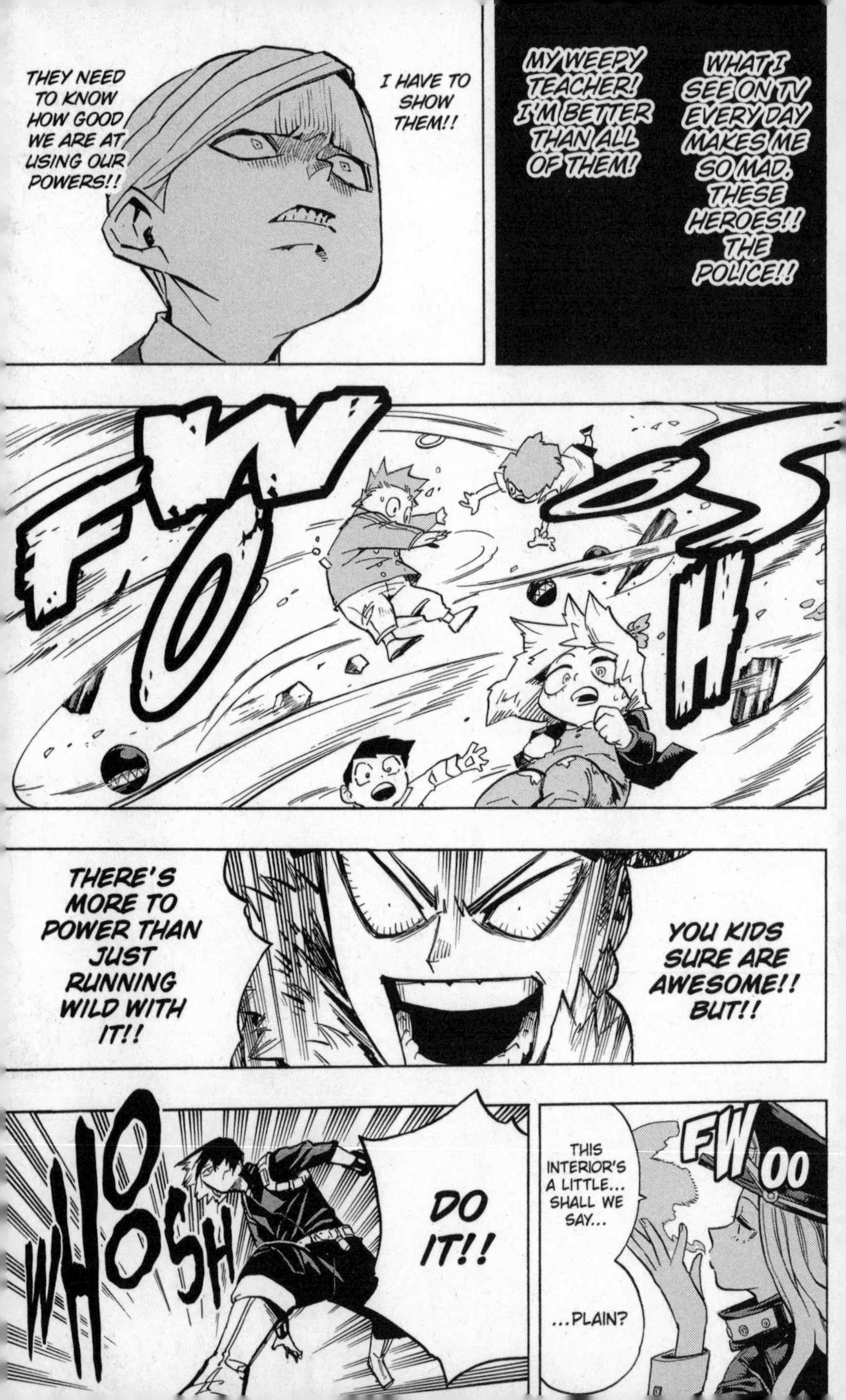
WHAT I SEE ON TV EVERY DAY MAKES ME SO MAD. THESE HEROES!! THE POLICE!!
MY WEEPY TEACHER! I'M BETTER THAN ALL OF THEM!
I HAVE TO SHOW THEM!!
THEY NEED TO KNOW HOW GOOD WE ARE AT USING OUR POWERS!!
FWOOSH
YOU KIDS SURE ARE AWESOME!! BUT!!
THERE'S MORE TO POWER THAN JUST RUNNING WILD WITH IT!!
FWOO
THIS INTERIOR'S A LITTLE... SHALL WE SAY...
...PLAIN?
DO IT!!
WHOOSH

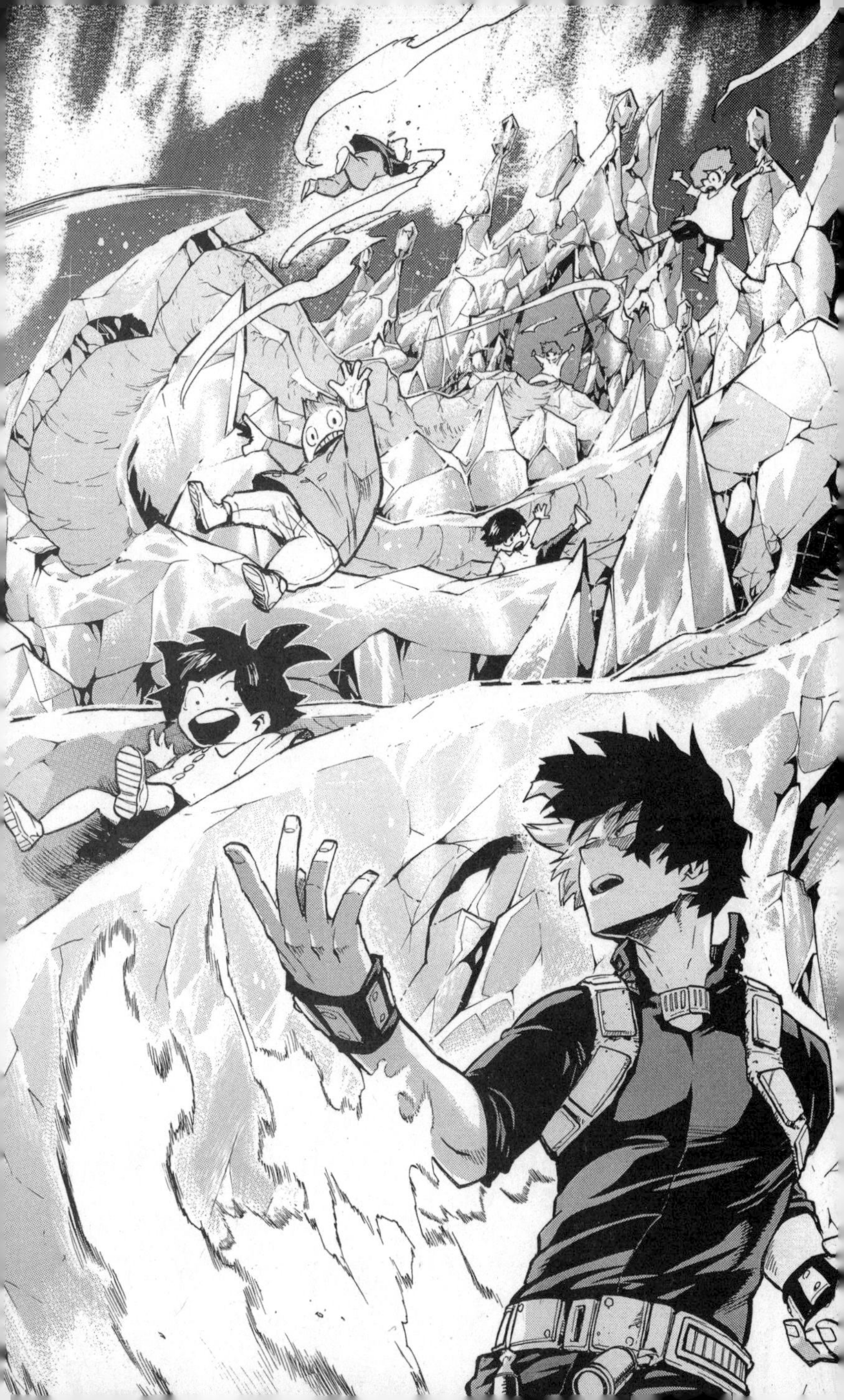

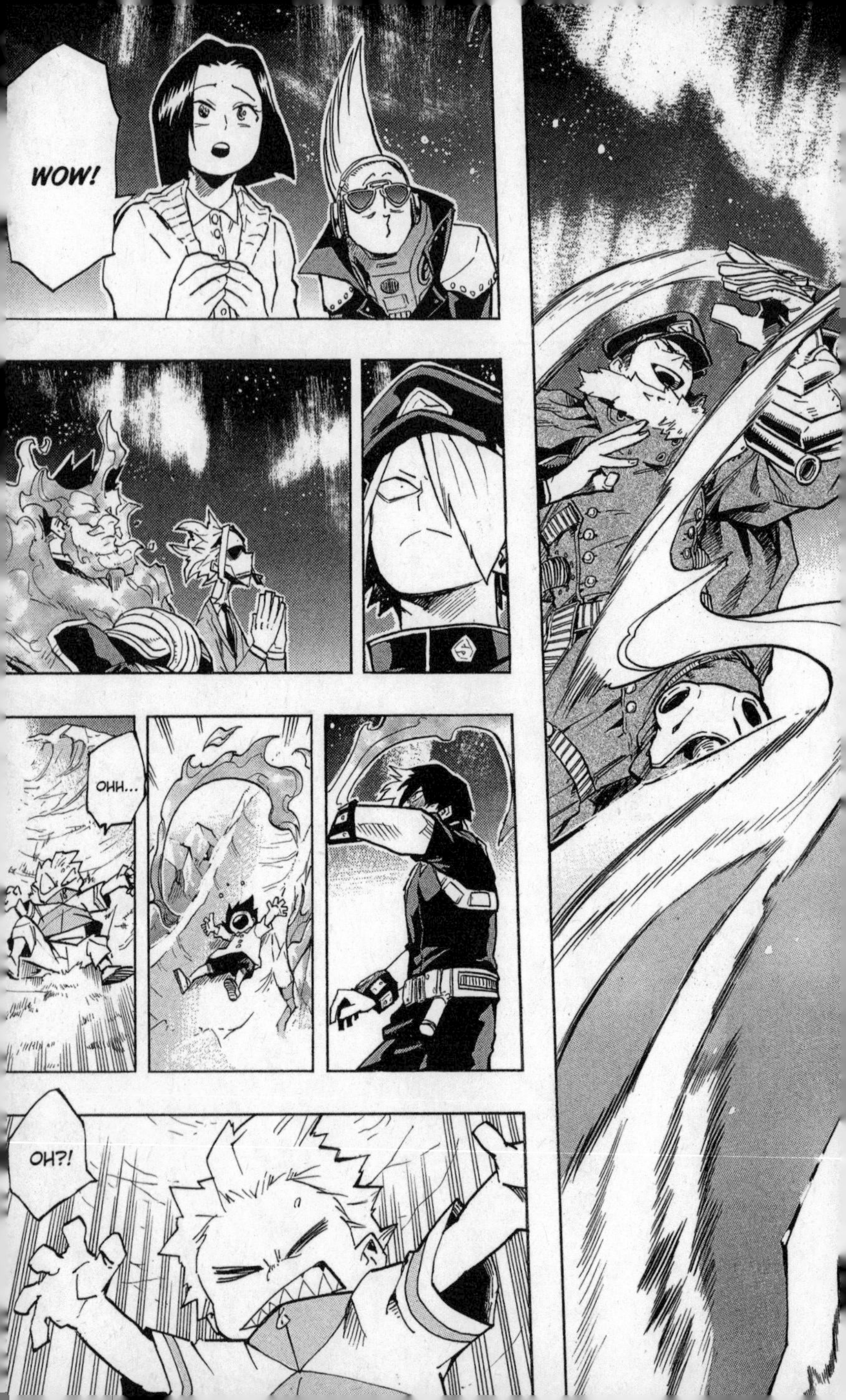
WOW!
OHH...
OH?!

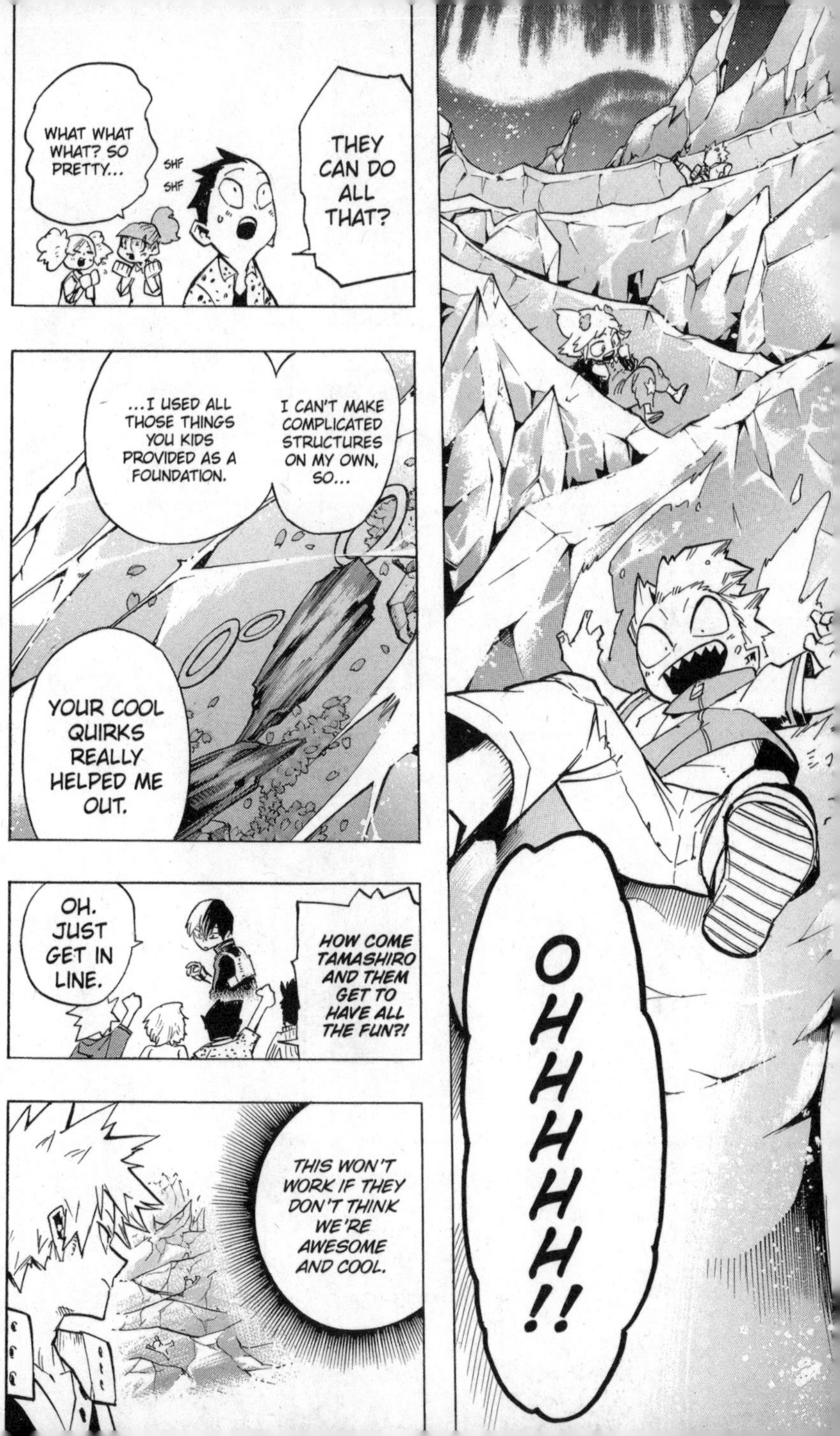
OHHHHHH!!
THEY CAN DO ALL THAT?
SHF SHF
WHAT WHAT WHAT? SO PRETTY...
I CAN'T MAKE COMPLICATED STRUCTURES ON MY OWN, SO...
...I USED ALL THOSE THINGS YOU KIDS PROVIDED AS A FOUNDATION.
YOUR COOL QUIRKS REALLY HELPED ME OUT.
HOW COME TAMASHIRO AND THEM GET TO HAVE ALL THE FUN?!
OH. JUST GET IN LINE.
THIS WON'T WORK IF THEY DON'T THINK WE'RE AWESOME AND COOL.

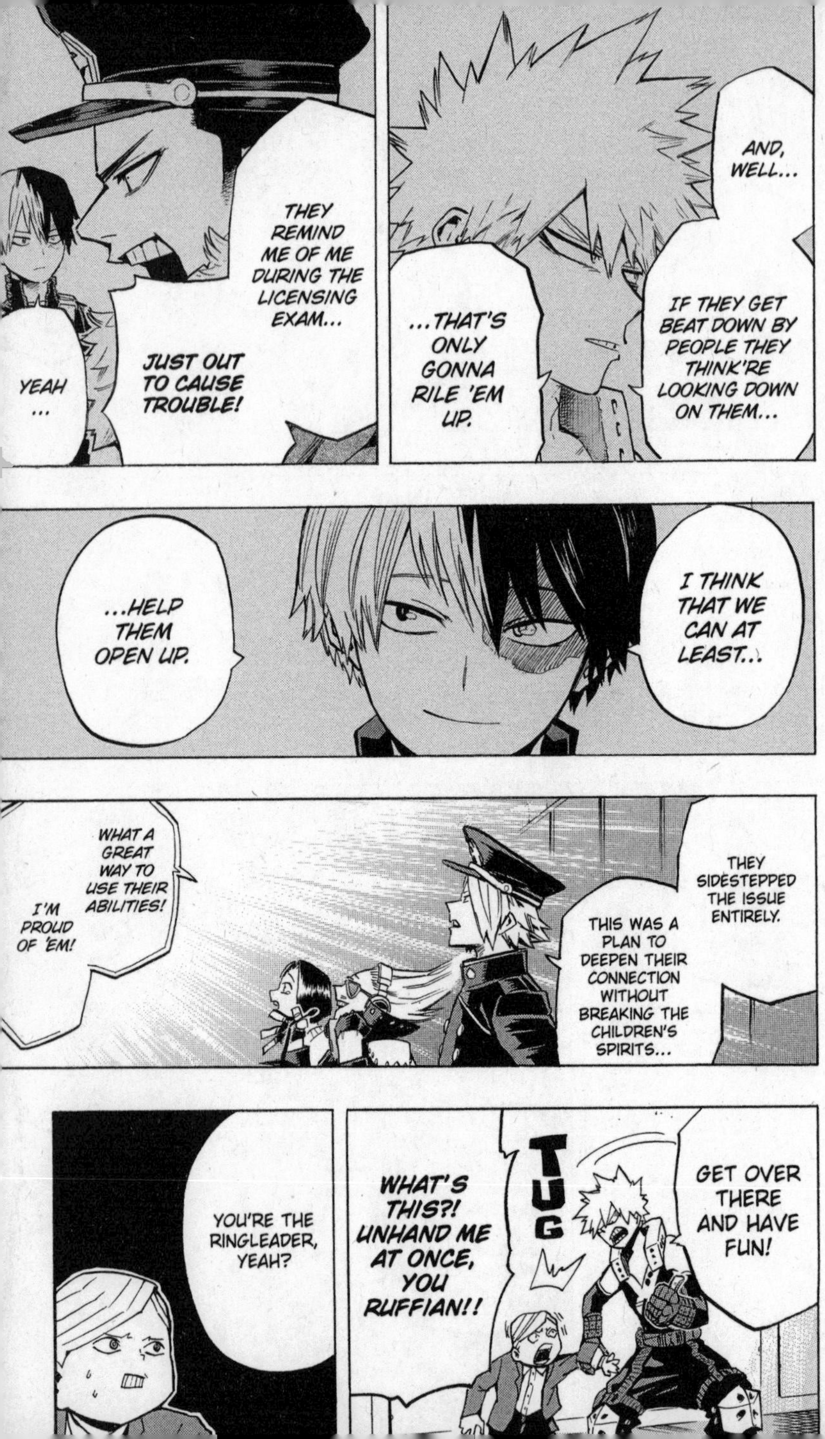
AND, WELL...
IF THEY GET BEAT DOWN BY PEOPLE THEY THINK'RE LOOKING DOWN ON THEM...
...THAT'S ONLY GONNA RILE 'EM UP.
THEY REMIND ME OF ME DURING THE LICENSING EXAM...
JUST OUT TO CAUSE TROUBLE!
YEAH ...
I THINK THAT WE CAN AT LEAST...
...HELP THEM OPEN UP.
THEY SIDESTEPPED THE ISSUE ENTIRELY.
THIS WAS A PLAN TO DEEPEN THEIR CONNECTION WITHOUT BREAKING THE CHILDREN'S SPIRITS...
WHAT A GREAT WAY TO USE THEIR ABILITIES!
I'M PROUD OF 'EM!
GET OVER THERE AND HAVE FUN!
TUG
WHAT'S THIS?! UNHAND ME AT ONCE, YOU RUFFIAN!!
YOU'RE THE RINGLEADER, YEAH?

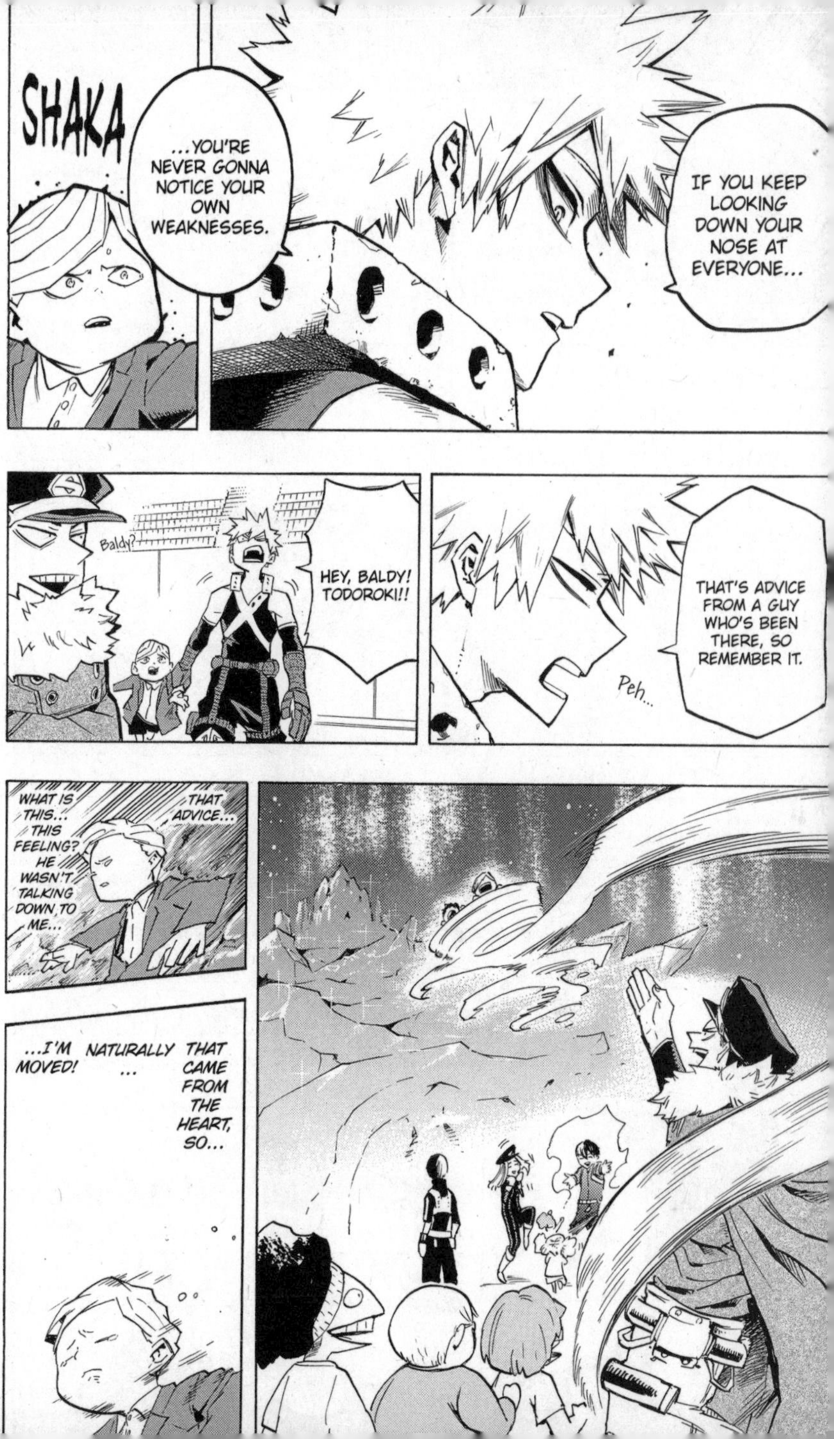

IF YOU KEEP LOOKING DOWN YOUR NOSE AT EVERYONE...
...YOU'RE NEVER GONNA NOTICE YOUR OWN WEAKNESSES.
SHAKA
THAT'S ADVICE FROM A GUY WHO'S BEEN THERE, SO REMEMBER IT.
Peh...
HEY, BALDY! TODOROKI!!
Baldy?
THAT ADVICE...
WHAT IS THIS... THIS FEELING? HE WASN'T TALKING DOWN TO ME...
THAT CAME FROM THE HEART, SO...
NATURALLY ...
...I'M MOVED!

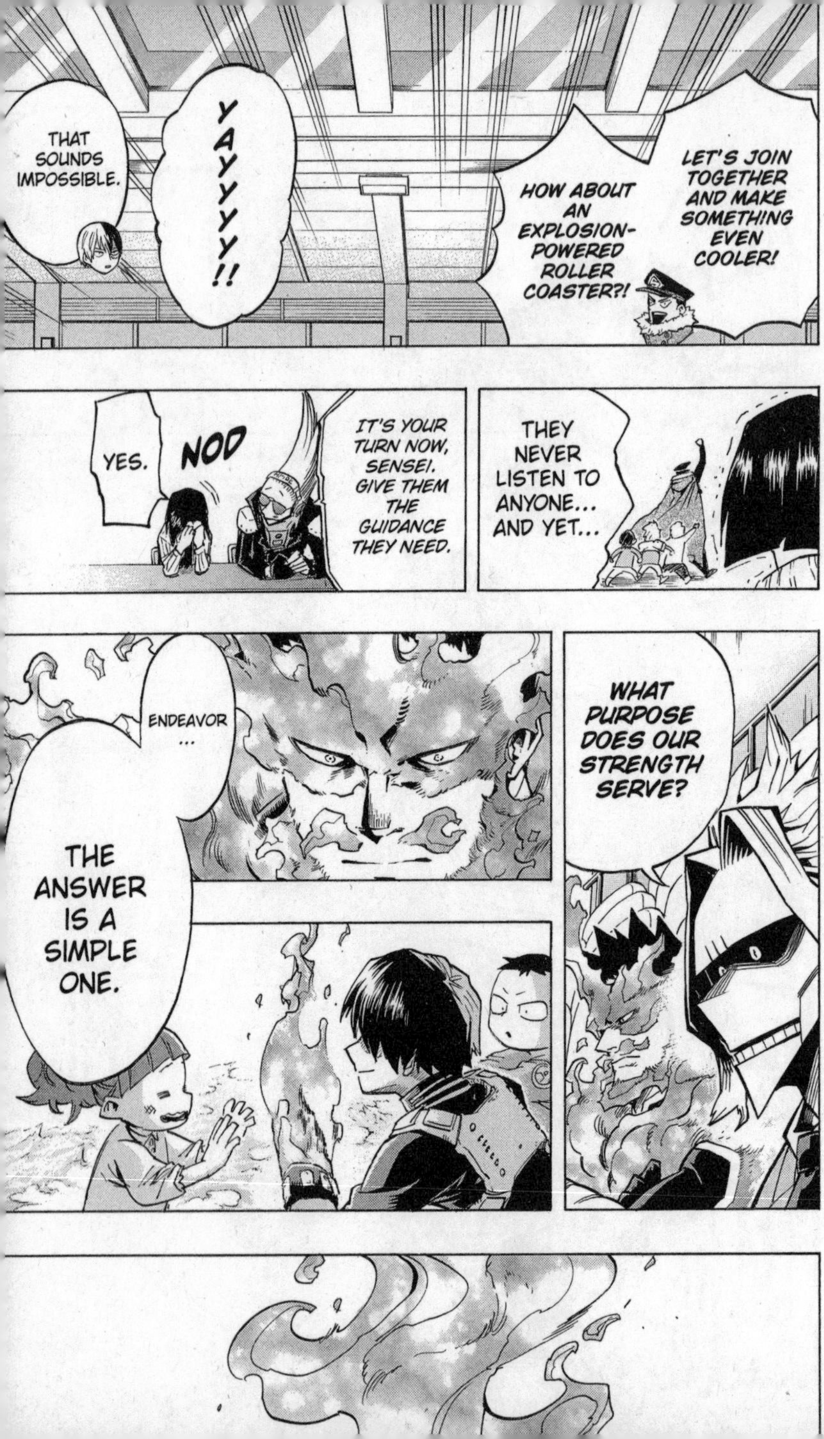
LET'S JOIN TOGETHER AND MAKE SOMETHING EVEN COOLER!
HOW ABOUT AN EXPLOSION-POWERED ROLLER COASTER?!
YAYYYY!!
THAT SOUNDS IMPOSSIBLE.
THEY NEVER LISTEN TO ANYONE... AND YET...
IT'S YOUR TURN NOW, SENSEI. GIVE THEM THE GUIDANCE THEY NEED.
NOD
YES.
WHAT PURPOSE DOES OUR STRENGTH SERVE?
ENDEAVOR ...
THE ANSWER IS A SIMPLE ONE.

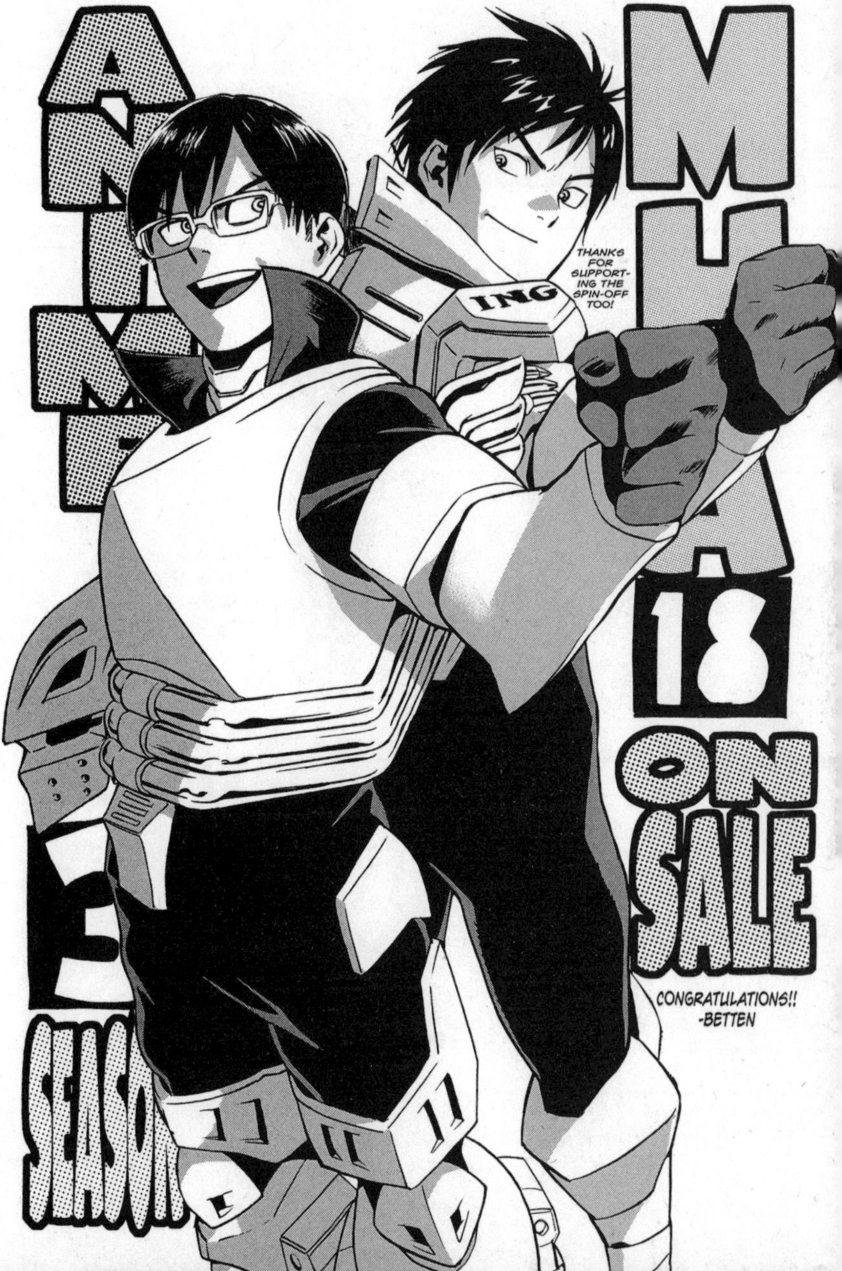
MHA
18
ON SALE
THANKS FOR SUPPORTING THE SPIN-OFF TOO!
ING
SEASON
CONGRATULATIONS!! -BETTEN

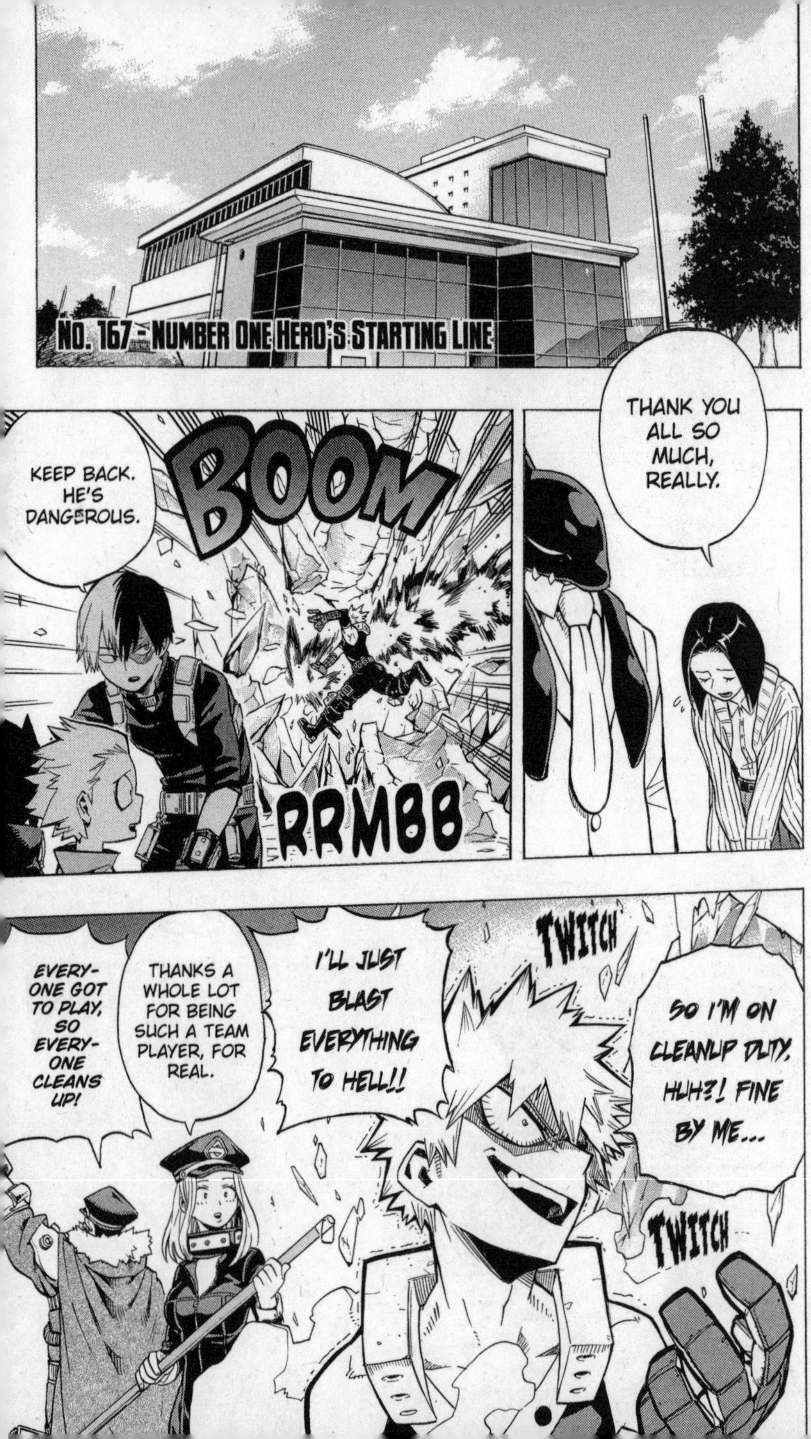
No. 167 - Number One Hero's Starting Line
THANK YOU ALL SO MUCH, REALLY.
KEEP BACK. HE'S DANGEROUS.
BOOM
RRMBB
TWITCH
SO I'M ON CLEANUP DUTY, HUH?! FINE BY ME...
I'LL JUST BLAST EVERYTHING TO HELL!!
THANKS A WHOLE LOT FOR BEING SUCH A TEAM PLAYER, FOR REAL.
EVERY-ONE GOT TO PLAY, SO EVERY-ONE CLEANS UP!
TWITCH

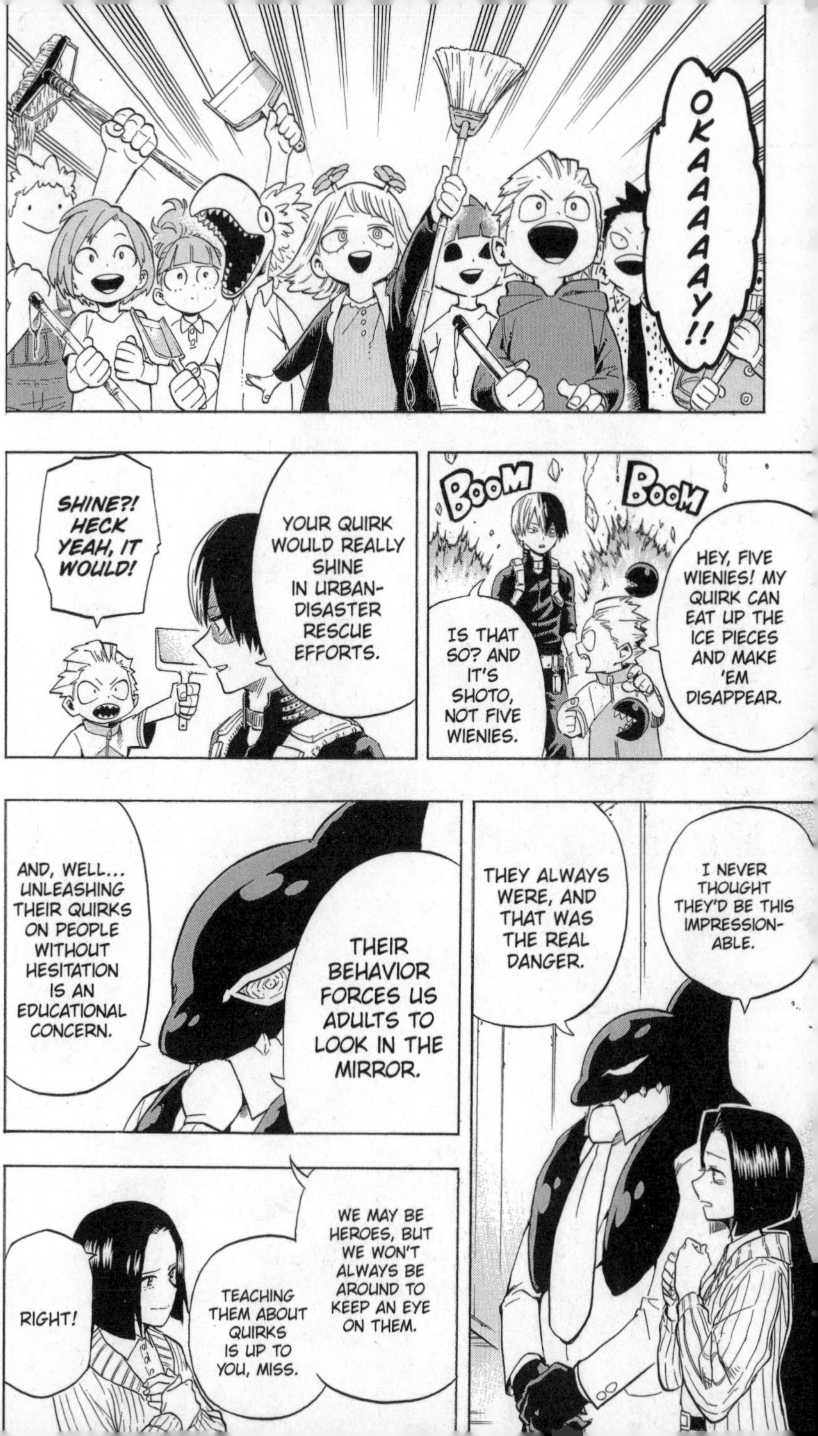
OKAAAAAY!!
BOOM
BOOM
HEY, FIVE WIENIES! MY QUIRK CAN EAT UP THE ICE PIECES AND MAKE 'EM DISAPPEAR.
IS THAT SO? AND IT'S SHOTO, NOT FIVE WIENIES.
YOUR QUIRK WOULD REALLY SHINE IN URBAN-DISASTER RESCUE EFFORTS.
SHINE?! HECK YEAH, IT WOULD!
I NEVER THOUGHT THEY'D BE THIS IMPRESSIONABLE.
THEY ALWAYS WERE, AND THAT WAS THE REAL DANGER.
THEIR BEHAVIOR FORCES US ADULTS TO LOOK IN THE MIRROR.
AND, WELL... UNLEASHING THEIR QUIRKS ON PEOPLE WITHOUT HESITATION IS AN EDUCATIONAL CONCERN.
WE MAY BE HEROES, BUT WE WON'T ALWAYS BE AROUND TO KEEP AN EYE ON THEM.
TEACHING THEM ABOUT QUIRKS IS UP TO YOU, MISS.
RIGHT!

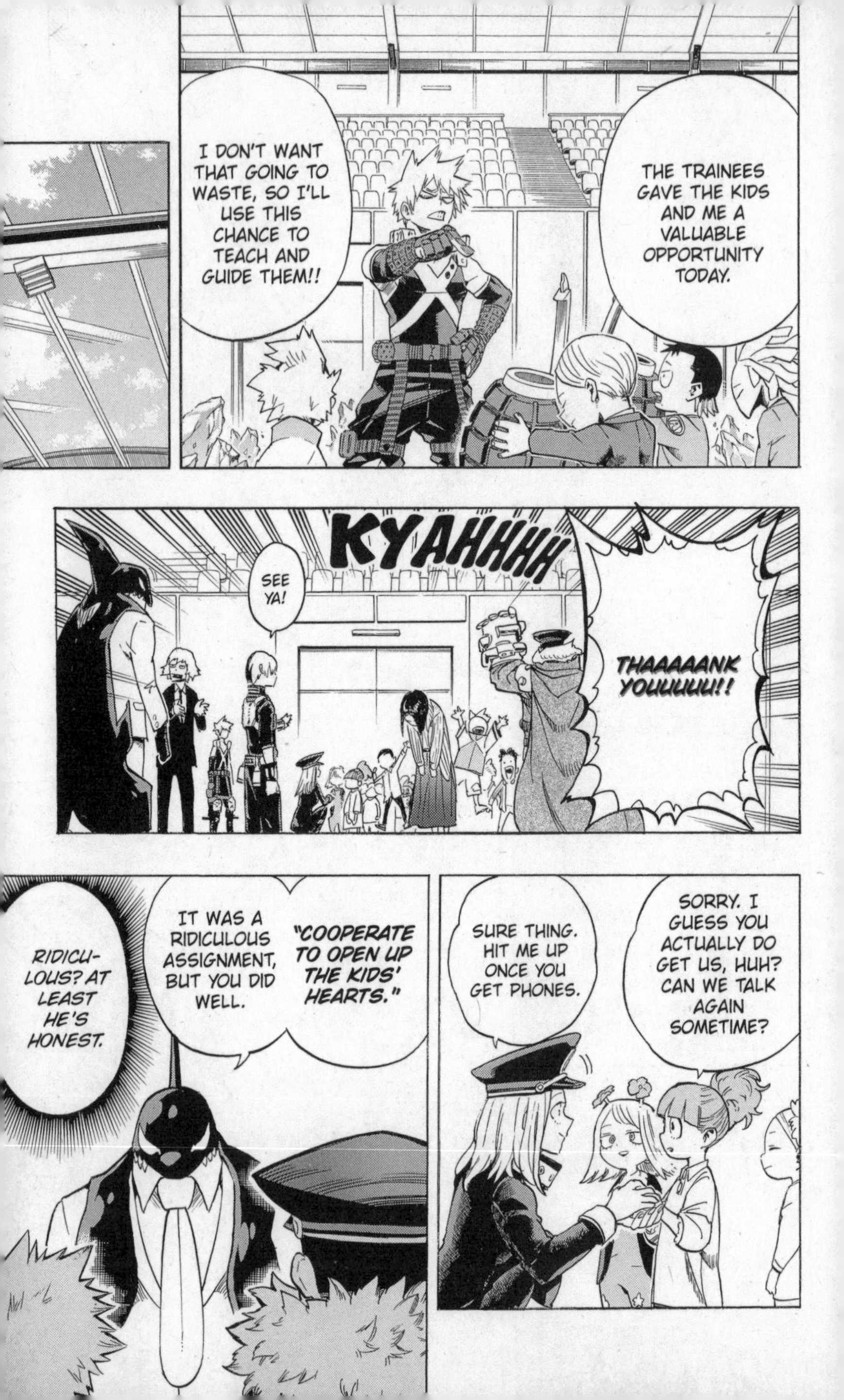
THE TRAINEES GAVE THE KIDS AND ME A VALUABLE OPPORTUNITY TODAY.
I DON'T WANT THAT GOING TO WASTE, SO I'LL USE THIS CHANCE TO TEACH AND GUIDE THEM!!
KYAHHHH
THAAAAANK YOUUUUU!!
SEE YA!
SORRY. I GUESS YOU ACTUALLY DO GET US, HUH? CAN WE TALK AGAIN SOMETIME?
SURE THING. HIT ME UP ONCE YOU GET PHONES.
"COOPERATE TO OPEN UP THE KIDS' HEARTS."
IT WAS A RIDICULOUS ASSIGNMENT, BUT YOU DID WELL.
RIDICU-LOUS? AT LEAST HE'S HONEST.

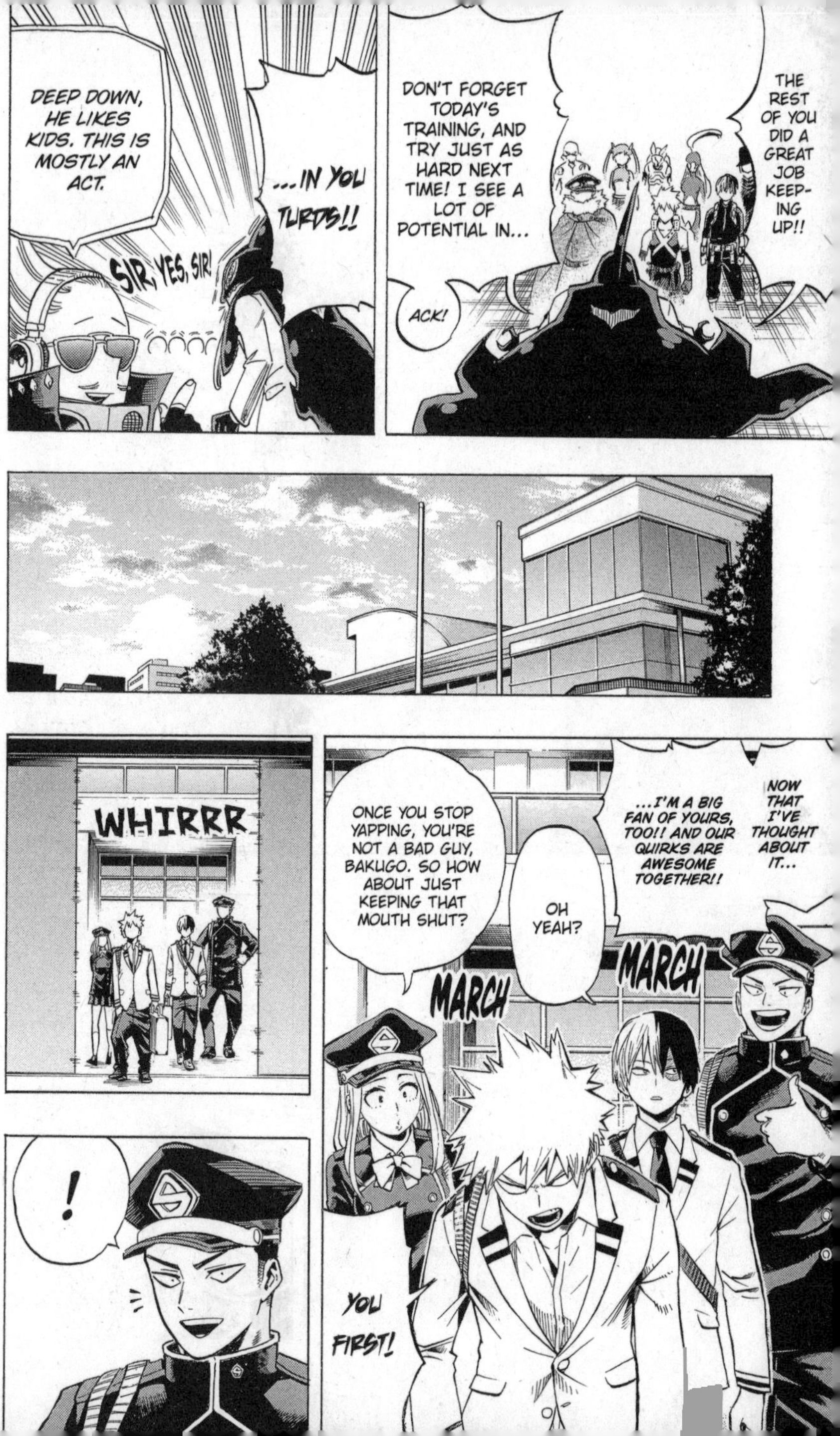
THE REST OF YOU DID A GREAT JOB KEEPING UP!!
DON'T FORGET TODAY'S TRAINING, AND TRY JUST AS HARD NEXT TIME! I SEE A LOT OF POTENTIAL IN...
ACK!
...IN YOU TURDS!!
SIR, YES, SIR!
DEEP DOWN, HE LIKES KIDS. THIS IS MOSTLY AN ACT.
NOW THAT I'VE THOUGHT ABOUT IT...
...I'M A BIG FAN OF YOURS, TOO!! AND OUR QUIRKS ARE AWESOME TOGETHER!!
MARCH
OH YEAH?
ONCE YOU STOP YAPPING, YOU'RE NOT A BAD GUY, BAKUGO. SO HOW ABOUT JUST KEEPING THAT MOUTH SHUT?
MARCH
YOU FIRST!
WHIRRR
!

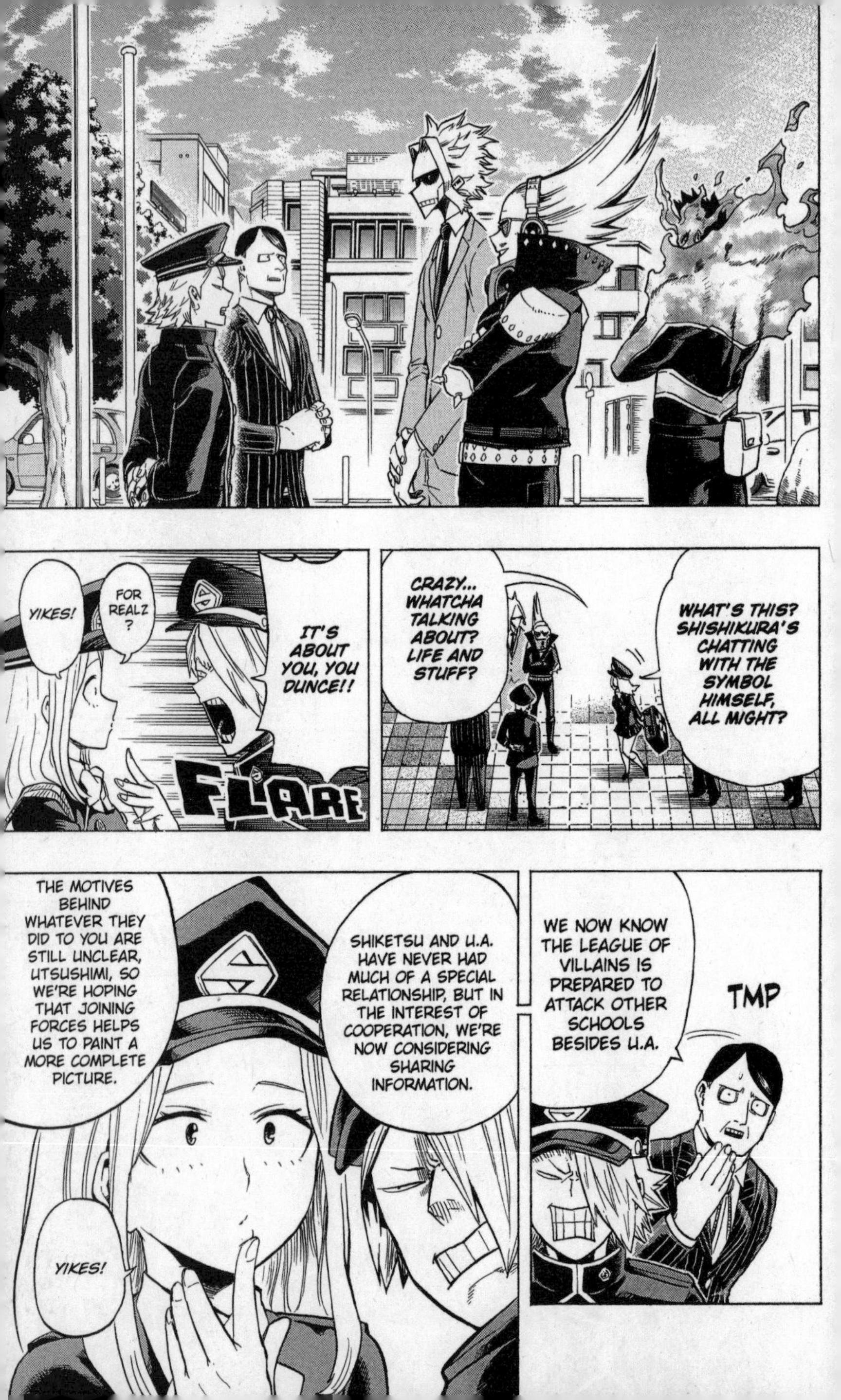
WHAT'S THIS? SHISHIKURA'S CHATTING WITH THE SYMBOL HIMSELF, ALL MIGHT?
CRAZY... WHATCHA TALKING ABOUT? LIFE AND STUFF?
IT'S ABOUT YOU, YOU DUNCE!!
FOR REALZ?
YIKES!
FLARE
WE NOW KNOW THE LEAGUE OF VILLAINS IS PREPARED TO ATTACK OTHER SCHOOLS BESIDES U.A.
TMP
SHIKETSU AND U.A. HAVE NEVER HAD MUCH OF A SPECIAL RELATIONSHIP, BUT IN THE INTEREST OF COOPERATION, WE'RE NOW CONSIDERING SHARING INFORMATION.
THE MOTIVES BEHIND WHATEVER THEY DID TO YOU ARE STILL UNCLEAR, UTSUSHIMI, SO WE'RE HOPING THAT JOINING FORCES HELPS US TO PAINT A MORE COMPLETE PICTURE.
YIKES!

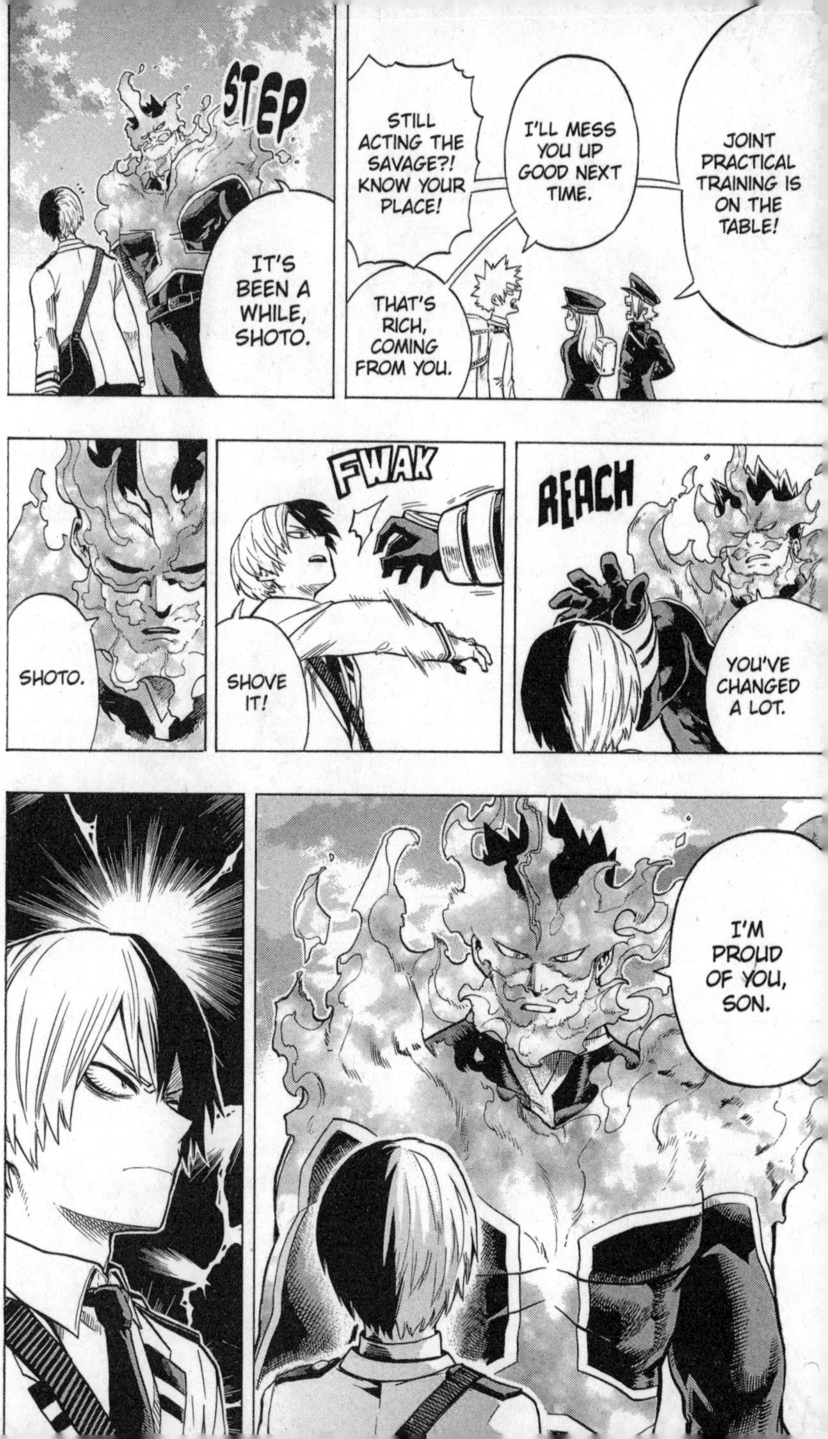
JOINT PRACTICAL TRAINING IS ON THE TABLE!
I'LL MESS YOU UP GOOD NEXT TIME.
STILL ACTING THE SAVAGE?! KNOW YOUR PLACE!
THAT'S RICH, COMING FROM YOU.
STEP
IT'S BEEN A WHILE, SHOTO.
REACH
YOU'VE CHANGED A LOT.
FWAK
SHOVE IT!
SHOTO.
I'M PROUD OF YOU, SON.

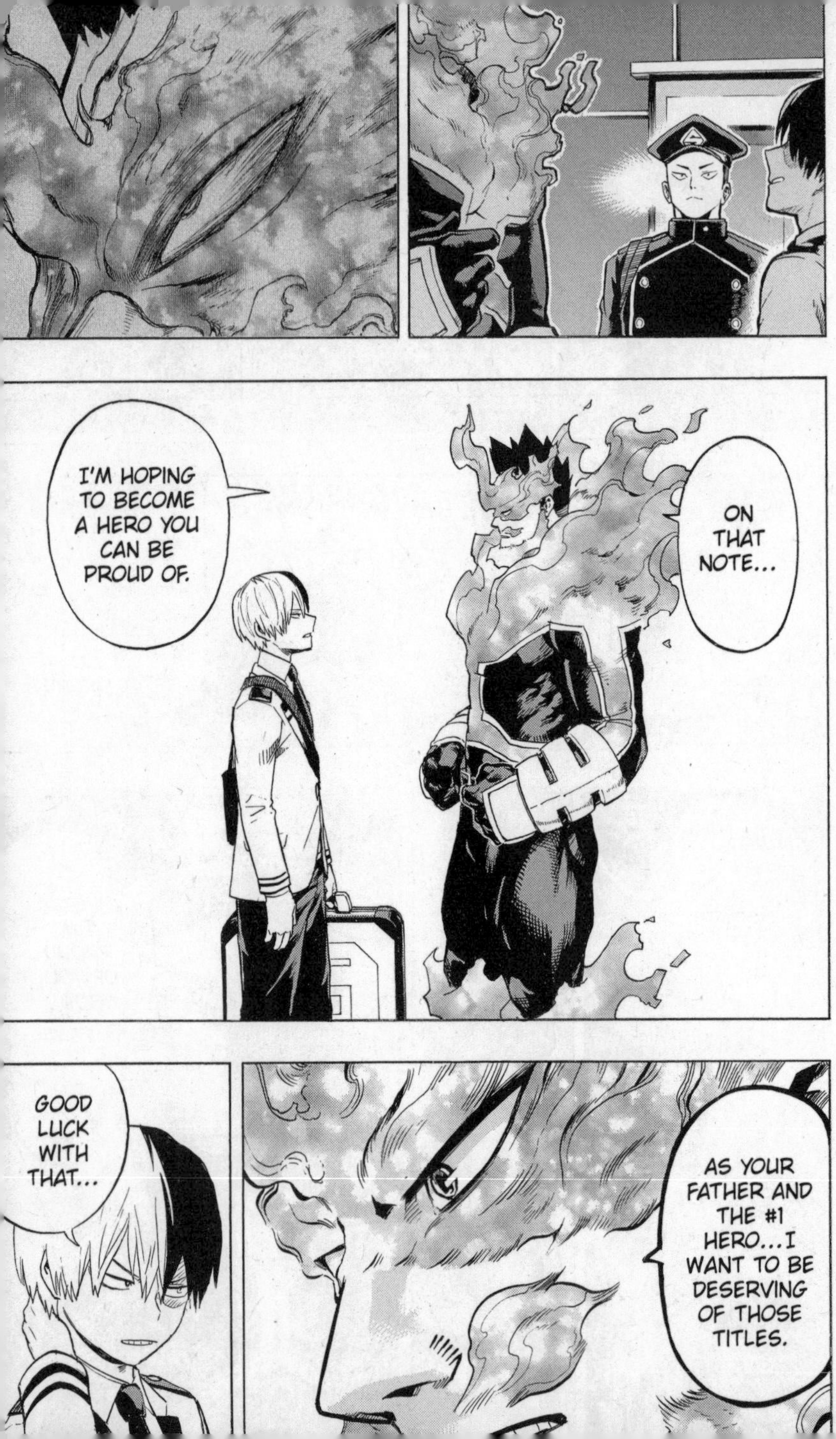
ON THAT NOTE...
I'M HOPING TO BECOME A HERO YOU CAN BE PROUD OF.
AS YOUR FATHER AND THE #1 HERO...I WANT TO BE DESERVING OF THOSE TITLES.
GOOD LUCK WITH THAT...

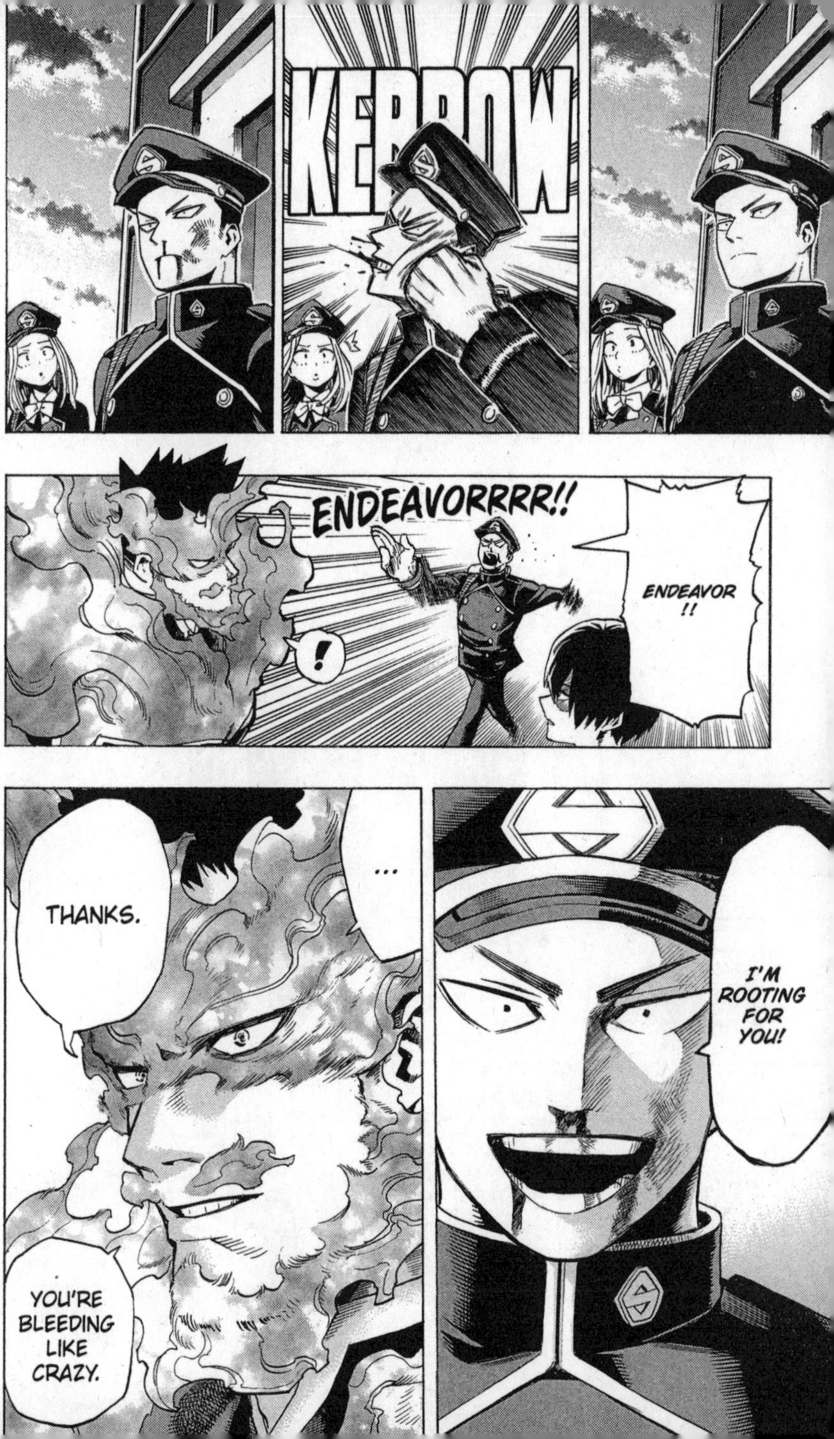
KERROW
ENDEAVOR !!
ENDEAVORRRR!!
!
I'M ROOTING FOR YOU!
...
THANKS.
YOU'RE BLEEDING LIKE CRAZY.

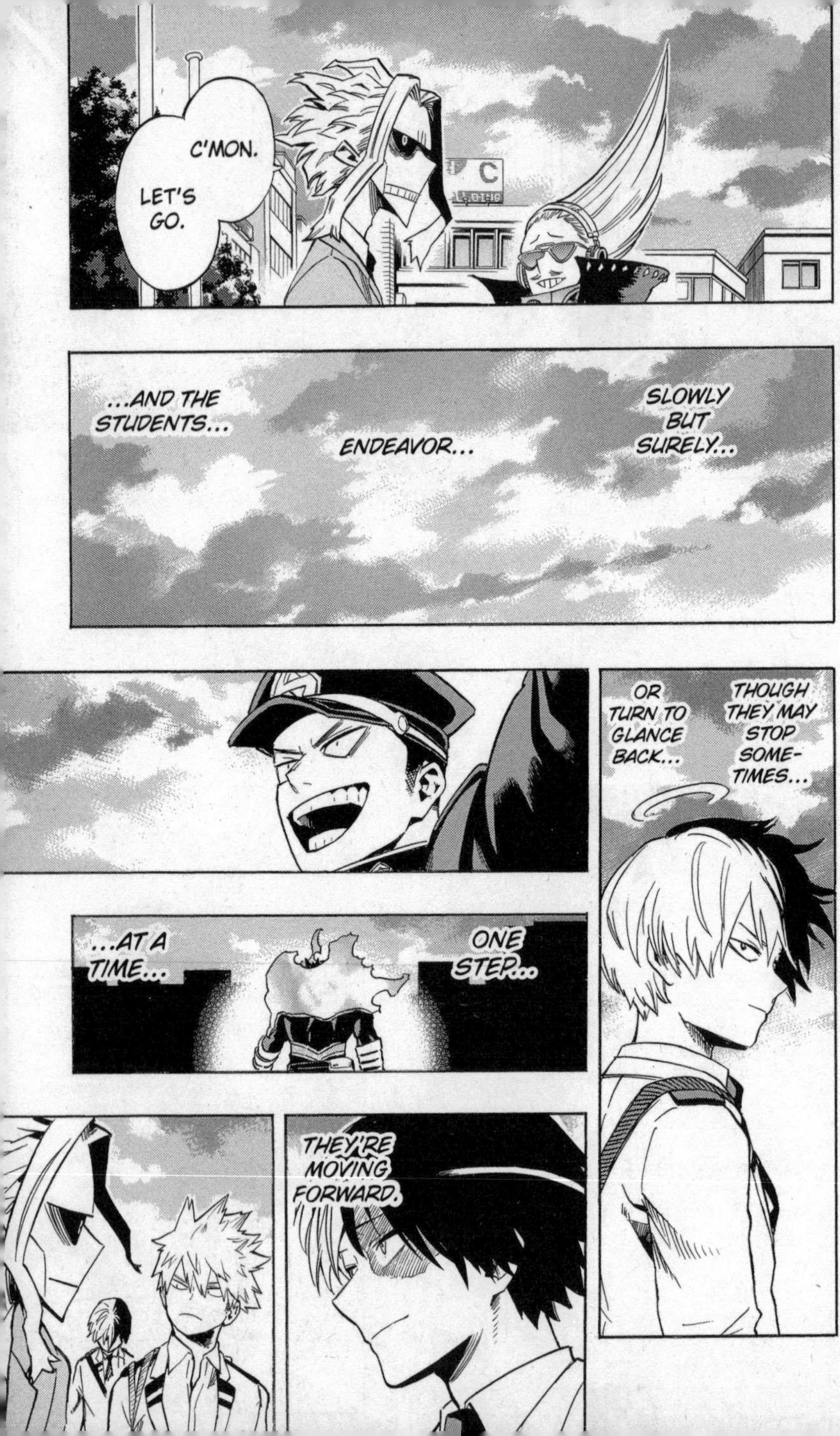

C'MON.
LET'S GO.
SLOWLY BUT SURELY...
ENDEAVOR...
...AND THE STUDENTS...
THOUGH THEY MAY STOP SOME-TIMES...
OR TURN TO GLANCE BACK...
ONE STEP...
...AT A TIME...
THEY'RE MOVING FORWARD.

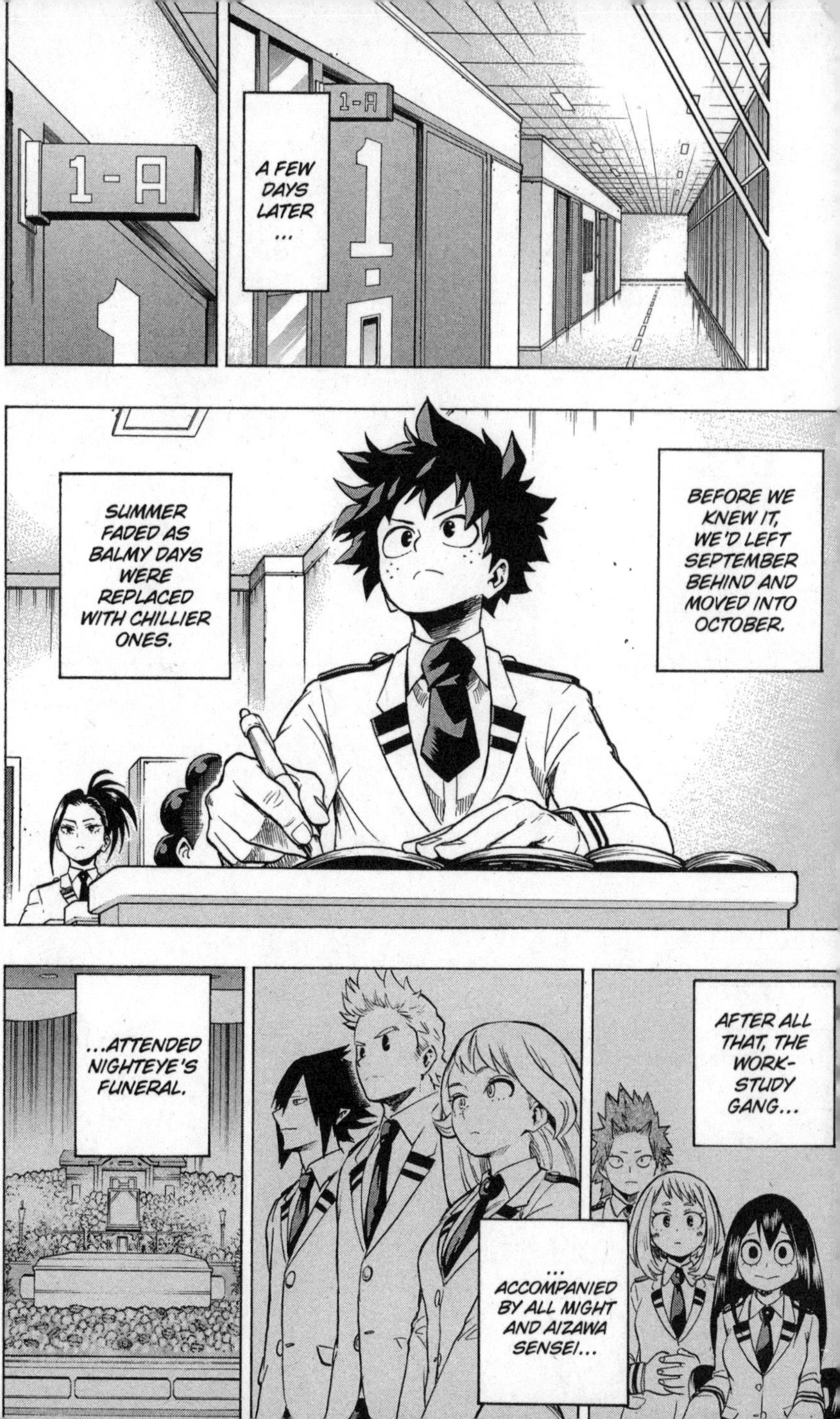
A FEW DAYS LATER ...
BEFORE WE KNEW IT, WE'D LEFT SEPTEMBER BEHIND AND MOVED INTO OCTOBER.
SUMMER FADED AS BALMY DAYS WERE REPLACED WITH CHILLIER ONES.
AFTER ALL THAT, THE WORK-STUDY GANG...
...ACCOMPANIED BY ALL MIGHT AND AIZAWA SENSEI...
...ATTENDED NIGHTEYE'S FUNERAL.

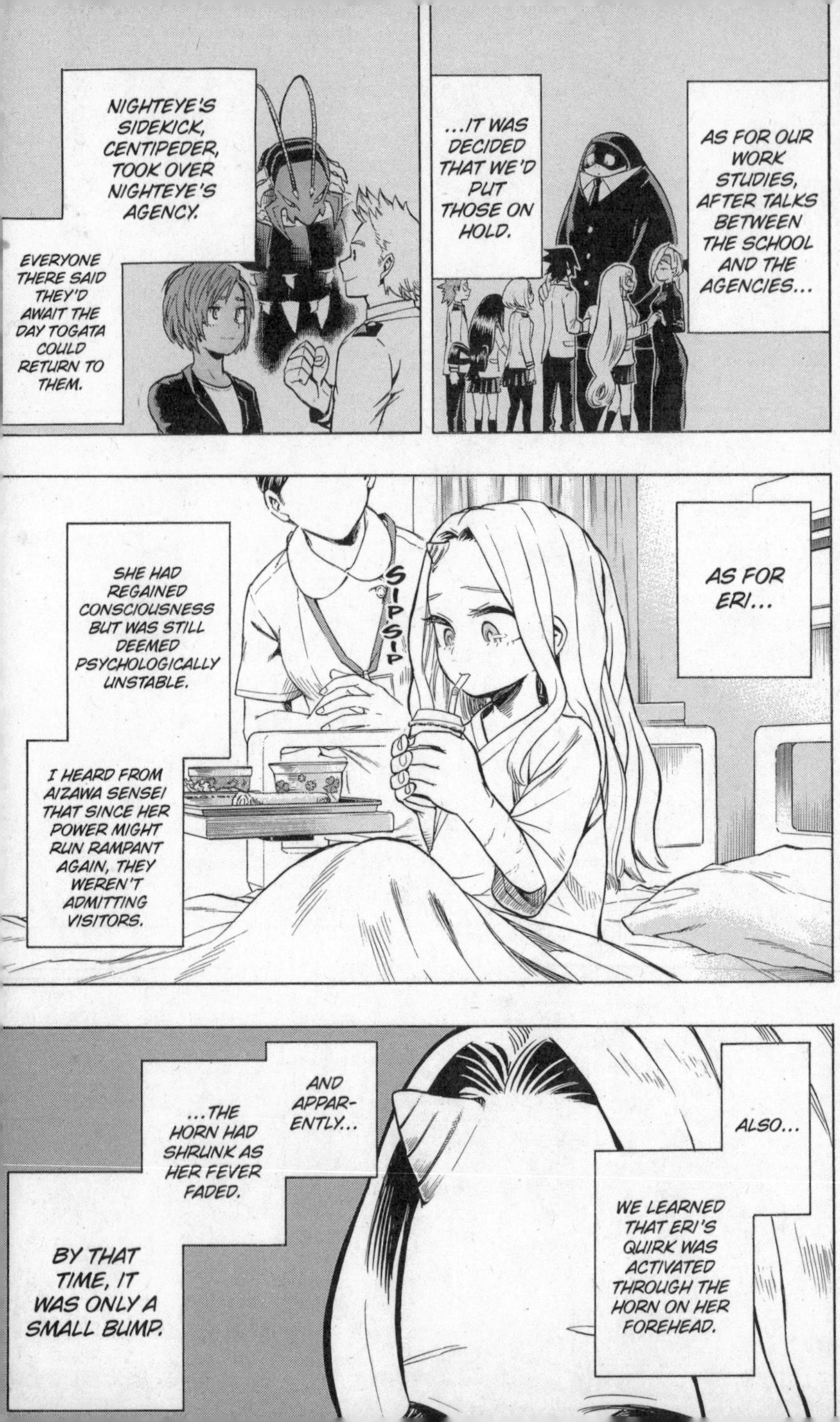
AS FOR OUR WORK STUDIES, AFTER TALKS BETWEEN THE SCHOOL AND THE AGENCIES...
...IT WAS DECIDED THAT WE'D PUT THOSE ON HOLD.
NIGHTEYE'S SIDEKICK, CENTIPEDER, TOOK OVER NIGHTEYE'S AGENCY.
EVERYONE THERE SAID THEY'D AWAIT THE DAY TOGATA COULD RETURN TO THEM.
AS FOR ERI...
SIP SIP
SHE HAD REGAINED CONSCIOUSNESS BUT WAS STILL DEEMED PSYCHOLOGICALLY UNSTABLE.
I HEARD FROM AIZAWA SENSEI THAT SINCE HER POWER MIGHT RUN RAMPANT AGAIN, THEY WEREN'T ADMITTING VISITORS.
ALSO...
WE LEARNED THAT ERI'S QUIRK WAS ACTIVATED THROUGH THE HORN ON HER FOREHEAD.
AND APPAR-ENTLY...
...THE HORN HAD SHRUNK AS HER FEVER FADED.
BY THAT TIME, IT WAS ONLY A SMALL BUMP.

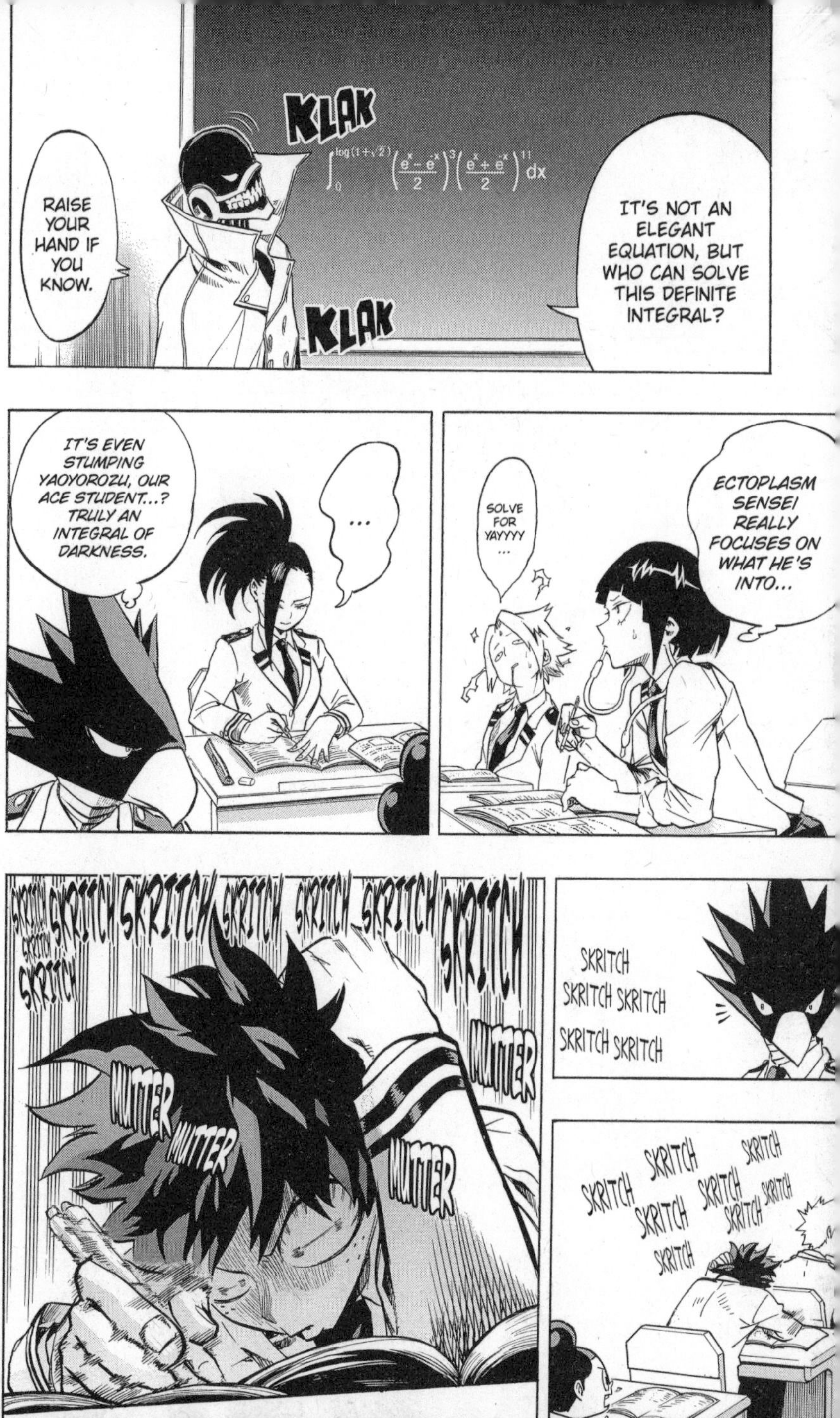
KLAK
$\int_0^{\log(1+\sqrt{2})} \left(\frac{e^x - e^{-x}}{2}\right)^3 \left(\frac{e^x + e^{-x}}{2}\right)^{11} dx$
IT'S NOT AN ELEGANT EQUATION, BUT WHO CAN SOLVE THIS DEFINITE INTEGRAL?
KLAK
RAISE YOUR HAND IF YOU KNOW.
ECTOPLASM SENSEI REALLY FOCUSES ON WHAT HE'S INTO...
SOLVE FOR YAYYYY ...
...
IT'S EVEN STUMPING YAOYOROZU, OUR ACE STUDENT...? TRULY AN INTEGRAL OF DARKNESS.
SKRITCH SKRITCH SKRITCH SKRITCH SKRITCH
SKRITCH SKRITCH SKRITCH SKRITCH SKRITCH SKRITCH SKRITCH SKRITCH SKRITCH
SKRITCH SKRITCH SKRITCH SKRITCH SKRITCH SKRITCH SKRITCH SKRITCH SKRITCH SKRITCH
MUTTER MUTTER MUTTER MUTTER

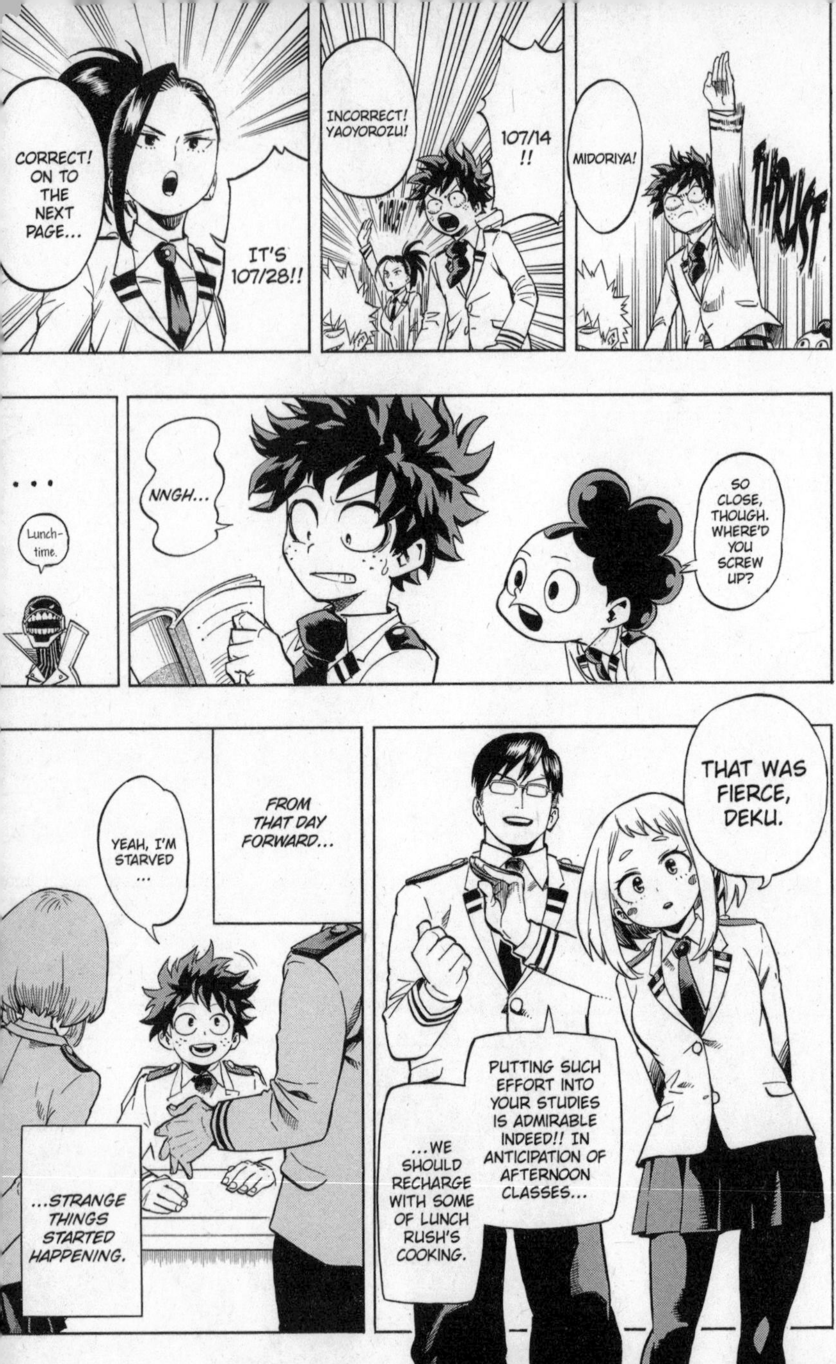
MIDORIYA!
THRUST
107/14 !!
INCORRECT! YAOYOROZU!
THRUST
IT'S 107/28!!
CORRECT! ON TO THE NEXT PAGE...
SO CLOSE, THOUGH. WHERE'D YOU SCREW UP?
NNGH...
...
Lunch-time.
THAT WAS FIERCE, DEKU.
PUTTING SUCH EFFORT INTO YOUR STUDIES IS ADMIRABLE INDEED!! IN ANTICIPATION OF AFTERNOON CLASSES...
...WE SHOULD RECHARGE WITH SOME OF LUNCH RUSH'S COOKING.
FROM THAT DAY FORWARD...
YEAH, I'M STARVED ...
...STRANGE THINGS STARTED HAPPENING.

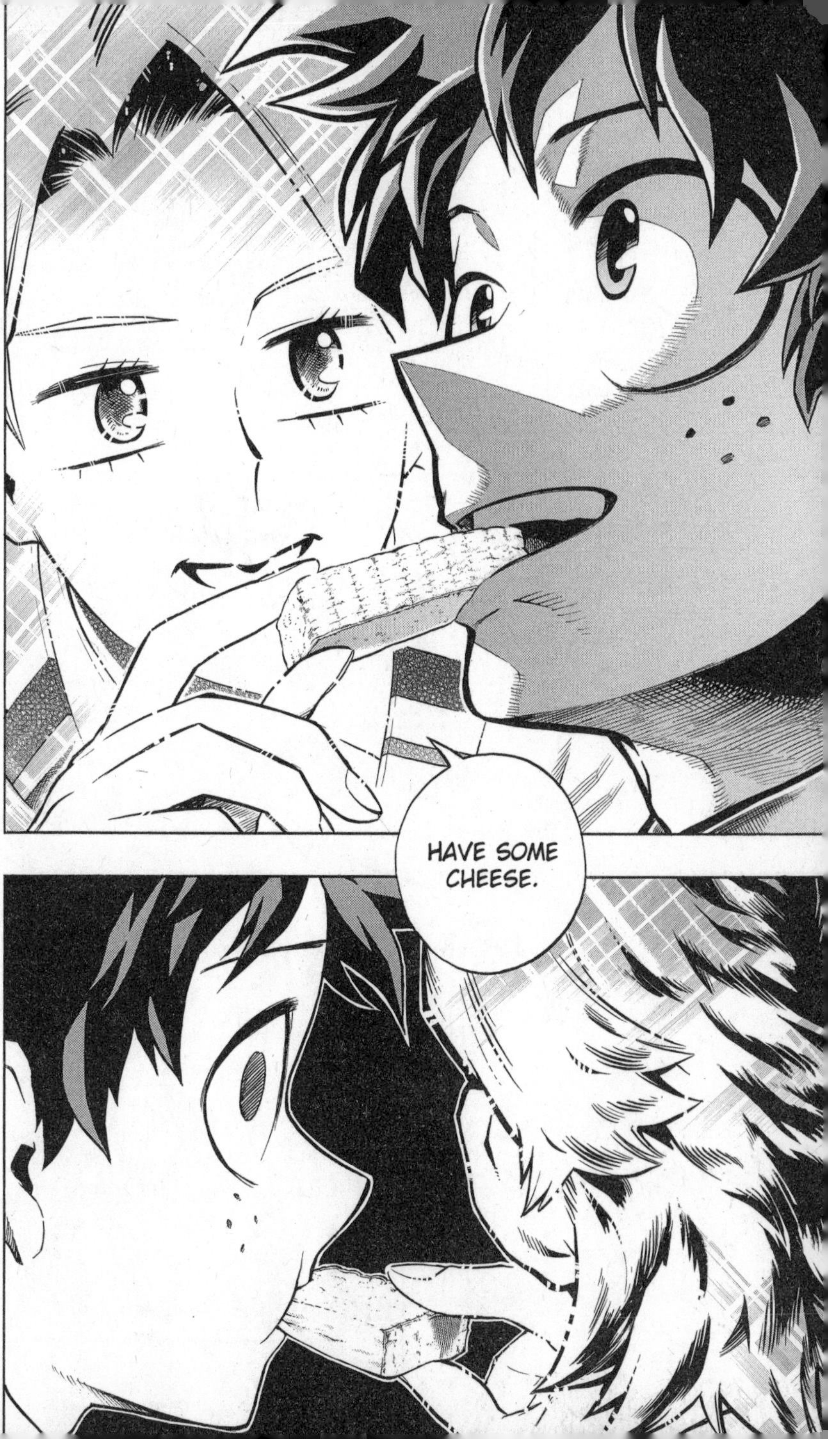
HAVE SOME CHEESE.

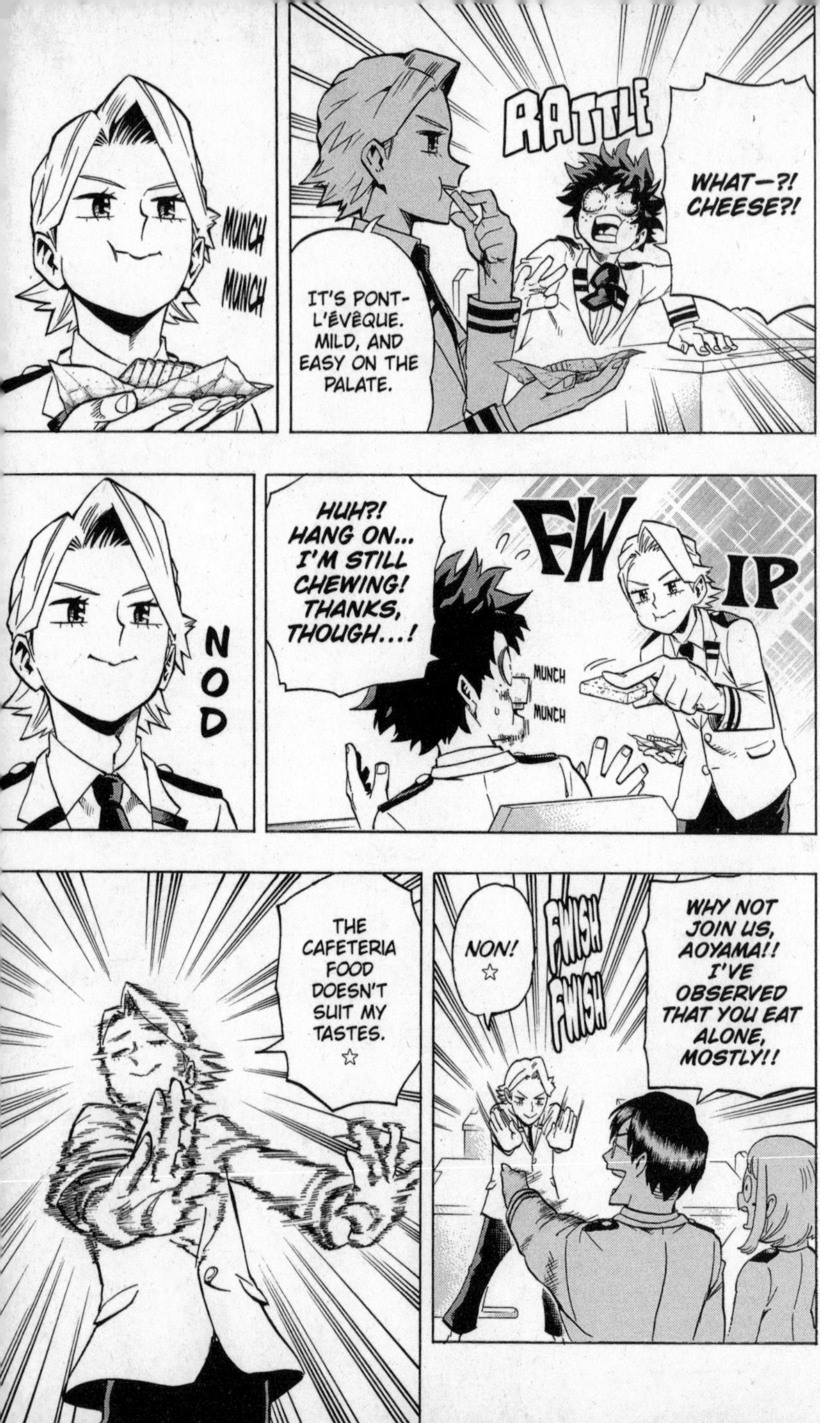
WHAT—?! CHEESE?!
RATTLE
IT'S PONT-L'ÉVÊQUE. MILD, AND EASY ON THE PALATE.
MUNCH
MUNCH
FWIP
HUH?! HANG ON... I'M STILL CHEWING! THANKS, THOUGH...!
MUNCH
MUNCH
NOD
WHY NOT JOIN US, AOYAMA!! I'VE OBSERVED THAT YOU EAT ALONE, MOSTLY!!
FWISH
FWISH
NON! ☆
THE CAFETERIA FOOD DOESN'T SUIT MY TASTES. ☆

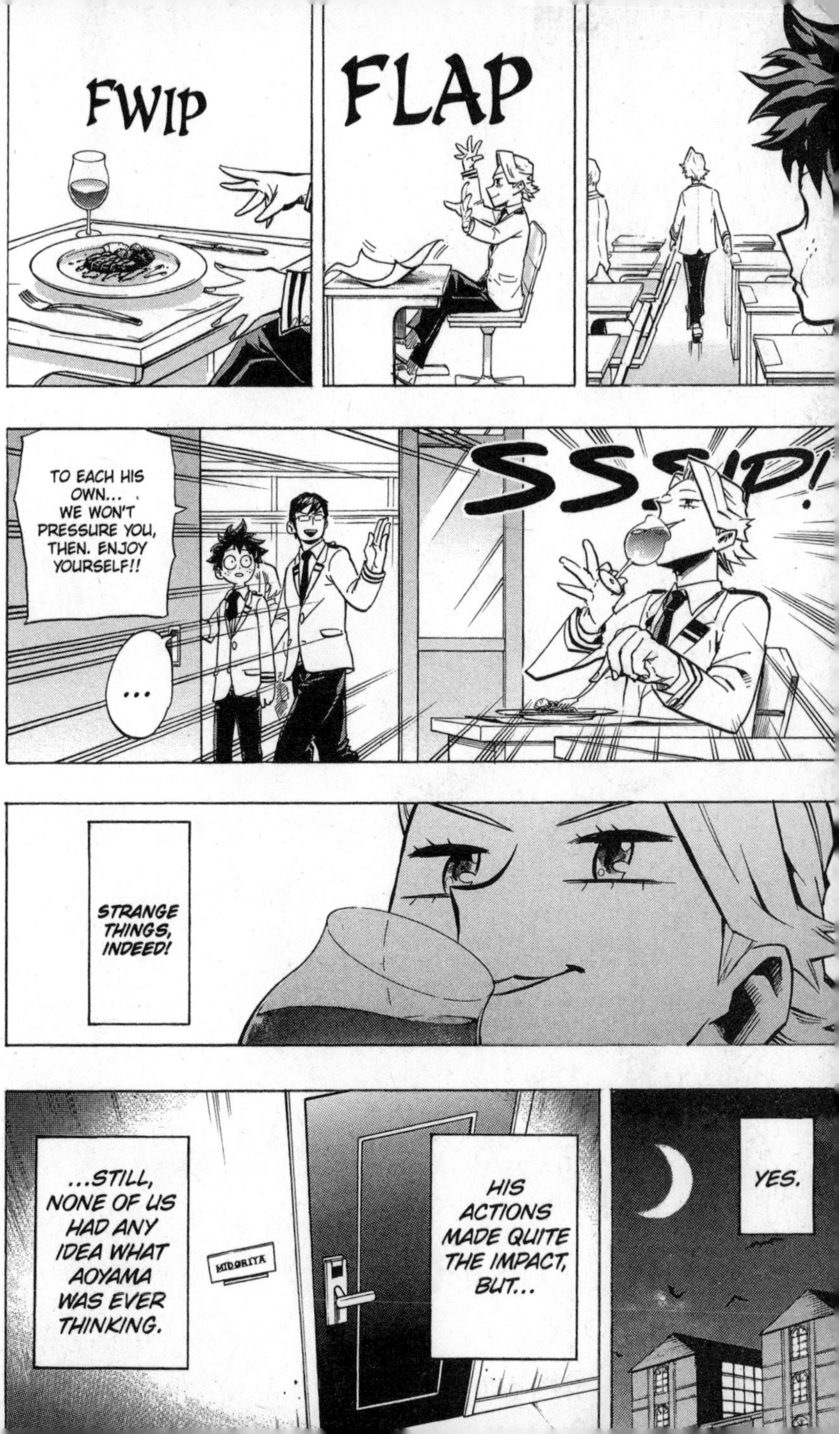
FLAP
FWIP
SSSIP!
TO EACH HIS OWN... WE WON'T PRESSURE YOU, THEN. ENJOY YOURSELF!!
...
STRANGE THINGS, INDEED!
YES.
HIS ACTIONS MADE QUITE THE IMPACT, BUT...
MIDORIYA
...STILL, NONE OF US HAD ANY IDEA WHAT AOYAMA WAS EVER THINKING.

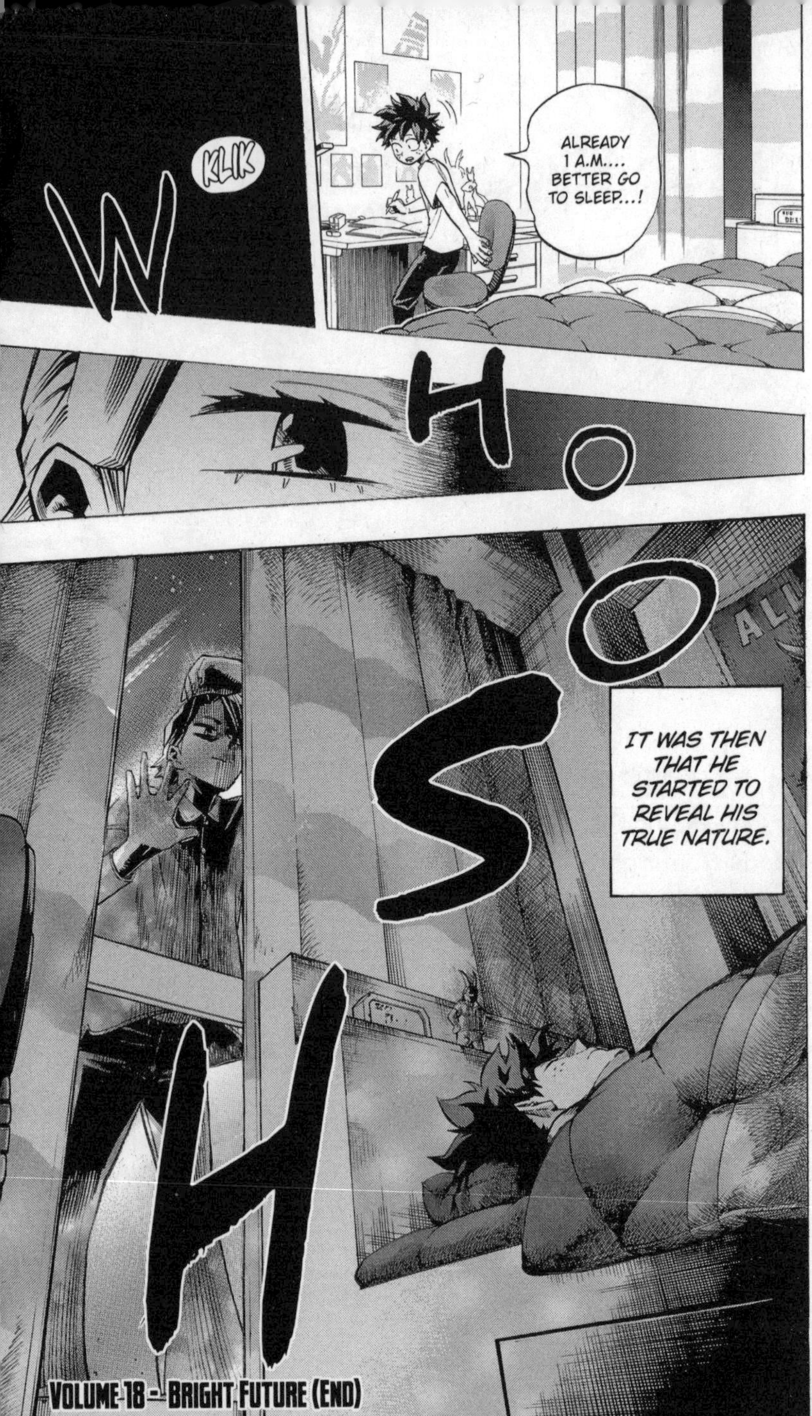
ALREADY 1 A.M.... BETTER GO TO SLEEP...!
KLIK
W
HO
OSH
IT WAS THEN THAT HE STARTED TO REVEAL HIS TRUE NATURE.
VOLUME 18 – BRIGHT FUTURE (END)

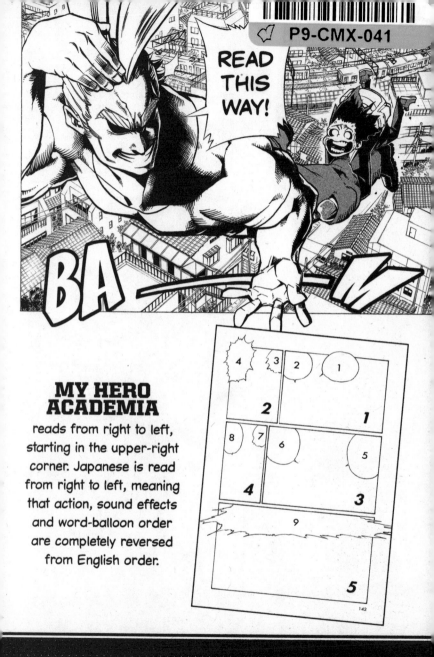

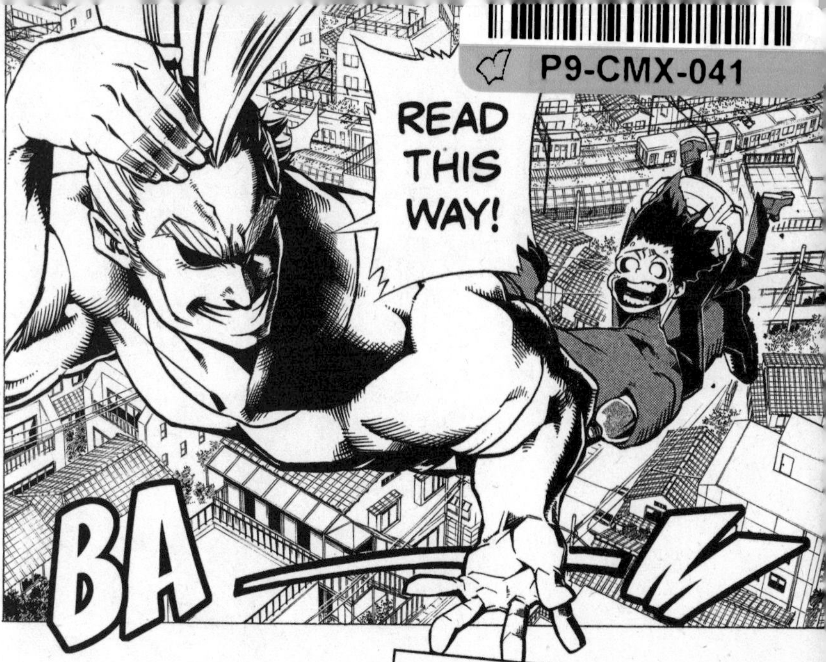
READ THIS WAY!
BA-M

MY HERO ACADEMIA

reads from right to left, starting in the upper-right corner. Japanese is read from right to left, meaning that action, sound effects and word-balloon order are completely reversed from English order.

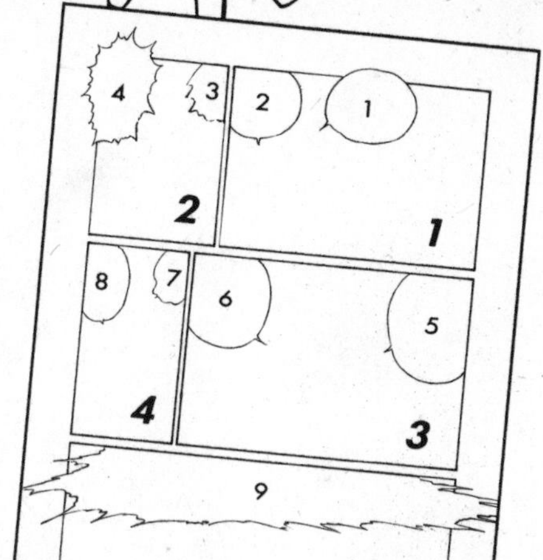
1
2
3
4
1
2
5
6
7
8
3
4
9
5
142